SOCIAL POLICY IN IRELAND

Principles, Practice and Problems

Revised and Updated Edition

Edited by
Seán Healy, Brigid Reynolds
and Micheál L. Collins

The Liffey Press

Published by
The Liffey Press
Ashbrook House
10 Main Street
Raheny, Dublin 5, Ireland
www.theliffeypress.com

© 2006 Individual contributors

A catalogue record of this book is
available from the British Library.

ISBN 978-1-905785-02-5

Printed in Ireland by ColourBooks

CONTENTS

FOREWORD

This second edition of *Social Policy in Ireland: Principles, Practice and Problems* has been produced to mark the twenty-fifth anniversary of the establishment of the Justice Commission of the Conference of Religious of Ireland (CORI Justice). In that twenty-five-year period, policy-making in Ireland has been much discussed. While specific issues such as poverty, unemployment and social exclusion have been addressed in detail, there has also been a broader focus on the framework and the emerging issues within which these discussions take place.

The "box" or framework within which society analyses itself will fundamentally determine how problems are identified and progress measured. Policy-makers in particular need to cultivate a healthy suspicion about the framework being used. Since its establishment in the early 1980s, this framework has been a central concern for CORI Justice. While we have dealt in great detail with the specific issues being considered, we have consistently emphasised the importance of this policy framework and the underlying paradigm which shapes the discussions and the decisions made. To ensure a comprehensive framework for analysis and policy-making we have argued constantly for the inclusion of groups affected by the decisions in the policy-making process.

The policy-making framework and the underlying paradigm determine, to a great extent, which issues are discussed and which ignored. Realities can be taken as inevitable, assumptions made and policy initiatives legitimated as a result of the unquestioned acceptance of the paradigm which underpins society's understanding of itself. A different paradigm and framework would open all of these to question. CORI Justice has long argued for a broadening of approach in the policy-making process, so as to incorporate ongoing discussion of this paradigm.

In each of the past eighteen years, CORI Justice has held a conference focusing on a specific issue or aspect of policy and published a book containing the papers of each conference. These conferences have dealt with topics such as work, income, participation, rural development, citizenship, progress, social partnership and taxation. Papers have been produced on each topic by a wide range of policy analysts, focusing on the present situation, how it emerged, how it should be adjusted and what could be done in specific policy terms to address the problems identified.

CORI Justice has sought out detailed solutions to specific problems identified in these conferences. In many cases, it has been involved in developing and piloting creative initiatives to tackle these and other issues. It has also argued for the inclusion of groups such as poor people, unemployed people and women in the policy development process.

This book continues the tradition of CORI Justice's previous social policy publications. Some of the following chapters look at issues of principle, some analyse practice, while others focus closely on specific problems. Many of the issues covered over the last eighteen years are revisited, in many cases by the same authors. Other issues are identified and analysed for the first time in this publication, while others still are omitted for want of space, although we intend to return to them in future years.

CORI is an organisation of religious women and men. It seems appropriate that it should be concerned not just with the specifics of problems, but with issues of principles, paradigms and guiding values. The religious quest, after all, seeks to deal with ultimate issues. CORI Justice has always seen this quest, however, as deeply rooted in the struggle to move the world from where it is towards a better place. This involves a number of things. It involves detailed analysis, linking of this analysis to the experience of people, articulating of viable alternatives and identifying pathways to move towards such alternatives. It also involves ongoing dialogue on these issues with as wide a range of groups, organisations and people as possible.

We do not claim to have all the answers. We do, however, argue that the issues we identify are important and need to be addressed in a comprehensive way if there is ever to be a world where human rights are respected, human dignity is protected, human development is facilitated and the environment is respected and protected. For CORI Justice, these are the core elements of a just society and all of our work is focused on developing such a world. We offer this book as a contribution to the public debate we believe is required if Ireland is to develop as a just society.

This is the second edition of *Social Policy in Ireland: Principles, Practice and Problems*. The first edition was published eight years ago. For this edition Micheál L. Collins has joined the editorial team. We are grateful that many of the previous authors were willing to update their chapters or write new ones. We wish to express our deep gratitude to all 28 authors who have produced the 22 chapters that follow. They contributed long hours and their obvious talent to preparing their chapters. Our gratitude is also due to Mary Coen of the Justice Office; to David Givens and Brian Langan at The Liffey Press, who saw the book through to publication quickly, calmly and with great professionalism; and to AIB Investment Managers, whose financial assistance made this publication possible.

Seán Healy, Brigid Reynolds
and Micheál L. Collins
August 2006

LIST OF CONTRIBUTORS

John Baker is Senior Lecturer and Coordinator for Equality Studies at University College, Dublin.

Noel Cahill is an economist with the National Economic and Social Council (NESC).

Charles M.A. Clark is a Professor of Economics at St John's University, New York, and was formerly visiting Professor at University College, Cork.

Patrick Commins is an independent consultant with long experience in rural and regional development.

Richard Douthwaite is an economist, author and economic adviser to the Global Commons Institute (London).

P.J. Drudy is a Professor at the Department of Economics, Trinity College, Dublin.

Tony Fahey is a research Professor at the Economic and Social Research Institute, Dublin.

Patrick Gillespie is in the Department of Economics at the National University of Ireland, Galway.

John Healy is an economist working in the area of philanthropy.

Tom Healy is senior statistician with the Department of Education. He is currently research associate at the TCD Policy Institute.

Catherine Kavanagh is a lecturer in economics at University College, Cork.

Kathleen Lynch is Professor of equality studies at University College, Dublin.

Piaras MacÉinrí is a lecturer in geography at University College, Cork.

Colin Menton is a public servant who has recently completed a Masters Degree in Public Policy Analysis.

Brian Nolan is a research Professor at the Economic and Social Research Institute, Dublin.

Rory O'Donnell is Director of the National Economic and Social Council (NESC).

Patricia O'Hara is senior policy analyst with the Western Development Commission.

Eamon O'Shea is a Professor in the Department of Economics at the National University of Ireland, Galway.

Emer Ó'Siochrú is a planning and development consultant.

Francis O'Toole is a lecturer in economics at Trinity College, Dublin.

Aidan Punch is senior statistician on demography in the Central Statistics Office.

Patrick Riordan SJ lectures in political philosophy at Heythrop College, University of London. He is Associate Director of the Heythrop Institute for Religion, Ethics and Public Life.

Damian Thomas is with the National Centre for Partnership and Performance.

Tony Varley is a lecturer in political science and sociology at the National University of Ireland, Galway.

Sean Ward is a public sector analyst working in the civil service.

Chapter 1

PROGRESS AND PUBLIC POLICY: THE NEED FOR A NEW PARADIGM

Seán Healy *and* **Brigid Reynolds**

We live in a world which promotes constant economic progress. Wealth, employment and production are growing steadily. The conventional economic wisdom argues that continuing on this path for the foreseeable future will produce a world where everyone has a stake and where the good life can be accessed by all. It is presumed that everyone, in a world population twice as large as now, can reasonably aspire to and achieve the high-consumption lifestyle enjoyed by the world's affluent minority at present. This is seen as progress.

This conventional economic vision of the future is unattainable. Environmental degradation, encroaching deserts, unemployment, starvation, widening gaps between rich and poor, exclusion from participation in either decision-making or development of society – these are the global realities confronting decision-makers today. Economic globalisation and environmental stress are accompanied by social inequality, endemic deprivation, social unrest and violence. Millions of people in the richer parts of the world recognise these problems and are seriously concerned about the plight of the billions of people on all continents whose lived experience is one of constant exclusion from the resources and the power that shapes this world.

People feel powerless. The media present one vision of the future and assume it is the only desirable or viable future. Politicians, more concerned about the next election, rarely discuss the fundamental causes of, or long-term solutions to, the issues and problems they confront every day. It is crucial that questions be asked concerning the core assumptions which underpin and support the present situation. What model of development is being followed? Is it likely to produce a good life for all the world's citizens? What constitutes progress? What are the underpinning values on which decisions are made in shaping the future? Are we at ease with these values and the structures which flow from them? Is it possible to envision a future where everyone really would have a stake, be respected, have meaningful work and adequate income, where all could genuinely participate? These are the questions addressed in this chapter.

Ireland is at a major crossroads. It has the resources and capacity to choose a wide range of different options. Decisions made now will have major effects on the generations of the future. Consequently it is essential that the questions addressed here be addressed by policy makers. The authors offer their views on these issues as a contribution to the public debate which is so badly needed at the present time.

Paradigms

The source of many of the problems lies in the development paradigm being followed and in its view of progress. Capra generalised Kuhn's definition of a scientific paradigm to that of a social paradigm, which he defined as

> . . . a constellation of concepts, values, perceptions, and practices shared by a community, which forms a particular vision of reality that is the basis of the way the community organises itself (Capra 1996).

A paradigm contains core beliefs and assumptions. It is a model or framework from which analyses, decisions and actions flow. "The world is flat" is a good example of a paradigm. If one accepts this, then one holds certain values, takes certain actions and expects certain results. On the other hand, if one's paradigm is that "the world is round" then one holds different values, takes different actions and seeks very different results. Moving from a framework which sees the world as flat to one that sees the world as round is a paradigm shift.

Paradigms are extremely powerful as they determine one's "world view". They underpin decisions concerning what constitutes a problem, how it should be approached, what action should be taken and what the desired outcome might be (Healy and Reynolds, 1993). History shows that if a paradigm is producing negative results, however, it is not always changed immediately. Thomas Kuhn (Kuhn, 1970) analysed how paradigm change was effected in the natural sciences. Changes did not occur through a process of cumulative research which brought people ever closer to a final solution to the problems encountered. Rather it happened through a "revolution in which a small group of scientists recognise that the existing frame of reference is inadequate for the resolution of newly emerging problems" (McCabe, 1996). They seek out a new paradigm. Change, however, is resisted and the transition is never smooth (Dunne, 1991). As the existing paradigm becomes more recognisably inadequate the new one attracts more and more support until the old one is finally abandoned. Tension and conflict are usually part of the transition process as are rearguard actions in defence of the outdated paradigm. Total acceptance of the new paradigm can take a long time as was the case for example in the world of science in the shift from the Copernican paradigm to the Newtonian one and again in the later shift to the Einsteinian one.

The dominant paradigm underpinning public policy-making today is mechanistic. Capra describes it as follows:

> The paradigm that is now receding has dominated our culture for several hundred years, during which it has shaped our modern Western society and has significantly influenced the rest of the world. This paradigm consists of a number of entrenched ideas and values, among them the view of the universe as a mechanical system composed of elementary building-blocks, the view of the human body as a machine, the view of life in society as a competitive struggle for existence, the belief in unlimited material progress to be achieved through economic and technological growth, and – last, not least – the belief that a society in which the female is everywhere subsumed under the male is one that follows a basic law of nature. All of these assumptions have been fatefully challenged by recent events. And, indeed, a radical revision of them is now occurring (Capra, 1996).

This world view dates back to the sixteenth century when developments in astronomy and physics resulted in a paradigm shift. Galileo, reflecting the focus of the time, taught that science should be restricted to the essential priorities of material bodies. By "essential" he meant priorities that could be measured like shapes, numbers, movements, etc. Colour, sound, taste and smell were excluded. In other words, the human senses and emotions were not considered reliable means of "measuring" the universe. Galileo's strategy of directing scientists' attention to the quantifiable properties of matter has been proved very successful. But it was a development in one direction only and has had its cost. As R.D. Laing has said:

> Out go sight, sound, taste, touch and smell and along with them has since gone aesthetics and ethical sensibility, values, quality, form; all feelings, motives, intentions, soul, consciousness, spirit. Experience, as such, is cast out of the realm of scientific discourse (Laing, 1982).

Isaac Newton formulated the fundamental laws of physical reality. This resulted in a shift from an organic view to a mechanistic view of the material universe (including people). Nature was seen as the perfect machine, composed of distinct parts and governed by exact laws. However there was no measurement to show that the whole is greater than the sum of the parts. Philosophers and sociologists followed in Newton's wake, drawing on his approach and sought to discover the basic axioms and principles of social reality. The machine was used as the basic model and was applied both to the state and to individuals. Mechanistic physics became the dominant paradigm of the modern world. It has had many positive effects and opened up great new possibilities ranging from the development of technology to the emergence of liberal democracy. But it also has had dramatic limitations which were unseen by the thinkers and policy-makers who adopted it with enthusiasm.

These limitations are especially obvious to people encountering current global problems. The ecological crisis, the emphasis on hierarchy, addressing the issue of difference through conflict and confrontation, defining work in a very narrow way, these are simply a few, very varied effects which flow from adoption of this mechanistic paradigm. One of its key outcomes, however, is in its impact on the understanding of progress.

Progress

Economics accepted Newtonian physics as the dominant paradigm. Progress came to be seen principally in terms of economic growth. Gross Domestic Product (GDP) became the measurement used by policy-makers. Growth in GDP came to be seen as the key indicator of progress. Everything with a market price, which was paid for, was assumed to add to the national well-being. The family and the local community are accepted by most people as essential components of their well-being. These are omitted, however, from this indicator. The natural environment is also accepted as being crucial for human survival, yet its plundering and destruction are added to this measure of progress as a plus while costs, such as the consumption of finite resources, are not deducted.

The adoption of an economic indicator as the widely accepted measurement of progress also had another side-effect: economists became the ultimate authorities on most areas of public policy. We see this clearly today in Ireland both in the context of Government decision-making and of media commentary. Over and over again the views of economists are accepted, often unquestioned, unless economists disagree among themselves. If there is no disagreement their views are given the status of absolute truth!

The end result of all of this is that growth in GDP, which is a measure and means of policy, became an end of policy in itself (Cobb, Halstead and Rowe, 1995). Because GDP growth was seen as the key to progress other aspects of policy development were not considered or given any real priority. Alternative analyses or ideas were most often dismissed without any serious consideration. The policy-making process assumed that everything people needed or wanted would follow once economic growth was sustained. Once growth is maintained, according to this approach, jobs will emerge for everyone seeking them. These in turn will produce adequate income which will see the end of poverty and the emergence of the good life for all.

There are some very serious problems with this approach, however. At the global level, economic growth has been dramatic yet the number of people living in poverty has never been higher. The redefinition of work as paid employment which has accompanied this approach has resulted in ever-larger numbers of people being excluded from meaningful work. Nor do the vast majority of people benefit from the growth which is produced. In fact, poverty, unemployment, exclusion, poor healthcare and inadequate accommodation are the lot of an ever larger number of people on this planet.

After decades of increasing unemployment in Ireland, recent years have seen a dramatic reversal in this trend as the number of jobs doubled, the unemployment level fell from 15 per cent to just over 4 per cent and the economy began to depend on migrants to fill many available jobs. Economic growth has been dramatic and unprecedented. But as Ireland negotiates its way through this new reality it faces a number of challenges in the context of building a society characterised by fairness and well-being. Two of these challenges stand out:

- Firstly, there is the challenge of improving people's sense of well-being. Growing incomes have not led directly to increased well-being for all those who are better off. In fact, the growing competitiveness and individualism in society have made some people unhappy.

- Secondly, there are many people who have benefited little from the economic growth of recent years and who are at risk of poverty and exclusion for a variety of reasons.

If there is to be genuine progress then sustainable pathways are required to secure fairness and well-being for all in a land that now has more than sufficient resources to secure both (Healy and Reynolds, 2005). While economic development is important there is more to progress. Economic development is a means to an end, not an end in itself. The New Economics Foundation (NEF, 2004, p. 5, emphasis in the original) argues that

> For people to lead truly *flourishing* lives they need to feel they are personally satisfied and developing, as well as functioning positively in regard to society. Unfortunately too many people are instead *languishing* – living unhappy, unfulfilled lives as well as lacking social and community engagement. Estimates from the US suggest that less than 20 per cent of the population are flourishing and over 25 per cent are languishing, with the rest being somewhere in between.

We need indicators of progress that measure fairness and well-being as well as economic development. The benefits of this growth have gone, however, principally to those already better off. Budget after budget produced by successive Governments has seen little being made available to those in poverty or on lower incomes while substantial gains were provided to the better off. The only difference between Governments tended to be the scale of the disparity in the allocations to the two ends of the spectrum. This skewing of the benefits towards the better off is justified on the basis that they are the ones who produced the growth and who will re-invest their gains in generating further growth in the economy. Meanwhile, the poor are told to wait!

Alternatives Needed

The paradigm underpinning decision-making in the social policy area is not adequate to the present situation. Likewise with the generally accepted measurements of progress. What could serve as a fundamental reference point when evaluating the present situation and making decisions concerning future directions? What should guide the choice of real progress indicators? Alternatives are required. Finding agreement on what these should be, however, is not easily achieved. What should provide the anchor for an alternative paradigm or framework or model? Capra suggests an approach:

> The new paradigm may be called a holistic worldview, seeing the world as an integral whole rather than a dissociated collection of parts. It may also be called an ecological view, if the term "ecological" is used in a much broader and deeper sense than usual. Deep ecological awareness recognises the fundamental interdependence of all phenomena and the fact that, as individuals and societies, we are all embedded in (and ultimately dependent on) the cyclical process of nature (Capra, 1996).

The present authors have long argued that underlying the guiding paradigm or the choice of measurements of progress lie sets of values. The shift of paradigms requires not only a change in our way of thinking but also of our values. The existence of such values is sometimes accepted, more often denied. Daly and Cobb summarise this situation and its implications succinctly:

One of the central limitations of the academic disciplines in contributing to wisdom is their professed aim of value neutrality. That there
is here a large element of self-deception has been pointed out frequently and convincingly. The ideal of value neutrality is itself a
value that is generally highly favourable to the status quo. Which
economic questions are taken up and in what terms, even within the
range allowed by the disciplines, often depends on the interests of
the economists or even of someone who has commissioned the
study. More objectivity is in fact obtained by bringing values out into
the open and discussing them than by denying their formative presence in the disciplines . . . as long as the disciplines discourage any
interest in values on the part of their practitioners, they inevitably
discourage the ordering of study to the solution of human problems
(Daly and Cobb, 1990, p. 131).

A similar position is enunciated by Fritjof Capra:

. . . there can be no such thing as a "value-free" social science. . . .
Any "value-free" analysis of social phenomena is based on the tacit
assumption of the existing value system that is implicit in the selection and interpretation of data. . . . Economics is defined as the discipline dealing with the production, distribution and consumption of
wealth. It attempts to determine what is valuable at a given time by
studying the relative exchange values of goods and services. Economics is therefore the most clearly value-dependent and normative
among the social sciences (Capra, 1982).

Uncovering the underpinning values and having them discussed, scruti-
nised and evaluated is crucial if there is to be any agreement or consensus on what constitutes real progress (Wogaman, 1986). This is an issue
that arises in many spheres and is the often unarticulated question at the
root of people's concerns. In policy-making today there is huge pressure
to accept only one way of thinking and to reject all alternatives as non-
viable (i.e. "the end of history" view). Attempts to challenge this view
meet with one of Hirschman's three classic reactions: alternatives are
dismissed as perverse, futile or putting one's own best interests in jeopardy (Hirschman, 1991).

In Search of a World Ethic

Despite frequent references to the Celtic Tiger and the economic boom being experienced, there is much unease. People are searching for security. The awareness of rapid social change causes great insecurity. People want assurance against the future. Even news media feel the need to speculate about what is going to happen rather than report on what has happened. Those in leadership give assurance that the future is under control. Labels like "New World Order", "Post Industrial Age", "Information Age", "World Government", "Global Village" etc. are used to give an impression of inevitable benign and manageable progression.

The future is not inevitable. It will be determined largely by the decisions that are being taken now. What are these decisions? Who is taking them and on what basis? What values underpin the decision-making processes? How are questions like: "What constitutes the good life for citizens?" or "What makes a life a good one for the person who lives it?" being answered? These questions raise the relationship of ethics to decision-making (Mieth and Vidal, 1997). In a pluralist society are universal values possible?

Michael Walzer, in his reflections on various events which have evoked international response (Prague, Beijing, Bosnia, Rwanda), shows that there is something like a "core morality", a whole set of elementary ethical standards, which include the fundamental rights to life, to just treatment (also from the state), to physical and mental integrity (Walzer 1994; Curran, 1998). While it is possible to identify similar type responses from people living in different geographical and cultural areas is it possible to devise a process which would arrive at an agreed articulation of this "core morality"? We can take heart from the efforts of eminent and committed international bodies to formulate a global ethic. Worthy of particular note is the work of the council of the Parliament of the World's Religions in Chicago (1993) which was supported in principle by a report of the InterAction Council of former State Presidents and Prime Ministers under the chairmanship of the former German Federal Chancellor Helmut Schmidt (1996). These statesmen are convinced that there will be no better global order without a global ethic.

The core of a global ethic adopted by this body of statesmen has two basic principles:

- Every human being must be treated humanely

- What you wish done to yourself do to others.

On the basis of these principles the InterAction Council affirms four irrevocable directives on which all religions agree.

- Commitment to a culture of non-violence and respect for all life. The age-old directive: You shall not kill! Or in positive terms: Have respect for life!

- Commitment to a culture of solidarity and a just economic order. The age-old directive: You shall not steal! Or in positive terms: Deal honestly and fairly!

- Commitment to a culture of tolerance and a life of truthfulness. The age-old directive: You shall not lie! Or in positive terms: Speak and act truthfully!

- Commitment to a culture of equal rights and partnership between men and women. The age-old directive: You shall not commit sexual immorality! Or in positive terms: Respect and love one another!

In 1992 the United Nations Organisation Commission on Global Governance was established. In its report in 1995, entitled "Our Global Neighbourhood", it highlights the connection of rights with responsibilities. Reflecting on this report Kung first summarises the rights of human beings as:

> . . . the right to a secure life, equitable treatment, an opportunity to earn a fair living and provide for their own welfare, the definition and preservation of their differences through peaceful means, participation in governance at all levels, free and fair petition for redress of gross injustices, equal access to information and to the global commons.

Having noted that "hardly ever has it been stated in an official international document that concrete responsibilities, human responsibilities, are associated with human rights", Kung goes on to quote the report (Commission on Global Governance, 1995):

At the same time, all people share a responsibility to:

– contribute to the common good;

– consider the impact of their actions on the security and welfare of others;

– promote equity, including gender equity;

– protect the interests of future generation by pursuing sustainable development and safeguarding the global commons;

– preserve humanity's cultural and intellectual heritage;

– be active participants in governance; and

– work to eliminate corruption (Quoted in Kung, 1997, p. 226).

He notes that responsibilities were formulated long before rights:

. . . in the debate on human rights in the French Revolutionary Parliament of 1789 the demand was made: if a declaration of the rights of man is proclaimed, it must be combined with a declaration of the responsibilities of man. Otherwise, in the end all human beings would have only rights which they would play off against others, and no one would any longer recognise the responsibilities without which the rights cannot function (Kung, 1997, p. 99).

Kung discusses the relationship of law with rights and responsibilities and concludes that:

. . . no comprehensive ethic of humanity can be derived from human rights alone, fundamental though these are for human beings; it must also cover the human responsibilities which were there before the law. Before any codification in law and any state legislation there is the moral independence and conscious self responsibility of the individual, with which not only elementary rights but also elementary responsibilities are connected (Kung, 1997, p. 103).

For Kung law has no permanent existence without ethics, so there will be no new world order without a world ethic which he defines as:

the basic moral human attitude, understood individually or collectively . . . a basic consensus on binding values, irrevocable criteria and personal basic attitudes, without which any community is sooner or later threatened with anarchy or a new dictatorship (Kung, 1997, p. 105).

Relationships

What should be the basis of this "world ethic"? What should be the fundamental paradigm to replace the present mechanistic one? We argue it is right relationships. Developments in "new physics" give huge support and credibility to the centrality of relationships in the universe. Einstein initiated two revolutionary trends in scientific thought: a) the theory of relativity; and b) electromagnetic radiation. He believed in nature's inherent harmony.

> The universe is no longer seen as a machine, made up of a multitude of objects but has to be pictured as one indivisible, dynamic whole whose parts are essentially interrelated and can be understood only as patterns of a cosmic process (Capra, 1982, p. 66).

Experimental work showed that not only were atoms not solid particles, the sub-atomic particles were nothing like the solid objects of classical physics. These subatomic units had a dual aspect. Sometimes they appeared as waves, sometimes as particles. Capra explains this very complex reality as follows:

> Subatomic particles, then, are not "things" but are interconnections between "things" and these "things" in turn are interconnections between other "things", and so on. In quantum theory you never end up with "things"; you always deal with interconnections. This is how modern physics reveals the basic oneness of the universe. It shows that we cannot decompose the world into independent existing smallest units. As we penetrate into matter, nature does not show us any isolated basic building blocks, but rather appears as a complicated web of relations between the various parts of a unified whole (Capra, 1982, pp. 69, 70).

Newton's work in developing the general laws of motion in the late seventeenth century was adopted by philosophers and opinion formers of the time. The universe was seen as one huge mechanical system operating according to exact mathematical laws. As pointed out earlier, this view influenced all disciplines and policy making. It was a static view of a world made up of parts which could be treated in isolation, a view where change was measurable and predictable and hence could be controlled and managed.

This world view did facilitate much progress in various areas. However, we must recognise its limitations. While it has facilitated increased specialisation it has also resulted in increased compartmentalisation and isolation. A new world view is required which recognises that not only living systems but also inanimate matter are interconnected. This idea of interlinkage calls us to form relationships. Human development is about forming right relationships.

Approaches to understanding human existence in the social and psychological sciences see it as made up of a series of relationships. These relationships can be divided into four categories which correspond to different levels of human existence.

- Relationship with self and God (*interior life*). By getting in touch with self and the Transcendent we grow and become more human.

- Relationship with people (*social life*). Our humanity is developed and enriched through our relationships with people.

- Relationship with institutions (*public life*). If institutional structures and relationships are right human development is facilitated by those social institutions and structures.

- Relationship with the environment (*cosmic life*). Each of us is related to all the generations that have gone before us and to the generations that will follow us. Also we have a relationship with all other people living at this time and with the environment. Life itself depends on basic elements like air, water and minerals to survive. We must recognise the intrinsic value of all living beings and see humans as one particular strand in the web of life.

We grow as persons through these four sets of relationships. A just society is one that is structured in such a way as to promote these right relationships so that human rights are respected, human dignity is protected, human development is facilitated and the environment is respected and protected.

Recognition and promotion of human rights are central to building a just society understood in terms of right relationships. This is highlighted by Mary Robinson, the former President of Ireland and UN High Commissioner for Human Rights, when she argues that "respecting human rights is the surest basis on which to build a culture of peace" (Boyle, 2006). She goes on to argue that with globalisation has come the growing sense that we are all responsible in some way for helping promote and protect the rights of our neighbours, whether they live on the next street or the next continent.

We cannot claim that right relationships are the norm in a world where immense wealth and power exist alongside widespread poverty and severe deprivation. Nation states have been failing to provide an enabling environment for addressing these contrasts and securing fairness and well-being for all. Sometimes the language of human rights is weakened by overuse or misuse. Kuper (2005) argues that we must begin to understand "the potential inherent in a new constellation of power, where multinational corporations, NGOs, intergovernmental institutions, cross-border networks and informal arrangements are shaping our lives in unprecedented ways". Kuper's book goes on to argue that the responsibilities approach to human rights where we demand, in every context, to know "who must do what for whom?" provides the conceptual resources to move beyond conventional understandings and reliance on the state alone to deliver people's human rights. In Kuper's book Onora O'Neill points out that most approaches to global justice assume that states are the primary agents – a concept that runs into difficulties when states are unjust or weak, as many are. This situation provides a range of challenges to developing a world ethic based on right relationships and the paradigm shift such a world would require.

Side by side with human rights there is also a need to recognise the importance of sustainability. There is a growing awareness that sustainability must be a constant factor in all development, whether social, economic or environmental. This fact was reiterated by Kofi Annan, the Secretary-General of the United Nations, at the opening of the World Summit on Sustainable Development in Johannesburg, South Africa (September 2002). There he stated that the aim of the conference was:

> . . . to bring home the uncomfortable truth that the model of development that has prevailed for so long has been fruitful for the few, but flawed for the many.

And he further added that

> ... the world today, facing the twin challenges of poverty and pollution, needs to usher in a season of transformation and stewardship – a season in which we make a long overdue investment in a secure future.

Sustainable development has been defined in many different ways. Perhaps the best-known definition is that contained in *Our Common Future* (World Commission on Environment and Development, 1987, p. 43):

> development that meets the needs of the present without compromising the ability of future generations to meet their own needs.

As we stated at the beginning of this section, we argue that the new paradigm should be right relationships and these relationships should include the personal (spiritual and social), institutional/public and cosmic areas. The work of building a just society should focus on the sustainability of these right relationships. In this context sustainability includes environmental, economic and social sustainability.

Citizenship

How might this new paradigm of right relationships and our earlier comments on the development of a global ethic and the balancing of rights and responsibilities be incarnated in a meaningful and tangible way? It is essential that this be done. Otherwise, these ideas may be deemed interesting or worthy but ultimately be ignored for want of a concrete means of accessing them. We suggest the concept of citizenship as the key to this end. Citizenship is hardly a new concept but it is one which is argued about and understood differently by different groups today.

Historically there are two major traditions (Heater, 1990; Oliver and Heater, 1994; Weld 1987). One sees citizenship in terms of rights (Marshall, 1950; Doyal and Gough, 1991; Ginsburg, 1994). This comes from the liberal political tradition which emerged in the seventeenth century. It views civil and political rights as the means by which the state guarantees the freedom and formal equality of individuals. The second tradition sees citizenship in terms of obligation (Mead, 1986; Novak et al., 1987). This emerged from the civic republican tradition of classical Greece. It goes back as far as Aristotle and views political participation as civic duty and emphasises responsibilities. These two different approaches have been conceptualised as "citizenship as a status" vs. "citizenship as a practice" (Oldfield, 1990). The first of these prioritises the individual citizen while the second emphasises the wider society (Heater, 1990).

Those who support the first of these approaches include classic liberals, who restrict citizenship to the formal and political rights needed to protect individual freedom. They also include people in the tradition of Marshall who see social rights as necessary in terms of promoting freedom (Marshall, 1950). Those who support the second of these approaches include those who argue that the real citizen is actively involved in political and civic affairs (present-day followers of civic republicanism). They also include those who insist on the obligation of (some?) citizens to take up paid employment or to engage in some service of the community. Those who argue for more responsible attitudes to the environment can also be placed in this approach.

Marshall identified three sets of citizenship rights: civil, political and social. These have underpinned the development of the dominant understanding of citizenship in Europe in the second half of the twentieth century. In the US, however, civil and political rights were highlighted while social rights were not emphasised (Turner, 1990; Fraser and Gordon, 1994). Discussion on the nature of rights and the status of social rights has become a major issue again in more recent years with the emergence of the new right which gives priority to property rights over all other forms of citizenship rights. This new debate is rooted in different understandings of freedom. The new right sees freedom in negative terms as the absence of coercion and interference. If this were accepted then the role of government would be confined to protecting the freedom of individual citizens. Involvement by government in promoting an understanding of freedom as the ability to participate in society as full citizens is rejected by the new right. The new right's understanding of freedom is too limited. If one asks what negative freedom is for, it is to enable people pursue their own ends. But this cannot be separated from the ability to pursue those ends. Consequently, the freedom and the ability to pursue chosen ends are inextricably linked (Plant, 1988). The right to participate in decision-making in social, economic, cultural and political life has been urged by Gould (Gould, 1998). Seven clusters of rights — health, social, cultural, civil, economic, pacific and political rights — have been identified by Held who argues that these are crucial in facilitating free and equal political participation (Held, 1987, 1989).

An interesting development along these lines in the Irish context can be seen in the concept of the developmental welfare state (DWS) developed by the National Economic and Social Council (NESC, 2005) which formed the core of the *Towards 2016* national social partnership agreement. The DWS approach involves a life-cycle approach to policy development. In each stage of the life-cycle provision is made to ensure service delivery, income adequacy and participation/activation. This approach can be seen as trying to ensure that people's rights are delivered and that participation is secured for all.

However, this emphasis on social rights as central to citizenship is often downplayed today and in its place far more emphasis is placed on duties under various headings. For example, there has been a movement which identifies taking up paid employment to support their families as the prime obligation faced by social welfare recipients (Mead, 1986; Novak et al., 1987). This approach has been gaining ground in some countries and many welfare-to-work and workfare programmes reflect this change of priorities. The obligation to work is often presented as uniting all citizens in making a contribution to the common good. However, its application varies in practice. Those with sufficient wealth or income from other sources can ignore this obligation if they so wish. Those targeted by welfare-to-work and workfare programmes are very often poor and the jobs available to them are usually low-paid, often dirty and unpleasant. Consequently, people's right to work is turned into an obligation (to take up whatever paid employment is available) which has to be met only by those already experiencing exclusion. What this does in practice is to reinforce the existing inequalities in the interests of the better off (Jordan, 1989). The identification of work with paid employment has also led to the downgrading of caring, particularly in the family context. In practice such work often is not seen as fulfilling the "paid employment" requirement. Such an approach is based on a very narrow understanding of the meaning of work and a denial of the social component of human rights and right relationships.

So we see that citizenship has two historical roots based in the traditions of liberalism and civic republicanism. One views citizenship as status carrying a range of rights. The other views it as a practice involving both obligations and political participation broadly defined. Ruth Lister argues that "while the rights and participatory approaches to citizenship remain conceptually different, they do not necessarily have to conflict; indeed, they can be seen as being mutually supportive, even if tensions between them remain". She draws them together in a critical synthesis around the notion of human agency (Lister, 1998). She argues that:

> . . . to act as a citizen requires first a sense of agency, the belief that one *can* act; acting as a citizen, especially collectively, in turn fosters that sense of agency. Thus, agency is not simply about the capacity to choose and act but it is also about a *conscious* capacity which is important to the individual's self-identity (Lister, 1998, p. 38).

Citizenship, then, both as a practice and in the relationship between practice and rights, can be seen as a dynamic process. We believe this synthesis provides the basis for putting some flesh on the new paradigm we have argued is necessary. It also enables the issues we raised concerning core moral values to be placed within an integrated framework. The issue of sustainability (environmental, economic and social) also needs to be included if our paradigm of right relationships is to be fully developed. We recognise that the outline contained here needs substantial development. We are constrained by space from writing further on the issue but we believe it offers great potential for useful investigation. The new relational paradigm we propose is consistent with the global ethic we outlined. It is also consistent with developments in the scientific field. Acceptance of this paradigm would open up new frontiers for full citizenship for all people (Healy and Reynolds, 1993).

New Progress Indicators

One issue remains to be addressed here. If a paradigm shift towards right relationships is required then how should progress be measured? We believe that much work needs to be done in this area. Progress indicators should be developed in four key overlapping areas and at a number of different levels. These four areas are economic, political, cultural and social.

In the area of economics the traditional indicators could be maintained. However, some modification would be required in measures such as GNP to ensure they included costs as well as benefits. Further indicators need to be adopted in this context, however. These would include measures of poverty, of income distribution and of wealth distribution. Every person has a right to have sufficient resources to live life with dignity (Healy and Reynolds, 1996). Indicators are needed to monitor this area.

In the political area new indicators are needed which would identify the real participation levels of people both in public decision-making and in the development of society. If interdependence is to have any meaning then indicators are also needed to measure how progress in one nation is affecting development in other countries. New forms of governance are beginning to emerge which seek to find a balance between representative democracy and a more participatory process of democracy. Progress indicators are needed in this context.

In the cultural area a wide range of indicators is needed. We accept the definition of culture developed by UNESCO:

> culture may now be said to be the whole complex of distinctive spiritual, material, intellectual and emotional features that characterise a society or social group. It includes not only the arts and letters, but also modes of life, the fundamental rights of the human being, value systems, traditions and beliefs (UNESCO, 1982).

Consequently progress indicators could be developed on the quality of life and work, on media, language, education, youth and popular culture, recreation, sport. This may seem very wide-ranging. However, it could be done by developing a national cultural policy and developing indicators to measure progress in this area.

In the social area progress indicators are needed on equality, most notably in the context of gender (Lister, 1998). In this context the conceptual framework outlined by the National Economic and Social Forum (1996) would be most useful. This comprises four stages:

1. Equality of formal rights, opportunities and access

2. Equality of participation

3. Equality of outcome or success

4.   Equality of condition.

These are not exhaustive and it is clear that the areas overlap. However, it is useful to focus on progress indicators in this way as it helps identify all the areas for which progress indicators need to be developed. It also helps to identify the policy areas within which these indicators should now be incorporated.

There is also a need to ensure progress indicators are developed for different levels of society ranging from the local to the global. One of the reasons for this is interdependence. The mechanistic view of the world and of society has resulted in increased compartmentalisation and isolation. Integration has not been a priority and its absence has produced many problems which could have been avoided.

We have already identified the central importance of sustainability (social, economic and environmental) in a world seeking to develop right relationships. Consequently, indicators are also required in this area. A central initiative in this context should be the development of "satellite" or "shadow" national accounts. Our present national accounts miss fundamentals such as environmental sustainability. Their emphasis is on GNP/GDP as scorecards of wealth and progress. These measures, which came into widespread use during the Second World War, more or less ignore the environment, and completely ignore unpaid work. Only money transactions are tracked. Ironically, while environmental depletion is ignored, the environmental costs of dealing with the effects of economic growth, such as cleaning up pollution or coping with the felling of rain forests, are added to, rather than subtracted from, GNP/GDP. New scorecards are needed. These scorecards also need to include other variables such as the value of unpaid work.

Some governments have picked up on these issues, especially in the environmental area. They have begun to develop "satellite" or "shadow" national accounts, which include items not traditionally measured. The national social partnership agreement *Towards 2016* (covering the period 2006–2015) commits the Irish government to examine the application of satellite accounts in the area of environmental sustainability. CORI Justice welcomes this development. One final point needs to be emphasised in this context. A wide range of groupings should be involved in choosing meaningful indicators and in deciding how these should be applied. It should not be acceptable that only professional elites or powerful institutes have the right to decide what constitutes progress or development (Healy and Reynolds, 1996). Agenda 21 recognises a range of major groups that should be involved in this process. These are women, children and youths, indigenous people, farmers, local authorities, workers and trade unions, business and employers, the scientific and technical community, and non-governmental organisations. This list provides a good starting point. We would add poor people and unemployed people.

Conclusion

In this chapter we identified major problems facing our world today. We argued that the source of many of these problems lies in the development paradigm being followed and in its inadequate understanding of progress. We highlighted the limitations of (a) the dominant mechanistic paradigm and (b) the emphasis on a narrow understanding of economic growth as the key measurement of progress. Having argued that alternatives are required we suggested what some of these might be. A global ethic is required and we suggested some elements which might form the core of such an ethic. We proposed that right relationships would be a better paradigm to underpin development than the current mechanistic one. Having outlined some of the key dimensions in such a paradigm we showed how these were linked to the building of a just society.

If this new paradigm, underpinned by a global ethic, were accepted by policy makers and others we suggested that the most tangible way of incarnating this, and ensuring the balancing of rights and responsibilities, would be in a broader understanding of the concept of citizenship. An argument was made for the development of genuine progress indicators in the (overlapping) economic, political, cultural and social areas as well as at different levels of society ranging from the local to the global and in the area of sustainability. Having outlined what some of these indicators might be we argued for the involvement of a wide range of groupings in choosing meaningful indicators and in deciding how these should be applied. We believe a public debate is urgently needed around the issues of progress, paradigms and policy. We offer this chapter as a contribution to that debate.

References

Agenda 21 (1993), *The Earth Summit's Agenda for Change*, Michael Kearing, Centre for Our Common Future.

Boyle, K. (ed.) (2006), *A Voice for Human Rights: Mary Robinson,* Philadelphia: University of Pennsylvania Press.

Capra, F. (1982), *The Turning Point,* London: Fontana Books.

Capra, F. (1996), *The Web of Life,* London: HarperCollins.

Cobb, C. Holstead, T. and Rowe, J. (1995), "If the GDP Is Up Why Is America Down?", *The Atlantic Monthly,* October 1995.

Curran, E. (1998), *Absolute Moral Norms in Christian Ethics*, Bernard Hoose, (ed.)

Daly, H.E. and Cobb J.B. (1990), *For the Common Good,* London: The Merlin Press.

Doyal, L. and Gough I. (1991), *A Theory of Human Need*, Basingstoke: Macmillan.

Dunne, J. (1991), "The Catholic School and Civil Society: Exploring the Tensions" in *The Catholic School in Contemporary Society*, CMRS Education Commission.

Erikson, R. (1993), "Descriptions of Inequality: The Swedish Approach to Welfare Research" in Nussbaum, M. and Sen, A. (eds), *The Quality of* Life, Oxford: Clarendon Press.

Fraser, N. and Gordon, L. (1994), "Civil Citizenship against Social Citizenship" in van Steenbergen, H. (ed.), *The Condition of Citizenship*, London: Sage.

Ginsburg, N. (1994), "Agendas and Prognosis for Social Policy " in Page, R. and Baldock, J. (eds), *Social Policy Review 6*, Canterbury: Social Policy Association.

Gould, C. (1988), *Rethinking Democracy*, Cambridge: Cambridge University Press.

Healy, S. and Reynolds, B. (2005), *Securing Fairness and Wellbeing in a Land of Plenty*, Dublin: CORI Justice Commission.

Healy, S. and Reynolds, B. (1996), "Progress, Values and Public Policy" in Reynolds, B. and Healy, S. (eds.), *Progress, Values and Public Policy*, Dublin, CORI, pp. 11-59.

Healy, S. and Reynolds, B. (1993), "Work, Jobs and Income: Towards a New Paradigm" in Reynolds, B. and Healy S. (eds.), *New Frontiers for Full Citizenship*, Dublin: CMRS.

Heater, D. (1990), *Citizenship*, London: Longman.

Held, D. (1987), *Models of Democracy*, Cambridge: Polity Press.

Held, D. (1989), *Political Theory and the Modern State*, Cambridge: Polity Press.

Interaction Council (1996), *In Search of Global Ethical Standards*, Vancouver, Canada, No. 2.

Jordan, B. (1989), *The Common Good: Citizenship, Morality and Self-Interest*, Oxford: Basil Blackwell.

Kelly, A. (1989), "A Cultural Policy for Ireland", *Administration*, Vol. 32, No. 3, 1989.

Kuhn, T. (1970), *The Structure of Scientific Revolutions,* Chicago: University of Chicago Press.

Kung, Hans (1997), *A Global Ethic for Global Politics and Economics*, London: SCM Press.

Kuper, A. (ed.) (2005), *Global Responsibilities; Who Must Deliver on Human Rights?* New York: Routledge.

Laing, R. D. (1982) *The Voice of Experience,* New York: Pantheon,.

Lister, R. (1998), *Citizenship: Feminist Perspectives*, London: Macmillan.

McCabe, M. (1997), "Clashing Paradigms: Leadership in the Church Today", *SMA Bulletin*, Christmas 1997, pp. 1-12.

Marshall, T.H. (1950), *Citizenship and Social Class,* Cambridge: Cambridge University Press.

Mead, L. (1986), *Beyond Entitlement: The Social Obligations of Citizenship*, New York: The Free Press.

Mieth, D. and Vidal, M. (1997), *Outside the Market No Salvation?* London: SCM Press.

National Economic and Social Forum (1996), *Equality Proofing Issues*, Dublin: NESF.

National Economic and Social Forum (1997), *A Framework for Partnership - Enriching Strategic Consensus through Participation*, Dublin: NESF.

New Economics Foundation (2004), *A Well-being Manifesto for a Flourishing Society*, London: NEF.

Novak, M., J. Cogan, B. Bernstein et al. (1987), *A Community of Self-reliance: The New Consensus on Family and Welfare*, Milwaukee: American Institute for Public Policy Research.

Oldfield, A. (1990), *Citizenship and Community, Civic Republicanism and the Modern World,* London: Routledge.

Oliver, D. and D. Heater (1994), *The Foundations of Citizenship*, Hemel Hempstead: Harvester Wheatsheaf.

Plant, R. (1988), *Citizenship, Rights and Socialism*, London: Fabian Society.

Reynolds, B. and S. Healy (eds.) (1993), *New Frontiers for Full Citizenship*, Dublin: CMRS.

Scott, S., Nolan, B. and Fahey, T. (1996), *Formulating Environmental and Social Indicators for Sustainable Development,* Dublin: ESRI.

Turner, B. (1990) "Outline of a Theory of Citizenship", *Sociology*, Vol. 24, No. 2.

UNESCO (1982), World Conference on Cultural Policies, Mexico.

Walzer, M. (1983), *Spheres of Justice: A Defence of Pluralism and Equality*, Oxford: Oxford University Press.

Walzer, M. (1994), *Thick and Thin: Moral Argument at Home and Abroad,* Terre Haute, Indiana: University of Notre Dame Press.

Wogaman, J.P. (1986), *Economics and Ethics: A Christian Enquiry*, London: SCM Press.

Chapter 2

EQUALITY

John Baker[1]

O n the face of it, equality is just another of those principles that Irish society is happy to endorse on ceremonial occasions so long as it doesn't impinge on real life. There it is in the Easter Proclamation: "The Republic guarantees . . . equal rights and equal opportunities to all its citizens, . . . cherishing all the children of the nation equally." The Constitution also pays its respects: "All citizens shall, as human persons, be held equal before the law" (Article 40.1). Meanwhile, back in the real world, Ireland is a deeply unequal country, marked by one of the most unequal distributions of income in Europe, by massive class inequalities in educational participation, by entrenched intolerance towards minorities such as Travellers and immigrants. So equality seems to be no more than a pious aspiration, an idea that is fine for the Constitution so long as it stays there.

This picture is complicated, however, in two major ways. First, despite the widespread complacency with which privileged people view Ireland's gross inequalities, the issue refuses to go away. Groups that have been oppressed and marginalised – women, Travellers, disabled people, gays and lesbians, working class communities and others – continue to assert their claim to equal treatment. The second complication, and the main concern of this chapter, is that equality has more than one meaning: there are many different types of equality. So it is not enough to demand "equality": we need to know what kind of equality we want.

In this chapter, I summarise the analysis of equality that Kathleen Lynch, Sara Cantillon, Judy Walsh and I put forward in *Equality: From Theory to Action* (2004), where we distinguish three different definitions or conceptions of equality: basic equality, liberal egalitarianism and equality of condition. These different ideas of equality place very different demands on Irish society, and by implication on the relations between Ireland and the rest of the world. However, it is not that easy to believe in basic equality without becoming a liberal egalitarian, or to be a liberal egalitarian without taking the next step to equality of condition.

Over the last century, there have been many attempts to define equality and to classify types of egalitarianism. The framework presented here is only one alternative, which is particularly relevant to contemporary Irish society. Although it is closely related to work by modern theorists of equality, the main aim is to distinguish broad approaches to equality rather than to analyse particular theories. Thinking about equality is constantly challenged both by new academic work and, more importantly, by social movements of the marginalised and oppressed. The framework below is meant for now, not forever, and is meant to be open enough to allow for different interpretations and perspectives.

Basic Equality

The idea of basic equality is the cornerstone for all egalitarian thinking: the idea that at some very basic level all human beings have equal worth and importance, and therefore are equally worthy of concern and respect. It is difficult to explain these ideas precisely, since many people who claim to hold them are happy to defend a wide range of other inequalities, including the view that some people deserve more concern and respect than others. Perhaps what is really involved in basic equality is the idea that every human being deserves some basic minimum of concern and respect, placing at least some limits on what it is to treat someone as a human being. At any rate, that is how basic equality is defined here.

The minimum standards involved in the idea of basic equality are far from trivial. They include prohibitions against inhuman and degrading treatment, protection against blatant violence, and at least some commitment to satisfying people's basic needs. In a world in which rape, torture and other crimes against humanity are a daily occurrence, and in which millions of people die every year from want of the most basic necessities, the idea of basic equality remains a powerful force for action and for change. Yet taken on its own, it remains a rather vague and minimalist idea. On its own, it does not challenge widespread inequalities in people's living conditions or even in their civil rights or educational and economic opportunities. It calls on us to prevent inhumanity, but it does not necessarily couch its message in terms of justice as distinct from charity. These stronger ideas only arise in more robust forms of egalitarianism, of the sort to which the rest of this chapter is devoted.

It is surprisingly hard to provide any *arguments* for basic equality. That is partly because it is an assumption of our age and therefore something we do not feel the need to justify, and partly because the people who reject basic equality in practice do not have any interest in arguments. (In fact, they commonly pay lip-service to equality at the same time as they are wielding the knife.) Most people willingly accept that there are such things as humane treatment and human needs; these ideas seem to be built into the very idea of morality. They are in any case the common assumptions of all modern political outlooks.

Liberal Egalitarianism

The idea of liberalism has itself been given many interpretations, all of them embracing basic equality but varying quite a lot in other ways. Liberal egalitarianism refers to those forms of liberalism that move well beyond basic equality in terms of social, economic and political equality: positions that might be called "left liberalism" and that are often found in social democratic political movements. But this still covers a wide range of outlooks.[2]

A key assumption of these views is that there will always be major inequalities between people in their status, resources, work and power. The role of the idea of equality is to provide a fair basis for managing these inequalities, by strengthening the minimum to which everyone is entitled and by using equality of opportunity to regulate the competition for advantage. Liberal egalitarians vary in both these respects. For some, the minimum to which all should be entitled barely differs from basic equality, while others have a more generous approach. The most ambitious minimum is set by Rawls's "difference principle", which states that "social and economic inequalities" should work "to the greatest benefit of the least advantaged" members of society (Rawls, 1971, p. 83; Rawls, 2001, pp. 42-43).

Liberal equality of opportunity means that people should in some sense have an equal chance to compete for social advantages. This principle has two main interpretations. The first, "formal" equal opportunity, prohibits discrimination on the basis of gender, "race", sexual orientation and other "irrelevant" differences. A stronger form of equal opportunity insists that people should not be advantaged or hampered by their social background and that their prospects in life should depend entirely on their own effort and abilities. Rawls calls this principle "fair equal opportunity" (1971, p. 73; 2001, pp. 43-44).

To make these ideas more concrete, it helps to focus on five key factors that affect nearly everyone's well-being or quality of life. These *dimensions of equality* are:

1. Respect and recognition

2. Resources

3. Love, care and solidarity

4. Power

5. Working and learning.

These five dimensions provide a framework that not only helps to map out the differences between liberal egalitarians and equality of condition, but also makes it easier to analyse inequality and to develop institutions and policies for the future.[3]

1. Respect and recognition: Universal citizenship, toleration and the private sphere

A fundamental element in the thinking of liberal egalitarians is their commitment to "social" equality in the sense of recognising the equal public status of all citizens and of tolerating individual and group differences, so long as they respect basic rights. Liberal egalitarians typically believe that citizenship should extend to all long-term residents, and the principle that in the public realm we all share an equal status as citizens is a long-standing democratic belief. The idea of toleration is another deeply entrenched part of the liberal tradition, arising from the religious conflicts of the sixteenth and seventeenth centuries. The citizens of modern, pluralist societies disagree in many ways about what matters in life and how we should live, but rather than suppress these differences, we should tolerate them and "live and let live".

These elements of the thinking of liberal egalitarians are related to the distinction they make between those aspects of human life that are subject to social and legal regulation and those that are protected against any such interference, a distinction sometimes phrased in terms of the "public" versus the "private". The idea of religious toleration was facilitated by thinking of religious belief and practice as a private concern in this sense. Another less explicit and now more controversial exemption was the realm of the family, preserving it as a central source of male dominance.

Although these ideas of universal citizenship, toleration and the private sphere are meant to define a sense in which every member of society has an equal status, they are generally considered by liberal egalitarians to be compatible with huge differences in social esteem. In this regard, as in others, it is more accurate to think of liberal egalitarianism as combining the idea of a minimum entitlement with the idea of equal opportunity than to see it as committed to strictly equal respect.

2. Resources: Poverty relief and the difference principle

The second dimension of liberal egalitarianism concerns the distribution of resources. The most obvious resources are income and wealth, and liberal egalitarians typically concentrate on those. Assuming that significant inequalities of resources are inevitable, liberal egalitarians again aim to regulate this inequality by combining a minimum floor or safety net with the principle of equal opportunity. Quite where the floor should be is a continuing issue for liberal egalitarians, illustrated in debates about whether poverty is "absolute" or "relative", but the focus remains on eliminating poverty rather than promoting equality. A more demanding liberal egalitarian principle, at least in theory, is Rawls's difference principle. Like other liberal egalitarians, Rawls assumes that there will be major inequalities of income and wealth. But rather than being satisfied with eliminating poverty, we should aim to make the worst off as well-off as possible.

Because liberal egalitarians take inequality of resources to be inevitable, they are concerned to ensure that the competition for advantage is as fair as possible and that it is governed by equal opportunity. One of the most difficult problems for liberal egalitarians is that this is a forlorn hope. Major social and economic inequalities inevitably undermine all but the thinnest forms of equal opportunity, because privileged parents will always find ways of advantaging their children in an unequal society.

3. Love, care and solidarity: A private affair

The third dimension of equality is conspicuous by its absence from the work of most liberal egalitarians. It is the dimension of love, care and solidarity. When we think of the conditions people typically need for even a minimally decent life, it is clear enough that relations of love, care and solidarity belong on the list. It is therefore an important equality issue to ask who has access to, and who is denied, these relations and whether the ways societies operate help to satisfy or frustrate these human needs.

The most plausible explanation of the liberal egalitarian neglect of love, care and solidarity is that liberals tend to see these as private matters that individuals should work out for themselves. That stance sits uncomfortably with the fact that many of the institutions of liberal societies are both dependent upon and have a direct impact on these relationships. All societies rely on the love and care typically provided by women to children and other dependents. At the same time, the organisation of work and transportation has an obvious effect on the amount of time workers can spend with their families. The way the state organises residential facilities for disabled people, or denies accommodation to Travellers or homeless people, also has a huge impact on their personal relationships.

Were we to construct a more adequate liberal-egalitarian approach to love, care and solidarity, the natural place to start would be with the ideas of a minimum standard and equal opportunity. We would have to consider how to enable every member of society to develop an adequate range of loving, caring and solidary relationships. We would also have to consider whether social arrangements systematically work in ways that make it harder for some groups of people to meet these needs than other groups, since this would be contrary to equal opportunity. But in keeping with the general shape of liberal-egalitarian ideas, we would consider it inevitable that some people would have much more satisfactory access to relations of love, care and solidarity than others.[4]

4. Power relations: Civil and personal rights and liberal democracy

The fourth dimension of liberal egalitarianism concerns relations of power. The protection of basic civil and personal rights against the powerful, particularly the state, is a central and long-standing idea within liberalism. These rights include the prohibition of torture, equality before the law, freedom of expression and the right to own property. Such civil and personal rights are familiar features of modern liberal regimes and are one way of setting limits on inequalities of power.

Liberalism has also had a long association with democracy and with a certain conception of political equality. The right to vote, and its extension over the past two centuries to workers, women and ethnic minorities, is clearly an egalitarian idea. But we need to contrast these equal political rights with the fact that privileged groups have much more influence on public policy in all liberal democracies than disadvantaged groups. Liberal democracy also tends to concentrate on conventional forms of politics, neglecting power inequalities in the economy, the family, religion and other areas. Liberal democracy and the conception of political equality that goes with it are thus themselves examples of the general idea that liberal equality is about regulating inequality rather than eliminating it.

5. Working and learning: Occupational and educational equal opportunity

Work is a central fact of human life, but it is double-edged. In some respects it is a burden, something people have to be induced to do by threat or reward. In other ways it is a benefit, not just because of its influence on status, resources and power but because it provides opportunities for social contact, personal satisfaction and self-realisation. Work is immensely varied, consisting of all forms of productive activity, whether paid or unpaid. It therefore includes the work people do in households, voluntary bodies and political organisations.

The process of learning is closely related to work, because work always involves learnt abilities. But there are many other forms of learning, relevant to the whole range of human activities. Like work, learning is both beneficial and burdensome. It can be a joy and can open up all kinds of doors, but not all learning is fun: it often involves hard work. Another similarity with work is the wide range of contexts in which learning takes place, not just in the formal educational system but in families, playgrounds, workplaces and politics.

Perhaps surprisingly, liberal egalitarians have paid little attention to minimum standards of work. Yet the idea that everyone has a right to work, under minimally decent conditions, is common enough in the modern world. By contrast, the aim of achieving certain minimum educational standards – of a universal right to basic education – does feature in the writings of liberal egalitarians (e.g. Walzer, 1985). In any case, the central liberal-egalitarian principle for dealing with working and learning is equal opportunity. The "formal" interpretation of equal opportunity inspires anti-discrimination legislation that makes it illegal to deny education or work to people because of their religion, sex or other specified characteristics. Rawls's principle of "fair equal opportunity" implies, more strongly, that the educational system should try to compensate for the obstacles faced by people from working class and other disadvantaged backgrounds in developing their talents. Since most educational systems do too little in this regard, another of its implications is the development of "affirmative action" policies in employment and higher education, as ways of correcting for unequal opportunities earlier in life.

The emphasis placed by liberal egalitarians on equal opportunity means that it is left to the operation of "fair" social institutions to decide who ends up in which occupations and how tasks are distributed among these occupations. The benefits and burdens attached to different kinds of work are taken as given, even though this has the effect of consigning some people to lives of unmitigated toil.

Reform of Existing Social Structures

The discussion so far has concentrated on the key principles endorsed by liberal egalitarians, but the picture would be incomplete without asking how they think of these principles as being implemented: what social structures or institutions are necessary to put them into practice? The vision liberal egalitarians have of how the world operates and of the possibility of change seems to be based on the assumption that the fundamental structures of modern welfare states are at least in broad outline the best we are capable of. Certainly, liberal egalitarians want to improve the ways we manage our societies. But they seem to believe that certain key features of modern welfare states – including representative government, a mixed economy, a developed system of social welfare, a meritocratic educational system, and a specialised and hierarchical division of labour – define the institutional framework within which any progress towards equality can be made, and that the task for egalitarians is to reform these structures rather than to alter them in fundamental ways. It is partly because these structures inevitably produce inequality that liberal egalitarians think that inequality is unavoidable, and that the egalitarian agenda must be defined in terms of regulating inequality rather than eliminating it.

Justifying Liberal Equality

The views of liberal egalitarians represent a tremendous challenge to the entrenched inequalities of the contemporary world. Can this challenge be morally justified? Many of the arguments put forward by liberal egalitarians are rooted in the idea of basic equality, the claim of every person to basic concern and respect. If we are to take these ideas seriously in modern societies, where people have complex and diverse needs and differ profoundly in their moral and political beliefs, we must surely take steps to tolerate their differences, to protect their personal freedoms and to enable them to participate in decision-making. The ideas of concern and respect also support the principle that everyone should have a decent standard of living, including the resources necessary for exercising their rights and freedoms. The most distinctive idea of liberal egalitarians, equal opportunity, can be seen as a way of showing basic respect and concern for human beings as rational agents with differing talents and ambitions. Of course, these remarks are not a fully developed argument for liberal egalitarianism: they merely indicate the ways in which many authors have attempted to construct one. In any case, the principles of liberal egalitarians are in fact widely accepted in contemporary welfare

states. But are these principles strong enough? It is argued below that
they are not.

Equality of Condition

Liberal egalitarianism is based on the assumption that many major inequalities are inevitable and that our task is to make them fair. The idea of
equality of condition sets out a much more ambitious aim: to eliminate
major inequalities altogether, or at least massively to reduce the current
scale of inequality.[5] The key to this radical agenda is to recognise that
inequality is rooted in changing and changeable social structures that
create, and continually reproduce, the inequalities that liberal egalitarians
see as inevitable. But since social structures have changed in the past, it
is at least conceivable that they could be deliberately changed in the future. Exactly how to name and analyse these structures and their interaction is a matter of continuing debate, but one way or another they clearly
include capitalism, patriarchy, racism and other systems of oppression.

Discussions of equality sometimes contrast equality of opportunity
with "equality of outcome". Although the distinction is a good shorthand
account of the difference between liberal egalitarianism and equality of
condition, it can be misleading, since equality of condition is also concerned with people having a wide range of choices, not with their all
ending up the same. The difference is in how equal opportunity is understood. Liberal equal opportunity is about fairness in the competition for
advantage. It implies that there will be winners and losers, people who
do well and people who do badly. Equality of condition is about opportunities in a much stronger sense, about enabling and empowering people
to exercise what might be called real choices among real options. Inevitably these choices would lead to different outcomes, which could have
profound effects on people's lives: wasting money on useless things, falling in love with the wrong person, choosing an occupation that doesn't
suit. But these outcomes, precisely because they would take place in a
context of continuing equality in the overall conditions of people's lives,
would not undermine people's roughly similar prospects for making further choices. These ideas can be made more concrete by returning to the
five dimensions of equality.

1. Equal respect and recognition

Like liberal egalitarianism, equality of condition includes the principle of the equal status of citizens. Where it differs from liberalism is in relation to the ideas of toleration and the public/private distinction. Critics of liberalism have pointed out that toleration is not always quite what it seems, since it is perfectly possible to tolerate someone while retaining a sense of one's own superiority. Thus, dominant cultures can "tolerate" subordinate ones, but not vice versa. There is no suggestion that the dominant view may itself be questionable, or that an appreciation of and interaction with subordinate views could be valuable for both sides.

For these reasons, supporters of equality of condition tend to talk about the appreciation or celebration of diversity and to say that differences from the norm are to be welcomed and learned from rather than simply permitted. They urge us to be glad to live in a multicultural society, to welcome differences in sexual orientation and so on. While this shift from "tolerate" to "celebrate" is of real value, it can mislead us into thinking that it is wrong to criticise beliefs we disagree with, that the politically correct view is to cherish all difference. That could not possibly be a coherent position, if for no other reason than that not every group is prepared to celebrate – or even to tolerate – others. In the end, we show more respect for others by engaging critically with their beliefs than by adopting a *laissez-faire* attitude. The real task is to engage in such criticism in an open and dialogical spirit, recognising the real effort that the privileged must make to understand the voices of members of subordinate groups and to open their own ideas to critical interrogation. Such a dialogue often reveals that there is more common ground between apparently divergent views than meets the eye, and that there are centres of resistance within even the most oppressive cultures. This relation of mutually supportive and critical dialogue between members of different social groups can be called "critical interculturalism". A commitment to critical interculturalism does not of itself resolve all the difficult issues raised by cultural conflict, but it creates a space in which they can be constructively addressed.

Equality of condition also seeks to redefine the contrast between public and private. It accepts that some aspects of life should be protected from public scrutiny, but it rejects the idea that whole spheres of life should be largely exempt from principles of justice. In particular, it highlights the oppression of women and children inside both families and religions (Cohen, 2000; Nussbaum, 2000; Okin, 1989). If we are truly committed to equality of recognition, we cannot cordon off these important spheres of life from critical scrutiny.

As noted above, liberal egalitarians are generally quite comfortable with inequality of social esteem based on personal achievement. The world looks very different from the point of view of people with low social status, who can recognise more clearly the contribution of accident, indoctrination and fashion in deciding who gets high esteem and who does not. Attitudes of admiration and disdain may be part of the human condition, but equality of condition calls on us to limit their range. Without such limits, inequality of esteem is all too easily translated into all of the other dimensions of inequality.

2. Equality of resources

In contrast to liberal egalitarianism, equality of condition aims at what can best be described as equality of resources. Like liberal egalitarianism, it recognises income and wealth as key resources. But the idea of resources naturally includes a number of other goods that people find useful in achieving their aims in life. For example, Bourdieu (1986) has emphasised the importance of what he calls social and cultural capital. Social capital consists of the durable networks of social relationships to which people have access, while cultural capital includes both people's embodied knowledge and abilities and their educational credentials. A person's resources also include non-financial conditions for accessing goods and services, such as the right to public services and the right not to be excluded from privately provided goods and services by discriminatory treatment, as well as environmental factors such as a safe and healthy environment, the geographical arrangement of cities, the accessibility of buildings and so on. Time, particularly leisure time, is another important resource in people's lives.

Equality of condition accepts the urgency of satisfying basic needs and providing a safety net against poverty. But its wider understanding of resources helps us to recognise a wider range of needs than some liberal egalitarians are inclined to attend to and to take a less market-oriented view of how these needs should be satisfied. For example, people with physical impairments not only need higher incomes than those without these impairments, but also changes in the physical environment that promote their inclusion into activities that others take for granted.

Beyond the level of need, equality of condition aims for a world in which people's overall resources are much more equal than they are now, so that people's prospects for a good life are roughly similar. This does not mean that everyone should have the same income and wealth, because people have different needs and because there are so many other important resources to take account of. There is also an egalitarian case for permitting modest inequalities in income to offset inequalities in the burdens of work – otherwise people who worked hard would be worse off than those who didn't. But if these are the only kinds of reason that can justify inequality of income and wealth, it follows that people who have similar needs and who work in similarly demanding occupations for similar amounts of time should have similar income and wealth. This implies, for example, that there should be no significant differences in income and wealth between manual workers and office workers, women and men or people of colour and whites, and that public services should serve these different groups equally well. So equality of condition would certainly involve a dramatic change in the distribution of income and wealth and in access to public services. To adopt this view is to reject the liberal belief that substantial inequalities of resources are inevitable.

3. Equality of love, care and solidarity

As already noted, human beings typically have both a need and a capacity for intimacy, attachment and caring relationships. The ability to recognise and feel some sense of affiliation and concern for others is a typical human trait. Being cared for is also a fundamental prerequisite for human development. All of us have urgent needs for care at various stages in our lives, as a consequence of infancy, illness, impairment or other vulnerabilities. In addition, relations of love, care and solidarity help to establish a basic sense of importance, value and belonging. Love, care and solidarity therefore constitute a family of distinct but similar relationships that are important for their own sake and for achieving a wide range of other goals.

Caring is both an activity and an attitude. In caring for others, we act to meet their needs in a way that involves an attitude of concern or even love. This duality is characteristic of the wider field of relationships of love, care and solidarity. So our needs for loving, caring and solidary relationships are needs to be enabled to do something for others as well as to feel attached to them.

These facts show that, at the very least, an adequate conception of equality must involve a commitment to satisfying basic needs for love, care and solidarity. But equality of condition involves a more ambitious goal: a society in which people are confident of having, if not equal, then at least ample prospects for loving, caring and solidary relationships. To achieve this goal, it is necessary to change structures and institutions that systematically impede people's opportunities to develop such relationships, including the organisation of paid work, processes of gender-stereotyping and the gendered division of labour, attitudes and institutional arrangements concerning disability, and of course the burdens of poverty and deprivation. Societies cannot *make* anyone love anyone else, and to this extent the right to have loving, caring and solidary relations is not directly enforceable. (Parents can be legally required to care *for* their children, but they cannot be forced to care *about* them.) But societies can work to establish the conditions in which these relationships can thrive. As noted below, a key element in this task is to make sure that the work involved in providing love and care is properly recognised, supported and shared.

4. Equality of power

A central obstacle to equality of condition is the pervasive network of power relations in all societies. In recognition of the dangers of state power, equality of condition retains the liberal commitment to basic civil and personal rights, including the right to personal private property. But since the general right to private property enshrined in some declarations of rights, including the Irish Constitution (Articles 40.3.2 and 43), can be used to protect the economic power of the privileged, equality of condition has to involve a more limited definition of what this right involves. And because social structures often involve the systematic oppression of social groups, equality of condition may entail creating certain group-related rights, for example the right of an ethnic minority to political representation. This is not a licence for social groups to behave as they choose towards their members. It is a recognition that specific group-based rights may sometimes promote equality of power.

As mentioned earlier, liberal democracies have had a strictly limited impact on power inequalities, leaving dominant groups largely unchallenged in conventional politics and neglecting many other types of power. Yet it is precisely these power relations that sustain inequality between privileged and disadvantaged groups. Equality of condition responds to these limitations on two fronts. First of all, it supports a stronger, more participatory form of politics in which ordinary citizens, and particularly groups who have been excluded from power altogether, can have more control over decision-making. Secondly, it challenges power in other areas such as the economy, the family, education and religion. In both cases, the aim is to promote equality of power rather than to regulate inequalities of power, recognising that power takes many forms, is often diffuse and has to be challenged in many different ways.

5. *Working and learning as equals*

In contemporary societies, both the burdens and benefits of work are unequally distributed. Those who shoulder the greatest burdens often receive the least benefit. The burdens of menial work are generally accompanied by the worst wages and working conditions. The burdens of caring in individual households are typically unpaid, unrecognised and carried out with little support. Equality of condition involves redressing these inequalities, requiring that both the burdens and the benefits of work are much more equally shared and that people's working conditions are much more equal in character. As suggested above, where some people continue to take on greater burdens, it is acceptable for them to receive greater benefits. But the central aim of equality of condition is to ensure that everyone has the prospect of satisfying work.

The most fundamental change entailed by equality of condition would be in the division of labour. To be sure, human life depends on the completion of many tedious and disagreeable tasks and will continue to do so. But it is a matter of social organisation whether these tasks are concentrated in particular occupations or fairly shared among the population as a whole. Equality of condition also requires us to recognise, support and share the work of loving and caring: work that is now done primarily by women and is usually unpaid. In particular, it entails a commitment to meeting the needs of those who care for dependents (Kittay, 1999). It also implies a rebalancing of other work so that everyone is able to engage in the work of love and care.

These principles about work have important implications for learning because they require educational systems that give everyone worthwhile occupational choices. But there are many other aspects of learning, including learning to develop personal relationships, to engage in literature and the arts, to participate in politics and so on. If equality of condition is about enabling people to exercise real choices, then equality in learning is about self-development in its broadest sense. And since learning is itself an activity that takes up a great deal of each person's life, we need to think of how to make it satisfying in its own right.

Challenge to Existing Structures

It seems clear enough that equality of condition challenges the basic structures of contemporary societies. Predominantly capitalist economies continually create and reproduce inequalities in people's resources, work and learning; they rely on and perpetuate inequalities of power and status; they place tremendous strains on relations of love, care and solidarity. Contemporary cultural systems embody and reinforce inequalities based on gender, class, disability, ethnicity, "race" and sexual orientation. Existing networks of care and solidarity – societies' affective systems – work together to the advantage of privileged groups while denying support to the most vulnerable. Established political systems reinforce the privileges of dominant groups throughout society. All of these systems pervade the social institutions that shape our lives.

Equality of condition would require very different institutions and structures, developing participatory, inclusive, enabling and empowering ways of cooperating in all areas of life. These structural changes would play a crucial role in ensuring that everyone had roughly equal prospects for a good life, largely through promoting greater equality in each of its five dimensions.[6]

Justifying Equality of Condition

Equality of condition presents a radical challenge to existing attitudes and structures, but many of the arguments in its favour come from basic and liberal egalitarianism. The most general way of putting the case is that the aims of both basic and liberal egalitarians are thwarted by the inequalities of wealth, status and power that they refuse to challenge. On the face of it, it seems a simple enough task to ensure that everyone in the world has access to clean water and decent food, but layers of entrenched inequality make even these minimal goals unattainable. On the face of it, it seems easy enough to ensure that everyone's basic rights are protected, but in practice the rights of powerless and marginalised people are easily violated. Liberal egalitarians are eloquent proponents of equal opportunity, but equal opportunity is impossible so long as privileged people can deploy their economic and cultural advantages on behalf of themselves and their families – as they will surely continue to do, so long as the consequences of success and failure are so spectacularly different.

Other arguments for equality of condition arise out of the internal tensions and contradictions of liberal egalitarianism. We have seen how the idea of toleration can involve the very inequality of respect it purports to reject. There is a similar contradiction in the "incentive" argument for inequality, namely that when privileged people demand an incentive for helping the worst off, they are taking resources away from the very people they pretend to be concerned about (Cohen, 2000, chapter 8). Another tension arises in arguments for fair equality of opportunity. This principle is often justified by appealing to the interest each person has in "experiencing the realisation of self which comes from a skilful and devoted exercise of social duties" (Rawls, 1971, p. 84). Yet it is clear enough that an unequal society provides precious few people with this experience.

Additional arguments for equality of condition come from reflections on the limited assumptions of liberal egalitarians, particularly their reluctance to confront the ways in which inequality is generated and sustained by dominant social institutions. A related problem is the liberal egalitarian emphasis on choice and personal responsibility, which plays an important role in supporting the idea of equal opportunity but tends to ignore the extent to which people's choices are influenced by their social positions.

These, then, are some of the key arguments for equality of condition.[7] If they are sound, they show that although most of the principles of liberal egalitarianism are worth defending, they do not go far enough. Western societies in particular, and the world more generally, are deeply unjust and need to be radically rebuilt.

Conclusion

This chapter has set out a framework for thinking about equality, distinguishing the basic egalitarianism that belongs to all modern political thinking from the ideas of liberal egalitarianism and equality of condition (see Table 2.1). It has outlined and contrasted the main ideas of liberal egalitarianism and equality of condition by identifying five key dimensions of equality – respect and recognition, resources, love, care and solidarity, power and working and learning – and by commenting on their relation to social structures. It has also sketched some reasons why a person who takes basic equality seriously is obliged to endorse liberal egalitarian ideas, and how the difficulties involved in holding those views provide grounds for equality of condition. But these arguments are far from complete. In particular, they allow for the possibility that someone could support equality of condition in some dimensions but not others.

In contemporary Ireland, basic egalitarianism is taken for granted at the level of moral and political rhetoric. The Irish left is primarily concerned with aspects of liberal egalitarianism. Unlike some leftists, I do not consider "liberal" to be a term of abuse. But I have tried to show that there is an alternative to liberal egalitarianism, and that this position is a natural extension of the concerns and difficulties involved in the liberal egalitarian outlook. If I am right in believing that equality of condition is a better view, this only emphasises the scale of the tasks ahead of us. We face the challenge not only of constructing plausible models of an egalitarian society, but also of developing a political movement for radical change.

Table 2.1: Basic Equality, Liberal Egalitarianism and Equality of Condition

Dimensions of Equality	Basic Equality	Liberal Egalitarianism	Equality of Condition
Respect and recognition	Basic respect	Universal citizenship Toleration of differences Public/private distinction	Universal citizenship "Critical interculturalism": acceptance of diversity; redefined public/private distinction; critical dialogue over cultural differences Limits to unequal esteem
Resources	Subsistence needs	Anti-poverty focus Rawls's "difference principle" (maximise the prospects of the worst off)	Substantial equality of resources broadly defined, aimed at satisfying needs and enabling roughly equal prospects of well-being
Love, care and solidarity	Protection against blatant violence	A private matter? Adequate care?	Ample prospects for relations of love, care and solidarity
Power relations	Protection against in-human and degrading treatment	Classic civil and personal rights	Liberal rights but limited property rights; group-related rights
		Liberal democracy	Stronger, more participatory politics Extension of democracy to other areas of life
Working and learning		Occupational and educational equal opportunity Decent work? Basic education	Educational and occupational options that give everyone the prospect of self-development and satisfying work

References

Baker, John (1987), *Arguing for Equality*, London: Verso.

Baker, John, Kathleen Lynch, Sara Cantillon, and Judy Walsh (2004), *Equality: From Theory to Action*, Basingstoke: Palgrave Macmillan.

Bourdieu, Pierre (1986), "The Forms of Capital" in J.G. Richardson (ed.), *Handbook of Theory and Research for the Sociology of Education*, Westport, CT: Greenwood, pp. 241-58.

Bubeck, Diemut Elisabet (1995), *Care, Gender, and Justice*, Oxford: Oxford University Press.

Cohen, G.A. (1995), *Self-Ownership, Freedom and Equality*, Cambridge: Cambridge University Press.

Cohen, G.A. (2000), *If You're an Egalitarian, How Come You're So Rich?* Cambridge, MA: Harvard University Press.

Dworkin, Ronald (2000), *Sovereign Virtue: The Theory and Practice of Equality*, Cambridge, MA: Harvard University Press.

Fraser, Nancy (1997), *Justice Interruptus: Critical Reflections on the "Post-Socialist" Condition*, Princeton: Princeton University Press.

Fraser, Nancy (2000), "Rethinking Recognition", *New Left Review*, No. 3, pp. 107-20.

Kittay, Eva Feder (1999), *Love's Labor: Essays on Women, Equality, and Dependency*, New York: Routledge.

Nielsen, Kai (1985), *Equality and Liberty: A Defense of Radical Egalitarianism*, Totowa, NJ: Rowman & Allanheld.

Norman, Richard (1987), *Free and Equal*, Oxford: Oxford University Press.

Nussbaum, Martha C. (2000), *Women and Human Development: The Capabilities Approach*, Cambridge: Cambridge University Press.

Okin, Susan Moller (1989), *Justice, Gender, and the Family*, New York: Basic.

Phillips, Anne (1999), *Which Equalities Matter?* Cambridge: Polity Press.

Rawls, John (1971), *A Theory of Justice*, Oxford: Oxford University Press.

Rawls, John (2001), *Justice as Fairness: A Restatement*, Cambridge, MA: Harvard University Press.

Sen, Amartya (1992), *Inequality Reexamined*, Oxford: Oxford University Press.

Walzer, Michael (1985), *Spheres of Justice*, Oxford: Blackwell.

Young, Iris Marion (1990), *Justice and the Politics of Difference*, Princeton: Princeton University Press.

Notes

---

[1] This chapter is based on Chapter 2 of Baker et al. 2004. We are grateful to many people, including Harry Brighouse, Vittorio Bufacchi, G.A. Cohen, Niall Crowley, Andrew Sayer and Erik Olin Wright for their detailed comments on that chapter. Readers are encouraged to consult that book for further elaboration of the ideas set out here and for more detailed references.

[2] The paradigm case of a liberal egalitarian is Rawls (1971; 2001). Other prominent liberal egalitarians are Dworkin (2000) and Walzer (1985).

[3] The five dimensions are chosen for ease of exposition and to provide a coherent framework. They draw particularly on the work of Rawls (1971; 2001) and Fraser (1997; 2000). Our discussion is also indirectly influenced by the capabilities approach of Sen (1992) and Nussbaum (2000), especially in respect to emphasising enabling rather than outcomes and to highlighting the category of love, care and solidarity.

[4] A few authors have attempted to incorporate love, care and solidarity into broadly liberal-egalitarian theories of justice, including Walzer (1985), Nussbaum (2000), Bubeck (1995) and Kittay (1999).

[5] The idea of equality of condition is meant to draw together insights from a range of radical egalitarians including Baker (1987), Cohen (1995; 2000), Fraser (1997; 2000), Nielsen (1985), Norman (1987), Okin (1989), Phillips (1999) and Young (1990). There are however many differences among these authors and not all would agree with equality of condition as specified here.

[6] See Baker et al., 2004, Ch. 4 and Part II, for a fuller explanation and discussion of these issues.

[7] For more arguments, see Baker, 1987; Cohen, 1995, 2000; Nielsen, 1985; Norman, 1987; Okin, 1989; and Young, 1990. One general upshot of these arguments is that, contrary to appearances, it is liberal egalitarians who are unrealistic or utopian, because their limited aims are in fact unrealisable in a world marked by severe inequality and because they neglect the real influence of social structures.

Chapter 3

THE COMMON GOOD OF
A PLURALIST SOCIETY

Patrick Riordan SJ

The controversy provoked by the celebration of the ninetieth anniversary of the 1916 Easter Rising in 2006 brought into public focus an ongoing debate about Ireland's culture and identity at this stage of its history. The symbolic significance of this particular event highlighted the issue of tradition in our current self-understanding. In particular, the still unresolved question of the viability of the Belfast Agreement as providing a way forward for Northern Ireland underlies the anxiety that political violence may not be relegated to the past. The ambivalence towards the celebration of this anniversary in contrast to the fiftieth anniversary in 1966, 40 years ago, is explained by the violence experienced on the island in the intervening decades. Who are we now? How do we stand towards our past? As we inevitably change and develop the traditions we have inherited, do we have a choice about the direction we take? How then do we wish to shape our future?

The many influences which are requiring adaptation and change are familiar but they warrant reflection. In the intervening decades since the fiftieth anniversary Ireland has joined a European community which is now an expanded Union of 25 states. We have experienced unprecedented prosperity. We have become a society which relies on foreign workers to perform the many tasks which keep life going, an amazing development considering the centuries during which Ireland was a land of emigration, providing people and skills for other countries and economies. Our health services, our hospitality industry, our building trade, three domains of activity with particular symbolic significance for Irish identity, cannot function at all now without workers from abroad. The traditional figures of the Irish barman, the Irish nurse and the Irish navvy belong to memory. Their roles are now likely to be taken by a charming young woman from Lithuania pulling your pint, a young Filipino or Filipina taking your temperature, the construction worker building a new hotel chatting with his mates in Polish. Ireland's international role has meant that it has had to play its part in accepting asylum seekers and refugees from war-torn and crisis-ridden parts of the world. Just like other European states it has accommodated a Muslim diaspora so that the public presence of religion in Ireland has a very different aspect. The country has not been able to avoid involvement in the debates concerning the major international events of the wars in Afghanistan and Iraq. The influences bringing change are unmistakeable. Given these pressures, what direction do we wish to take? What changes are required of our political culture in the broad sense, and how can our education system in particular facilitate the training of citizens for participation in the political process?

What kind of society do we wish to construct, given our present situation? What kind of politics do we desire? What are the characteristics which we would wish our public life and political culture to exhibit, and which qualities would we want citizens to exemplify in their participation in public debate and political process? These are the questions guiding my reflections in this chapter. In other words, what is, or can be, the common good of a pluralist society with democratic institutions? My object is to explore the values which could be the basis of agreement in a society which is otherwise diverse in relation to fundamental religious and moral commitments.[1]

The system of education in any society is central to the process of its reproduction and development. Faced with the question of our social direction, we have to consider the ultimate purposes of education, and this must include a consideration of the models of human person and citizen which are the intended products. These in turn cannot be adequately considered without an attempt to articulate the ideals of political culture and the quality of social, economic and public life which we wish to bring about. I begin with a consideration of issues arising in the context of education policy, and show how these can be opened up to more fundamental questions about the goals of society. In a second section I will draw from a North American debate on issues of education in order to further sharpen the issues for our political culture. In a third part I will outline the political assumptions behind my delineation of the problem, and in a final fourth part briefly sketch the values which could be part of an overlapping consensus, and which could in turn guide thinking on the ultimate purposes of education within a pluralist and democratic society.

Educating Citizens for Ireland's Future

The restructuring of the university sector in the last decade provided the occasion for a serious reflection on the role of the university in relation to more ultimate purposes.[2] The *Universities Act* (1997), while radically reorganising the institutional and legal structures governing university life in Ireland, also managed to address the question of purpose. But it is remarkable that this section of the Act has been the least problematic, and the least discussed. And yet the question at stake here is a most important one for a society, and especially one confronted by enormous changes, such as Ireland is facing today.

Section 12 of the 1997 *Universities Act* lists eleven different purposes which the University might serve. It is to be noted that the formulation does not see this list as exhaustive; rather, it asserts

The objects of a university shall include:

(a) to advance knowledge through teaching, scholarly research and scientific investigation,

(b) to promote learning in its student body and in society generally,

(c) to promote the cultural and social life of society, while fostering and respecting the diversity of the university's traditions,

(d) to foster a capacity for independent critical thinking amongst its students,

(e) to promote the official languages of the State, with special regard to the preservation, promotion and use of the Irish language and the preservation and promotion of the distinctive cultures of Ireland,

(f) to support and contribute to the realisation of national economic and social development,

(g) to educate, train and retrain higher level professional, technical and managerial personnel,

(h) to promote the highest standards in, and quality of, teaching and research,

(i) to disseminate the outcomes of its research in the general community,

(j) to facilitate lifelong learning through the provision of adult and continuing education, and

(k) to promote gender balance and equality of opportunity among students and employees of the university.[3]

I reproduce this section in full, because as a piece of recent legislation it allows me the possibility of discussing the quality of our political reflection on fundamental questions concerning our ultimate social objectives. I wish to highlight a number of issues which arise from this text, and which can open up more radical questions.

Knowledge and Education

Many traditional educators are consoled to find that the advancement of knowledge and research and the promotion of learning head the list of objects of the university, although it must be admitted that no prioritisation is intended in the ordering of the list. Fearful that the demands of the economy and the labour market's need for skilled workers has become too influential in setting the agenda for education, traditionalists will be reassured by this reaffirmation of the value of knowledge and learning. One would almost expect the phrase ". . . for its own sake" to be added to the last sentence. But the Act does not presume that knowledge is for its own sake. It gives no clear reason why knowledge and research are valuable for our society. Why are knowledge and learning and research to be fostered? Is it for their own sake, or for the sake of something else? In either case, what reasons can be given to make sense of this and to justify the dedication of significant social and economic resources to this purpose? The Act does not answer this question, but it is not clear that in our political culture there is an overlapping consensus on an answer to the question either.

Vocational Function

Alluded to in the previous paragraph is the tension between the vocational and the educational functions of the university. The training of students in the skills and expertise required in the range of professions from engineering to teaching is a recognised part of the university's role, but it is in tension with its other roles. Everyone can see easily enough the rationale behind the training of good technicians, scientists, lawyers, doctors and architects, but how do we explain the importance of educating good people and good citizens? The latter cannot be the object of certification, and yet a society which is organised politically in a democratic system must be at least as concerned about the quality of its voters as it is about the quality of its pharmacists. All the more so when it is no longer possible to assume that all citizens share the same broad cultural heritage. Yet, while reflecting this tension, the wording of the Act suggests no way of managing the tension. This remains as a task for political discourse.[4]

Social and Cultural Roles

An innovation in the Act is the assertion of responsibility on the part of the university towards society. Against any tendency there might be for the university to become an ivory tower, comfortably isolated from the society around it, the Act imposes on the university the obligation "to promote the cultural and social life of society". Admittedly, this is qualified with a clause which allows the diversity of the university's traditions to be fostered and respected. In a further listed object, in which the promotion of the Irish language is given special place, the obligation to preserve and promote the distinctive cultures of Ireland is imposed. But which cultures are to be preserved and promoted? All which can be identified as existing in Ireland, including the culture of political violence? This example reflects the treacherous ambiguity of the term "culture". It is frequently used with a normative connotation, implying that culture is good. At the same time it can be used purely empirically, without any evaluative implication, as when one speaks of the "drugs culture" or "the cultural subjugation of women". Because drug addiction or oppression of women can be identified as cultural phenomena does not entitle them to automatic approval. How does the Act use and understand the term? Is the cultural and political life of society to be understood also in a non-normative fashion? If not, what criteria are available to delimit the extent of the obligation which the Act imposes on the university?

Recognition of the diversity of cultures seems impossible without at the same time facing the fact that cultures can be in conflict with one another. Different cultural and political traditions view one another as opponents and the ideals and purposes they pursue are mutually incompatible. And yet the Act speaks as if it were possible for the university to promote all cultures. How ought the university, and indeed society in general, deal with this social and political reality of conflicted diversity? What contribution can the university make to society's handling of conflict? These are the fundamental questions which arise, and which ought to be part of a background discussion of the aims of education.

The Role of Religion

The absence of any explicit mention of religion from the list of purposes of the university, which may have made sense when originally drafted, now ten years later seems like a glaring omission. Our European neighbours have experienced considerable difficulties in dealing with the Islamic diaspora and it is naïve to think that Ireland will not be challenged also in attempting to accommodate religious and cultural groups which resist integration. Among the resources which the political culture must have available to it to deal with these challenges will be reliable knowledge of the religious beliefs and traditions of the relevant groups. This has two aspects. One aspect is the capacity of the existent political system to absorb the radically other – to do so requires of it that it have an adequate literacy in the values and concerns of that other. The second aspect is the capacity of the incoming group to occupy an appropriate place in the host society – fostering that capacity requires of it that it engage in the public reflection on its values and concerns, for which appropriate space and facilities must be provided.

Political and Economic Roles

There is a delightful irony in the way in which the Act identifies the cultivation of independent critical thinking amongst students as a purpose of the university, while at the same time requiring the university to "support and contribute to the realisation of national economic and social development". It appears as if the university is simply to accept the goals of national economic and social development having been set by some other entity, the government perhaps, and to contribute to the national endeavour in a supportive capacity. But could its contribution be critical? Is it part of its function to provide independent critical thinking on the direction and goals of economic and social development? Should it hold up for analysis the social and economic trends which are the consequences of political decisions and apply its critical faculties? And if so, what criteria should it rely on for the critique of national development? Can it use principles of social justice other than those adopted in the national project?

This brief review of one section of the *Universities Act* has highlighted basic questions which may not be avoided in any serious attempt to articulate the purposes of education and to delineate the kind of product of the educational system which is envisaged. I move on now to consider a debate from North America, in which similar questions were addressed.

Cultivating Humanity

Tradition and change have set the parameters of the debate about the political and cultural role of education elsewhere also. Martha Nussbaum (1997) has attempted to defend developments in North American college education against the kinds of criticisms made, for example, by Allan Bloom (1987).[5] Critics of developments in liberal education such as Allan Bloom are fearful that a fostering of tolerance for a plurality of religious and philosophical traditions will lead to relativism among young people. Brought up to show tolerance and respect for groups and ideas with which their own tradition is in conflict, students are likely to regard their own inherited convictions and value-commitments as merely one possible candidate among many, without any superior claim to truth or validity. The resulting culture would tend to homogenisation without any representation of strong religious or moral convictions, and the consequent elimination of the very plurality which was the favoured quality of society. These are the kinds of arguments one also hears from Muslim advocates of a distinct Islamic education.

In the course of her defence, Nussbaum sketches the role which education should play in training citizens who are capable of participating in a richly diverse society and political system. Her main focus is on the role of education in producing citizens. This is a classical focus, as befits a scholar of Aristotle and of Stoicism. Her title, *Cultivating Humanity*, is borrowed from Seneca. If university education produces citizens, then the most fundamental question in order to specify the purpose of education is to identify what the good citizen in the present day should be and should know. Diversity of culture and background and lifestyle characterises the contemporary world. To be capable of contributing to handling the kinds of problems which arise in this world of differences requires capacities for dialogue in search of intelligent cooperative solutions. Cultivation of these capacities is the aim of a liberal, as distinct from a technical or vocational, education.[6] Nussbaum subscribes to the Stoic ideal of the "world citizen" and the "cultivation of humanity" as the aim of liberal education. She lists three capacities which are essential. The first is the capacity for critical examination of oneself and one's traditions, so that one can live the "examined life" in Socrates' sense. This means the ability to subject inherited meanings and values and authorities to critical review. A second ability is the capacity to understand oneself as sharing a common humanity with all other men and women. While local identity and loyalty is easily known and expressed, it requires a deliberate process of education to inculcate the awareness of a solidarity with others of differing racial and national backgrounds, religious affiliation, and with other differences including gender and sexuality. The third ability which she emphasises is narrative imagination, namely, the ability to think and imagine oneself in the place of another, and to understand the emotions and wishes and desires of those very different from ourselves. She admits that these three abilities do not exhaust the requirements for intelligent citizenship, but they are central to the role to be played by a liberal education in preparing citizens for today's world.[7]

If people are to be capable of acting as responsible citizens in a very complex world, they must have learned to live alongside differences of many kinds. They must have learned to understand themselves and their traditions as situated in a plural and interdependent world.[8] This means that they must be capable of operating at two levels: they must be comfortable in their own tradition and be at home with their distinctive identity; on the other hand, they must be capable of meeting others from differing backgrounds in the public forum on a basis of understanding, respect and tolerance. There is a tension between these two, which is not always well managed. One tendency is to regard the public forum as a market place or bargaining table, where the differing identity and interest groups meet in order to compete for power. Nussbaum contrasts her ideal of the world-citizen and its corresponding form of politics with that of interest-group politics:

> The world-citizen view insists on the need for all citizens to understand differences with which they need to live; it sees citizens as striving to deliberate and to understand across these divisions. It is connected with a conception of democratic debate as deliberation about the common good.[9]

Debate and dialogue is contrasted with bargaining and deal-making.[10] A recent publication by the renowned political philosophy Michael Walzer argues that liberal political philosophy has neglected the dimension of passion in politics, and with its typical abstraction to the autonomous individual it overlooks the myriad ways in which persons' identities are shaped by the pre-choice allegiances of their encumbered selves.[11] Precisely in the context of such a passionate diversity there is a need for a commitment to fostering an alternative space for political engagement than the competition for power in forms in which the stronger (more passionate, more numerous, better organised and mobilised) is sure to win. This is Nussbaum's agenda.

As a defence of a form of education, Nussbaum's book is somewhat anecdotal, relying on descriptions of what is being done in various universities. She includes a number of universities which have strong religious affiliations, including the Catholic Notre Dame, and the Mormon Brigham Young University. She notes that colleges and universities with religious affiliation have a dual mission: "advancing higher education in a pluralistic democracy, and perpetuating their specific traditions".[12] Her argument is that both tasks can be fulfilled and that for both to be done well the essentials of world-citizenship must be present. These essential qualities are, first, the ability to reflect critically on oneself and one's own tradition; second, the ability to understand oneself as bound by ties of recognition and concern with all other women and men, and third, the capacity to imagine oneself in the shoes of another. Her response therefore to Bloom's anxiety is to argue that there is no necessary link between a fostering of plurality and relativism. The cultivation of understanding and tolerance for diversity which is essential to the education of the world-citizen is not necessarily to the detriment of local and particular identity. Rather, the sense of solidarity with others based on common humanity merely means that one must accept limits in the name of reason and humanity to what one would do in the name of some local or particular loyalty.

> The goal of producing world-citizens is profoundly opposed to the spirit of identity politics, which holds that one's primary affiliation is with one's local group, whether religious or ethnic or based on sexuality or gender.[13]

This is a frequently reiterated theme in her book:

> . . . we need not give up our special affections and identifications, whether national or ethnic or religious; but we should work to make all human beings part of our community of dialogue and concern, showing respect for the human wherever it occurs, and allowing that respect to constrain our national or local politics.[14]

The Political Context

Nussbaum is writing about education in a society and a world which is increasingly multicultural. Ireland is not as rich in variety as the United States of America, but neither is it homogeneous. We are diverse, we are different, we are complex. What then is the basis of our cooperation in political and legal institutions? What can we be said to share, in terms of beliefs and values, which can be the basis of our public life? What is our common good?

John Rawls (1996) has used the term "overlapping consensus" to name this range of agreement in an otherwise diverse situation.[15] In a pluralist society, in which citizens are divided by reasonable though incompatible religious, philosophical and moral doctrines, what basis can there be for their cooperation in maintaining a system of law and of government? The comprehensive philosophical or religious world-view of any one group as a basis for political and legal order could not expect to evoke allegiance from adherents of other comprehensive doctrines. It would seem that an overlapping consensus in support of the basic structures of a political and legal system could only be achieved by an articulation of that order which was not tied to any one comprehensive doctrine yet was capable of receiving the support of all.[16]

Within pluralist societies which are made up of groups of differing and even conflicting religious and philosophical views, there is no possibility of achieving commitment by each citizen to a civil and political system if that system is identified with only one of the competing groups. There is need for a language to express the rationale of the civil and political order which is accessible to all citizens equally. Much of the literature in the contemporary political philosophical debate is devoted to finding and clarifying the necessary language. Dr Attracta Ingram of UCD states the problem well:

> . . . as citizens of modern republics, we meet as strangers without a common good except whatever we can forge together for the advancement of our diverse ends.[17]

Given this complexity in our social situation, there is a need to find common ground which could be a foundation on which to build political and legal arrangements, capable of enjoying the support of citizens who have differing moral and religious traditions and therefore diverse substantive ideals of human flourishing. In her book she argues for a conception of rights rooted in the good of autonomy to fill the role of agreed starting point. Autonomy refers to the idea of self-government, and it reflects a respect for free persons as capable of ruling themselves. The rights to be accorded persons as autonomous citizens would mark out those conditions and means which anyone would have to enjoy in order to live a meaningful and independent life.[18] Her approach finds echoes in other thinkers who address similar questions as to how agreement might be constructed in a situation in which disagreement on ends and purposes prevails. For instance, a common approach is to argue that people who otherwise have independent if not conflicting goals will nonetheless be prepared to cooperate to secure the conditions which must obtain if they are to succeed in achieving their goals. Thus John Rawls (1971) focused on primary social goods of liberties, rights and opportunities, income and wealth and the bases of self-respect, as goods which anyone would wish to have, whatever their ultimate ends turn out to be.[19] A comparable notion is that of need, defined as the conditions of life, speech and action: "such conditions include not only the conditions of physical-biological life, but also the conditions for technical and practical deliberation and the setting of goals".[20] Autonomy, need, primary social goods, these are various attempts to identify a common starting point from which agreement in an overlapping consensus could be achieved in a pluralist society. In the following section I sketch out a set of values which one could expect to belong to this overlapping consensus. It must be emphasised that the philosophical reasoning to justify these conclusions would have to be more elaborate than is attempted here.[21]

Shared Values

Quality of Public Debate and Political Process

What values might belong to the overlapping consensus? Since I began with a consideration of what we would desire as purpose and product of our educational system, it is useful to continue from there. My reflections allow me to list the qualities which we would wish citizens to exhibit in their participation in public debate. Since the context is the construction of agreement on shared institutions, as well as the maintenance and development of such political and legal institutions, citizens would have to possess the necessary skills of literacy and debate in order to participate. Fostering these skills would require considerable investment and coordination in order to ensure that everyone has access to the required levels of education and to the relevant means of communication in which public debate is conducted. However, the qualities required would have to go beyond minimal literacy skills. Citizens would have to exhibit attitudes of equal respect. They would have to be prepared to treat one another as having equal entitlement to speak. But they would also have to be prepared to listen and respond to one another, and be prepared to give an account of their own positions. The readiness to relinquish manipulative interventions, the willingness to allow others their opportunity to speak and to grant them a respectful hearing, and the submission to the discipline of accepting the better argument are acquired qualities which would tend to enable people to achieve the truth and validity which they pursue in the practice of debate.

Quality of Educational System

It is evident, however, that these qualities cannot be legislated for or commanded. Yet it must be part of the common good of such a political community that the educational system would cultivate such citizens, both by effective training, and by modelling through the example of actual practice in schools and universities the kind of rational encounter which is desired. Accordingly, it will be part of the common good of concerned citizens in a liberal state that the practice of discourse be fostered, and that participants acquire the necessary willingness and attitudes for conducting argument. Concretely this will mean not only a concern about the institutional means of excluding threats to open discussion, such as the protection of the freedom of speech, but more positively a concern for the quality of education of citizens in the practice of argument.

Quality of Legal Arrangements

The common good of citizens in a pluralist but liberal and democratic society will include other institutional and structural elements. Political and legal institutions are fundamental. Citizens may well pursue different ends and may disagree on what constitutes a good life; but they can have a common interest in there being a state which respects their liberties, which does not favour the interests of some over others, and which guarantees some measure of security and protection. The acknowledgement of rights, and their protection in law, the rule of law and maintenance in practice of due process, these will be part of their common good.

Cultural Diversity

Part of the overlapping consensus among citizens participating in a liberal democratic system in a pluralist society would be an agreement that the diversity and plurality of the society is to be fostered, while at the same time the common conditions for public life are to be sustained. Education therefore would aim at both supporting the identity and distinctiveness of each group and sub-section of society, while at the same time inculcating the habits required for mutual understanding and tolerance and the functioning of common institutions. This would mean ensuring that all citizens and groups have access to the resources which are necessary for them to function well. So the political system commensurate with the ideal of the world-citizen would be designed to ensure that citizens receive the institutional, material and educational support that is required if they are to become capable of functioning well according to their own judgement and choice.

Quality of Economic Life

This is the area of social life which is liable to produce the most problems when it comes to translating agreed values into concrete policies or programmes of action. Nevertheless, it should be possible to delineate some values which could belong to the overlapping consensus. A major concern today is certainly the protection of the physical and biological environment so that it in turn will continue to be capable of sustaining human life and society. Another value widely recognised today is participation: that all have the possibility of participating according to their level of competence in society's wealth creating and distributing activity. This means having access to training, technology and markets. At this level of abstraction it is also possible to get agreement that work tasks be so designed and organised that they are compatible with workers' health and welfare, as well as dignity. An open market for goods and services ensures competition, and therefore it also provides some element of choice for the consumer as well as some safeguard against inefficiency and associated waste. Accordingly, structures and institutions which maintain open markets and which facilitate ease of access to them would be valued in a pluralist society.

Quality of Social Welfare and Health Care

Nussbaum (1990) has elsewhere elaborated the implications of the requirements that citizens have the material support necessary to ensure they are capable of functioning well according to their own judgement and choice. Focusing on what the citizen requires in order to function well, she maintains that a state's welfare system should not be understood primarily as residual, picking up those who have fallen through various nets and have not been able to fend for themselves. Rather, it should be understood as aimed at facilitating all citizens by means of a comprehensive support scheme of health care and welfare support for their functioning in a range of areas over a complete life. Treating citizens as free and equal means moving all of them across a threshold into capability to choose well, should the available resources permit this. People must be allowed scope to determine for themselves how precisely they will realise the various aspects of their good. Therefore it cannot be the concern of government to decide people's good for them, or to make them good. However, government does need some conception of what constitutes good human functioning in order to create and sustain the appropriate conditions which enable people to identify and pursue their own good. A lively, shared understanding of what constitutes good human functioning therefore is a prerequisite for this purpose and it would be part of the overlapping consensus in a pluralist society that this shared understanding be fostered.

Conclusion

Any conclusions arrived at in these reflections are very tentative. Tentative, because the argument from the role of overlapping consensus in a pluralist society to the sort of values which might be expected to make up the content of the overlapping consensus would have to be elaborated and discussed at greater length. Furthermore, the articulated values would have to be tested in attempts to translate those values into policies, and such practical attempts may reveal unwelcome implications which do not arise at the abstract level. And they are tentative, most especially because the content of overlapping consensus is not to be determined by abstract philosophical reflection, but rather through the process of political debate and public discussion. All that academic reflection can offer for this public debate is the service of clarification of both method and argument. But in the last analysis, agreement on the values which animate and guide our political and economic life must be hammered out in a process of public discussion, such as the Justice Commission of the Conference of Religious of Ireland has stimulated and facilitated through two decades of Social Policy Conferences and related publications. Sean Healy and Brigid Reynolds, through their position papers, have offered for public scrutiny and review proposals on social policy which are rooted in an articulate set of values.[22] For their arguments to succeed, this set of values must be accepted in the wider political community and achieve overlapping consensus among diverse groups. The project is precisely what is required in an evolving Ireland which is becoming more and more conscious of its diversity and of its need for a public culture. The questions about education policy highlight the need for such a project and for a more extended reflection on the values and purposes guiding social, economic and political life.

References

Bloom, A. (1987), *The Closing of the American Mind: How Higher Education Has Failed Democracy and Impoverished the Souls of Today's Students*, New York: Simon and Schuster.

Hoey-Heffron, A. and Heffron, J. eds. (2001) *Beyond the Ivory Tower: The University in the New Millennium*, Convocation of The National University of Ireland, Cork: Mercier Press.

Ingram, A. (1994), *A Political Theory of Rights*, Oxford: Oxford University Press.

Nussbaum, M. (1997), *Cultivating Humanity: A Classical Defense of Reform in Liberal Education*, Cambridge, Mass.: Harvard University Press.

Rawls, J. (1971), *A Theory of Justice*, Oxford: Oxford University Press.

Rawls, J. (1996), *Political Liberalism*, paperback edition, New York: Columbia University Press.

Reynolds, B. and Healy, S. (1992), "Participation: A Values Perspective", in Reynolds, B. and Healy, S. (eds.), *Power, Participation and Exclusion*, Dublin: Justice Commission, CMRS.

Riordan, P. (1991), *The Practical Philosophy of Oswald Schwemmer*, Lanham, MD: University Press of America.

Riordan, P. (1996), *A Politics of the Common Good*, Dublin: Institute of Public Administration.

Riordan, P. (2003a), "The Limits of Pluralism" in *Studies* 92, pp. 42-50.

Riordan, P. (2003b), "Citizenship: Burden or Challenge?" *Administration,* 51 pp. 58-72.

Riordan, P. (2004) "Permission to Speak: Religious Arguments in Public Reason", *Heythrop Journal* XLV, pp. 178-96.

"The Role of the University in Society: Proceedings of the Conference held in Dublin Castle on 20-21 May 1994", Dublin: National University of Ireland.

The Universities Act (1997), Dublin: The Stationery Office.

Walzer, M. (2004) *Politics and Passion: Toward a More Egalitarian Liberalism*, New Haven and London: Yale University Press.

Notes

---

[1] On pluralism see Riordan (2003a).

[2] For example, see *The Role of the University in Society: Proceedings of the Conference held in Dublin Castle on 20-21 May 1994*, Dublin: National University of Ireland. See also Hoey-Heffron and Heffron, (2001).

[3] *Universities Act*, 1997, p. 11.

[4] For an outline of the challenges to citizenship today, see Riordan (2003b).

[5] M. Nussbaum (1997), A. Bloom, (1987).

[6] Nussbaum (1997), p. 9.

[7] Ibid., pp. 9-14.

[8] Ibid., pp. 298f.

[9] Ibid., p. 110.

[10] I deal with this contrast in Riordan (1996) (Chapter 9, "Discourse and the Process of Politics").

[11] Walzer (2004).

[12] Nussbaum (1997), p. 258.

[13] Ibid., p. 109.

[14] Ibid., pp. 60f.

[15] Rawls (1996).

[16] For a discussion of the implications of this position for a religious world-view see Riordan (2004).

[17] Ingram (1994), pp. 3f.

[18] Ibid., p. 112.

[19] Rawls (1971), sect. 15.

[20] Riordan (1991), p. 47.

[21] See Riordan (1991) and Riordan (1996) for more elaborate attempts.

[22] See, for example, Reynolds and Healy (1992).

Chapter 4

EVIDENCE-BASED SOCIAL POLICY-MAKING

Micheál L. Collins *and* **Colin Menton**

There is now little challenge to the idea that good policy requires good information. This is particularly true in an era where public policy is becoming increasingly complex, diverse and interconnected. In the social sphere public policy is challenged by a range of diverse problems. These social problems require complex and innovative solutions.

To respond successfully to these challenges there is a need to establish, through analysis and evaluation, "what works" in terms of policy responses. There is a need to review existing policy responses in order to establish whether such interventions are working effectively, whether they are worth continuing and what scope there is for improvement or reform. Equally, it is important to examine new ways of doing things. In the context of social expenditure, there is a need to know whether expenditure is being used effectively and whether value for money is being achieved. For these reasons, it is now generally accepted that an evidence-based approach to policy-making, one where policy is made on foot of factual information, is required.

The growing importance of evidence-based policy-making in Ireland largely stems from the process of public sector reform that commenced in the 1990s with the launch of the Strategic Management Initiative (SMI). That process of reform advocated the need for an evidence-based approach to policy formulation and the assessment of policy outcomes.

An evidence-based approach which focuses on key long-term goals and outcomes is central to the social policy perspective proposed by the National Economic and Social Council (NESC) in their *Developmental Welfare State* report and the Lifecycle Framework adopted by the 2006 social partnership agreement, *Towards 2016*.

The National Statistics Board (NSB, 2003) suggests that the demands of evidence-based policy-making are creating new pressures for data to allow policy-makers to analyse and understand what is a complex and fast-changing environment. The need to improve information for policy and measuring progress on key indicators are essential to the successful implementation of an evidence-based policy approach (NESC, 2002).

NESC (2001) propose that comprehensive evidence-based policy-making is contingent on a public service-wide commitment to developing appropriate information for policy. This supposes the maximum use of existing data sources and a commitment to fully exploiting the potential of administrative data not only at the policy formation stage but also in monitoring implementation of policy. NESC stress that for such a system to work an effective system of indicators on which progress is to be assessed must first be identified.

This chapter examines issues around the selection of social indicators to provide the "evidence" required for social policy-making. In doing so the contribution of research concerning indicators in areas other than socio-economic assessments is included. In particular, the extensive literature on compiling sustainability measures provides many lessons and techniques which can be incorporated into a discussion on social indicators.

The structure of the chapter is to examine what social indicators are, the role they should play, the type of indicators that should be used, the sources of the data used to produce them and the properties which social indicators should possess.

Social Indicators

The late 1990s witnessed a revival of interest in social indicators. The growth of interest in sustainability, and the necessity to provide some social indicators towards its assessment, helped fuel this revival. However, the European Union (EU) principally drove it. Following the Maas-

tricht treaty the EU made deliberate moves to focus attention on the social obligations of union membership. This process culminated in March
2000 when the European Council meeting at Lisbon, Portugal declared
that the EU was to begin a process of drawing up "structural indicators"
to assess "employment, innovation, economic reform and social cohesion". Ultimately they presented 27 indicators as well as proposing a set
of seven "basic principles" used to select them (European Commission,
2000a, p. 9). As part of that process the EU commissioned the most
comprehensive recent assessment of social indicators which was performed by Atkinson et al. (2002). They examined indicators of social
inclusion in a pan-European context and drew on previous social measurement literature to evaluate the properties which individual indicators,
and portfolios of indicators, should possess.

The 1992 United Nations Earth Summit adopted *Agenda 21* which
made sustainable development a universally accepted goal. Its adoption
gave further impetus to the process of measuring sustainability. Therefore, throughout the 1990s an increased awareness of sustainability issues engendered a discussion of how it might be measured and what type
of indicators could be used (Moldan and Billharz, 1997, pp. 1-7). Institutions that were to the fore in this dialogue include the United Nations
Environment Programme (1994, 1995), the United Nations (1996), the
Scientific Committee on Problems of the Environment (SCOPE)
(Moldan and Billharz, 1997), the UK Round Table on Sustainable Development (1997), the World Bank (1997), The Sustainability Institute
(Meadows, 1998), the UK Department of Environment, Transport and
the Regions (DETR, 1999) and the OECD (2000).

The most significant contribution made by the sustainability literature
to indicator methodology is the Bellagio Principles. These are a set of ten
principles agreed by an international group of measurement practitioners
and researchers from five continents who met in Bellagio, Italy in November 1996. Their principles are broadly defined and serve to guide the
choice and design of sustainability indicators, their interpretation and the
communication of their results (Hardi and Zdan, 1997, pp. 1-5; Hardi,
1997, p. 28; Hodge and Hardi, 1997, pp. 7-20). The remainder of this
chapter incorporates the contributions of these principles, in addition to
those of the aforementioned institutions and social indicator researchers.

The Definition and Purpose of Social Indicators

The term indicator derives from the Latin verb *indicare* meaning "to disclose or point out, to announce or make publicly known, to estimate or put a price on" (Hardi et al., 1997, p. 8). Therefore its role is to facilitate the understanding and communication of something.

Establishing a definition for what a social indicator is has engendered sustained debate since the emergence of the social indicator movement in the late 1960s. Across the literature there have been numerous brief definitions, generally stating that an indicator represents a simplified version of reality, and a limited number of comprehensive assessments. The latter include discussions by Carlisle (1972), Carley (1981), Miles (1985) and Gallopin (1997).

Carley defines a social indicator as both a *surrogate* and a *measure* (1981, p. 2). In ideal circumstances the availability of complete information on society would eliminate the requirement to construct social indicators, simply the outcome would be known and consequently an indicator would be of no value. However, given that such a scenario is purely idealistic and unachievable, a social indicator is intended to act as a representative substitute, or *surrogate*, for the full information. In effect it operationalises "abstract and unmeasurable social concepts, like safe streets" by turning them into measurable proxies that facilitate the consideration and assessment of a concept (Carley, 1981, p. 2; Carlisle, 1972, pp. 25-28). Intuitively an indicator can never represent what it is attempting to measure in its totality; rather it can only act as a credible guide.

Achieving the translation from abstract to operational requires a social indicator only to be concerned with information that it is possible to quantify. Therefore, as a *measure*, Carley maintains that a social indicator must be quantifiable and avoid using information which cannot be expressed in some ordered scale.

Facilitating the transition of a statistic into a social indicator requires it to be identified as contributing information to our understanding of society. That understanding is normally theoretical, involving a conceptual system of some sort, and the transition to become a surrogate measure of a particular element of that system is only possible if an indicator is clearly identifiable as representing an aspect of that social system (Miles, 1985, p. 19). Furthermore, Carlisle notes that a social indicator becomes an element of the information system used to understand and evaluate those parts of the social system over which it is possible to exert some power (1972, p. 26).

The purpose of a social indicator is twofold: it evaluates and monitors. Firstly, a social indicator evaluates the extent, nature or causes of a phenomenon. It does this by capturing and quantifying an issue, so that it becomes possible for academics, policy-makers and the public to understand it. Secondly, it monitors changes within society and informs discussion on the effectiveness of particular policy initiatives. That effectiveness may be observed against stated pre-determined targets or by the size and direction of change in an indicator. The existence of an indicator also facilitates the creation of such targets and the framing of policy towards achieving them (Miles, 1985, p. 75; Bennett and Roche, 2000, p. 24; European Commission, 2000a, pp. 5-6). In many cases a social indicator simultaneously serves both these purposes.[1]

Accordingly, a social indicator may be defined as a surrogate measure chosen to "summarise or otherwise simplify relevant information, make visible or perceptible phenomena of interest, and quantify, measure, and communicate relevant information", where that relevant information concerns the reality of the society it is assessing (Gallopin, 1997, p. 15).[2]

The Types of Social Indicators

In spite of the extensive literature on indicators, be they social or sustainable, it is possible to identify the leading types of indicators. Principally, the distinction between different types of indicators is related to their intended use.

Type A: Descriptive Indicators

The first type of social indicators are descriptive indicators. These consist of indicators which portray society, and what is happening within it. They are "collections of apparent fact" such as a variable or number revealing the total amount of people unemployed or are a function of variables such as the percentage of the labour force who are unemployed (Carley, 1981, p. 24; Hardi et al., 1997, p. 8). Also these types of indicators can be problem-orientated, meaning that they are constructed to reveal information about a particular problem. Generally, this type of social indicator is the most prevalent, as it includes the regularly produced data on socio-economic issues collected by governments.

Type B: Performance Indicators

The second type of social indicators are performance indicators. These are indicators which measure society against targets or ideals, such as achieving a 5 per cent unemployment level. They also include programme evaluation indicators, meaning indicators used to assess the effectiveness of a particular policy programme given its stated aims. Performance indicators isolate the impact of a specific policy intervention and allow its efficiency and effectiveness to be assessed (NESC, 2005).

In addition, this category includes relative performance indicators, which are indicators that move relative to society. The number of individuals or households below a relative income poverty line serves as an example. As society's income levels change so too does the poverty line, but the performance target (e.g. remove all from below the line) remains the same.

Type C: Total Welfare Indicators

The third type of social indicators are total welfare indicators. These are indicators which gather together the results of a number of individual indicators and express the information they portray collectively. Prime examples included indices of well-being and so called "baskets of indicators", which without aggregating the individual indicators use them collectively to assess society.

Often total welfare indicators are used to assess how a particular area/region is performing or how a specified group is doing within society. This type of indicator is in effect a by-product of the aforementioned types A and B. Both are likely to be included in the aggregation facilitating the creation of a total welfare indicator. Table 4.1 summarises the three types of social indicators.

Table 4.1: The Three Types of Social Indicators

Type A	*Descriptive Indicators:*	Variables and functions of variables which portray society and what is happening within it.
Type B	*Performance Indicators:*	Indicators which measure society against targets or ideals (or which benchmark progress under social policy interventions).
Type C	*Total Welfare Indicators:*	Indicators which gather together the results of a number of individual indicators and express the information they portray collectively.

A further suggested type of social indicators are predictive indicators. Carlisle (1972, pp. 26-27) suggests that these are indicators incorporated into models of the social system to facilitate predictions of future trends. However, such indicators are in effect the results of using either/both type A and B indicators to reach a policy conclusion. Therefore it seems inappropriate to classify them as a separate category. In the longer term, following a significant advancement in the provision of sound intertemporal social indicator data, it may be possible for the development of scientifically appropriate models which could facilitate reliable predictions of societal outcomes. In such a context, these could be classified as "predictive indicators"; however at this stage such a development seems far off.

The Sources of Social Indicator Data

The statistics, or data, which act as the sources of social indicators principally include national statistics, surveys and administrative data. The manner in which the data is collected is of significance to the quality and potential usefulness of the eventual indicator. Consequently, an examination of all the possible sources of social indicators is worthwhile. This section categorises those potential sources, none of which is mutually exclusive, and in doing so discusses the appropriateness of each of them.

Objective and Subjective Data

Miles employs an example of a measure of people's health to distinguish between subjective and objective data. Health statistics, derived from an aggregation of the post-examination judgements of medical practitioners, are considered objective due to the fact that the individual supplying the data is autonomous. The doctor expresses an informed professional opinion on the health of an individual, and so cumulatively it is possible to get data reflecting the overall level of health among persons. Alternatively, if health statistics are collected following the questioning of people with regard to how satisfactory their state of health is, a subjective measure is achieved. It is subjective as it relies on individuals' own views of themselves, a view which may not be based on medical science (1985, pp. 66-67).

The debate among social indicator researchers, with regard to whether indicators formed from either objective or subjective indicators are optimal, is ongoing. The major proportion of indicators currently used are objective, and tend to be sourced from available evidence on societal phenomena. This ensures they are also readily verifiable. However, the feasibility of rapidly validating a measure does not mean that it should be the only source of social indicators. Subjective data, primarily sourced via surveys, have been recognised as useful in providing a further insight into social problems. Generally they concentrate on recording individual's opinions, attitudes and emotional states. It is now commonplace to use both objective and subjective data in assessments of society. Both types of data possess the potential to bring relevant, and often different, information to the fore.

Input, Throughput and Output Data

Carley suggests that social indicator data can be measures of inputs, throughputs or outputs (1981, p. 25). Measures based on inputs assess the resources made available to society to deal with some issue/problem. An example might be the number of remedial teachers per thousand pupils, or the expenditure per head of population on health care. While this type of data is easy to access, it usefulness to assessments of society is regularly questioned. Just because a certain amount of resources is made available does not guarantee that those resources are used to best effect in dealing with a particular issue. Measuring inputs takes no account of what happens after the inputs are put in place (Miles, 1985, p. 65).

Throughput measures are typically based on workload data, such as the number of prisoners or the amount of doctor visits for flu shots. Similar criticisms to those made against the input indicators are produced against these. Again, they measure what is happening rather than the quality of what is happening.

Output data is divided by Carley into two parts, intermediate output data and final output data (1981, p. 25). The former facilitates the provision of results for particular activities performed, in other words it measures what has happened in society. An example would be data on the reduction in infant mortality levels or illiteracy levels. Examples of final output data are measures of concepts such as a "healthy" population or a "better" environment. These are in effect subjective aggregate measures.

While some researchers, including Carley (1981, p. 25) and Miles (1985, p. 66) argue for the use of all these types of measures, recent assessments have focused on the primacy of intermediate output measures. It is maintained that because these measures represent actual outcomes, and not the means by which they are achieved, they reflect a more comprehensive and informative source of data (Atkinson et al., 2002, p. 20). The NSB (2003) argue that, while programme indicators relating to specific policy interventions are essential to policy evaluation, the main focus must be on social outcomes because it is these that ultimately allow us to gauge the nature and extent of social change and progress.

However, outcome measures are more difficult to attain than input measures. Input data, on expenditure and staffing levels, tends to be readily available whereas output data is limited and in many cases requires new data collection procedures (NSB, 2003). This lays down a further challenge to assessing social phenomena.

While social outcome indicators are essential to supporting evidence-based social policy, they must not be seen in isolation. The NSB (2003) propose that such indicators will be more informative when combined with both programme/policy indicators and with measures which capture the context in which the outcomes are emerging. The example cited is of a change in the proportion of elderly people in the population which, while not representing a social goal in itself, may be essential to understanding other trends relating to specific goals associated with the well-being of the elderly.

Direct and By-product data

The results of specific investigations designed to assess social conditions produce direct data. These include data from census and from surveys. Both seek to obtain information directly from the population and if properly designed can "provide wide-ranging and detailed material concerning social conditions and changes" (Miles, 1985, p. 62). In contrast, by-product data draws on data produced from administrative records. It uses those records to generate data on social outcomes. This type of data is therefore produced within "a framework of meanings which is dictated by administrative accounting needs" rather than within the context of identifying specific elements of society and constructing techniques to examine them, as is the case with direct data (Miles, 1985, p. 61). However, Bilderman (1966, pp. 113-116) critiques by-product data as being potentially misleading. He uses measures of crime levels to compare administrative data, collected from police records, to direct data collected from statistically sound societal surveys. The latter indicate a higher level of criminal activity as they capture both reported and unreported crimes, including petty theft and minor vandalism. Administrative data may therefore under-report the true situation in society, and so its use necessitates careful consideration.

In the context of the critiques of these potential sources of social indicator data it seems clear that appropriate and acceptable data should be derived from a limited number of sources. Ideally, a social indicator should be constructed from data which is directly collected, is either objective or subjective and is concerned with societal outcomes. Choosing data which meets these requirements minimises the potential for challenging the indicators produced from them.

The Properties of Social Indicators

As different disciplines make use of indicators to assess progress, policy and problems, there exists an interdisciplinary body of literature on their properties.[3] Drawing on both the sustainability and social measurement literature it is possible to identify a set of 14 principles for social indicators. Collectively, these principles indicate the necessary properties which any indicator, or group of social indicators, should possess. Following the DETR (1999), Atkinson et al. (2002) and NESC (2002), this set of principles may be divided into those which apply to individual in-dicators (10 principles) and those which apply to collections, or groups, of indicators (4 principles).

Principles for Individual Social Indicators

Each of the 10 principles is outlined individually below. Given that these principles apply collectively there are clear similarities between some of them. However, while the lines of division may be blurred, each princi-ple establishes a necessary criterion which any potential indicator should meet.

(1) Interpretable. As a social indicator is intended for the consumption of the public and policy-makers, it should be easy to understand and clear in what it is measuring. Meadows (1998, p. 18) further states that indicators should be "physical", meaning that they should be expressed in units which people can relate to. Similarly, an indicator should also have a "clear and accepted normative interpretation" (Atkinson et. al, 2002, p. 21). It should be obvious which direction of change in the indi-cator reflects a positive improvement, and therefore the direction in which public and policy-makers alike would wish to see it move.[4]

(2) Policy Relevant. Carley (1981, p. 30) concludes that an understand-ing of the policy formation process is one of the two most important ele-ments of any effort to produce a social indicator.[5] Consequently, it should be relevant to existing policy goals as well as to policy ideals. Therefore, a social indicator may not necessarily be restricted to moni-toring *ex-post* policy effectiveness but could also be proactive in high-lighting deficiencies within areas of society which existing policy does not address. As such, social indicator selection should be "issue-driven", by being focused on providing a means of assessing a social problem, rather than driven by a desire to assess only current policy or to use available data (Parris, 2000, p. 129; Hodge and Hardi, 1997, p. 16).

(3) Methodologically Appropriate. A further property requiring fulfil-ment before choosing an indicator is that it is methodologically appropri-ate or scientifically sound. An indicator should be representative of the information it is trying to capture and express. It should therefore be sensitive to change and responsive in both scale and direction to an adjustment in welfare. Consequently, if there is an improvement in what the indicator is measuring, such as lower income inequality or lower education disadvantage, the indicator when calculated after that improvement should reflect both its occurrence and positive impact. Meadows (1998, p. 17) describes this quality as the indicator being "clear in value".

Similarly the indicator should adhere to the population principle, meaning that were two populations compared, where the second replicates the first, then the indicator would be unchanged.[6]

Given that changes to social indicators are used within the political process to assess political achievement, or lack of it, there is an implicit attraction for policy makers to manipulate indicators via artificial changes. Atkinson et al. (2002, p. 22) note this phenomenon, and consequently suggest that a necessary consideration for a social indicator is that it is open to minimal, and ideally no, artificial manipulation which generates an improved indicator result.

(4) Intuitively Valid. Alongside being methodologically appropriate, an indicator should also be intuitively valid. It should make logical sense to those members of the public and policy-makers who will use it. Accordingly an indicator should be representative of the scale of the problem it is attempting to summarise, with its result seeming reasonable and not misleading. Atkinson et al. (2002, p. 22) illustrate this requirement by citing the hypothetical example of a pan-European Union poverty indicator, which records more than 50 per cent of its population living in poverty. Clearly, in spite of the scientific structure of such an indicator, its result may be seen to be unreasonable and therefore its use is undesirable. Analogously, all movements in an indicator in response to changes in society should follow directions which are reasonable and reflective of that change.

(5) Feasible. A social indicator should be feasible, meaning that it should be possible, both in practical and cost terms, to measure it. It may be impossible to construct a data collection method for a particular variable, and hence it may not be feasible to measure it. Similarly, while it might be practical to propose a collection methodology, the costs associated with gathering and/or processing that information would result in the indicator being impracticable.

Discussion within the literature on indicator feasibility splits between two groups. The first, including the European Union (2000b) and Parris (2000), suggest that indicators should be derived from currently available or planned data, rather than from new sources. However, most of these assessments are made within the context of collecting either data relating to poverty or data for the limited number of social indicators required to measure sustainability. This is also a view that violates the aforementioned requirement of indicator selection being issue rather than data driven. The second view, held by Meadows (1998), the DETR (1999) and Atkinson et al. (2002), favour the collection of new data where necessary, though they emphasise the matter of avoiding unnecessary costs.

In the context of a growing demand for evidence upon which to build and judge policy the latter view is certainly acceptable. It is apparent that in the years to come new indicators will have to be proposed and collected. Therefore the feasibility of their creation, in both cost and measurement terms, must be borne in mind. However, the primacy of indicator selection being issue- rather than data-driven must be recognised, and so the exclusion of a particular indicator due to the impracticality of data collection is a decision that requires comprehensive justification.

(6) Timely. The relevance of a social indicator to assessments of policy effectiveness or policy absences depends on it timeliness. Ideally, an indicator should be as up-to-date as possible. Meadows (1998, p. 18) further adds that an indicator should be "leading", meaning that it should provide information fast enough for it to be assessed and acted upon before it becomes dated.

Traditionally, there has been a clear tendency on the part of statistical collection agencies to focus on the collection of economic data, such as prices and national income, rather than on producing timely statistics in the wider socio-economic sphere. For example, in general Irish income data has tended to be up to two to three years out of date, and data on household composition is derived from a census which occurs once every five years. While indicators using such data may provide an empirical value (or a qualitative description), their analytical benefit is undermined. The availability of timely data is therefore an important consideration in indicator choice.

(7) Acceptable. An indicator should be acceptable in its structure, measurement and result to three groups within society: the public, academics and policy-makers.

The willingness of the general public to accept an indicator as sensible and understandable may be regarded as central. An indicator is unlikely to retain what Hills (2001, p. 6) describes as "public credibility" if the result it produces is out of line with what the affected people themselves think. In that case, there is probably something erroneous about the indicator. Similarly, if an indicator is not understood by the public due to its ambiguity or broad definition, it will receive neither public support nor credibility. The significance of public credibility cannot be understated, indeed the UK Round Table on Sustainable Development describe it as the most important type of credibility an indicator should attain (1997, p. 14).

Acceptance amongst academics of an indicator is based on its methodological appropriateness as well as the reliability of the data it uses and the logic of its result given existing information sources. Therefore, the data used should be derived from a reliable source, be of known quality and have all its assumptions, judgements and uncertainties adequately documented (European Commission, 2001, p. 5; DETR, 1999, p. 17; Hodge and Hardi, 1997, p. 17). This implies that the use of new data, sourced via methods such as a survey, requires comprehensive scientific justification to legitimise the associated indicator's academic acceptance.

Finally, a social indicator should have, or be in the process of attempting to create, political acceptance of its purpose. Given the policy significance of social indicators it is essential that they are accepted and hence can influence policy. After all, "indicators that are not acceptable by decision-makers are unlikely to influence decisions" (Gallopin, 1997, p. 25).

Evidently there are synergies between each of the three types of acceptability and some of the aforementioned indicator properties. Public acceptability clearly links with the properties of interpretability and intuitive validity. Similarly, the connection is apparent between academic acceptability and the property of methodological appropriateness, and between political acceptability and policy relevance.

(8) Replicable. A social indicator serves minimal long-term purpose if it is not possible to replicate its measurement of the same group or place over time, and accordingly facilitate intertemporal comparisons. Additionally, it should be possible to replicate an indicator across different groups and over other areas or regions (Apthorpe, 1978, p. 22).

(9) Decomposable. Where feasible and relevant, a social indicator should be sufficiently decomposable so that it may be broken down and examined by sub-region, age, gender, social group, etc. The implications of this demand are on the data collection process. The construction of data sampling methodologies should take into account the requirement that where possible an indicator is decomposable.

(10) Updateable. Given that our understanding of socio-economic phenomena is continually changing, an indicator should, on an ongoing basis, be capable of being revised and updated. If there is a change in the concepts underpinning an indicator, naturally it requires alteration. Atkinson et al. (2002, p. 23) term this property as an indicator being "susceptible to revision", while Meadows (1998, p. 18) describes it as an indicator being "tentative".

Meadows further notes that an indicator should be prevented from becoming "institutionalised", meaning that in spite of the development of techniques and thought which suggests its replacement the indicator has become so established it is near impossible to remove. In the context of indicators for sustainable development, she cites gross national product (GNP) as a classic example of an institutionalised indicator (1998, p. 18). In Ireland, the deprivation items used to measure consistent poverty between 1987 and 2003 could be recognised as having become institutionalised.

Accepting that an indicator should be subject to update comes at the cost of data continuity. Alterations to the definition of an indicator, and therefore to the data collected, are likely to result in discontinuous longitudinal data sets. However, as the trade-off is between enhanced understanding of the problem under investigation and data set continuity, the former is a necessary victor.

Principles for Groups of Social Indicators

While individual indicators should each adhere to the ten principles above, there are four further properties that should apply to situations where groups of indicators are collectively used. Such groups generally reflect attempts to establish a more comprehensive insight into societal outcomes (such as the EU Laeken indicators) or to measure multi-dimensional phenomena such as social exclusion. The properties apply irrespective of whether that group is presented simply as a basket of indicators or more complexly as an index.

(1) Balance between the Dimensions. Where a group of indicators are attempting to measure across a number of areas or dimensions (e.g. labour market participation, health status and income levels) it is important that each of these dimensions is adequately represented within the group of indicators chosen. Given the easier availability of data within some dimensions, it is clear that there will be an uneven distribution of information across the overall portfolio of dimensions (DETR, 1999, p. 17). However, once each dimension is adequately represented, meaning that the essential elements within it are assessed, the overall indicator group may be regarded as balanced. Atkinson et al. (2002) note that one way to assess that adequacy is to consider whether the selection commands general support such that it is regarded as a balanced representation of the concerns being examined.

(2) Hierarchical. Rather than adopting a random method of presenting a group of social indicators, they should be presented in a structured hierarchical manner. This implies that some indicators within the group are less important than others, and so should receive relatively reduced attention. For example, an indicator representing the scale of relative income poverty is likely to be more informative to an assessment of social exclusion than an indicator identifying the number of individuals who do not possess a bank, building society, credit union or post office account (financial exclusion). However, both these indicators may be included within the overall group.

There are two established methods by which a hierarchical structure can be implemented. The first ranks a basket of indicators into primary and secondary indicators, or Level A, B, C, . . . indicators, with the importance of each indicator reflected in its position within the ranking. However, although the relative importance of each indicator vis-à-vis other indicators is implied it is not quantified. Atkinson et al. (2002) and the EU Laeken indicators have adopted this tiered approach.

A second method is to create a weighted index using a group of indicators. Allocating a weight to each indicator explicitly, and quantifiably, ranks them by order of importance – the larger the weight the more important the indicator. By using a system of individual indicators classified within specific dimensions, it is possible to rank the indicators vertically within dimensions and to rank the dimensions horizontally relative to each other. The United Nations Human Development Index has been compiled using this approach.

Implementing either of these methodologies necessitates the adoption of value judgements. In some cases it may be apparent that one indicator is more important than another, while in other cases the ranking of indicator A over indicator B may be controversial. In presenting a hierarchical group of indicators it is necessary that any value judgements adopted are adequately justified and "are such as to meet with fairly general approval" (Drewnowski, 1972, p. 85).

(3) Avoids Double Counting. Double counting occurs when an item is assessed (at least) twice during an evaluation process. Accordingly, its double-inclusion exaggerates its significance and biases the results of the evaluation. Thus policy initiatives which target a social policy issue that is double counted may achieve exaggerated reductions due to the construction of the measurement mechanism rather than as a result of corresponding societal improvements. Avoiding double counting is therefore necessary both within and across the groups of dimensions.

Although double counting is an established problem within national accounting literature, it has received very limited attention from those who assess socio-economic issues. For example, the EU Laeken indicators double count some of those who are at risk of poverty by assessing those currently living below the poverty line and those who are persistently poor (living below the poverty line in the current year and for two of the previous three years).

Where groups of social indicators are being collectively used to assess a societal outcome it is necessary to avoid double counting. Otherwise its existence biases these assessments.

(4) Easy to Read and Understand. The European Commission states that an indicator should be "easy to read and understand" (2001, p. 5; Atkinson et al., 2002). This feature is clearly one that applies at both the individual and cumulative level of indicator presentation. A group of indicators should reflect a clear message and be accessible to those who wish to consult them. This implies that the overall set should not be too expansive, for instance by including hundreds of relatively uninformative indicators, and that every step, value judgement or assumption taken in collecting or presenting the indicator group be clearly and simply explained. A priority in presenting groups of social indicators must therefore be to "increase transparency and reduce complexity" (Obst, 2000, p. 15), a task described by Miles (1985, p. 196) as "demystification".

If a social indicator group is to successfully achieve its aim of enhancing the academic, political and public understanding of social exclusion, then throughout the indicator construction process it must be conscious of its audience, continually maintain the aim of clarity and produce well-explained apparent conclusions.

A further property suggested for groups of indicators is that they be internally coherent or mutually consistent (NESC, 2002, p. 7). This property suggests that an indicator set should contain related variables, a property previously acknowledged, and that those variables be consistent in their results throughout the overall indicator group. However, as it is possible that some indicators may be increasing while others are decreasing, consistency is unlikely to be either achieved or desirable. The primary purpose of each indicator is to be reflective of what it measures, irrespective of the movement elsewhere within the indicator portfolio.

These 14 principles set out a list of requirements that each social indicator, or group of indicators, should meet if they are to be used to assess any socio-economic phenomenon or situation. Collectively, the principles are summarised in Table 4.2 below.

Table 4.2: The Principles of Social Indicators

Principles of Individual Social Indicators	
(1)	Interpretable
(2)	Policy Relevant
(3)	Methodologically Appropriate
(4)	Intuitively Valid
(5)	Feasible
(6)	Timely
(7)	Acceptable
(8)	Replicable
(9)	Decomposable
(10)	Updateable
Principles for Groups of Social Indicators	
(1)	Balanced Between the Dimensions
(2)	Hierarchical
(3)	Avoids Double Counting
(4)	Easy to Read and Understand

Conclusion

Given the role played by social indicators in capturing the nature and changes of a society, and in providing evidence as to the progress being made to overcome key social problems, their appropriate construction requires careful consideration. A central challenge to the successful implementation of a system of social indicators and an evidence-based approach to social policy-making is the availability of appropriate, accurate and timely data. In Ireland, the statistical system is responding to the need to develop social policies on the basis of sound evidence and data by introducing a number of important new surveys such as the special modules of the Quarterly National Household Survey (QNHS). Furthermore, at EU level the EU-SILC survey is providing data to support the Laeken suite of social indicators.

This chapter attempts to present the guidelines to which the indicator construction process should adhere. An indicator should satisfy the definition of a social indicator as an informative surrogate measure of society, it should be derived from well-chosen data and it should abide by the list of principles outlined above. Meeting all these requirements sets the bar high for each social indicator; however an indicator that possessed all these qualities provides the informed scientific assessment needed to comprehensively assess a societal condition.

References

Apthorpe, R. (1978), *Social Indicators: Definitions, Properties, Uses, Representations,* University of East Anglia: Development Studies Discussion Paper No. 26.

Atkinson, A.B., Cantillon, B., Marlier, E. and Nolan, B. (2002), *Social Indicators – The EU and Social Inclusion*, Oxford: Oxford University Press.

Bennett, F. and Roche, C. (2000), "Developing Indicators: The scope for participatory approaches", *New Economy,* Vol. 7, issue 1, pp. 24-28.

Bilderman, A.D. (1966), "Social Indicators and Goals" in Bauer R.A. (ed.) *Social Indicators,* Cambridge, MA: MIT Press.

Carley, M. (1981), *Social Measurement and Social Indicators: Issues of policy and theory*, London: Allen & Unwin.

Carlisle, E. (1972), "The conceptual structure of social indicators" in Shonfield A. and S. Shaw (eds.) *Social Indicators and Social Policy*, London: Social Science Research Council and Heinemann.

Collins, M.L. (1998), *Decompositions of Irish Household Income Inequality, 1987-1994/95.* Unpublished M.A. Thesis, Department of Economics: University College Cork.

Cowell, F.A. (1995), *Measuring Inequality – LSE Handbooks in Economic Science (second edition)*, London: Prentice Hall/Harvester Wheatsheaf.

Department of Environment, Transport and the Regions (DETR) (1999), *Quality of Life Counts – Indicators for a Strategy for Sustainable Development for the United Kingdom: a baseline assessment*, London: Stationery Office.

Department of the Taoiseach (2006), *Towards 2016 – Ten-Year Framework Social Partnership Agreement 2006-2015,* Dublin: Stationery Office.

Drewnowski, J. (1972), "Social Indicators and Welfare Measurement: Remarks on Methodology", *The Journal of Development Studies,* Vol.8, No.3, pp. 77-90.

European Commission (2000a), *Structural Indicators*, Communication from the Commission, COM(2000) 594 final, Brussels: European Commission.

European Commission (2000b), *Non-monetary Indicators of Poverty and Social Exclusion,* Brussels: European Commission.

European Commission (2001), *Structural Indicators*, Communication from the Commission, COM(2001) 619 final, Brussels: European Commission.

Gallopin, G.C. (1997), "Indicators and their use: information for decision-making" in Moldan, B. and Billharz, S. (eds.) *Sustainability Indicators: Report of the Project on Indicators of Sustainable Development*, Chichester: Wiley.

Hardi, P. (1997), "Measurement and Indicators Program of the International Institute for Sustainable Development" in Moldan, B. and Billharz, S. (eds.) *Sustainability Indicators: Report of the Project on Indicators of Sustainable Development*, Chichester: Wiley.

Hardi, P. and Zdan, T. (1997), *Assessing Sustainable Development: Principles in practice*, Canada: The International Institute for Sustainable Development.

Hardi, P., Barg, S., Hodge, T. and Pinter, P. (1997), Measuring Sustainable Development: Review of Current Practice. *Occasional Paper No. 17*. Ontario: Industry Canada.

Hills, J. (2001), "Measurement of Income Poverty and Deprivation: The British Approach" in CASE report 13, *Indicators of Progress: A discussion of approaches to monitor the Government's strategy to tackle poverty and social exclusion*, London: London School of Economics.

Hodge, R.A. and Hardi, P. (1997), "The Need for Guidelines: The Rationale Underlying the Bellagio Principles for Assessment" in Hardi, P. and Zdan, T. (eds.), *Assessing Sustainable Development: Principles in practice*, Canada: The International Institute for Sustainable Development.

Jenkins, S. (1991), "The Measurement of Income Inequality" in Osberg, L. (ed.), *Economic Inequality and Poverty, International Perspectives*, New York/ London: M.E. Sharpe.

Meadows, D. (1998), *Indicators and Information Systems for Sustainable Development*, Vermont: The Sustainability Institute.

Miles, I. (1985), *Social Indicators for Human Development*, London: Frances Pinter.

Moldan, B. and Billharz, S. (eds.) (1997), *Sustainability Indicators: Report of the Project on Indicators of Sustainable Development*, Chichester: Wiley.

National Economic and Social Council (2001), *Review of the Poverty Proofing Process*, Dublin: NESC.

National Economic and Social Council (2002), *National Progress Indicators*, Dublin: NESC.

National Economic and Social Council (2005), *NESC Strategy 2006 – People, Productivity and Purpose*, Dublin: NESC.

National Economic and Social Council (2005), *The Developmental Welfare State*, Dublin: NESC.

National Statistics Board (2003), *Developing Irish Social and Equality Statistics to meet Policy Needs: Report of the Steering Group on Social and Equality Statistics*, Dublin: Stationery Office.

Obst, C. (2000), "Report of the September 1999 OECD expert workshop on the measurement of sustainable development" in *Frameworks to Measure Sustainable Development*, Paris: OECD.

OECD (2000), *Framework to Measure Sustainable Development*, Paris: OECD.

Palmer, G. and Rahman, M. (2002), *Monitoring Progress on Poverty: A Policy Guide on the Use of Social Indicators*, Dublin: Combat Poverty Agency.

Parris, K. (2000), "OECD agri-environmental indicators" in *Frameworks to Measure Sustainable Development*, Paris: OECD.

UK Round Table on Sustainable Development (1997), *Getting the Best out of Indicators*, London: Round Table on Sustainable Development.

United Nations (1996), *Indicators of Sustainable Development: Framework and Methodologies*, New York: United Nations.

United Nations Environment Programme (UNEP) (1994), *An Overview of Environmental Indicators: State of the art and perspectives*, Nairobi: UNEP.

United Nations Environment Programme (UNEP) (1995), *Scanning the Global Environment: A framework and methodology for integrated environmental reporting and assessment*, Nairobi: UNEP.

World Bank (1997), *Expanding the Measure of Wealth: Indicators of Environmentally Sustainable Development*, Environmentally Sustainable Development Studies and Monographs Series No. 17, Washington, DC: World Bank.

Notes

---

[1] Palmer and Rahman (2002) also reach this conclusion.

[2] Both Gallopin (1997, p. 14) and Hardi et al. (1997) draw from semiotics (the general theory of signs) and define an indicator as a sign.

[3] Throughout the literature the properties of indicators are also referred to as: rules for indicators; scientific and technical criteria; specific features; qualities; principles; and desirable properties.

[4] Atkinson et al. (2002, p. 21) note that while this property applies to social indicators it may not apply to all forms of indicators. As an example they cite labour productivity and fertility as indicators whose direction of "a positive improvement" is unambiguous.

[5] The other being methodological appropriateness.

[6] Both these properties reflect two axioms used when assessing indicators to measure income inequality, namely the Pigou-Dalton condition and the population principle (see Jenkins, 1991; Cowell, 1995, pp. 54-60; and Collins, 1998, pp. 58-60).

Chapter 5

PROJECTING IRELAND'S POPULATION AT A TIME OF MAJOR DEMOGRAPHIC CHANGE

Aidan Punch

This chapter reviews the most recent official population projections published by the Central Statistics Office (CSO) for Ireland.[1] The projections, which were published in December 2004, were based on the results of the 2002 census.

At the time of writing – June 2006 – the fieldwork for the 2006 Census of Population has been completed. The first results of the census carried out on 23 April 2006, which are due for publication in July, will provide a comprehensive assessment of the current state of our population. The definitive demographic data is due for publication in April 2007 at which stage the raw material for a revised set of population projections will be available. Meanwhile, the focus of the present chapter is on the projections based on the 2002 census results.

The simplest method of projecting the population is to extrapolate past trends forward into the future. For instance, projecting the change in population between 1980 and 2005 forward a further 25 years would yield a population of 4.86 million in 2030 based on the derived absolute change in population or just over 5 million using the percentage change. However, this would not provide any indication of the reasons behind the projected increase in population. In order to get this assessment we need to make assumptions concerning how each of the components of population change – births, deaths, immigrants and emigrants – are likely to behave and then gauge what the combined effect of these assumptions would be for our population.

The CSO uses such an approach in its official population projections. The model used in the official report – the so-called demographic component method – projected the base 2002 population forward to 2036 under chosen assumptions governing births, deaths and net migration. The inter-relationship between the various components is illustrated in Appendix 5.1. A summary of the factors, which informed the assumptions, is given in the next section.

Assumptions

In formulating its assumptions for the 2002 based population projections the CSO was assisted by an expert group made up of academics and officials of relevant Government departments. The expert group deliberated on each of the components of population change and put forward their suggestions for incorporation into the projection model. The main deliberations under each of the appropriate headings are set out in the remainder of this section.

Fertility

Under this heading the target variable for the projections model is births classified by sex. The number of births is dependent on the number of women aged 15-49 years and the fertility levels of these women. The latter is best estimated using age-specific fertility rates – the number of births to women in the relevant age group per 1,000 females in the same age group. At the overall level the total fertility rate (TFR) provides a summary measure of the number of children which a woman would be likely to have based on the prevailing age specific fertility rates. Table 5.1 provides a summary of the evolution of fertility rates from 1960 to 2004. The data for all but the most recent year was available to the expert group when they were finalising their assumptions on fertility.

Table 5.1: Age-specific Fertility Rate and Total Fertility Rate, 1960 to Date

Year	Live Births per 1,000 Women at Specified Ages							TFR
	15-19	*20-24*	*25-29*	*30-34*	*35-39*	*40-44*	*45-49*	
1960	8.8	103.9	209.6	213.1	156.3	56.0	4.2	3.76
1965	14.0	125.1	236.1	218.9	150.3	57.6	4.2	4.03
1970	16.3	145.5	228.7	201.9	131.9	45.3	3.7	3.87
1975	22.8	138.5	216.0	162.2	100.2	36.8	2.6	3.40
1980	23.0	125.3	202.3	165.7	97.3	29.6	2.3	3.23
1985	16.6	87.2	158.6	138.4	75.3	21.6	1.5	2.50
1990	16.7	63.3	137.6	126.2	63.1	15.4	1.1	2.12
1995	15.1	50.3	106.7	123.5	60.3	13.1	0.8	1.85
2000	19.5	51.6	95.1	129.3	71.3	13.6	0.5	1.90
2001	19.9	53.3	95.1	134.1	75.3	13.9	0.7	1.96
2002	19.6	53.0	93.6	134.3	79.9	14.7	0.6	1.98
2003	18.8	50.8	93.6	134.5	81.4	15.6	0.5	1.98
2004	17.6	49.1	87.9	133.4	84.6	15.8	0.6	1.95

As women in the age groups 20-39 years account for 90 per cent of births it will suffice for the present analysis to focus on these. By 2003 the fertility rate of women in their early twenties had declined by 65 per cent compared with the corresponding 1970 value, while the decline for women aged 25-29 years was 59 per cent over the same period. The decline in fertility of women in their early thirties bottomed out during the mid-1990s and following subsequent increases has stabilised since 2001. For women aged 35-39 years the downward trend in fertility was arrested in 1995 and has since been upwards. At the overall level the total fertility rate has declined from over four children per woman in 1965 to less than two almost 40 years later.

By examining the trends in Irish fertility rates and comparing them with trends elsewhere in Europe, where Ireland tops the EU fertility table, the expert group was of the opinion that the most likely range for the total fertility rate into the future was 1.7 to 2.0. On this basis three fertility assumptions were chosen.

- **F1:** TFR to increase from its 2003 level to 2.0 by 2011 and to remain constant thereafter

- **F2:** TFR to decrease to 1.85 by 2011 and to remain constant thereafter

- **F3:** TFR to decrease to 1.7 by 2011 and to remain constant.

The average annual assumed changes in the TFR are also applied to the various age-specific fertility rates. Applying the derived fertility rates in turn to the relevant female population groups results in projected births. These births are then apportioned between male and female births on the basis of the ratios experienced for recent years.

Mortality

The most recent figures for 2002 show female life expectancy at birth to be 80.3 years – an excess of 5.2 years over the corresponding male figure of 75.1 years. Back in 1926, when the first Irish life table was compiled, female life expectancy at birth was 57.9 years – just 0.5 years ahead of the male figure of 57.4 years. The computed average annual gains are given in Table 5.2 for the period as a whole and for each of the sub-periods indicated.

Table 5.2: Average Annual Gains in Life Expectancy at Various Ages, 1926–2002

	Males			Females		
Period	*Birth*	*5 Years*	*70 Years*	*Birth*	*5 Years*	*70 Years*
1926-1946	0.16	0.10	-0.04	0.23	0.17	-0.03
1946-1961	0.51	0.28	0.03	0.63	0.43	0.05
1961-1971	0.07	-0.02	0.00	0.16	0.10	0.05
1971-1981	0.13	0.06	0.00	0.21	0.15	0.07
1981-1986	0.18	0.14	0.02	0.22	0.18	0.08
1986-1991	0.26	0.24	0.14	0.24	0.22	0.18
1991-1996	0.14	0.12	0.04	0.16	0.12	0.06
1996-2002	0.35	0.35	0.22	0.28	0.28	0.18
1926-2002	0.23	0.15	0.03	0.29	0.22	0.05

The 1946-1961 period showed the greatest gain in life expectancy at birth for both males and females. A significant part of this was due to a reduction in infant mortality. However, general improvements in medical treatment including more systematic immunisation programmes also played a part.

The rate of improvement tapered off in the 1960s due in part to increased mortality of persons of working age from heart disease and most forms of cancer. The most recent period has witnessed gains of 2.1 and 1.7 years in life expectancy at birth for males and females respectively, due mainly to improvements in the mortality of older persons.

However, despite the marked improvements in life expectancy Ireland still stands in the bottom half of the wider European league table – a position it has occupied over the last 30 years. The expert group therefore felt that there was scope for some catching up in life expectancy over the course of the projection period to 2036, notwithstanding the widespread belief among European demographers that improvements in life expectancy are likely to continue for most countries for the foreseeable future. Specifically, the expert group proposed that the average rate of improvement in life expectancy over the 16-year period 1986 to 2002 should be maintained over the lifetime of the projections yielding a projected life expectancy at birth in 2036 of 86.9 years for females and 82.5 years for males.

- Mortality rates are assumed to decrease which will result in gains in life expectancy at birth from 75.1 years in 2002 to 82.5 years in 2036 for males and 80.3 years in 2002 to 86.9 years in 2036 for females

Migration

The final and most uncertain component of the projections is net migration – the difference between inward and outward migration. The annual gross flows for the 1983 to 2005 period are given in Table 5.3. The data for 2005 was not available when the projections were being finalised.

Table 5.3: Migration Flows, 1983–2005 (000s)

Year	Immigration	Emigration	Net Migration
1983	15.6	29.6	-14.0
1984	15.4	24.4	-9.0
1985	13.6	33.6	-20.0
1986	17.2	45.2	-28.0
1987	17.2	40.2	-23.0
1988	19.2	61.1	-41.9
1989	26.7	70.6	-43.9
1990	33.3	56.3	-23.0
1991	33.3	35.3	-2.0
1992	40.7	33.4	7.3
1993	34.7	35.1	-0.4
1994	30.1	34.8	-4.7
1995	31.2	33.1	-1.9
1996	39.2	31.2	8.0
1997	44.5	25.3	19.2
1998	46.0	28.6	17.4
1999	48.9	31.5	17.4
2000	52.6	26.6	26.0
2001	59.0	26.2	32.8
2002	66.9	25.6	41.3
2003	50.5	20.7	29.8
2004	50.1	18.5	31.6
2005	70.0	16.6	53.4

The table clearly shows how net migration has oscillated in the period under review. During the late 1980s annual net emigration flows of over 40,000 were being experienced. The early to mid-1990s was a period when net migration was in the range −5,000 to +8,000. However, since then we have witnessed large net immigration. In particular since 2000 immigration has averaged 58,000 a year compared with emigration of 22,000 a year resulting in net inward migration of approximately 36,000 annually. The recent situation is clearly linked to the strong performance of the Irish economy and labour force.

When the expert group was framing its assumptions it was guided by expectations in relation to national and international developments. The main factors were the continuing strength of the economy and the declining domestic labour supply situation. It therefore formed the view that the recent strong net immigration picture was unlikely to be reversed to any sustained degree over the projection period.

Two migration assumptions were used. The highest of these (M1) assumed a continuation of the then-prevailing average net inward migration of 30,000 per annum for the next decade, to be followed by 20,000 per annum for the following decade and finally by 15,000 per annum during 2026-2036. Such an assumption would be warranted if the Irish economy were to continue to perform strongly. The lower migration scenario (M2), which assumed that net immigration would decrease at a faster rate, is consistent with a more modest growth path for the Irish economy – in line with prevailing EU rates. The assumed gross migration flows consistent with these two scenarios are given in the following table.

Table 5.4: Assumed Average Annual Migration Flows, 2002–2036 (000s)

Scenario	2002–2006	2006–2011	2011–2016	2016–2021	2021–2026	2026–2031	2031–2036
M1							
Immigration	51	51	51	41	40	35	35
Emigration	21	21	21	21	20	20	20
Net migration	30	30	30	20	20	15	15
M2							
Immigration	51	41	30	25	25	25	25
Emigration	21	21	20	20	20	20	20
Net migration	30	20	10	5	5	5	5

How Have the Assumptions Behaved?

The period that has elapsed since the publication of the population projections report is a mere 18 months. However, it is worth examining how the assumptions of the expert group have behaved in this period.

The total fertility rate resumed its downward path and stood at 1.95 in 2005 compared with 1.98 in 2004 – the main influence being the decline in the age-specific rates of women aged 20-34 years. The continued fall in fertility points towards assumption F2 probably being the most likely of the three scenarios chosen. Furthermore, it is in line with the experience of other northern European countries.

Only one mortality scenario was used. Experience from previous projections for Ireland and elsewhere suggests that demographers tend to underestimate the likely gains in life expectancy. However, maintaining the reasonably strong growth in survivorship rates experienced in the 16 years to 2002 for a further 29 years probably represents an abandonment of the overly cautious approach adopted in previous official projections.

In the 12 months to April 2005 immigration was estimated at 70,000, which taken in conjunction with emigration of 16,600 resulted in record net immigration of 53,400. The evidence so far in the remainder of 2005 and early 2006 points to this level of net immigration being at least sustained if not exceeded. While the preliminary results of the 2006 census will indicate whether the net migration picture for the inter-censal period is correct, it would be fair to assume that on the basis of present trends the M1 scenario is the most likely out-turn for the projections, at least in the short to medium term.

A final point on assumptions is that projections can sometimes be poor in forecasting the immediate future but accurate in the medium to long term. The main advantages which projections offer are an insight into changes in the structure of the population as well as an indication of the overall magnitude of the changes involved. The next section will look at these issues for the 2002-based exercise.

Projection Results

The three fertility assumptions taken in conjunction with the single assumption concerning mortality and the two migration assumptions yield six different population outcomes. These are designated M1F1, M1F2,

M1F3, M2F1, M2F2 and M2F3. The 2002 census results by single year of age and sex are used as the starting point of the projections. The assumed gross migration flows, also classified by single year of age and sex, are incorporated into the model while applying the fertility and mortality assumptions yields the projected annual births and deaths figures. These latter components are analysed first.

Figure 5.1: Projected Births, 2004–2036

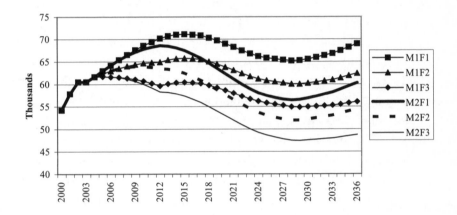

Projected Births

Figure 5.1 shows the projected number of births under each of the six scenarios. The wave-like effect from 2011 to the end of the projection period results from earlier female birth cohorts entering the prime child-bearing age groups of 20-39 years. The difference between the two scenario extremes M1F1 and M2F3 attains its maximum value of 20,000 births in 2035 and is 13,000 on average over the entire projection period. For migration scenario M1 the high fertility assumption F1 would yield 9,000 additional births on an annual average basis compared with fertility assumption F3. The corresponding figure for M2 is 8,000 additional births annually.

Additional migrants will in turn lead to an increment in the number of births. In the absence of migration (inflows equal to outflows) births would average 52,000 a year in the period to 2036 compared with an average projected 63,000 births under M1. In this context it should be borne in mind that in the absence of information to the contrary it is assumed that the fertility rates of immigrants are identical with those of the indigenous population. The question in the 2006 census on the number of children born to women is expected to throw some light on whether any differential exists.

Projected Deaths

The number of deaths projected to occur in the period to 2036 will not vary to any significant extent according to the fertility assumption chosen given that less than 4 per cent of deaths are to persons aged under 35. Neither will migration affect the projected number of deaths in any major way mainly because of the relatively young age profile of immigrants. The major determinants of the projected number of deaths are the existing age structure of the population and the assumed improvements in mortality rates. The annual number of deaths is projected to increase from the 2003 level of 30,000 to around 40,000 by 2036, with most of the increase taking place towards the end of the projection period.

Regardless of the combination of fertility or migration assumptions used the total number of deaths is projected to average around 33,000-34,000 per annum in the period to 2036 – on a par with the average number of deaths registered for the previous 35 years. While the number of older persons will undoubtedly increase the reduced mortality rates which these persons will experience will keep average deaths at the level pertaining since the mid-1960s.

Natural Increase

Subtracting the projected number of deaths from the corresponding births gives the natural increase, which taken in conjunction with the assumed net migration gives the derived change in population. The various components of population change are shown in Table 5.5 for five-year periods to 2036 in respect of scenario M1F2, with the period since 1966 included for comparison purposes. The figures shown are average annual inter-censal amounts in thousands.

Table 5.5: Historical and Projected (M1F2) Components of Population Change (000s)

	Period	Births	Deaths	Natural Increase	Net Migration	Change in Pop.
Actual	*1966–1971*	63	33	30	-11	19
	1971–1979	69	33	35	14	49
	1979–1981	73	33	40	-3	38
	1981–1986	67	33	34	-14	19
	1986–1991	56	32	24	-27	-3
	1991–1996	50	31	18	2	20
	1996–2002	54	31	23	26	49
Projected	*2002–2006*	62	30	32	30	62
	2006–2011	64	30	34	30	64
	2011–2016	65	31	35	30	65
	2016–2021	64	32	32	20	52
	2021–2026	61	35	27	20	47
	2026–2031	60	38	23	15	38
	2031–2036	62	41	20	15	35

The natural increase in the population is positive throughout the whole period under review. The peak value occurred in the 1979-1981 period coinciding with the 74,000 peak in births in 1980. With the fall-off in births the natural increase declined to 18,000 on average in the early 1990s but has since recovered. Under M1F2 it is projected to reach an annual average of 35,000 during 2011-2016 before again declining, on this occasion due to a projected increase in deaths.

The volatility of net migration is clearly illustrated for the period since 1966. The late 1960s represented a continuation of the previous experience of net outward migration, albeit on a reduced scale compared with the emigration of the 1950s. The 1970s witnessed net inward migration for the first time on record but a resumption of net emigration was to follow in its wake with the late 1980s being particularly pronounced in that regard. These net outward flows have since been reversed and in the 1996-2002 inter-censal period net immigration averaged 26,000 per annum. The amounts shown as net migration for the duration of the projection period, as already explained, represent the assumptions of the expert group under migration scenario M1.

The late 1980s was the only inter-censal period since 1966 to show a decline in population – the natural increase in population not being sufficient to counterbalance the net outward migration which occurred during that period. By way of contrast the decade of the 1970s has yet to be surpassed in terms of population growth. The average annual increase in population of 49,000 recorded, which was replicated between 1996 and 2002, represented a higher percentage increase as it was on a lower population base.

Looking to the future, the population is projected to continue to grow as a result of positive natural increase supplemented by assumed net inward migration. The projected increase will peak at 65,000 per annum during 2011-2016 and decline steadily to reach an annual average of 35,000 during 2031-2036. The next section looks at how the projected components of population change will affect the overall population total.

Total Population

Table 5.6 shows the projected population under all six scenarios at five-year intervals from 2006 to 2036.

Table 5.6: Projected Population 2006-2036 (000s)

	Strong Net Migration (M1)			Declining Net Immigration (M2)		
Year	*F1*	*F2*	*F3*	*F1*	*F2*	*F3*
2006	4,168	4,166	4,164	4,168	4,166	4,164
2011	4,505	4,487	4,469	4,452	4,435	4,416
2016	4,854	4,810	4,765	4,688	4,645	4,601
2021	5,140	5,070	4,999	4,870	4,803	4,736
2026	5,399	5,304	5,208	5,016	4,927	4,838
2031	5,613	5,492	5,370	5,140	5,029	4,917
2036	5,820	5,669	5,518	5,259	5,121	4,983

From 2011 onwards, after which fertility is assumed constant, the projected population follows the sequence M2F3 → M2F2 → M2F1 → M1F3 → M1F2 → M1F1 in ascending order for any particular year chosen. This is illustrated in Figure 5.2.

Figure 5.2: Population Projections to 2036

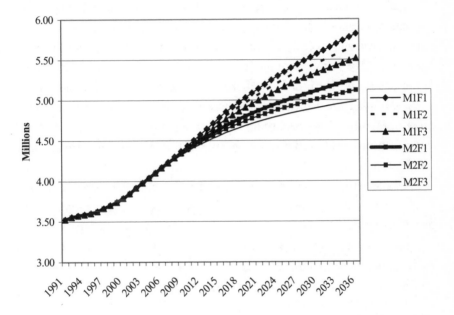

By the end of the projection period the projected population will range from a low of 4.983 million for M2F3 to a high of 5.82 million for M1F1. The range of 837,000 can be decomposed into a migration effect (M1F1–M2F1) and a fertility effect (M2F1–M2F3). As expected, the migration effect is the dominant one and accounts for two-thirds of the overall range in 2036.

The projected annual population growth rate varies from 0.7 per cent for M2F3 to 1.2 per cent for M1F1 for the period 2002-2036. This compares with a growth rate of 0.8 per cent for the period 1961 to 2002, bearing in mind that the population was at an all time low of 2.8 million in 1961. In the absence of migration the population is projected to continue to grow but at a reduced rate of 0.5 per cent per annum.

One of the advantages of the demographic component method of projecting population is the insight it offers on the age structure effects. These are considered in the next section.

Age Structure

For the population as a whole three broad categories are distinguished. These are the young population aged 0-14 years, the population of working age which is taken as those aged 15-64 years and the old population aged 65 year and over. With increasing education participation at older ages it could be argued that the lower boundary of the working age population should be increased. Similarly, arguments about early retirement, or on the other hand the need for increased labour force participation at older ages, might suggest a redefinition of the upper boundary of this age group. Regardless of redefinition, however, the same general conclusions can be drawn.

A further two age groups will also be of interest – children aged 5-12 years, broadly corresponding to the primary school-going population, and teenagers aged 13-18 years approximating persons in secondary education.

Table 5.7 provides a summary of the projections under M1F2 for each of these age groups at five-year intervals up to 2036, with the 2001 data shown as a benchmark for comparison purposes.

Table 5.7: Population Projections, 2006-2036 (000s)

	Population				Population of School-going Age	
Year	*0-14*	*15-64*	*65 years and over*	*Total*	*"Primary" 5-12*	*"Secondary" 13-18*
2001	827.5	2589.8	429.8	3847.2	433.9	375.3
2006	866.2	2834.0	465.6	4165.8	447.4	341.3
2011	943.1	3012.8	531.1	4487.0	500.2	331.1
2016	1002.1	3176.7	631.1	4809.9	542.3	365.1
2021	1016.3	3312.2	741.3	5069.9	551.7	406.4
2026	997.5	3439.9	866.2	5303.6	546.0	417.5
2031	966.9	3522.6	1002.3	5491.8	522.8	418.2
2036	950.8	3572.6	1145.3	5668.7	507.0	403.6

The number of persons aged 0-14 years reached a peak of 1,044,000 in 1981 and has since been in decline. The 1981 peak was the culmination of the build-up in births experienced during the 1970s supplemented by the children of returning Irish migrants – mainly from Britain. The downward path in the number of young persons has now bottomed out and numbers in this age group are projected to increase in the period to 2021. For the part of this period to 2016 some of those aged 0-14 will have been born already while the remainder will be projected future births.

Beyond 2016, however, the population aged 0-14 years will arise solely as a result of projected births. Given the F2 assumption that the total fertility rate will be maintained at 1.85 from 2011 onwards, the main determinant of the young population beyond that year will be the number of women of childbearing age.

It is estimated that the young population will increase to 1,016,000 by 2021 – not far off the 1981 peak of 1,044,000. This would represent an increase of nearly 190,000 or 23 per cent in the 20-year period 2001-2021. A modest decline is projected to occur between 2021 and 2036.

The population of primary school-going age, being a sub-set of the young population, will follow a similar path to it. Numbers will steadily increase from the 2001 level of 434,000 to reach a peak level of about 550,000 by 2021 – an increase of over a quarter in 20 years. Thereafter, the numbers will gradually decline towards a level of 507,000 by 2036 – still about 17 per cent higher than the 2001 level.

For the first half of the projection period the population of secondary school-going age will be determined by births which have already oc-curred, with due allowance being made for the effects of migration. It is only in the latter stages of the projection period that the numbers will be affected by the fertility assumptions. Numbers are projected to decline by about 12 per cent between 2001 and 2011, to increase by 26 per cent in the following 20 years before beginning to decline again. Clearly, the actual numbers in secondary education will also depend on education participation of older teenagers being maintained.

The population aged 15-64 years, which broadly corresponds to those of working age, has increased at every census since 1961, when it was at a low point of 1,626,000, to reach a level of 2,590,000 by 2001. Numbers in this age group are directly affected by migration assumptions and by the difference between those entering at young ages and those exiting at older ages. The differences in birth cohort size will therefore play a significant role especially if earlier birth cohorts (those in the older age groups) are already depleted through past emigration.

Under the M1 migration assumption the number of persons aged 15-64 years will continue to grow for the duration of the projection period. However, the rate of growth will decline over time, mainly reflecting the downward path in the M1 assumption. To highlight the impact which the migration assumption exerts on the projected population of working age it is worth bearing in mind that the working age population would increase by 28,000 per annum under the M1 assumption compared with just 5,300 in the absence of migration. While a discussion on employment rates is outside the scope of the present chapter, a key determinant of future migration will undoubtedly be the extent to which the economy will continue to grow and whether the commensurate changes in the labour force can be satisfied from domestic sources.

One of the strongest results of the projections exercise is in respect of the old population, i.e. those aged 65 years and over. Regardless of the assumption chosen this population subgroup is projected to increase from its 2001 level of 430,000 to over 1.1 million by 2036. The factors that will contribute to this increase will be the ageing of earlier larger birth cohorts coupled with the assumed improvements in mortality. The projected increase in the very old population (i.e. those aged 80 years and over) will be even more pronounced increasing from 98,000 in 2001 to over 320,000 by 2036.

The projection period will see major changes occurring in the structure of the population. The young population will continue to outnumber the old population until 2026 after which the old population will be numerically superior. The age structure effects are best illustrated by means of population pyramids. Figure 5.3 compares the population pyramid for 2001 with the 2036 version under M1F2.

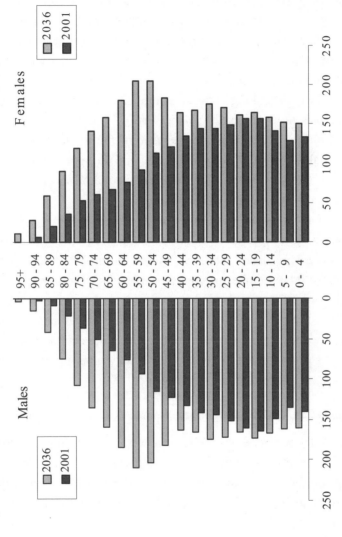

Figure 5.3: Population Pyramids for 2001 and 2036 (M1F2), thousands by age group

The projected population for each five-year age group in 2036 will exceed the corresponding 2001 figure with the greatest excess occurring in the 55-59 year age group. This corresponds to the birth cohorts of the late 1970s supplemented by assumed migration occurring in the period to 2036. The figure illustrates the considerable bulge that will occur in the middle and older age groups.

Another way of looking at the structural changes which are projected to take place is to examine dependency ratios. These ratios express the young and old populations as a percentage of the working age population. The total ratio, which sums the young and old ratios, gives an indication of the likely pressure which will be exerted on those of working age to support the young and old populations.

Figure 5.4 charts the historical trends in dependency ratios since 1926 along with the projected trends to 2036 under M1F2. The graph shows that the dependency ratio was highest during the 1960s mainly as a result of the large number of young people. The current period represents a low point for total dependency. However, future increases in the total dependency ratio will arise as a direct result of the increases in the number of older persons more than outweighing the decline in the number of young people taken in conjunction with a tapering off in the rate of increase in the population of working age.

Conclusions

The pace of demographic change experienced in this country in the last quarter of a century has been unparalleled elsewhere. The outlook is for continued population growth, which, even in the absence of net immigration, is likely to be well in excess of that projected for our European counterparts.

On the basis of the high migration assumption the proportion of foreign-born persons could exceed 1 million by the end of the projection period compared with 400,000 at the time of the 2002 census. This would equate to about 18 per cent of the population in 2036, higher than the present rate in the following high immigration countries: Sweden, United States, Germany and Austria; though lower than the present rates in Canada, New Zealand, Switzerland, Australia and Luxembourg.

Figure 5.4: *Actual and Projected (M1F2) Dependency Ratios*

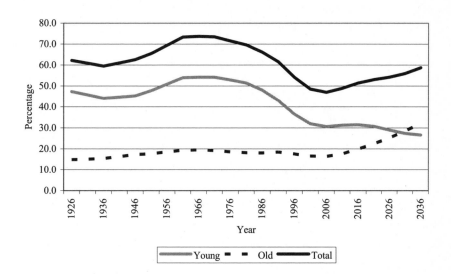

Ireland will be an older country in 2036. As recent as 1981 just over 30 per cent of the population was aged under 15 years while the relevant proportion aged over 65 years was 10.7 per cent. At present these percentages are 20.9 per cent and 11.2 per cent, respectively. By 2036 it is projected that the young will make up 16.8 per cent of the projected 5.7 million population, while older persons will account for 20.2 per cent of the total.

In short, if the assumptions put forward in the projections exercise prove accurate then the demographic profile of the Ireland of 2036 will differ significantly from the present profile.

Appendix 5.1 — Diagram of Population Projection Model

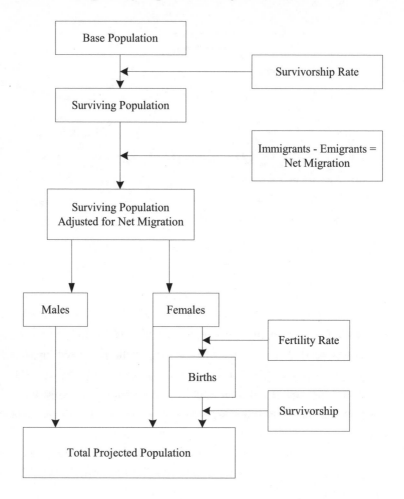

Notes

---

[1] Central Statistics Office, 2004. Population and Labour Force Projections, 2006-2036, Pm 4017

Chapter 6

SOCIAL PARTNERSHIP AND THE POLICY PROCESS

Rory O'Donnell *and* **Damian Thomas**

This chapter describes social partnership and its role in Irish public policy since 1987. Section 2 gives a brief outline of social partnership in Ireland, listing the partnership programmes and identifying the main institutions. Section 3, the main content of the chapter, fleshes out that summary by tracing the evolving analysis which underpinned partnership and the associated partnership programmes. Section 4 identifies the main questions that have been debated by those with conflicting views of partnership.

The focus of the chapter is on partnership and the national policy process. Consequently, it does not provide a detailed account of the industrial relations dimension and the organisations involved in managing industrial relations and organisational change. Nor does the chapter provide an account of local partnership structures and processes, although these form an important part of the overall story of partnership.

The chapter aims to provide an objective account of the partnership process and programmes. However, it is only fair to state at the outset that each of the authors have been involved in the work of partnership bodies, the National Economic and Social Council and the National Centre for Partnership and Performance, respectively.

Partnership in Outline

The opening and modernisation of the Irish economy in the 1960s in-cluded elements of tripartism in Irish public institutions and policy. Rep-resentatives of trade unions and business were appointed to many of pub-lic bodies established during those years. The National Industrial Eco-nomic Council was created in 1963 and was succeeded in 1973 by the National Economic and Social Council (NESC). NESC contained repre-sentatives of employers' associations, trade unions, farmer's organisations and senior civil servants. Its mandate was to seek agreement on issues of economic and social policy and to advise government, through the Tao-iseach. Effort at national pay determination was made in the 1960s, and this approach became dominant in the 1970s, with a series of National Wage Agreements and National Understandings. Significant economic and social progress was made in those decades. Yet, by the late 1970s Ire-land was experiencing increased economic difficulties – reflecting struc-tural adjustment to free trade, increased need for social services, a turbu-lent international economy and recourse to foreign borrowing to fund both capital and current spending. The national approach to pay determination was abandoned in 1980 and during much of that decade successive gov-ernments failed to achieve control of the public finances.

In a context of deep despair in Irish society, the social partners un-dertook intensive discussion in NESC and reached an agreed analysis of Ireland's situation and a strategy to escape from the vicious circle of stagnation, unemployment, emigration, rising taxes and debt. The Coun-cil's 1986 report, *A Strategy for Development,* formed the basis upon which a new government and the social partners negotiated the Pro-gramme for National Recovery (PNR), which ran from 1987 to 1990. This was to be the first of seven agreements that will soon bring Ireland to more than two decades of negotiated economic and social governance (see Box 6.1). Following the influence of NESC's 1996 report and the success of the PNR, the negotiation of each subsequent partnership pro-gramme has been preceded by a NESC report – widely referred to as the NESC "Strategy"– which sets out a shared analysis of economic and so-cial trends and the parameters within which a new programme should be negotiated (NESC, 1990, 1993, 1996, 1999, 2003, 2006). The NESC Strategy report is the main input into the negotiation of the partnership programmes. These negotiations take place in the Department of the Taoiseach and are chaired by the Secretary General of that department, assisted by his officials and those from other departments[1].

Box 6.1: Seven National Agreements

- Programme for National Recovery (1987-1990)

- Programme for Economic and Social Progress (1991-1993)

- Programme for Competitiveness and Work (1994-1996)

- Partnership 2000 for Inclusion, Employment and Competitiveness (1997-2000)

- Programme for Prosperity and Fairness (2001-2003)

- Sustaining Progress (2003-2005)

- Towards 2016

An important feature of partnership has been the widening of the organisations involved in the process. In 1993, the government established a new partnership body, the National Economic and Social Forum (NESF), to focus specifically on issues of long-term unemployment and social exclusion. Its membership included the traditional social partners – trade unions, employers associations and farm organisations – and representatives of the community and voluntary sector, as well as members of the Oireachtas. Through the latter half of the 1990s, the membership of NESC was widened and, by 1997, the community and voluntary sector had full representation on NESC and full social partner status.

A number of other institutional developments are worthy of note. Under the first partnership agreement, government and the partners established a process for monitoring the programme, located in the Department of the Taoiseach. This has continued, in various guises, ever since and means that that department is, to a significant degree, the guardian of the partnership programme and the partnership process. In addition, at various times, government and the partners have created working groups or committees to analyse and address specific problems. While most of these have a defined life-span, some have become institutionalised, such the Housing Forum. In 1997, government created the National Centre for Partnership (NCP) to monitor and promote partnership at enterprise and organisational level and, following a review in 2000, this body was replaced by the National Centre for Partnership and Performance (NCPP) (O'Donnell and Teague, 2000). In 2004, government stated its intention to link the three partnership bodies – NESC, NESF and NCPP – more closely within a new National Economic and Social Development Office (NESDO) and in 2006 legislation was passed establishing NESDO and its constituent bodies on a statutory footing.

Evolving Analysis and Partnership Programmes

The 1986 NESC Strategy Report and the Programme for National Recovery

While NESC's 1986 report, *A Strategy for Development*, discussed a wide range of problems, its major contribution was probably its analysis of the public finances and creation of a shared understanding that correction of the public finances was an imperative. It achieved this by shifting the focus from the annual budget deficit and annual borrowing to the ratio of national debt to GNP. This revealed the hard arithmetic of debt, the role of international interest rates and, most significantly, the critical role of economic growth. This allowed all partners to escape from a short-term and ideological focus on this year's budgetary stance, to a medium-term focus on competitiveness, growth and employment.

That NESC report was the basis on which government and the social partners negotiated the PNR in 1987.[2] It involved agreement on wage levels in both the private and public sectors for a three-year period. Moderate wage growth was seen as essential to international competitiveness and to achieving control of the public finances. Indeed, the PNR enlisted trade union support for a radical correction of the public finances. In return, the government accepted that the value of social welfare payments would be maintained, and that public spending cuts would not be extended to these transfer payments. In addition, it undertook to introduce reforms in income tax which were of benefit to union members. The Irish Congress of Trade Unions put the agreement to a vote at a special delegate conference where it was ratified. This democratic procedure is an important feature of partnership which has been repeated in all subsequent agreements.

The PNR, and its successors, involved far more than centralised wage bargaining. They covered a wide range of economic and social policies – including tax reform, the evolution of welfare payments, trends in public spending, structural adjustments and Ireland's adherence to the narrow band of the ERM. On the macroeconomic front, each partner agreed that they would not generate inflationary pressures, which would warrant devaluation, and would not seek devaluation when external problems arose.

NESC 1990 and Programme for Economic and Social Progress (PESP)

In its 1990 report, *A Strategy for the Nineties: Economic Stability and Structural Change*, NESC set out an analytical framework that informed its subsequent work and the partnership programmes. It argued that there are three requirements for a consistent policy framework in a small, open, European democracy:

- **Macroeconomic:** the economy must have a macroeconomic policy approach which yields low inflation and steady growth of aggregate output;

- **Distributional:** there must be an evolution of incomes which ensures competitiveness, which handles distributional conflict in a way which does not disrupt the functioning of the economy and which is fair; and

- **Structural or Supply-Side Policy:** there must be a set of policies which promote structural change in order to maintain competitiveness, eliminate barriers to participation and achieve social cohesion in an ever-changing environment (NESC, 1990).

Policies in each of these three areas must be consistent and must be suitable for the economy and society to which they are applied.

The Council argued that, in the Irish case, the macroeconomic requirement is best met by adherence to the European Exchange Rate Mechanism (ERM) and transition to EMU, as well as sustained reduction of the debt/GNP ratio.[3] NESC argued that the distributional requirement is best met by a negotiated determination of incomes and that, to be really effective, such a negotiated approach must encompass not only the evolution of pay, but also taxation, the public finances, exchange rate and monetary policy and the main areas of public provision and social welfare.[4] In pursuit of the third requirement, the Council and others advocated a number of structural reforms. NESC argued that such reforms are best achieved with the active consent and participation of those who work in public agencies and with the participation of affected citizens and groups.

Among the supply-side measures proposed by NESC in 1990 was a new area-based approach to long-term unemployment and disadvantage. This was reflected in the new partnership agreement, the *Programme for Economic and Social Progress* (PESP). Partnership companies were established, on a pilot basis, in 12 areas of particular disadvantage in order to design and implement a more coordinated, multi-dimensional, approach to social exclusion. This pilot initiative was subsequently extended to a larger number of areas and has been the subject of numerous studies and lively debate.

In other respects, the Programme for Economic and Social Progress (PESP) – and the subsequent agreements in the 1990s – had a broadly similar form to the PNR. Each has covered a three-year period, and has set out agreed pay increases for that period. Increasingly, as economic recovery yielded abundant tax revenue, the partnership agreements saw an exchange of wage moderation for reduction in personal income tax.

NESC's 1993 Strategy Report and the Programme for Competitiveness and Work

While policy adjustment, partnership and other factors had achieved a significant recovery of the Irish economy after 1987, unemployment remained extremely high. Indeed, it increased during the 1992-93 crisis of the ERM and the associated rise in interest rates. NESC's 1993 report, *A Strategy for Competitiveness, Growth and Employment*, opened with a sombre assessment:

> The extent of unemployment in Ireland, and especially long-term unemployment, casts a dark shadow over the performance of the economy. Unemployment is a powerful symbol of the under-development of the economy. The low level of employment in the Irish economy,

relative to our neighbours, is the root cause of income levels per head which continue to lag behind the European average. Furthermore, had emigration not relieved labour market pressures in the late 1980s, unemployment would be substantially higher than it is now.

These realities constitute an inescapable backdrop to the formulation of public policy. The acceleration of employment growth and the reduction of unemployment constitute the over-riding objective for the Council as it prepares its recommendations for the conduct of economic and social policy in the medium term (NESC, 1993, p. 3).

In February 1994, government and partners agreed the *Programme for Competitiveness and Work* (PCW), which ran from 1994 to 1996. The PCW extended the focus on increasing the number of people at work and reducing the level of unemployment.

The NESF and Ending Long-term Unemployment

The intense focus of the social partners on employment and unemployment was reflected in, and reinforced by, the NESF's 1994 report, *Ending Long-term Unemployment* (NESF, 1994). That report played an important role in promoting the development of active labour market policies in Ireland. It is widely seen as having prompted the development of the Local Employment Service, which aimed to assist the transition from welfare to work.

NESC's 1996 Strategy Report and Partnership 2000

The analytical framework set out in 1990 was developed in two directions in NESC's 1996 report, *Strategy into the 21st Century*. First, by 1996 the Irish economy was well into the Celtic Tiger phase. Investment was strong, exports were booming, employment was growing strongly and unemployment was falling. This raised the question: was social partnership still appropriate outside of the crisis context that had prevailed in the late 1980s and early 1990s? To answer that question, the report opened with a review of the Irish economy and Irish society since 1960. This led the Council to the following interpretation:

Although the Irish economy achieved significant economic growth, adjustment, modernisation and inward investment since 1960, these successes are qualified in important ways. Growth was not handled

well, giving rise to inconsistent claims on the Irish economy. Awareness of the international environment was incomplete. The adjustment of indigenous enterprises to international competition failed
more often than it succeeded. Job creation was insufficient, old jobs
were lost at a remarkable rate and unemployment increased. High
levels of savings and corporate profits were not matched by investment in the Irish economy. Inevitable adversities were allowed to
become divisive and produced delayed and insufficient responses.
Overall, there was an insufficient appreciation of the interdependence in the economy – between the public and private sectors, between the indigenous economy and the international economy, and
between the economic and the political.

A core argument of this chapter – which informs the whole report – is
that these problems arose as much in periods of strong economic
growth, as in periods of international recession. An understanding of
these weaknesses, and the possibility of repeating them in a period of
high growth, is critical in current circumstances (NESC, 1996, p. 21).

A second concern was to place Ireland's consistent policy approach in a
global context. It argued that while globalisation has undermined many
elements of national economic policy, it is possible to identify areas of
national policy that remain vital and effective. In a small, open, European democracy like Ireland:

(i) Most of the policies which affect Ireland's prosperity and social
cohesion are *supply-side* policies – i.e. those that improve quality,
quantity and allocation of resources and capabilities;

(ii) Given rapid economic change, national policies must produce
flexibility; and

(iii) Successful national supply-side policies – directed towards innovation, competitiveness and inclusion – depend on the high level social
cohesion and co-operation that the state can both call upon and develop.

This suggested that once a consensus on macroeconomic policy is in place
– and is reflected in government policy, wage bargaining and management
– the main focus of policy analysis and development should be the supply-
side measures that influence competitive advantage, social cohesion and
societal well-being, and the creation of institutional arrangements which
encourage discovery and implementation of such measures.

The 1996 NESC Strategy contained a more detailed analysis of wage bargaining than the previous reports. This was necessary because of the strong recovery of the Irish economy, the revival of the EMU project at European level, and increased awareness of the need to ensure that public pay determination was consistent with economic performance and served public sector modernisation. While Irish wage bargaining and economic management made the difficult transition to the euro in the years from 1997 to 2002, several of the concerns which motivated NESC's 1996 analysis – how to combine wage discipline with a dynamic enterprise sector, and how to keep public pay growth in line to economic reality and service quality – have remained live issues in partnership up to the present.

Another focus of the 1996 NESC report was enterprise-level partnership. Trade union representatives argued that the high level of partnership at national level was not adequately reflected at enterprise level. Reflecting NESC's recommendations, *Partnership 2000* made provision for the establishment of the National Centre for Partnership (NCP) to develop partnership at enterprise level and to provide encouragement, training, information and support to employers' and employees' representatives. As noted in the introduction, the NCP was replaced by the NCPP in 2001 and given a wider remit focused on supporting and fostering organisational change and innovation through partnership-based approaches (see www.ncpp.ie).

Partnership 2000 also contained a significant measure of agreement on action to modernise the public service, enlisting the social partners in support of the Strategic Management Initiative (Government of Ireland, 1987). This reflected an anxiety to ensure that the pay moderation and improved performance delivered by the private sector after 1987 was matched in the public sector. This too was to become an enduring theme of both discussion within partnership and commentary on partnership.

In reviewing the analytical basis of partnership, a final aspect of the 1996 Strategy should be noted. While the practical benefits of partnership were evident, there was considerable uncertainty among some about how partnership related to traditional forms of national industrial relations, policy advocacy and politics. In addition, the inclusiveness of partnership was hotly debated by community and voluntary organisations. To clarify these issues, NESC characterised partnership, as follows:

- The partnership process involves a combination of *consultation, negotiation* and *bargaining;*

- The partnership process is heavily dependent on a *shared understanding* of the key mechanisms and relationships in any given policy area;

- The *government* has a unique role in the partnership process. It provides the arena within which the process operates. It shares some of its authority with social partners. In some parts of the wider policy process, it actively supports formation of interest organisations;

- The process reflects *interdependence* between the partners. The partnership is necessary because no party can achieve its goals without a significant degree of support from others;

- Partnership is characterised by a *problem-solving* approach designed to produce consensus, in which various interest groups address joint problems;

- Partnership involves *trade-offs* both between and within interest groups;

- The partnership process involves different participants on various agenda items, ranging from national macroeconomic policy to local development (NESC, 1996, p. 66).

Shared understanding and problem solving became accepted as key features of a successful partnership process.

Following the recommendations of both NESC and NESF, the *Partnership 2000* agreement continued the process of widening inclusion. The government invited eight community and voluntary organisations to be part of the negotiations, forming the Community and Voluntary pillar. The negotiation of the programme was undertaken in a new manner, with a range of voluntary and community organisations involved. *Partnership 2000* included an action programme for greater social inclusion. In addition to the general pay and tax provisions of the programme – which were designed to promote employment – this included the National Anti-Poverty Strategy, reforms of tax and welfare designed to improve the incentives for and reward from work, an expansion of targeted employment measures, further measures to address educational disadvantage and consolidation of the local partnership approach to both economic and social development.

The 1997 NESF Report A Framework for Partnership

Soon after the negotiation of *Partnership 2000*, the nature of partnership and the conditions for making a widened partnership process effective were further examined in the NESF report *A Framework for Partnership – Enriching Strategic Consensus Through Participation* (1997). Preparation of that report involved not only discussion within the Forum, but a series of in-depth discussions among a wide set of social partners and government departments. That discussion revealed a number of problems and frustrations with the partnership process. An important argument of the NESF analysis was that many of these problems – particularly the problems of linking national participation to the local level and effective implementation – were experienced by all the social partners.

Building on NESC's 1996 characterisation, the Forum report distinguished two different conceptions, or dimensions, of partnership:

- Functional interdependence, bargaining and deal-making, and

- Solidarity, inclusiveness and participation.

While effective partnership involves both of these, it cannot be based entirely on either. There is a third dimension that transcends these two. Partnership involves the players in a process of deliberation and interaction that has the potential to shape and reshape their understanding, preferences and identity. This third dimension has to be added to the hardheaded notion of bargaining (and to the idea of solidarity) to adequately capture the process. Indeed, the NESF argued that despite the difficulties of an inclusive partnership system, there are fewer preconditions for effective and inclusive partnership than might be imagined. The key, it argued, would seem to be adoption of a problem solving approach.

The Forum report combined that analysis with observation of three trends which demand a further revision of conventional ideas of "neo-corporatism". First, the nature and role of social partners are changing, in ways which accentuate mobilisation, information and action, rather than power resources. Second, the role of national government is changing, in ways that weaken traditional policy-making and administration, and accentuate its role as policy entrepreneur and facilitator of information-pooling and deliberation. Third, the relationship between policy-making, implementation and monitoring is changing, in ways which place monitoring of a new sort at the centre of policy development, and require a new combination of all three.

This analysis was used to define a new division of labour between NESC and NESF. It was agreed that NESC would continue to undertake strategic analysis of overall policy and of selected sectoral issues, and NESF would undertake in-depth examination of issues of implementation, using project teams including both Forum members and experts from within the relevant sectors (see www.nesf.ie).

The 1999 NESC Strategy and the Programme for Prosperity and Fairness

In its 1999 Strategy report, NESC proposed a new vision for Ireland. It argued that the foundations of a successful society are:

- A dynamic economy, and

- A participatory society,

- Incorporating a commitment to social justice,

- Based on consistent economic development that is socially and environmentally sustainable,

- Which responds especially to the constantly evolving requirements of international competitiveness, understood as the necessary condition of continuing economic and social success.

This vision had several dimensions, including economic inclusion based on full employment, social inclusion, successful and continuing adaptation to change, commitment to lifelong learning, commitment to the further development of the European Union and international solidarity, and an entrepreneurial culture. This vision was endorsed in the *Programme for Prosperity and Fairness,* and in subsequent NESC Strategy reports and partnership programmes.

The *Programme for Prosperity and Fairness* encompassed a very broad policy agenda. This reflected the wide range of structural or supply-side issues which partners saw as a relevant to either competitiveness or social inclusion.

NESC's 2003 Strategy and Sustaining Progress

In its 2003 strategy report, *An Investment in Quality: Services, Inclusion and Enterprise*, NESC once again addressed the task of developing a shared understanding of Ireland's long-run economic and social development as a basis for agreement on medium-term policy approaches. This was particularly important, and difficult, because of the combination of economic and social realities that existed at that time. Economically, Ireland had experienced an unprecedented boom in employment, earnings and general prosperity from 1993 to 2000. Yet the international recession between 2000 and 2002 and the bursting of the dot.com bubble had a particularly sharp impact on the Irish public finances, if not on employment. Socially, soaring employment, falling unemployment and increased social spending represented real advances. Yet a number of acute social problems remained obvious and wider deficits in services and social protection were becoming increasingly apparent.

The analysis of long-run economic and social development revealed undoubted progress and strengths, but also significant vulnerabilities. On the economic side, the vulnerabilities largely reflect the fact that the Irish economy has some of the characteristics of a regional economy. On the social side, the vulnerabilities arise from three general sources: the legacy of the past and public policy, the economic context and the limits of bureaucratic delivery. Therefore, NESC argued, "there is no comprehensive doctrine – of the market, the state, society or globalisation – that uniquely explains Ireland's current social situation and unambiguously guides action" (NESC, 2002, p. 39). Acceptance of the core elements of Ireland's economic strategy demands recognition of the associated social and economic vulnerabilities.

NESC argued that a critical aspect of vision is clear sight of how public policy, the social partners and others have influenced the economy and society, and how they can influence it in future. Ireland's experience suggests that:

- Ireland does not fit neatly into any existing model or category of socio-economic development;

- Much greater economic and social progress occurred than was deemed possible within the models that informed earlier analysis;

- Ireland has succeeded with an eclectic approach that seeks to adopt the best features of different socio-economic models;

- Many of the new economic and social possibilities were discovered by experimental problem-solving action involving government, the social partners and others; and

- Changes in many parts of the economy, society and the state can amount to significant change in the whole.

NESC argued that the final aspect of vision is seeing new possibilities. Among the new possibilities sketched in the 2003 NESC strategy report was the Developmental Welfare State (DWS). This idea emerged from intense discussion within both the Council and the NESC Secretariat on how to interpret Ireland's increasing level of relative income poverty and on whether Ireland's social deficits could be addressed by one of the classic European "models" of welfare: universalist Scandinavian, insurance-based Continental and liberal/residual.

The starting point of the DWS was to escape from the ongoing debate about these models of welfare by recognising that any welfare system can be seen as containing three over-lapping elements: income transfers (via welfare or tax), the provision of services and innovative policy measures. The question is, how effectively do these three elements address risks and social disadvantages, support participation and identify and tackle unmet needs? The report posed the possibility of a Developmental Welfare State, which would provide better social protection and yet connect more fully with Ireland's dynamic economy. NESC emphasised that the DWS was, at that stage, "a sketch of a new possibility, rather than a list of recommendations that the Council has agreed" (NESC, 2002, p. 54). But a new way of thinking about Ireland's social policies and social deficits had begun to emerge, and this was to become a major theme of the Council's work from 2003 to 2005, and a central element of its 2006 strategy report (see below).

Within NESC, there was debate on socio-economic rights and the potential of a "rights-based approach" to social problems. The Council agreed a new perspective on this (NESC, 2002, pp 106-113; 2003, pp 355-371).

The agreement negotiated in early 2003, *Sustaining Progress*, was shaped by two factors, referred to above. One was the economic and budgetary situation. Government made it clear that its budget of December 2002 defined the resources available. This limited negotiation on additional resources or new programmes. The agreement was also shaped by the experience of the previous agreement, the *Programme for Prosperity and Fairness,* which ran from 2001 to 2003. Its extensive agenda had given rise to so many working groups and committees that the partners and government felt overburdened. Consequently, beyond the main themes of macroeconomic policy, economic development and social inclusion, *Sustaining Progress* confined itself to ten "Special Initiatives": (a) housing and accommodation; (b) the cost of insurance; (c) migration and interculturalism; (d) long-term unemployment and vulnerable workers; (e) educational disadvantage; (f) waste management; (g) care of children, people with disabilities and older people; (h) alcohol and drug misuse; (i) including everyone in the information society and (j) ending child poverty. These were seen as cross-cutting issues that required the mobilisation of a range of resources across sectors, organisations and at different levels of government. The agreement emphasised that:

> In approaching such issues, the emphasis should be on working together, building consensus and adopting a problem-solving approach to finding practical solutions (Government of Ireland, 2003, p. 17).

After negotiation of the agreement, two organisations in the community and voluntary pillar – the National Women's Council of Ireland and the Community Platform – felt unable to endorse *Sustaining Progress*. The other six organisations ratified the programme. This was a significant split in the community and voluntary sector. Government adopted the position that only organisations that were in partnership could be appointed to partnership bodies, such as the NESC and NESF. Consequently, in reappointing these and other bodies, it reconstituted the pillar, confining it to organisations that had endorsed *Sustaining Progress*.

The Developmental Welfare State

In April 2005, NESC published *The Developmental Welfare State* (NESC, 2005a). The report re-analysed Ireland's social deficits, placing poverty and other indicators in the context of employment trends, inequalities (of both opportunity and outcome) and service needs. It highlighted a most important and troubling fact: the continuing high level of benefit dependency among working-age adults and the long duration for which many remain on social welfare. It reviewed the relation between economic performance and social protection and examined Ireland's welfare system in a comparative context. It examined the principal strategies commonly advanced for reforming Ireland system – more universalism, a stronger insurance system and more targeting – and argued that changed circumstances make it unwise to rely on any one of them. In any case, it has proved impossible to build a consensus on any one of these reform strategies, delaying the building of a coalition to achieve urgent reforms. While significant learning is possible from each of the more sharply defined welfare models in Europe, the hybrid character of Ireland's system is, more than before, a potential strength.

The study outlined three overarching objectives for social policy and Ireland's welfare state:

- To revise systems that reflect low expectations and achieve low outcomes for a minority;

- To support the employed population more adequately in changed times;

- To institutionalise wholly new standards of participation and care for society's most dependent and vulnerable members.

It proposed that the core structure of Ireland's welfare system should consist of three overlapping areas of welfare activity – services, income supports and activist or innovative measures – as shown in Figure 6.1.

> Its character would derive from the approach taken in each of these
> spheres and the integration of them in ways that are developmental
> for individuals, families, communities and the economy (NESC,
> 2005a, p. xvii).

It argued that good economic performance and improved social protection are not intrinsically opposed, but neither do they inevitably occur together. Rather, they can be made to support each other where there is sufficient shared understanding and commitment. This depends critically on recognising that social policy is not simply an exercise in redistributing a surplus, there to be creamed off *after* successful economic performance. The composition and manner of social spending are as significant as its level.

Figure 6.1: Core Structure of the Developmental Welfare State

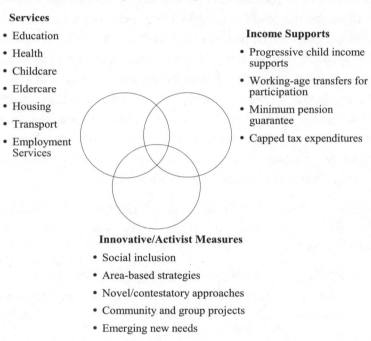

Services

- Education
- Health
- Childcare
- Eldercare
- Housing
- Transport
- Employment Services

Income Supports

- Progressive child income supports
- Working-age transfers for participation
- Minimum pension guarantee
- Capped tax expenditures

Innovative/Activist Measures

- Social inclusion
- Area-based strategies
- Novel/contestatory approaches
- Community and group projects
- Emerging new needs

The analysis showed that the radical development of services is the single most important route to improving social protection in Ireland over the coming years. It has a triple logic: supporting people in employment, redressing the marginal position of socially disadvantaged groups and according autonomy and respect to people with disabilities and in institutional care.

NESC Strategy 2006 and Towards 2016

In its seventh triennial Strategy report, *NESC Strategy 2006: People, Productivity and Purpose*, the Council suggested the need to find a new understanding of the relation between Ireland's economy, society and environment.

A new shared understanding of the Irish economy must incorporate the increasing role of services, knowledge and skills in a successful regional economy, the enhanced role of domestic demand, the importance of participation by those with low levels of educational attainment and with disabilities, and the impact of migration on the economy. This implies a significant adaptation of earlier thinking about national economic development. For several decades, Ireland's ultimate economic, social and cultural goals were reflected in the proximate goal of employment. Anything that promoted employment – especially employment in the traded sector – was also likely to contribute to export growth, business strength, domestic prosperity and wider social progress. Now, our ultimate and proximate goals do not coincide so neatly. This has implications in a range of economic and social policy areas.

> Through much of the past decade and a half, there was a real sense that the economic reality set limits to the social possibilities. Now, the medium and long term strength of the economy seems to depend critically not only on increased investment in physical infrastructure and scientific research, but also on a deepening of capabilities, even greater participation, internal as well as external connectivity, more social mobility and successful handling of diversity, including immigration (NESC, 2005b, p. xv).

The Council argued that the development of a dynamic, knowledge-based economy has social implications that can serve social justice and a more egalitarian society, but also that the development of Ireland's welfare state is integral to sustaining the dynamism and flexibility of its economy.

NESC suggested that economic and social progress in Ireland is now more broadly based and has deeper roots than in the past, or than is sometimes recognised. At the same time, this progress continues to be uneven in certain respects and is vulnerable in a number of ways, some of which are new. It suggested that this modified picture of Ireland's situation demands that its goals should be modified:

- To focus more on *GNP per head* than the growth of *total GNP*;

- To focus more on the overall *employment rate* and the *employability* of individuals than the absolute level of job creation;

- To encompass not only export growth but also the *competitive advantage in a networked world economy*;

- To build on successful *adoption* and *operation* of advanced technologies to achieve much wider *innovation* in products, processes and organisation;

- To aim less for targeted programmes for disadvantaged groups and more for the responsiveness and flexibility of publicly-funded services, securing adequate income and improving participation;

- To build on successful control of a *small number of large-scale polluters* and an improving waste management infrastructure, to achieve *widespread adoption of environmental quality* through more effective conflict resolution and governance.

Based on this analysis, NESC identified strategies to achieve these goals in a range of policy areas: enterprise and innovation, training, migration, participation and fairness, pensions, infrastructures of care, housing and sustainable settlements, health, education, regional and rural development, agriculture, infrastructure and a new national development plan, the environment and policy to enable voluntary activity.

Not surprisingly, many of its recommendations were based on its in-depth analysis in *The Developmental Welfare State*. In particular, it reiterated the proposal for a life-cycle approach, as illustrated in Figure 6.2. For each life-cycle group it is now necessary to identify an effective combination of income supports, services and innovative policy initiatives. To design and deliver these it is necessary to address issues of governance and leadership. More responsive and integrated "participation packages" will require the articulation of rights and responsibilities the definition of standards that give meaning to those rights.

Figure 6.2: The Developmental Welfare State: The Life Cycle Approach

Who?	What?	How?	
	Integration of services, income support and activist measures	*Governance and leadership*	*Standards and rights*
0-17			
18-29			
30-64			
65+			
People challenged in their personal autonomy			

NESC closed its 2006 Strategy report with a discussion of policy-making, implementation and partnership. It noted the perception that Irish public governance, including partnership, confronts a problem of action or "implementation". Since negotiated policy is likely to continue in many spheres, the quality of policy depends critically on the nature and outcomes of various negotiations: Will they produce deadlock? Will the outcome be the lowest common denominator agreeable to insiders, with limited care for the public good? Or will negotiation involve an open-minded search for better solutions with a sharing of gains and costs?

The answer, NESC suggests, depends to a large degree on government's use of its legitimate authority to shape the engagement of interest groups in ways that support problem-solving negotiation and agreement on policy solutions that serve the public good. Effective negotiated agreements require that government use its authority to structure engagement and confront stakeholders with the need to go beyond partial and adversarial approaches and to take responsibility for jointly identifying and implementing agreed policy initiatives.

In late 2005, towards the end of NESC's preparation of its 2006 Strategy report, the Irish Ferries dispute created significant tension with Irish industrial relations and partnership. The proposal by Irish Ferries to replace its crew with workers from outside Ireland and to re-register its vessels created fears that labour standards in the Irish economy were being significantly undermined by migration and globalisation. The opening of negotiations on a successor to *Sustaining Progress* were delayed and, once negotiations began, they were protracted, as ICTU, IBEC and government sought agreement on labour standards.

In mid-2006, government and the partners agreed a new partnership programme *Towards 2016* (Government of Ireland, 2006). While the social partner organisations have yet to ratify the new agreement, it seems that the programme significantly advances partnership. Instead of a three-year programme, the partners have agreed a ten-year framework agreement, covering the period 2006 to 2016, to realise the NESC vision by:

- Nurturing the complementary relationship between social policy and economic prosperity;

- Developing a vibrant, knowledge-based economy and stimulating enterprise and productivity;

- Re-inventing and repositioning Ireland's social policies;

- Integrating an island-of-Ireland perspective;

- Deepening capabilities, achieving higher social and economic participation rates and more successfully handling diversity, including immigration.

It identifies a range of measure to enhance Ireland's competitive advantage in a changing world economy and sets out principles that will underlie the new National Development Programme. The programme commits the government and partners to building a new social policy approach. At the heart of this lies the life cycle approach and strategies to re-cast key services, income supports and activation measures requiring new and innovative responses.

On the issue of labour standards, *Towards 2016* outlines a "New Compliance Model", based on effectiveness, fairness and impartiality and ease of understanding and use. This will involve a new Office of the Director for Employment Rights Compliance, better monitoring and a strengthening of penalties and redress. More generally, the parties are agreed on the need to monitor changing patterns of employment, includ-

ing that of workers from overseas, and to keep under review the effectiveness of the new measures.

Perspectives on Partnership and Public Policy

This chapter has provided a basic account of the analytical foundations
of Irish social partnership and a summary of the partnership programmes
since 1987. Needless to say, there are conflicting interpretations and
evaluations of partnership. These revolve around five main questions:

- Is partnership the correct approach to economic policy?

- Can partnership address social issues adequately?

- Is partnership a form of corporatism or an example of new governance?

- Is partnership consistent with democracy and how has it altered Irish
  democracy?

- Has national partnership strengthened enterprise-level partnership
  and participation and supported organisational change?

Each of these issues is actively debated in social and economic organisations, in political parties, in the media and in academic publications. This
chapter has, we hope, demonstrated that they are debated most actively
in the partnership process itself.[5] Partnership has tried to apply its deliberative and problem-solving method to itself. As the NESC said at the
close of its 2006 Strategy report, "Partnership is only worthwhile and
legitimate if it helps in the solution of economic and social problems.
Indeed, if partnership is not part of the solution, it will very quickly become part of the problem" (NESC, 2005b, p. xxvii).

References

CORI (1999) *Social Partnership in a New Century*, CORI Justice Commission,
Dublin.

CORI (2002) *Choosing a Fairer Future: A Social Partnership After the Celtic
Tiger*, CORI Justice Commission, Dublin.

CORI (2005) *Securing Fairness and Wellbeing in a Land of Plenty*, CORI Justice Commission, Dublin.

Government of Ireland (1987), *Programme for National Recovery,* Dublin: Stationery Office.

Government of Ireland (1991*), Programme for Economic and Social Progress,* Dublin: Stationery Office.

Government of Ireland (1994), *Programme for Competitiveness and Work*, Dublin: Stationery Office.

Government of Ireland (1996), *Partnership 2000 for Inclusion, Employment and Competitiveness*, Dublin: Stationery Office.

Government of Ireland (2000), *Programme for Prosperity and Fairness*, Dublin: Stationery Office.

Government of Ireland (2003), *Sustaining Progress*, Dublin: Stationery Office.

Government of Ireland (2006), *Towards 2016*, Dublin: Stationery Office.

NESC (1986), *A Strategy for Development, 1986-1990*, Dublin: NESC.

NESC (1990), *A Strategy for the Nineties*, Dublin: NESC.

NESC (1993), *A Strategy for Competitiveness, Growth and Employment*, Dublin: NESC.

NESC (1996), *Strategy into the 21st Century*, Dublin: NESC.

NESC (1999), *Opportunities, Challenges and Capacities for Choice,* Dublin: National Economic and Social Council.

NESC (2002), *An Investment in Quality: Services, Inclusion and Enterprise – Conclusions and Recommendations,* Dublin: NESC.

NESC (2003), *An Investment in Quality: Services, Inclusion and Enterprise,* Dublin: NESC.

NESC (2005a), *The Developmental Welfare State,* Dublin: NESC.

NESC (2005b), *NESC Strategy 2006: People, Productivity and Purpose,* Dublin: NESC.

NESF (1994), *Ending Long-Term Unemployment*, Dublin: NESC.

NESF (1997), *A Framework for Partnership – Enriching Strategic Consensus through Participation*, Dublin: NESC.

O'Donnell, R. (1994), "European Integration" in Norton, D. (ed.), *Economics for an Open Economy*, Dublin: Oak Tree Press.

O'Donnell, R. and O'Reardon, C. (1997), "Ireland's Experiment in Social Partnership 1987-96" in Fajertag, G. and Pochet, P. (eds.), *Social Pacts in Europe*, Brussels: European Trade Union Institute.

O'Donnell, R. and O'Reardon, C. (2000), "Social Partnership in Ireland's Economic Transformation" in Fajertag, G. and Pochet, P. (eds.), *Social Pacts in Europe: New Dynamics*, Brussels: European Trade Union Institute.

O'Donnell, R. and Thomas, D. (1998) "Partnership and Policy-Making" in S. Healy and B. Reynolds (eds) *Social Policy in Ireland: Principles, Practice and Problems*, Oak Tree Press, Dublin

O'Donnell, R. and Thomas, D. (2002), "Ireland in the 1990s: Policy Concertation Triumphant" in Berger, S. and Compston, H. (eds.), *Policy Concertation and Social Partnership in Western Europe: Lessons for the 21st Century*, New York and Oxford: Berghahn Books.

Notes

---

[1] The text of the social partnership programmes are available on the Irish Government website at www.taoiseach.gov.ie. The NESC Strategy reports since 1999 are available on the NESC website (www.nesc.ie) and all are available in hard copy from either NESC, 16 Parnell Square, Dublin 1 or the Government Publications Sales Office.

[2] A more detailed account of these negotiations, and a list of the organisations that participated in each partnership programme, can be found in O'Donnell and Thomas (1998 and 2002).

[3] Here NESC drew on its 1989 study, *Ireland in the European Community*. In its analysis of the impact of economic integration on weaker and peripheral regions, NESC had rejected the older economic view that it is the *monetary* stage of integration which poses the greatest threat to weaker regions and member states, and instead focused on the *economic* forces unleashed by free trade and the mobility of labour and capital (NESC, 1989; O'Donnell, 1994).

[4] The connections between monetary, fiscal and distributional issues, and the advantages of a negotiated approach, are discussed in O'Donnell and O'Reardon (1997 and 2000).

[5] The views of various social partners and others can be found in CORI (1999, 2002 and 2005). References to the wider economic and political analysis of partnership in Ireland and elsewhere can be fond in the texts cited here and in the papers at www.nesc.ie/organisation/papers.asp?authorId=88.

Chapter 7

POVERTY: MEASUREMENT, TRENDS AND FUTURE DIRECTIONS

Micheál L. Collins

Addressing poverty continues to be identified as a major challenge for Irish society. Commitments in the National Anti Poverty Strategy, National Action Plans on Social Inclusion and various social partnership documents underscore that view. A government office, the Office of Social Inclusion, has also been established with overall responsibility for developing, coordinating and driving policy responses to poverty and social exclusion. This chapter considers the issue of poverty over three sections. First, the chapter examines the measurement methods used to assess poverty. It then uses data spanning ten years (1994-2004) to assess trends in Irish poverty. The distribution of poverty risk and a comparison of Irish poverty rates with those experienced in the 24 other EU state is also included. A third section considers the direction that poverty measurement and policy is likely to take in the years ahead.

Measuring Poverty

Assessments of poverty focus on living standards and are concerned with those in society unable to achieve a selected standard. Over the past century two broad schools of thought have emerged on how to establish these standards. The "absolute poverty" approach uses fixed benchmarks while the "relative poverty" approach selects thresholds that are variable and adjust as contemporary living standards change. While absolute approaches, such as the United Nation income of $1.00 a day measure, remain relevant for less developed countries, societies in the developed world are such that these concepts have been superseded by relative approaches to poverty.

The 1997 Irish National Anti-Poverty Strategy definition reflects the relative approach and defines poverty as follows:

> People are living in poverty if their income and resources (material, cultural and social) are so inadequate as to preclude them from having a standard of living that is regarded as acceptable by Irish society generally. As a result of inadequate income and resources people may be excluded and marginalised from participating in activities that are considered the norm for other people in society (1997, p. 3).

Moving from such a definition to a practical and feasible measure is both challenging and controversial. While income is mentioned, so too are material, cultural and social resources. Across most countries, the primary approach to implementing a poverty measure has been to adopt an income-based measure. In these cases an assumption is made that the possession of a certain income level will be sufficient to allow an individual to achieve a standard of living regarded as acceptable by society.[1]

There have been many approaches to establishing what this income measure, or relative income poverty line, should be. Irrespective of the approach taken there is always an arbitrary element of judgement involved and as Callan and Nolan (1998, p. 148) have pointed out, "life will not be very different for those with incomes just above or just below any such line". Across the European Union the most common method of establishing this threshold is to draw a line at 60 per cent of median income, where the income used is disposable income (earned income minus taxation and plus any government transfers), adjusted for household size and composition, and where the median income is the income of the middle person in the income distribution.

A poverty line derived in this way will change as income in society changes – specifically it is changes to income levels at the centre of the income distribution that drive movements in the poverty line. Those recording income levels above the line are considered to be outside poverty while those with incomes below the threshold are recorded as being poor. In recent years two interchangeable phrases have been used to describe those who are living on incomes below the poverty line, namely, those "living in poverty" and those "at risk of poverty". The latter of these terms is the most recent, and was introduced following a European Council meeting in Laeken in 2001. There the Indicators Sub-Group of the EU Social Protection Committee suggested that the phrase is a more appropriate description of those below the relative income poverty line. In particular, they noted that the possession of a low income cannot by itself guarantee that a person is unable to achieve an acceptable standard of living, a feature that reflects the aforementioned role of income as a proxy measure of living standards.

This chapter uses data from two sources to trace poverty over a decade from 1994. The first three years of data (1994, 1998 and 2001) come from the Living in Ireland Survey. This survey was carried out by the Economic and Social Research Institute (ESRI) up until 2001. Since mid-2003, income and poverty data for Ireland has been collected by the European Union Survey on Income and Living Conditions (EU-SILC). That survey, which is carried out by the Central Statistics Office (CSO), runs throughout the year with approximately 130 households surveyed each week, implying an annual sample of between 5,000 and 6,000 households.[2] Data from the years 2003 and 2004 are used in this chapter.

Poverty in Ireland

In 1994, 15.6 per cent of the Irish population was living with incomes of less than 60 per cent of the median. Since then the proportion of the population who are at risk of poverty has grown, reaching a peak of almost 22 per cent in 2001. As Table 7.1 shows, by 2004 almost one in every five people were living below the poverty line.

The table also reports information on the proportions of the population who have incomes at less than 50 per cent of the median and 70 per cent of the median. Given the aforementioned difficulties associated with the use of a single equivalised income figure as a poverty line, the reporting of these results has traditionally been used to lend robustness to assessments of poverty. The 50 per cent figures also provide some insight into the depth of poverty, given that they indicate how many are just below the poverty line (between 50 per cent and 60 per cent) and what proportion of the population are well below that threshold. Over the decade examined the proportion living below the 50 per cent threshold considerably increased from 6 per cent in 1994 to over 11 per cent in 2004. Similarly, the figures for 70 per cent threshold also provide information on those living on incomes just above the poverty line. Over the decade this figure increased by 2 per cent.

Table 7.1: Percentage of Population below Relative Income Poverty Lines, 1994-2004

	1994	1998	2001	2003	2004
50% median income line	6.0	9.9	12.9	11.6	11.1
60% median income line	**15.6**	**19.8**	**21.9**	**19.7**	**19.4**
70% median income line	26.7	26.9	29.3	27.7	28.7

Source: CSO, 2005, p. 5 and Whelan et al., 2003, p. 12.

Looking at the 2004 data, the CSO reported that the median equivalised income per adult in Ireland was €309.18 (2005, p. 15). Consequently, the income poverty lines for a single adult derived from this average were: 50 per cent line – €154.59 a week; 60 per cent line – €185.51 a week; and 70 per cent line – €216.43 a week. As it is sometimes difficult to comprehend the true meaning of population proportions, it is useful to translate the poverty percentages into numbers of people. Using population statistics from the CSO (2006, p. 52) the 19.4 per cent living below the poverty line in 2004 corresponds to a figure of 784,497 people.[3]

Taken together, the nominal value of the poverty line, and the number of people with incomes below it, combine to underscore the scale of poverty in Ireland. These numbers also raise an important public policy question, one best posed at the conclusion of an editorial in *The Irish Times* (5 September 2002) when it commented following the publication of the 2000 poverty figures (these figures reported a poverty rate of 20.9 per cent). Given the scale and growth of Ireland's poverty it asked, "how viable is such a society in the long run?"

Who Are the Poor?

In forming policy responses to these figures, information is required on the profile of those individuals below the poverty line. Table 7.2 examines the 2004 data and presents figures for the risk of poverty facing people when they are classified by their principal economic status (the main thing that they do). These risk figures represent the proportion of each group that are found to be in receipt of a disposable income that is less than the 60 per cent median income poverty line. Apart from a small group classified as "others" (those who cannot be described under the six principal status headings), the group of the Irish population that are at highest risk of poverty are the ill and disabled. Almost one in every two people who are classified as ill/disabled live in poverty. The next biggest group at risk of poverty are the unemployed. Thirty-seven per cent of this group live in poverty and when broken down by gender the table shows that the risk levels are much greater for unemployed males. Almost one in three of those on home duties (primarily women) live with incomes below the poverty line while 26 per cent of the retired are in poverty. A closer assessment of the poverty risk levels among the retired reveals that their risk of poverty rate has climbed to its current level from a rate of 8.2 per cent in 1994 (see Whelan et al., 2003, p. 24). Students, whether living in poor families while completing their secondary education or while attending post-secondary education, also have a high poverty rate at 23.6 per cent. The lowest poverty risk figure is recorded for those at work (employees, self-employed, farmers) with 7 per cent of this group living below the poverty line. One obvious conclusion to draw from Table 7.2 is that the highest risk of poverty is concentrated among those dependent on government transfers.

To complement the data in Table 7.2, it is worthwhile considering the 2004 poverty figures for a number of groups: workers, children, the elderly, the ill and disabled, and women. Examining poverty in this way also assists in identifying targeted policy interventions which could lower risk levels for these groups.

Table 7.2: Risk of Poverty among All Persons Aged 16 Years+ by Principal Economic Status, 2004

	Male	Female	Overall
At work	7.5	6.4	7.0
Unemployed	41.0	25.9	37.2
Students and school attendees	19.7	27.8	23.6
On home duties	*	31.8	32.1
Retired	27.9	20.1	26.1
Ill/Disabled	52.9	38.2	47.3
Other	*	53.5	52.3
Total	**18.0**	**20.8**	**19.4**

Source: CSO (2005, p. 11).

Note: * no recorded figure as sample occurrences were too small for estimation

Workers

The transformation of the labour market in Ireland over the past decade has been dramatic. Increases in employment have been significant, yet the segmentation of the labour market is reflected in the poverty figures. Among the employed are a group in receipt of low incomes – the "working poor". As Table 7.2 indicates, 7 per cent of those at work are living at risk of poverty. Translating this into numbers of people suggests that among the 1.89 million workers in Ireland in 2004, just over 132,000 were at risk of poverty.[4] From a policy perspective, addressing poverty among this group can be achieved through policies which remove those on minimum wages from having any income tax liabilities, and by addressing issues of underemployment and enhancing the provision and take-up of supplementary welfare payments such as the Family Income Supplement. In the longer term, reforming the taxation system such that all tax credits are made refundable would offer an opportunity to significantly address poverty experiences among this group.[5]

Children

Children are amongst the most vulnerable groups in any society and consequently the issue of child poverty receives particular attention. The impact of child poverty on children is regarded as "doubly serious", given that it tends to impose restrictions on a child's social, educational and civic upbringing while simultaneously imposing a burden of responsibility for that poverty on a child who can hardly be held responsible for it (Nolan and Farrell, 1990, p. 1). Child poverty is measured as the proportion of all children aged less than 16 years who live in households that have an income below the 60 per cent of median income poverty line. The age category of 0-15 years is chosen to measure child poverty as it corresponds to the international definition of children used by the International Labour Office (ILO). In 2004 there were approximately 865,000 children aged between 0 and 15 years living in Ireland.[6] Of these, Table 7.2 indicates that 21.9 per cent were at risk of poverty. This amounts to 189,530 children.

The fact that such a large proportion of Ireland's children are living in households with incomes below the poverty line has obvious implications for the education system and the success of these children within it. Targeted policies, such as through increases in child benefits to low income families, are among the primary policy responses open to society in addressing this issue.

The Elderly

The CSO have indicated that 11.2 per cent of the Irish population are aged over 65 years – some 452,960 people (CSO, 2006, p. 52). Results from Census 2002 also indicated that almost three in ten of this group live alone. When poverty is analysed across the age groups dramatic differences between the young, middle aged and old are visible. The 2004 figures show that 17.6 per cent of all those aged 15-64 live in relative income poverty, while 27.1 per cent of those aged 65 and over are in this situation. Over time the risk of being in poverty has increased sharply for the elderly. In 1994 this stood at 5.9 per cent, by 1998 it had risen to 32.9 per cent and in 2001 it peaked at 44.1 per cent. The figures for 2004 suggests that this has decreased slightly to a position where over one in four of Ireland's elderly are at risk of poverty.[7]

The Ill and Disabled

As Table 7.2 shows, the ill and disabled are the group with the highest risk of poverty at 47.3 per cent. Over time the situation of this group has visibly deteriorated with previous poverty studies by the ESRI showing that this group's risk of poverty has increased rapidly, climbing from 29.5 per cent in 1994 (Whelan et al., 2003, p. 24). This increase in the risk of poverty implies that in 1994 approximately three out of every ten persons who are ill or disabled were at risk of poverty and that by 2004 this had increased to almost five out of every ten. Consequently, although the ill and disabled only account for a small proportion of those in poverty (see Table 7.3), among themselves their experience of poverty is notably high. Since 2004 there have been some developments in addressing the needs of this group. Further policy responses which address issues of job creation, retraining and welfare supports for this group are likely. There also remains a case for addressing poverty among the disabled by introducing a non-means tested cost of disability allowance. Research on the disabled regularly highlights the additional costs faced by those living with a disability. These include higher overall medical costs, the cost of home adaptations and disability aids, transport costs and caring/assistance costs (Berthoud et al., 1993; Jones and O'Donnell, 1995; Zaidi and Burchardt, 2003). A proposal to introduce such a scheme has been researched and costed by the National Disability Authority. They have proposed an extra weekly payment of between €10 and €40 to somebody living with a disability (calculated on the basis of the severity of their disability).

Women

Consistently, the results of income surveys indicate that among all adults, women in Ireland experience a greater risk of poverty than men. The CSO poverty data for 2004 shows that across all age groups, females are at a higher risk of poverty than males (2005, p. 11). Among those over 65 years it is likely that the greater dependency of elderly women on social welfare payments and pensions, whose growth has lagged behind average income growth, is a central part of the reason behind this trend. As noted earlier in Table 7.2, the 2004 data record that 32 per cent of those working full time in the home were at risk of poverty. Since

1994 this figure has climbed from 20.9 per cent (see Whelan et al., 2003, p. 24). The 2004 EU-SILC results also indicate that 35.7 per cent of all single-adult households and 48.3 per cent of single-parent households are at risk of poverty (CSO, 2005, p. 11). All these classifications are house-holds primarily headed by women and can help to explain the growth and scale of female poverty risk.

Table 7.3: Incidence of Persons below 60% of Median Income by Principal Economic Status, 2003 and 2004

Principal Economic Status	2003	2004
At work	16.0	14.8
Unemployed	7.6	6.4
Student and school attendees	8.6	9.8
On home duties	22.5	23.1
Retired	9.0	9.1
Ill/Disabled	9.1	8.8
Children	25.4	25.3
Others	1.9	2.7
Total	**100.0**	**100.0**

Source: Menton (2006, p. 108).

A further insight into the nature of poverty in Ireland is to examine the composition of those below the poverty line – the incidence of poverty. Table 7.3 reports data from Menton's analysis of Irish poverty data and classifies all those at risk of poverty by their principal economic status (2006, p. 108). In 2004 the largest group are children (25.3 per cent) fol-lowed by those working in the home (23.1 per cent). Some 30 per cent of the poor are associated with the labour market (at work, unemployed or ill/disabled) while 70 per cent of Ireland's poor are outside the labour market.[8]

Where Are the Poor?

The 2004 EU-SILC results show that poverty is more likely to occur in rural areas than in urban areas. As Table 7.4 shows, the risk of poverty in rural Ireland was 7.5 per cent higher than in urban Ireland with at risk rates of 24.1 per cent and 16.6 per cent respectively. Poverty levels were also greater in the BMW (Border, Midland and Western) region than in the Southern and Eastern region with at risk rates of 26 per cent and 17.2 per cent respectively.

Table 7.4: Risk of Poverty among All Persons Aged 16 Years + by Location and Tenure Status, 2004

	Male	Female	Overall
Region			
Border, Midland and Western	24.4	27.8	26.0
Southern and Eastern	15.8	18.5	17.2
Urban/Rural Location			
Urban areas	15.0	18.1	16.6
Rural areas	22.8	25.5	24.1
Tenure Status			
Owner	14.9	17.1	16.0
Rented or rent free	33.2	36.3	34.8

Source: CSO (2005, p. 11).

Using Living in Ireland survey data from 2000 Watson et al. (2005) also examined the spatial distribution of poverty across Ireland's 26 counties. While the differences were small the study did point out that the highest levels of poverty were to be found in Donegal, Leitrim and Mayo with the lowest in counties around Dublin. Overall the study suggested that the structural issues driving poverty were unemployment, non-participation in the labour market due to illness/disability or old age, lone parenthood, low levels of education and social class background. It also highlighted the association between different housing tenures and poverty, an association also reflected in the 2004 EU-SILC data in Table 7.4.

Poverty: A European Perspective

Since the arrival of the EU-SILC it has become possible to compile a commonly defined comparable set of income figures for all 25 EU states.[9] These figures are used in Table 7.5. In each country the nominal value of the poverty line will vary in accordance with the level of median income in that country, a feature reflective of numerous factors such as the income distribution, wage levels, price levels, taxation and redistribution policies. As such, each country's poverty line is defined relative to where it is as a society and thereby reflects the earlier assumption that the possession of 60 per cent of that country's median income will be sufficient to allow an individual to achieve a standard of living regarded as acceptable by that society.

Table 7.5: Comparable EU-25 Poverty Indicators for 2004[#]

Country	Poverty Risk (%)	Country	Poverty Risk (%)
Ireland	**21**	Lithuania*	15
Portugal	21	Malta**	15
Slovakia	21	France	14
Greece	20	Austria	13
Spain	20	Hungary*	12
Italy	19	Netherlands*	12
Estonia*	18	Denmark	11
UK*	18	Luxembourg	11
Poland*	17	Finland	11
Germany	16	Sweden	11
Latvia*	16	Slovenia*	10
Belgium	15	Czech Republic*	8
Cyprus*	15	**EU-25 Average**	**16**

Source: Eurostat on-line database

Notes: [#] income data equivalised using the OECD modified scale; * indicates data from 2003; ** indicates data from 2000.

The average risk of poverty in the EU-25 is 16 per cent. Irish people experience the highest risk of poverty when compared to all the other EU member states; a position Ireland shares with Portugal and Slovakia. The risk of poverty which Irish people face is 3 per cent higher than that in the UK, 5 per cent higher than Germany, and 10 per cent higher than in

Luxembourg, Denmark, Finland and Sweden. The lowest poverty risk levels are in the Czech Republic (8 per cent).

Future Directions

Improvements in the availability of income data look set to drive developments in the area of poverty measurement and policy over the next decade. In particular, the CSO collected EU-SILC data offers the potential to monitor poverty trends in a timely way on an annual basis. Within that survey the collection of data needed to measure the EU Laeken indicator of persistent poverty is of major significance. Persistent poverty is defined as the percentage of persons below the 60 per cent of median income poverty line in the current year and for at least two of the preceding three years. Persistent poverty, therefore, identifies those who have experienced sustained levels of poverty, an experience which is assumed to seriously harm their quality of life and standard of living.

Given the definition, data spanning the same households over four years is required to measure persistent poverty. To achieve this, the CSO have established a longitudinal element within the EU-SILC sample where 30 per cent of households are revisited each year, thereby tracking their income levels over time. As the 2003 EU-SILC commenced in the middle of that year, the first full year of data is available for 2004 (CSO, 2005, pp. 20-21). Therefore, while some indications of persistent poverty levels will be available in late 2007 (using data from mid 2003-2006), the first complete set of persistent poverty results spanning four years will become available in late 2008 (using full year data from 2004-2007).[10]

The significance of this poverty indicator cannot be overstated. As a measure, persistent poverty rates can be seen as analogous to long-term unemployment rates. Both measures separate out those experiencing short-term poverty/unemployment from those trapped in such situations. As such it is crucial that when published, the CSO provide persistent poverty figures not just at a national level but also by principal economic status, age group, area and for specified vulnerable groups (e.g. the disabled, single parents). The persistent poverty figures will also imply the need for, and possibility of, a new set of poverty targets. Some discussion and preparation among the social policy community is needed to establish these targets, but it is likely that they should include policy commitments to achieve zero per cent persistent child poverty and zero per cent persistent poverty among those of working age.

Among those groups identified as being most at risk of poverty, further information is needed to complement these relative income measures. One innovative approach is to identify the amount of expenditure necessary for such groups to participate in society. Since Rowntree's 1901 study of poverty in the UK city of York, a budget standards literature has evolved with this aim in mind. In Ireland, the Vincentian Partnership for Social Justice (2004) applied this approach to compile "a low-cost but acceptable" budget for three households: a lone parent with two children, an unemployed couple with two children and an elderly couple reliant on income from state pensions. Although an expenditure-based approach, this method offers a further way of estimating a baseline income figure for certain disadvantaged groups.

The NAPS definition of poverty highlights resources as well as income. In an attempt to simultaneously capture both of these a combined income and deprivation measure titled "consistent poverty" was developed using 1987 data for the 1997 National Anti Poverty Strategy (Nolan and Whelan, 1996). Through the presence of various problems (among others, the use of a static set of items over a 16-year period, variations in measurement approaches and a change of question and survey format) the measure faded from use. However, information on the enforced lack of basic necessities due to a shortage of income (deprivation) continues to offer potential to inform assessments of poverty. As such there remains potential for the development of an appropriately defined updateable set of deprivation indicators for Ireland.[11]

Conclusion

The phenomenon of poverty remains a major issue for Irish society, a point which stands irrespective of whether we examine poverty levels over time, in a comparative European context or through using nominal income values of the poverty line. Looking to the future, there are challenges for policy makers to address this issue. Similarly, there are challenges to further inform our understanding of poverty and in particular to use new data sources to form targeted policies addressing low incomes among certain groups. A period of change and challenge lies ahead.

References

Berthoud, R., Lakey, J. and S. McKay (1993), *The Economic Problems of Disabled People*, London: Policy Studies Institute.

Callan, T. and Nolan, B. (1998), "Poverty and Policy", in Healy, S. and Reynolds, B. (eds.) *Social Policy in Ireland: Principles, Practice and Problems*, Dublin: Oak Tree Press.

Central Statistics Office (2003), *Census 2002: Volume 2 Ages and Marital Status*, Dublin: The Stationery Office.

Central Statistics Office (2005), *EU Survey on Income and Living Conditions*, Dublin: The Stationery Office.

Central Statistics Office (2006), *Measuring Ireland's Progress 2005*, Dublin: The Stationery Office.

Central Statistics Office (2006), *Quarterly National Household Survey (February)*, Dublin: The Stationery Office.

Collins, M.L. (2006). *Exploring the Experience and Nature of Deprivation in a Disadvantaged Urban Community: A socially perceived necessities approach*. Paper presented to the Combat Poverty Agency Research Seminar Series, Dublin, June 28.

CORI Justice (2006), *Developing a Fairer Ireland – Socio-economic review 2006*, Dublin: CORI.

Gordon, D., Adelman, L., Ashworth, K., Bradshaw, J., Levitas, R., Middleton, S., Pantazis, C., Patsios, D., Payne, S., Townsend, P. and Williams, J. (2000), *Poverty and Social Exclusion in Britain*, York: Joseph Rowntree Foundation.

Hills, J. (2004), *Inequality and the State*, Oxford: Oxford University Press.

Jones, A. and O'Donnell, O. (1995), "Equivalence Scales and the Costs of Disability", *Journal of Public Economics*, Vol. 56, pp. 273-289.

Menton, C. (2006), *An Investigation of Key Difficulties Associated with the Measurement of Poverty in an Irish Context*. Unpublished M.Econ.Sc. Thesis, Dublin: Institute of Public Administration.

National Anti-Poverty Strategy (1997), *Sharing in Progress*, Dublin: The Stationery Office.

Nolan B. and Whelan, C.T. (1996), *Resources, Deprivation and Poverty*, Oxford: Clarendon Press.

Nolan, B. and Farrell, B. (1990), *Child Poverty in Ireland: A report prepared for the Combat Poverty Agency*, Dublin: Combat Poverty Agency.

Rowntree, B.S. (1901), *Poverty: A study of town life,* London: Macmillan.

United Nations Development Program (2005), *Human Development Report – 2005,* New York: United Nations Publications.

Vincentian Partnership for Social Justice (2004), *Low Cost but Acceptable Budgets for Three Households*, Dublin: Vincentian Partership.

Watson, D., Whelan, C., Williams, J. and Blackwell, S. (2005), *Mapping Poverty: National, Regional and County Patterns,* Dublin: IPA and Combat Poverty Agency.

Whelan, C.T., Layte, R., Maitre, B., Gannon, B., Nolan, B., Watson, D. and Williams, J. (2003) *Monitoring Poverty Trends in Ireland: Results from the 2001 Living in Ireland Survey*, Dublin: ESRI.

Zaidi, A. and Burchardt, T. (2003). "Comparing Incomes When Needs Differ, Equivalisation for the Extra Costs of Disability", *CASE Paper No. 64*, London: Centre for the Analysis of Social Exclusion LSE.

Notes

---

[1] Although income based measures remain the primary approach to measuring poverty, a growing literature has attempted to develop alternative methods. For a review, see Hills, 2004, pp. 39-43.

[2] For more information on the Living in Ireland Survey see Whelan et al. (2003, pp. 5-7; pp. 75-87) and for the EU-SILC see CSO (2005, pp. 16-23).

[3] The CSO record the population of Ireland in 2004 to have been 4,043,800 (2006, p. 52). See CORI Justice (2006, p. 24) for similar calculations for the years between 1994 and 2003.

[4] Figures calculated using the risk of poverty figures in Table 7.2 and results from the Quarterly National Household Survey (CSO, February 2006, p. 7).

[5] A refundable tax credit is one where, if a taxpayer has insufficient income to use up all of their tax credits, the unused portion of the tax credit is refunded to the taxpayer by means of a cash transfer.

[6] This figure is calculated from a combination of data from the CSO (2006, p. 52) and results from Census 2002 (2003, volume 2, p. 27).

[7] Data from Whelan et al. (2003, p. 28) and CSO (2005, p. 10).

[8] The analysis assumes that those who are ill/disabled are likely to want to participate in the labour market.

[9] The EU definition of income differs from that used in the Irish calculations presented earlier. The EU analysis also uses a difference equivalence scale. Both combine to provide a poverty risk of 21 per cent for Ireland in 2004. For more details see CSO (2005, pp. 17-18).

[10] The ESRI did examine this issue using data from the Living in Ireland Surveys for 1997, 1998, 2000 and 2001. They found that in 2001 15.6 per cent of persons in Ireland were persistently poor. They also found that the rate of persistent poverty has increased across the period from 10.1 per cent in 1997 to 15.6 per cent in 2001 (Whelan et al., 2003, p. 46).

[11] Approaches include that of Gordon et al. (2000) for Britain and Collins (2006) for Ireland.

Chapter 8

THE CHANGING PATTERNS OF INCOME DISTRIBUTION AND INEQUALITY IN IRELAND, 1973–2004

Micheál L. Collins *and* **Catherine Kavanagh**

An imbalance between the rich and poor is the oldest and most fatal ailment of all republics. — Plutarch, circa 45-125AD

Ireland has become increasingly wealthy over the past 15 years. However, it is not clear that everyone is sharing in the benefits of a wealthier society. There are concerns that the impressive economic boom in Ireland has raised the living standards of only some and has widened income gaps. The distribution of income, inequality and poverty are central issues for policy-makers, not least because of the ability of policy-makers to influence them.

One thing is clear. No assessment of the well-being of a society can have much credibility unless it takes account of the distribution of income as well as aggregate GDP levels and other such indicators. The distribution of income in the economy, whether among persons or households, affects consumption, saving, growth, inflation and taxation. Additionally, the degree of income inequality is often regarded as an important aspect of the "fairness" of the society we live in (however defined). Income inequality refers to the extent of disparity between high and low incomes. The higher this measure, the greater the level of inequality. It is often argued that a high level of income inequality may also be detrimental to the level of social connectedness across society.

In a free market, the distribution of income may be highly unequal. Moreover, market imperfections will tend to make inequality greater. The initial distribution of income in society is determined by the market value placed on the services rendered by different individuals and households in the production of national output, and on the distribution of skills, talents and wealth within the community. Because this initial distribution of income may not be deemed "fair" by society, the government, by intervening – via the tax and benefit system, for example – can change the pattern of distribution to produce a more "equitable" distribution. Indeed, many taxation and benefit spending programmes are often explicitly directed at addressing issues of inequality and redistribution. Society is also therefore concerned with the extent to which the distribution of income is changed by government policies.

Whether the distribution of income in society is desirable or not is a normative question. The political right argues that a certain amount of inequality is the inevitable price paid for an efficient and growing economy. Inequality has an important economic function related to the operation of factor price differences. Factor prices are the price signals that encourage resources to move to sectors of the economy where demand is growing, and away from sectors where demand is declining. The political right argues that government intervention with this process may discourage people from acquiring greater human capital and distort the mobility of workers. The undermining of incentives may in turn reduce growth and efficiency. The political left, however, sees fewer dangers in reducing incentives and stresses the moral and social importance of redistribution from rich to poor. They argue that growth and employment are best encouraged by direct state support for investment.

Economists cannot settle the normative debate over how much the government should redistribute incomes from the rich to the poor. They can, however, identify the extent of inequality and analyse how it has changed over time. This is precisely the purpose of this chapter. We investigate how the distribution of household income in Ireland has changed over a period of three decades from 1973-2004. Confining the analysis to the distribution of direct and disposable income allows us to comment on the redistributive efforts of the tax and social welfare systems. We also estimate total household inequality using two different indices: the Gini coefficient and the Theil index.

The period assessed is one of contrasts for Ireland, running from the first oil crisis of 1973, through the prolonged recession of the early and mid 1980s, on to the golden age of economic growth from 1995-2001, before reaching the relatively slower, yet strong, growth years of 2003 and 2004. The period is also characterised by a series of economic transitions: from unemployment to full-employment, from emigration to immigration, and from high, and crippling, income taxes to one of the lowest income tax levels in the OECD (OECD, 2006a). While the story of that transformation has been well documented elsewhere,[1] the experience of such profound change suggests many interesting questions. One of these is the focus of this chapter. Against such a changing macroeconomic environment, how has the distribution of income fared?

This chapter is structured as follows. In the next section, we examine the changing distribution of household income by decile groups over the period. Although this analysis is partial, it allows us to comment on the extent to which certain categories of income recipients have fared over the past 30 years. The third section expands on the analysis by presenting total measures of inequality that relate to the whole distribution of household income. It also compares the Irish income distribution to that of other European countries. The final section concludes with a summary of the main points.

Income Distribution

The distribution of income can be examined at a number of levels. These include:

- The size distribution of income (looking at how evenly incomes are distributed)

- The functional distribution of income (analysing income according to the source of that income) and

- The distribution of income by recipient (examining income by classifications of people, e.g. women, men, age group, etc.).

Each seeks to highlight a different aspect of inequality. In this chapter we focus on the first category and examine the extent of inequality among Irish households.[2]

The Data

The data used in this chapter derives from two national household surveys, namely, the Household Budget Survey (HBS) and the EU Survey on Income and Living Conditions (EU-SILC). The HBS is conducted every five years (previously every seven years) by the Central Statistics Office (CSO) and is a random sample of over 7,000 urban and rural households throughout the country. The purpose of the survey is primarily to determine in detail the current pattern of household expenditure in order to update the weighting basis of the Consumer Price Index, but other information, including household income, is also collected. The first HBS was carried out in 1973, with subsequent surveys in 1980, 1987, 1994/95 and 1999/2000.[3] We employ all five HBSs.

Since mid-2003 the CSO has been a participant in EU-SILC, an EU-wide survey established under European legislation (Council Regulation no. 1177/2003) to collect information on the income and living conditions of different types of households. The survey is carried out throughout the year with approximately 130 households surveyed each week, implying an annual sample of between 5,000 and 6,000 households. To date this data has been collected in 2003 and 2004. As the survey commenced in June 2003 the sample for that year is smaller, comprising 3,090 households. The 2004 sample size was 5,477 households.[4] EU-SILC data from both these years has been used in this chapter. Taken together, the HBSs and the EU-SILC provide household income data for seven years between 1973 and 2004. We stress that, while it is impossible to summarise the trends over three decades by picking seven isolated years, the analysis does give an indication of the changes in the distribution of income over the period.

The income unit used in both surveys is the household. It is defined as "a single person or group of people who regularly reside together in the same accommodation and who share the same catering arrangements" (CSO, 2002, p. 173). Both surveys distinguish three different household income concepts. *Direct household income* is defined by the CSO as "all money receipts of a recurring nature which accrue to the households at annual or more frequent intervals, together with the value of any free goods regularly received by the household, and the retail value of own farm or garden produce produced by the household" (CSO, 2002, p. 176). Direct income is composed of earned income, employee's wages and salaries, self-employed farming and non-farming income, property income, investment income, retirement pensions, own garden or farm produce and "other" direct income, which includes income-in-kind, trade union sick or strike pay and income from securities, trusts and covenants. *Gross income* is defined as direct income plus state transfer payments (that is, unemployment benefits, children's allowances, old age pensions, etc.). *Disposable income* is defined as gross income less direct taxes (that is, income tax and employee share of social insurance contributions).

We confine our analysis to direct and disposable income. This is because direct income is analogous to the initial income allocation, and is determined by the returns in the market to the factors of production of national output. Disposable income corresponds to how much each household has to spend each week and, as such, is probably the most important income concept. It includes the redistributive efforts of the government. By comparing the distribution of direct income to that of disposable income we can comment on the effectiveness of the tax and benefit system.

Two further issues warrant mention. First, it should be emphasised that we are primarily examining cross-sectional surveys and, with the exception of a small number of households in the EU-SILC survey, the households in each survey differ.[5] Hence caution should be exercised in interpreting our results. Second, all household incomes in the analysis are *unequivalised*. This means that differences in household size and composition have not been accounted for. While changes in the family size and composition are unlikely to be significant in the short run, they are likely to change in the longer run. In order to provide a common basis for comparison between households of varying composition and income level, household income is often adjusted by weighting household incomes using an appropriate equivalence scale. Equivalence scales are attempts to control for relative consumption needs of households with differing composition, and represent the proportionate change in income necessary to maintain a constant standard of living as household composition changes. The choice of an appropriate equivalence scale is a matter of some debate.[6] Although the use of equivalised income would perhaps produce more reliable results, we nevertheless feel that an examination of the seven surveys using unequivalised income allows us to draw some important conclusions regarding the distribution of income in Ireland.[7]

A further household income data source which is worthy of note, though not used in this analysis, is the ESRI's Living in Ireland Survey (LIIS). That survey occurred annually between 1994 and 2001 and was part of the European Community Household Panel Survey. As a panel survey, the same households were surveyed in successive years to assist in monitoring households over time. One shortcoming of such surveys is that they are prone to attrition as a certain number of respondents drop out. For example, Corrigan et al. (2002) point out that only 67 per cent of the original 4,000 households surveyed in 1994 participated in the 1998 survey. Furthermore, O'Donoghue (2006) notes that attrition rates in the LIIS were highest in those households with income in the bottom decile (10 per cent).

Problems with Data Collected in Household Surveys

There are a number of problems with the reliability of the income data collected in household surveys. These include:

- As noted by Atkinson (1974, p. 44), the adoption of a household basis assumes that income sharing takes place within the household, and to the extent that it does not, inequality will be underestimated;

- Problems of under-reporting (income is generally understated in surveys of this type) and sampling error are present;[8] and

- Certain employer benefits and rent from home owner-occupation (imputed rent) are excluded, which understates the overall total income.

These problems do not mean that one should not use household data for distribution purposes; rather, such data should be used with care.

The Distribution of Income by Decile, 1973-2004

Tables 8.1 and 8.2 illustrate the changing distribution of income by decile across all seven surveys. Deciles are established by ranking households from the lowest to the highest income and then splitting them into ten equal-sized groups, starting with a group containing the 10 per cent of households with the lowest incomes.

Table 8.1 shows that the bottom two deciles received less that 1.4 per cent of the total earned income during the entire period, while if we take the bottom three deciles, we find their share of income has experienced a notable decline over the period, from 5 per cent to 1.7 per cent. Taken together, the bottom five deciles received 18.7 per cent of total income in 1973, and by 2004, this had declined significantly to 10.6 per cent. At the other end of the distribution, the top two deciles have steadily increased their share of direct income, from 46.9 per cent in 1973 to almost 55 per cent in 2004. By itself, the top decile received 29 per cent of total income in 1973 and increased its share to over 35 per cent by 2004. This portrayal of the distribution of direct income indicates an exceptionally high degree of concentration of incomes among the top tenth or top fifth of households. More importantly, there has been a marked increase in the level of direct income inequality over the past 30 years.

Table 8.1: The Distribution of Direct Income, 1973-2004 (%)

Decile	1973	1980	1987	1994/95	1999/00	2003	2004
Bottom	1.20	0.50	0.38	0.29	0.26	0.22	0.19
2nd			1.00	0.92	0.81	0.53	0.48
3rd	3.80	2.80	1.39	1.27	2.07	1.11	1.05
4th	6.10	5.70	3.26	3.10	4.22	3.33	2.64
5th	7.60	7.70	6.05	5.92	6.60	6.23	5.70
6th	9.30	9.50	8.73	8.80	9.07	9.30	8.65
7th	11.30	11.50	11.55	11.76	11.52	11.96	11.49
8th	13.80	14.30	15.09	15.43	14.61	15.46	14.96
9th	17.70	18.30	20.08	19.90	19.01	19.59	19.54
Top	29.20	29.70	32.46	32.61	31.84	32.28	35.31
Totals	**100.00**	**100.00**	**100.00**	**100.00**	**100.00**	**100.00**	**100.00**

Source: Rottman and Reidy (1988, p. 135), Household Budget Survey, various issues; EU-SILC (CSO, 2005).

Note: Values for the bottom two deciles in 1973 and 1980 are combined.

State transfer payments and direct taxes necessarily reduced the level of inequality in direct income in each year, but the net effect of state redistribution measures is limited. In Table 8.2, the distribution of disposable income (which reflects the relative spending power of households), shows that the bottom decile received 1.7 per cent of income in 1973, and although this share rose slightly to almost 2.3 per cent by 1987, it declined again to 2.1 per cent in 2004. In 1973, the bottom two deciles received 5 per cent of income and by 2004 this had marginally increased to 5.1 per cent. At the other end of the income distribution, the share of the top 20 per cent climbed slightly from 42.6 per cent in 1973 to 43.6 per cent in 2004, an increase primarily driven by the growing share held by the top decile.[9] In 2004, the top 10 per cent of households received their biggest ever share of the total disposable income at 27.1 per cent, exceeding the 22.5 per cent share received by the bottom 50 per cent and representing a share that is almost 13 times greater than that received by those in the lowest decile.

Table 8.2: The Distribution of Disposable Income, 1973-2004 (%)

Decile	1973	1980	1987	1994/95	1999/00	2003	2004
Bottom	1.70	1.70	2.28	2.23	1.93	1.85	2.10
2nd	3.30	3.50	3.74	3.49	3.16	2.92	3.04
3rd	5.00	5.10	5.11	4.75	4.52	4.38	4.27
4th	6.50	6.60	6.41	6.16	6.02	5.86	5.69
5th	7.80	7.90	7.71	7.63	7.67	7.69	7.43
6th	9.20	9.30	9.24	9.37	9.35	9.57	9.18
7th	10.90	11.00	11.16	11.41	11.20	11.50	11.11
8th	13.00	13.00	13.39	13.64	13.48	13.74	13.56
9th	16.20	16.20	16.48	16.67	16.78	16.84	16.47
Top	26.40	25.70	24.48	24.67	25.90	25.66	27.15
Totals	**100.00**	**100.00**	**100.00**	**100.00**	**100.00**	**100.00**	**100.00**

Source: Household Budget Survey, various issues; EU-SILC (CSO, 2005).

Table 8.3 provides a further insight into these income trends by assessing how decile shares have changed across four periods. These are the overall period from 1973-2004, during the high economic growth years between 1994 and 2004, during the "Celtic Tiger" years from 1994 to 2000 and over the first few years of this century.

Table 8.3: Changes in the % Share of Disposable Income for Various Periods

Decile	1973-2004	1994-2004	1994-2000	2000-2004
Bottom	+0.40	-0.13	-0.30	+0.17
2nd	-0.26	-0.45	-0.32	-0.12
3rd	-0.73	-0.48	-0.23	-0.25
4th	-0.81	-0.47	-0.15	-0.32
5th	-0.37	-0.20	+0.04	-0.24
6th	-0.02	-0.19	-0.01	-0.17
7th	+0.21	-0.30	-0.21	-0.09
8th	+0.56	-0.07	-0.16	+0.09
9th	+0.27	-0.20	+0.11	-0.31
Top	+0.75	+2.48	+1.24	+1.25
Totals	**0.00**	**0.00**	**0.00**	**0.00**

Two conclusions emerge from the analysis. First, it is clear that even after government redistribution efforts, the distribution of disposable income remained highly concentrated at the top of the income distribution. Second, inequality in direct income is more pronounced than inequality in disposable income, suggesting that redistributive efforts have succeeded in stemming the growth in income inequality to some extent. However, in comparing the degree of inequality across income distributions, it is generally more informative to adopt summary measures of inequality, which we do below.

Inequality

Several different methods exist for measuring the extent of inequality. One widely used method is the Lorenz curve, a device that plots cumulative proportions of the population from the poorest to the richest against the proportions of total income that they hold. The Lorenz curve proves a useful tool, since it gives a pictorial representation of the degree of income inequality. In the case of perfect equality, the Lorenz curve is a 45-

degree line, but otherwise, it will be bowed out below the 45-degree line. The degree to which the Lorenz curve lies below the 45-degree line gives an impression of the severity of the inequality in income distribution. If one distribution has a Lorenz curve everywhere above that of a second and the same total income, then there is good reason to think of inequality as being lower in the first than in the second, because this will occur if and only if the former distribution could be obtained from the latter by a series of income transfers from richer to poorer individuals. Figure 8.1 illustrates the Lorenz curve.

Figure 8.1: The Lorenz Curve

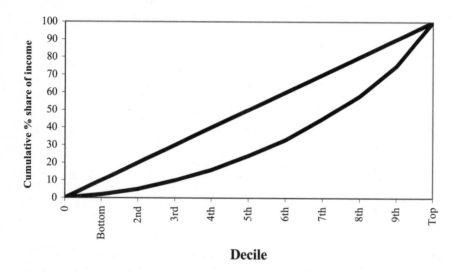

Although the Lorenz curve is useful for showing the change in income distribution over time, the problem with simply comparing Lorenz curves by eye is that it is imprecise. This problem is overcome by using the Gini coefficient, manifested by the Lorenz curves. The Gini coefficient summarises inequality in terms of an index and is calculated as the lens-shaped area between the Lorenz curve and the diagonal, expressed as a proportion of the complete triangle below the diagonal. The higher the Gini coefficient, the greater the degree of inequality.

While all-inclusive measures such as the Gini coefficient are more informative measures of inequality, it is important to note that condensing changes in inequality into movements in a single statistic inevitably obscures much of what is going on. However, they do make quantitative comparison possible. Although they provide a clear way of comparing income distribution in the same country at different times, there are several drawbacks associated with such summary measures. First, a single measure cannot take into account all the features of inequality. Second, there is the question of what statistics to use in calculation – whether to employ pre- or post-tax income, to include benefits, and to use households or individuals as the unit of investigation. Third, it is important to recognise, as noted by Atkinson, that when examining indices, "there is no reason to believe that they correspond to any values that we should like to hold regarding equity" (Atkinson, 1974, p. 51) – they are statistical not moral measures.

The performance of any index is frequently gauged by the extent to which it satisfies a set of axioms which are general enough to be accepted by most economists. The first axiom is the principle of transfers, also known as the Pigou-Dalton condition. It states that "if a transfer of income occurs form a poorer person to a richer one, *ceteris paribus,* then the measure of inequality should increase" (McGregor and Borooah, 1991, p. 84). Sen (1973, p. 27) proposed this condition's name based on the work at the beginning of the century by both Pigou and Dalton. The second axiom demands that the index be symmetric. This implies that if the same incomes are redistributed between individuals, the index would be unchanged. The third axiom is the population principle, which maintains that in comparing two income distributions where the second replicated the first, then the inequality index will be unaltered. Finally, the homogeneity principle requires that the index be homogenous of degree zero in incomes, thereby satisfying the fourth axiom. This implies that, were the income levels expressed in different units, the measure would remain unchanged.

The Gini Coefficient

The Gini coefficient is one of the most widely used summary measures of inequality. It satisfies all of the above four axioms, and has the advantage of being relatively simple to understand and use. This measure rises with rising inequality and varies between zero (everyone has the same income) and one (one person has all the income).

Over time some criticisms have been directed at the Gini measure which have undermined its once principal position as the main inequality measure (Osberg, 1984, pp. 18-22). Osberg (1984) and Atkinson (1970) challenge its ability to reflect changes in income distributions. They both maintain that the Gini measure is more sensitive to income changes which occur in the middle ranges of income distributions. This implies that a transfer of €100 for one rich individual to another rich individual will have little effect on the Gini coefficient, whereas the same €100 if transferred to a lower decile household would have a larger effect on the Gini. This occurs as such changes broaden the differences between income shares, thereby decreasing the variance and changing the Gini.

A further critique of the Gini coefficient is that, via its calculation, it assumes equality exists within distributions, implying that within each decile income is distributed evenly. Such an assumption is basically untenable, and undermines the Gini's reliability. Despite these criticisms, the Gini coefficient stands as the central index of inequality.

Theil "Entropy" Index

Theil's "entropy" index (1967) derives from the notion of entropy in statistical information theory (Osberg, 1984, p. 22). The Theil index spans from zero, where perfect equality exists, to a maximum of *log n* (where *n* represents the number of income groups), implying complete inequality. There are two versions of the Theil index, an income-weighted version that is used in this chapter and a population-weighted version.[10]

Similar to the Gini index, the Theil index satisfies the established axioms by meeting the Pigou-Dalton condition, symmetry, the population principle and homogeneity. Theil notes that the index could be aggregated in a simple manner over groups, and numerous economists have found that the index "naturally" decomposes into inter- and intra-group components of inequality (Theil, 1967; Murphy, 1984; Collins, 1998).[11]

The Theil index has also been the source of some criticism. It has been suggested that the Theil proves more sensitive to movements in the middle part of the income distribution, thereby implying a bias in its assessment of changes in inequality (Osberg, 1984, p. 23; Mookherjee and

Shorrocks, 1982, p. 892). Further, it has been argued that the index relies on relative rather than absolute income changes, which once again undermine its reliability (Jenkins, 1991, p. 18). However, the Theil remains a popular inequality measure (Osberg, 1984, p. 32).

Hence, both of these measures provide a useful indicator of the extent of inequality. None of the problems associated with each index causes major difficulties in the analysis of Irish households incomes. We now turn to the estimation of these two measures.

Estimated Measures of Inequality

The results for the two measures of inequality are presented in Table 8.4. It should be noted that the measures presented here consistently underestimate the extent of inequality to some degree, because the within-decile income inequality is not taken into account.

In the case of direct income, both measures exhibit a similar pattern. Over the period for which full decile data is available (1987-2004), the Gini climbed from 0.52 to 0.55 while the Theil increased from 0.47 to 0.55. These changes represent a significant rise in direct income inequality.[12] Both indicators suggest that there was a reduction in direct income inequality in the late 1990s, perhaps paralleling the large increase in employment during that period. Since then, direct income inequality has increased past its 1987 level to reach new heights in 2004.

The result in Table 8.4 also highlights the growth in inequality of disposable income. Over three decades the Gini coefficient increased from 0.37 to 0.38 while the Theil index climbed from 0.24 to 0.26. Both measures record a decline in inequality from 1973-1987 but that since then inequality has risen. Given that disposable income incorporates post-tax and transfer income, it is likely that the reductions in taxation (income and capital) during that period, combined with a rapid growth in earnings, to increase the income shares of the top deciles. Table 8.2 shows that between 1987 and 2003 the disposable income shares of each of the top five income deciles increased while those in the bottom five deciles all saw their share decline.[13] Overall, the results in Table 8.4 confirm the less formal decile analysis: rising inequality in market incomes was counteracted by the redistributive effort, but disposable income remains highly concentrated.

Table 8.4: Measures of Inequality for Direct and Disposable Income,
1973-2004 (unequivalised data)

Year	Gini Coefficient	Theil Index
1973 Direct*	–	–
1980 Direct*	–	–
1987 Direct	0.518	0.472
1994/95 Direct	0.523	0.480
1999/2000 Direct	0.498	0.435
2003 Direct	0.523	0.473
2004 Direct	0.548	0.550
1973 Disposable	0.367	0.237
1980 Disposable	0.359	0.223
1987 Disposable	0.346	0.203
1994/95 Disposable	0.356	0.213
1999/2000 Disposable	0.373	0.238
2003 Disposable	0.377	0.239
2004 Disposable	0.384	0.260

Note: * Complete direct income decile data prevents calculations for 1973 and 1980.

As noted earlier, the data used in the above tables are not adjusted to take account of household size and composition (equivalised). As part of the 2005 release of EU-SILC data the CSO provided a value for the Gini coefficient that is calculated using equivalised income, where the adjustment has been made using the OECD modified equivalence scale. Their results reflect the trend outlined in Table 8.4 and record the equivalised disposable income Gini coefficient increasing from 0.308 in 2003 to 0.316 in 2004 (CSO, 2005, p. 5).

In order to further examine the extent of inequality over the period 1987-2004, and identify the impact of redistribution on inequality, we attempt to illustrate the effectiveness of the state transfer payments. A straightforward numerical approach is to compare the value of the Gini coefficient before and after the provision of welfare payments. The results of this analysis are presented in Table 8.5.

Table 8.5: The Impact of Social Transfers on Income Inequality

	1987	1994/95	1999/00	2003	2004
Pre-Transfers Gini	0.488	0.496	0.473	0.497	0.521
Disposable income Gini	0.346	0.356	0.373	0.377	0.384
Change in Gini	-0.142	-0.140	-0.100	-0.120	-0.137

While the average impact of transfers across the period is to decrease inequality by 12.8 percentage points, the annual amounts vary. Between 1987 and 2000 the effect of transfers decreased to a point where they were only responsible for a 10 per cent reduction in inequality levels in 1999/2000. The data for 2003 and 2004 suggests a reversal of this trend, perhaps reflective of the increases in state welfare payments in recent budgets.

A European Perspective

To complement the above analysis, it is interesting to assess the distribution of Irish income in the context of distributions of income elsewhere. Given that countries differ, and so too do their income levels and consumer prices, nominal comparisons of income are often inappropriate. However, comparisons of the relative distribution of income within countries can be informative. To date there has been limited opportunity to make such a comparison,[14] but the arrival of the EU-SILC has made it possible to compile a commonly defined comparable set of income figures across all 25 EU states.

   Table 8.6 presents results for two of the Laeken indicators concerned with income distribution. The income quintile ratio, known as S80/S20, is the ratio of total income received by the 20 per cent with the highest income to that received by the 20 per cent with the lowest income. As such, the indicator attempts to capture the scale of the gap between both ends of the income distribution. The second indicator is the Gini coefficient and is calculated using a common EU definition of income (which differs from the Irish data used earlier).

Table 8.6: EU Income Distribution Indicators in 2004[#] (equivalised using OECD modified scale)

Country	S80/S20	Gini	Country	S80/S20	Gini
Belgium	4.0	0.26	Luxembourg	3.7	0.26
Czech Rep.*	3.4	0.25	Hungary*	3.3	0.27
Denmark	3.4	0.24	Malta**	4.5	0.30
Germany	4.4	0.28	Netherlands*	4.0	0.27
Estonia*	5.9	0.34	Austria	3.8	0.26
Greece	6.0	0.33	Poland*	5.0	0.31
Spain	5.1	0.31	Portugal	7.2	0.38
France	4.2	0.28	Slovenia*	3.1	0.22
Ireland	**5.0**	**0.32**	Slovakia	5.8	0.33
Italy	5.6	0.33	Finland	3.5	0.25
Cyprus*	4.1	0.27	Sweden	3.3	0.23
Latvia*	6.1	0.36	UK*	5.3	0.34
Lithuania*	4.5	0.29	**EU-25 Average**	**4.8**	**0.30**

Source: Eurostat on-line database

Notes: [#] income data equivalised using the OECD modified scale; * indicates data from 2003; ** indicates data from 2000.

In the case of both indicators Ireland records an indicator score above the EU-25 average. The top 20 per cent of Irish income earners receive five times that received by the bottom 20 per cent, while the Gini coefficient comes in two percentage points higher than the EU average. On both measures there is higher income inequality in Estonia, Greece, Italy, Latvia, Portugal, Slovakia and the UK. The most unequal European income distribution is in Portugal where the top quintile get 7.2 times that of the bottom quintile, and the Gini coefficient is 0.38.

The most equal income distribution in Europe is recorded for Slovenia. Elsewhere, a cluster of Scandinavian states record very low levels of inequality with Sweden, Finland and Denmark reporting quintile ratios of between 3.3-3.5 and Gini coefficients of 0.25 or less.

The income distribution comparisons in Table 8.6 suggest that Ireland is placed in the top third most unequal European income distributions by both measures. This finding underscores Nolan and Smeeding's conclusion that "Ireland remains something of an outlier among rich European nations in its high degree of income inequality" (2004, p. 32).

Conclusion

This chapter has tracked the level of inequality over the past three decades by examining seven household surveys from 1973-2004. Throughout this period, Ireland has undergone a dramatic economic transformation and become one of the wealthiest countries in the EU. However, this turnaround has been accompanied by a rise in inequality. Our analysis of two inequality indexes yields the same conclusion: taking direct income as a measure of income, the gap between the rich and the poor has increased since 1973. Although redistribution through the combination of the tax and benefit systems has stemmed the growth in inequality, disposable income remains highly concentrated at the top of the income distribution.

The chapter has also examined Ireland's income distribution in a comparative context. The results show that within the EU, Ireland resides in the top third most unequal countries, according to both measures of inequality examined. Given that other successful EU states record lower inequality levels (e.g. France, Germany, Netherlands and Austria), these findings suggest that achieving a more equal income distribution is certainly feasible.

Thus, the findings also imply a choice facing Irish society: do we wish to pursue the objective of a more equal income distribution or are we happy to let inequality persist in the future? If the answer is the former, then an increasing proportion of the fruits of our current economic prosperity will have to be allocated towards achieving that goal.

References

Atkinson, A.B. (1970), On the Measurement of Inequality, *Journal of Economic Theory,* Vol. II, pp. 244-63.

Atkinson, A.B. (1974), "Poverty and Income Inequality in Britain", in Wedderburn, D. (ed.) *Poverty, Inequality and Class Structure,* London: Cambridge University Press.

Blundell, R. and Preston, I. (1995), "Income Expenditure and Living Standards of UK Households", *Fiscal Studies*, Vol. 6, No. 3, pp. 40-54.

Callan, T. and Nolan, B. (1999), "Income Inequality in Ireland in the 1980s and 1990s", in F. Barry (ed.), *Understanding Ireland's Economic Growth*, Basingstoke: Macmillan.

Callan, T., Walsh, J. and Coleman, K. (2006), *Budget 2006: Impact on Income Distribution and Relative Income Poverty*, Quarterly Economic Commentary, Spring 2006, Dublin: ESRI.

Central Statistics Office, *Household Budget Survey,* Various editions, Dublin: The Stationery Office.

Central Statistics Office (2002), *Household Budget Survey 1999-2000 Final Results*, Dublin: The Stationery Office.

Central Statistics Office (2005), *EU Survey on Income and Living Conditions*, Dublin: The Stationery Office.

Collins, M.L. (1998), *Decompositions of Irish Household Income Inequality, 1987-1994/95*, Unpublished M.A. Thesis, Department of Economics: University College Cork.

Collins, M.L. and Kavanagh, C. (1998), "For Richer, For Poorer: The Changing Distribution of Household Income in Ireland, 1973-94", in Healy, S. and Reynolds, B. (eds.) *Social Policy in Ireland: Principles, Practice and Problems,* Dublin: Oak Tree Press.

Corrigan, C., Fitzgerald, E., Bates, J. and Matthews, A. (2002), *Data Sources on Poverty*, Dublin: Institute of Public Administration.

Cowell, F.A. (1995), *Measuring Inequality: London School of Economics Handbooks in Economics Series*, second edition, London: Prentice Hall/ Harvester Wheatsheaf.

Cussen, M.L. (2004), *Inequality in Ireland: A comparison using income and expenditure distribution data, 1994/95 and 1999/2000*, Working paper, Department of Economics, University College Cork.

Cutler, D. and Katz, L. (1992), "Rising Inequality? Changes in the Distribution of Income and Consumption in the 1980s", *American Economic Review*, Vol. 82, pp. 546-51.

Honohan, P. and Walsh, B. (2002) "Catching Up with the Leaders: The Irish Hare" Brookings Papers on Economic Activity – 2002, 1, pp. 1-77, Brookings Institution Press.

Houghton, J. (2005), "Growth in Output and Living Standards", in O'Hagan, J. and Newman, C. (eds.) *The Economy of Ireland: National and Sectoral Policy Issues*, Dublin: Gill and Macmillan.

Jenkins, S. (1991), "The Measurement of Income Inequality" in Osberg, L. (ed.), *Economic Inequality and Poverty, International Perspectives*, New York: M.E. Sharpe Inc.

Leddin, A. J. and Walsh, B.M. (2003), *The Macroeconomy of the Eurozone: An Irish perspective*, Dublin: Gill and Macmillan.

Madden, D. (1996), "Sources of Income Inequality in Ireland" *Working Paper Series*, Centre for Economic Research, University College Dublin.

McGregor, P.P.L. and Borooah, V.K. (1991), "Poverty and the Distribution of Income in Northern Ireland", *The Economic and Social Review,* Vol. 22, No. 2, pp. 81-100.

Mookherjee, D. and Shorrocks, A. (1982), "A Decomposition Analysis of the Trend in UK Income Inequality", *The Economic Journal*, Vol. 92, pp. 886-902.

Murphy, D.C. (1984), "The Impact of State Taxes and Benefits on Irish Household Incomes", *Journal of the Statistical and Social Inquiry Society of Ireland*, Vol. XXV, Part I, pp. 55-120.

Nolan, B. (1978), "The Personal Distribution of Income in the Republic of Ireland", *Journal of the Statistical and Social Inquiry Society of Ireland*, Vol. XXIII, Part V, pp. 91-161.

Nolan, B. and Maitre, B. (2000), "Income Inequality", in Nolan, B., O'Connell, P.J. and Whelan, C.T. (eds.) *Bust to Boom? The Ireland Experience of Growth and Inequality*, Dublin: Institute of Public Administration.

Nolan, B. and Smeeding, T. (2004), *Ireland's Income Distribution in a Comparative Perspective*, Working Paper No. 395, Luxembourg Income Study.

Nolan, B., Maître, B, O'Neill, D. and Sweetman, O. (2000), *The Distribution of Income in Ireland*, Dublin: Combat Poverty Agency and Oak Tree Press.

O'Connell, P.J. (1982), "The Distribution and Redistribution of Income in the Republic of Ireland", *The Economic and Social Review,* Vol. 13, No. 4, pp. 251-278.

O'Donoghue, C. (2006), *"The Impact of Macro-Economic Growth on the Income Distribution in Ireland 1987-2003"*, Paper to the Statistical and Social Inquiry Society of Ireland, 25 May.

OECD (2003). *Economic Survey - Ireland*, Paris: OECD.

OECD (2006a). *Taxing Wages 2004-2005*, Paris: OECD.

OECD (2006b). *Economic Survey - Ireland*, Paris: OECD.

Osberg, L. (1984), *Economic Inequality in the United States,* New York: M.E. Sharpe Inc.

Poterba, J. (1989), "Lifetime Incidence and the Distribution Burden of Excise Taxes", *American Economic Review*, Vol. 79, pp. 325-30.

Rottman, D. and Reidy, M. (1988), *Redistribution through State Social Expenditure in the Republic of Ireland 1973-1980*, Report No. 85, Dublin: National Economic and Social Council.

Sen, A.K. (1973), *On Economic Inequality,* Oxford: Clarendon Press.

Slesnick, D. (1993), "Gaining Ground: Poverty in Post-war United States", *Journal of Political Economy*, Vol. 101, pp. 1-38.

Theil, H. (1967), *Economics and Information Theory*, Amsterdam: North Holland.

Notes

---

[1] See Haughton (2005); OECD (2003, 2006b); Leddin and Walsh (2003) and Honohan and Walsh (2002).

[2] The following analysis implicitly assumes income as a measure of household welfare. Despite the widespread use of income as a proxy, it has been argued that consumption expenditure may better reflect expected lifetime resources (Poterba, 1989; Cutler and Katz, 1992; and Slesnick, 1993). The choice of any measure of living standards will inevitably exclude perspectives which could be gained from the choice of other measures. See Blundell and Preston (1995) for a discussion of measures of household welfare and Cussen (2004) for an analysis of the distribution of expenditure using Irish household data.

[3] A further HBS was conducted in 2005 but its results had not been released in time for inclusion in this chapter.

[4] For more information on this survey see CSO, 2005, pp. 16-23.

[5] Of the 2004 EU-SILC sample 1,659 households, or 30%, had also been surveyed in 2003.

[6] For example, in Ireland there are two different equivalence scales used to interpret EU-SILC data. An Irish scale derived on the basis of the relative values of social welfare payments and the OECD modified equivalence scale which the EU have decided should be used for compiling pan-European comparisons of income distribution statistics (see CSO, 2005, p. 18).

[7] As we shown later in this chapter, the trends established by the unequivalised data are reflected by those established using equivalised income data.

[8] For a discussion of these problems and their impact on the income statistics, see Nolan (1978), O'Connell (1982) and Nolan et al. (2000).

[9] Nolan and Smeeding (2004) have used tax returns data to study the income of the top 1 per cent during the 1990s and show how their share grew from 4.84 per cent in 1990 to 7.86 per cent in 2000.

[10] Collins and Kavanagh (1998), Callan and Nolan (1999) and Nolan and Maitre (2000) all use the population-weighted Theil.

[11] The decomposability of an index is useful attribute, as it helps in our understanding of the pattern of inequality. In Ireland, advances in decomposing the Theil index have been made by Murphy (1984) and for the Gini coefficient by Madden (1996). See also Cowell (1995, p. 66) and Osberg (1984, p. 22) for a discussion of the decomposition advantages of Theil.

[12] With ten decile groups n =1 and the Theil ranges from 0 to a maximum of 1.

[13] See also Callan, Walsh and Coleman (2006) who analyse the impact of budgetary decisions during some of this period.

[14] There have been some notable attempts to compile such comparisons, in particular via the Luxembourg Income Study. For example, see Nolan and Smeeding (2004).

Chapter 9

THE EU'S SOCIAL INCLUSION INDICATORS
AND THEIR IMPLICATIONS FOR IRELAND

Brian Nolan

P olicy co-ordination at European Union (EU) level, which in the past was mostly applied to economic and employment policy, is increasingly being applied in the social field as well. Agreeing goals and monitoring progress towards achieving them is central to such co-ordination. Core common objectives in the social area were agreed at the European Council in Nice in 2001, namely, facilitating participation in employment and access by all to resources, rights, goods and services; preventing the risks of exclusion; helping the most vulnerable; and mobilising all relevant bodies. A further important staging-point was then reached in 2001 when the European Council held at Laeken in Belgium adopted a set of commonly agreed and defined indicators relating to social inclusion. These indicators are intended to allow the Member States and the European Commission to monitor national and EU progress towards the key EU objectives in the area of social inclusion, and to support mutual learning and exchange of good practices in terms of both processes and policies. This chapter discusses these indicators, their role and their implications for Ireland. We start with how the indicators were selected, and then turn to the indicators themselves.

Agreeing Common EU Social Inclusion Indicators

While under subsidiarity the design and implementation of social policies
– including promoting social inclusion – remains the responsibility of individual Member States, the European Union has in recent years had an
increasing role in co-ordination, with an increasing focus on the linkages
between economic and social policies and outcomes, The 1997 Amsterdam Treaty assigned the fight against social exclusion an important role,
embedded by the Social Policy Agenda adopted by the Nice European
Council. The headline target adopted at the March 2000 Lisbon European
Council was that Europe become by 2010 "the most competitive and dynamic knowledge-based economy in the world capable of sustainable economic growth with more and better jobs and greater social cohesion".
Strengthening the role of social policy as a productive factor, and the need
for a balanced relationship between it and the economic, employment and
environment pillars of the Lisbon strategy, have remained key themes (although challenged on occasion, notably in the 2004 Kok report[1]).

In seeking to make a decisive impact on the eradication of poverty
and social exclusion by 2010, the Lisbon European Council also agreed
to adopt what is known as the "open method of coordination". Key elements is this approach have been the agreement of common objectives
on poverty and social exclusion; the preparation of National Action
Plans on social inclusion (NAPs/inclusion) that Member States have to
submit to the Commission; the exchange of good practices across Member States through peer reviews; and the adoption of common indicators
to monitor progress towards the common objectives and encourage mutual learning. The preparation of a Joint Report on Social Inclusion
(more recently on Social Inclusion and Social Protection), drafted by the
Commission on the basis of the NAPs/inclusion and then finalised between the Commission and the Council, is a critical element (see European Commission, 2002, 2004b, 2006). The aim is to improve performance of all the Member States to bring them all to a high level.

In seeking to implement the open method of co-ordination, a monitoring framework was required. A set of social inclusion indicators was
developed in 2001, with the Social Protection Committee comprising
high level officials from the relevant ministries in each Member State,
and more specifically its Indicators Sub-Group set up in February 2001,

playing the central role, assisted by Eurostat, the Statistical Office of the European Communities. As a contribution to the complex exercise of reaching this agreement within such a short period of time, the Belgian Government commissioned a scientific study (subsequently published as Atkinson, Cantillon, Marlier and Nolan, 2002) that fed into the work of the Sub-Group. The fruits of the Social Protection Committee's labours, summarised in the Report subsequently endorsed by the Laeken European Council in December 2001, included an agreement on a set of indicators for social inclusion – generally referred to since then as "the Laeken indicators".

A methodological framework to guide the further development of common indicators was also set out. This stressed that the portfolio of indicators should command general support as a balanced representation of EU and national social concerns, and recommended that they focus on social outcomes rather than the means by which they are achieved. Individual indicators should also be robust and statistically validated, have a clear normative interpretation, be measurable in a comparable way across countries, and be timely, while the indicators as a set should be as transparent and accessible as possible to the citizens of the European Union.

The Laeken Indicators of Social Inclusion

Recognising that a large number of indicators are needed to properly assess the multidimensional nature of social exclusion, the Social Protection Committee recommended that they be presented in tiers:

- *Primary indicators* consisting of a restricted number of lead indicators which cover the broad fields that have been considered the most important elements in leading to poverty and social exclusion;

- *Secondary indicators* supporting these lead indicators and describing other dimensions of the problems.

Both these levels comprise commonly agreed and defined indicators, to be used in the NAPs/inclusion and the Joint Report on social inclusion. Member States can also include a *third level* of indicators in their NAPs/inclusion, which need not be harmonised at EU level, to highlight specific areas and help interpret the primary and secondary indicators.

The Social Protection Committee and its Indicators Sub-Group grappled with an intimidating variety of conceptual, methodological and data-related issues, and recommended a set consisting of 10 primary and 8 secondary common indicators, subsequently adopted at the Laeken European Council (SPC, 2001).

The Indicators Sub-Group has continued working on indicators for social inclusion since then with a view to refining and consolidating the original set, and has also worked on the development of indicators in the fields of pensions and healthcare and long-term care. In the first half of 2006 it undertook a comprehensive review and reorganisation of all these indicators, producing a new, integrated monitoring framework for a "streamlined" open method of co-ordination. This includes a set of indicators for each of the social "strands" – social inclusion, pensions, and health and long-term care – together with a set of "overarching" indicators (Indicators Sub-Group, 2006). The streamlined social inclusion indicators are now to comprise eleven primary indicators and three secondary indicators; in addition, a further set of eleven statistics has been introduced to provide "context" information to help in interpreting trends in the primary and secondary indicators.[2] These indicators are listed in Tables 9.1a, 9.1b and 9.1c respectively.

An in-depth discussion of the individual indicators and how they have evolved since Laeken is beyond the scope of this chapter, but some key features are worth highlighting. The primary indicators begin with the most widely-used indicator of poverty, namely the percentage of persons falling below a relative income threshold set at 60 per cent of median income.[3] The Indicators Sub-Group emphasised that this was to be seen as a measure of people who are "at risk of poverty", not a measure of poverty *per se*. This reflects the recognition that low income, on its own, may not always be a reliable indicator of poverty and social exclusion.[4] This means that low-income households are best considered as being at high risk of poverty rather than "poor". The focus is on thresholds related to the median income of the country in question (rather than of the EU as a whole, for example) and that move over time in line with that median (although the percentage falling below a low income threshold anchored at one point in time and updated over time only in line with prices is included as one of the "context" indicators). The percentage persistently falling below this threshold over a number of years, and a measure of the average "gap" or shortfall of those below the threshold, are other primary indicators. Various breakdowns of those falling below the 60 per cent of median threshold are then also included as secondary indicators.

Table 9.1a: EU Primary Social Inclusion Indicators (from mid-2006)

Indicator	Definition
1. At-risk-of-poverty rate + illustrative values of at-risk-of-poverty threshold	Percentage of persons living in households with an income below 60% of national median income (with breakdowns by age and gender)
	The value of the 60% median threshold in PPS, Euro and national currency for single person households and households with two adults and two children.
2. Persistent at-risk-of-poverty rate	Percentage of persons with an income below the at-risk-of-poverty threshold in the current year and in at least two of the preceding three years
3. Relative median poverty risk gap	Difference between the median income of persons below the at-risk-of poverty threshold and the threshold itself, expressed as a percentage of the at-risk-of-poverty threshold
4. Long-term unemploy-ment rate	Total long-term unemployed population (≥ 12 months; ILO definition) as a proportion of total active population aged 15 years or more
5. Population living in jobless households	Proportion of people living in jobless households (for age group 1-17 and 18-59)
6. Early school leavers not in education or training	Percentage of persons aged 18 to 24 who have only lower secondary education and have not received education or training in the previous four weeks
7. Employment gap of immigrants	Percentage point difference between the employment rate for non-immigrants and that for immigrants
8. Material deprivation	To be developed
9. Housing deprivation	To be developed
10. Health	To be developed
11. Child well-being	To be developed

Table 9.1b: EU Secondary Social Inclusion Indicators (from Mid-2006)

Indicator	Definition
1. At-risk-of-poverty rate	Percentage of persons living in households with an income below 60% of national median income, with full breakdown by age
1a. Poverty risk by household type	Percentage of persons living in households with an income below 60% of national median income, by household types (one adult no children, two adults no children etc.)
1b. Poverty risk by the work intensity of the household	Percentage of persons living in households with an income below 60% of national median income by work intensity (the number of months all working-age household members worked during the year as a proportion of the total they could have worked.)
1c. Poverty risk by most frequent activity status	Percentage of adults (aged 18 years or over) living in households with an income below 60% of national median income in: employment, unemployment, retirement and other inactivity for more than half the months in the year.
1d. Poverty risk by accommodation tenure status	Percentage of persons living in households with an income below 60% of national median income in owner-occupied or rent free housing and in rented housing
1e. Dispersion around the at-risk-of-poverty threshold	Percentage of persons with an income below 40%, 50% and 70% of the national median income
2. Persons with low educational attainment	Percentage of the adult population (aged 25 years and over) whose highest level of education or training is ISCED 0, 1 or 2 (breakdowns by age and gender)
3. Low reading literacy performance of pupils	Percentage of 15 year old pupils who are at level 1 or below on the PISA combined reading literacy scale

Table 9.1c: EU "Context" Social Inclusion Indicators (from mid-2006)

Indicator	Definition
1. Income quintile ratio (S80/S20)	Ratio of total income received by the 20% of the country's population with the highest income to that received by the 20% of the country's population with the lowest income
2. Gini coefficient	Summary measure of income inequality with values ranging from 0% (complete equality) to 100% (complete inequality)
3. Regional cohesion	Standard deviation of regional employment rates at NUTS level 2 divided by the weighted national average
4. Life expectancy at birth and at 65.	Number of years a person aged 0 and 65 may be expected to live by gender, and by socio-economic status where available
5. At-risk-of-poverty rate anchored at a moment in time	Percentage of persons with an equivalised disposable income below the at-risk-of-poverty threshold calculated in year 2004, up-rated by inflation over subsequent years
6. At-risk-of-poverty rate before social cash transfers (other than pensions)	Percentage in households falling below 60% of the median national income (after social cash transfers) on the basis of their income excluding all social cash transfers other than retirement and survivors pensions
7. Jobless households by household type	Proportion of persons living in jobless households by household type
8. In-work poverty risk	Percentage of individuals aged 16 years and above who are classified as employed according to the definition of most frequent activity status and are living in households with an income below 60% of national median income
9. Making work pay indicators	Indicators of unemployment trap, inactivity trap, low-wage trap
10. Net income of social assistance as % at-risk-of-poverty threshold	Income of people living in households that rely on "last resort" social assistance benefits (including related housing benefits) as a percentage of 60% median at-risk-of-poverty threshold for their household type

Unemployment and household joblessness are seen as key determinants of poverty so the proportion of "jobless" households – containing no-one at work – and the long-term unemployment rate are included as primary indicators. The employment rate for migrants (relative to non-migrants) has also been introduced recently as a primary indicator in order to capture a key aspect of their often-disadvantaged situation. Low educational attainment is also seen as a key influence so the share of 18-24-year olds with only lower secondary level education or less and not in education or training is a primary indicator, while the proportion of the population of working age with a lower secondary or less, together with the proportion of 15-year old pupils with low reading literacy performance, are included as secondary indicators.

Two health-related indicators were initially included among the primary set, namely life expectancy at birth and a survey-based measure of inequality in self-assessed health across the income distribution. However, neither is very satisfactory in the social inclusion context, so life expectancy has been transferred to the "context" set and the self-assessed health measure has been dropped, with an alternative primary indicator to capture health and health care under development. Similarly the need for a primary indicator to capture housing and homelessness has been recognised from the outset, but an appropriate indicator is still being developed. The primary set currently includes two other indicators that are under development, one relating to material deprivation and the other to child well-being.

It is also worth noting that two indicators that focused on the distribution of income, namely, the ratio of the share of total income going to the top versus the bottom quintile and the Gini co-efficient, were originally adopted as primary and secondary indicators respectively but have now been moved to the "context" set. A measure of regional dispersion in unemployment, also originally a primary indicator, is now in the new "context" set, and this is also the case for the at-risk-of-poverty rate anchored at a moment in time and the at-risk-of-poverty rate calculated before social cash transfers, both of which were originally secondary indicators. Other "context" indicators focus on work and incentives/adequacy, namely, the poverty risk for those in work, indicators of unemployment/inactivity and low-wage "traps", and the level of social assistance support as a percentage of the at-risk-of-poverty threshold.

The Role of EU Social Inclusion Indicators

The role which the commonly agreed indicators are intended to play in the EU's Social Inclusion Process has several dimensions. The indicators are intended to allow the Member States and the Commission to monitor progress towards the goal set by the Lisbon European Council of making a decisive impact on the eradication of poverty by 2010, to improve the understanding of poverty and social exclusion in the European context, and to identify and exchange good practice in terms of how best to address poverty and social exclusion. Increasing attention is also being paid to their potential role in setting concrete targets as part of anti-poverty strategies.

In the absence of commonly defined and agreed indicators, Member States used national measures, or in some cases hardly any quantified outcome indicators at all, in their first National Action Plans on Social Inclusion submitted in mid-2001 (see European Commission, 2002). By contrast, all the second round of NAPs/inclusion submitted in 2003 did make use of the Laeken indicators, in various ways and to various degrees. The 2004 Joint Report on Social Inclusion notes that many Member States presented an extensive analysis of their national situation on the basis of both the Laeken indicators and national indicators, but often without integrating this into the core of the national action plan, that is, the formulation of the policy strategy against social exclusion and poverty. So to date the common EU indicators are most often seen in the NAPs/inclusion as tools for cross-country comparisons on poverty and social exclusion, not for policy monitoring, planning purposes or target setting.

As far as target-setting is concerned, the Barcelona European Council in Spring 2002 "invited" Member States set targets in their National Action Plans for significantly reducing the number of people at risk of poverty and social exclusion by 2010. The Social Protection Committee in its Common Outline for the 2003/2005 NAPs/inclusion suggested that a small number of headline targets should be set for 2010, accompanied by a series of more detailed targets. In the 2003 round of NAPs/inclusion some countries did set targets but these were mostly framed in terms of national indicators; Greece, Spain and Portugal were exceptions in setting quantified targets in terms of a commonly agreed indicator, the at-risk-of-poverty risk rate. However, looking to the future the logic of agreeing common indicators in the first place is that Member States should be working towards a situation where targets are framed in terms of those commonly agreed indicators (see the discussion in Atkinson, Marlier and Nolan, 2004). This would facilitate mutual learning and exchange of good practices between Member States, which is a key rationale of the open method of coordination.

Ireland and the EU Social Inclusion Indicators

The fact that common indicators for the EU have been agreed in the social inclusion field has major implications for Member States, including Ireland. First of all, this provides Member States and the Commission with a way of comparing performance across countries and measuring progress over time. It is worth illustrating the power of such comparisons by looking at some key indicators from the primary set and seeing where Ireland ranks, using up-to-date figures for the EU-25 for 2003/2004 produced by Eurostat.

First, Figure 9.1 shows the at-risk-of-poverty rate, that is, the percentage falling below 60 per cent of median income (adjusted for household size) in the country in question. We see that Ireland has one of the highest at-risk rates in the EU, together with Portugal and Slovakia, at over 20 per cent. At the other end of the spectrum, countries with at-risk rates that are only half that figure include the Czech Republic, Slovenia and Denmark. The EU-25 average is about 16 per cent. A very different picture is shown in Figure 9.2 for the long-term unemployment rate. Now Ireland is among the best performers, with a rate of under 2 per cent. The highest rates of long-term unemployment are in Poland and Slovakia, where it exceeds 10 per cent.

Figure 9.3 shows the other employment-related primary indicator, which focuses on households rather than individuals. We see that in Ireland the proportion of households that are "jobless" is below the EU-25 average, but Ireland's ranking is not as good as it was with long-term unemployment. Finally, Figure 9.4 shows the proportion of 18-24 year olds who are early school-leavers. Ireland ranks about the middle of the EU-25, but it is striking that the best performers now include some countries that did particularly poorly on other indicators, notably Poland and Slovakia.

Figure 9.1: At-Risk-of-Poverty Rate for EU-25 (2003)

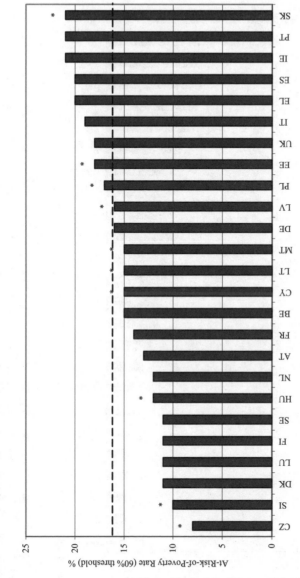

* New Member States

– – – EU 25 Average

Source: European Commission (2006b) – Annex 1c. Statistical Tables.

Notes: At-risk-of-poverty rate income reference year 2003, except for CZ: income year 2002; Malta: income year 2000.

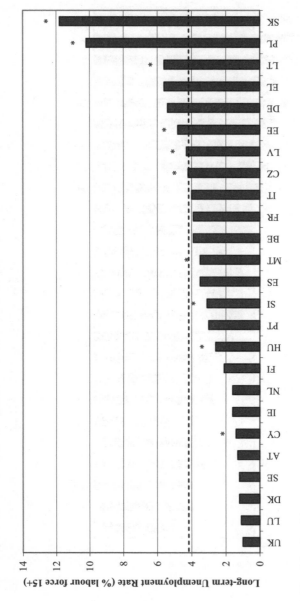

Figure 9.2: Long-term Unemployment Rate for EU-25 (2004)

* New Member States

– – EU 25 Average

Source: European Commission (2006b) – Annex 1c. Statistical Tables.

Notes: Long-term unemployment is unemployment for at least 12 months on the ILO-definition, expressed as a proportion of the total active population aged 15 years and over.

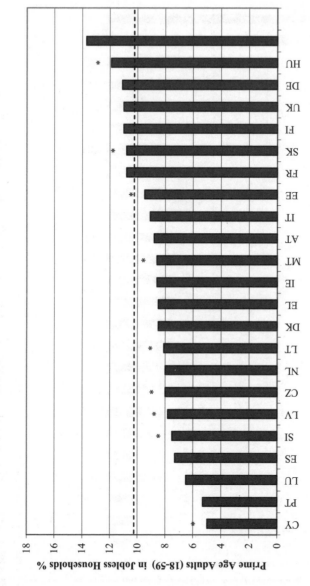

Figure 9.3: Prime Age Adults Living in Jobless Households for EU-25 (2004)

* New Member States
– – – EU 25 Average
Source: European Commission (2006b) – Annex 1c. Statistical Tables.

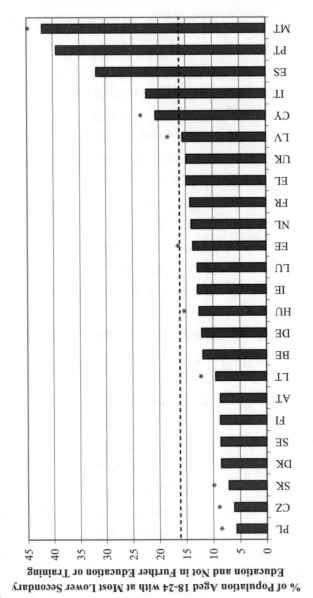

Figure 9.4: Early School Leavers not in Education or Training for EU-25 (2004)

* New Member States

– – – EU 25 Average

Source: European Commission (2006b) – Annex 1c. Statistical Tables

Notes: Proportion of the total population aged 18-24 who have at most lower secondary education and are not in further education or training. SI not included.

This brings out a key feature of the Laeken indicators, namely, their multi-dimensional focus. This represents a real strength: the phenomena to be captured are too complex to be summarised in a single number or target. A multidimensional set of indicators facilitates a more nuanced understanding of the relationships involved and can be more easily linked to policy and to mutual learning.

As far as using the EU indicators is concerned, at the point the indicators were agreed at Laeken different Member States were at rather different stages in the development of explicit anti-poverty strategies. Ireland was among the most advanced in this respect, the initiative to develop a formal National Anti-Poverty Strategy (NAPS) having being put in train in the mid-1990s. This meant that meeting the emerging demands of the EU's Social Inclusion Process in terms of framing National Action Plans against Poverty and Social Exclusion (NAP/incl) has meant in the Irish case adapting the pre-existing NAPS.

Furthermore, Ireland's anti-poverty strategy from its inception was highly unusual in having a number of key outcome targets at its centre. The global poverty reduction target originally adopted relates to a measure of "consistent" poverty that has played an important role in monitoring poverty in Ireland. This seeks to identify those who both fall below conventional relative income poverty thresholds and are experiencing rather basic forms of deprivation, as evidenced by specific non-monetary deprivation indicators. The logic behind this measure, developed at the Economic and Social Research Institute, is that low income on its own is not a reliable measure of exclusion due to lack of resources, for a variety of reasons (including difficulties in measuring income accurately, the importance of savings and other assets and unmeasured differences in "needs" across households). The same logic led the EU to label its income-based social inclusion indicators as capturing those "at risk of poverty" rather than "poor". However, the consistent poverty measure in effect tries to combine such information on low income with non-monetary indicators to identify those who are not simply "at risk" but are actually experiencing what would commonly be regarded as poverty.

The key target in the current Irish anti-poverty strategy is thus "to reduce the numbers of those who are 'consistently poor' below 2 per cent and, if possible, eliminate consistent poverty, under the current definition of consistent poverty". Considerable progress has been made in this re-gard, with the numbers measured as "consistently poor" declining sig-nificantly since the mid-1990s as economic growth surged and employ-ment levels rose sharply. By contrast, the numbers measured as being "at risk of poverty" using relative income thresholds alone have risen, as the incomes of those relying on social welfare payments (although increas-ing substantially in terms of purchasing power) have failed to keep pace with very rapidly rising incomes from work and profits. So the headline target in the Irish anti-poverty strategy is framed in terms of an indicator that is not among the commonly-agreed Laeken set, and there is no Irish target in relation to the at-risk-of-poverty rate that plays an important role among those agreed EU indicators – indeed, there is no explicit po-litical commitment to trying to bring that rate down.

The Irish strategy includes a range of other supporting targets cover-ing specific areas of concern. These include, for example, reducing illit-eracy and early school leaving, eliminating long-term unemployment, and reducing the gaps in premature mortality and low birthweight rates between the lowest and highest socio-economic groups. There are also stated targets for the level of social welfare payments. While these tar-gets are not framed explicitly in terms of the commonly agreed EU indi-cators, there is a good deal of convergence in terms of focus and it would not appear to be a major leap to align them in the future. It would also seem relatively unproblematic to extend the setting of targets to include some areas covered by the common indicators where there are currently no targets – notably the proportion of "jobless" households, now one of the primary Laeken set. The more challenging task is to find a way of incorporating the at-risk-of-poverty rate into target-setting in a way which takes its limitations as a measure of poverty (particularly in a rap-idly growing economy) into account but nonetheless recognises its im-portance as a long-term indicator of risk.

A fruitful way to approach this is to think in terms of a set of tiered targets (as discussed in Layte et al, 2001; Nolan et al 2001; Whelan et al, 2003) along the following lines:

- Priority is given to ensuring that those on low incomes see their real incomes rise, and their deprivation levels using a fixed set of indica-tors decline;

- Next, relative incomes and deprivation levels using a set of deprivation indicators which changes as far as possible in line with expectations should produce a decline in the combined income/deprivation measure;

- Finally, the proportion of the population falling below relative income poverty lines should be declining.

Each of these tiers can be regarded as encapsulating a necessary but not sufficient condition for a sustainable reduction in poverty. The first reflects the assumption that if real incomes of the poor are falling, and their deprivation levels rising, then even if their relative positions were improving most people would see poverty as increasing. The second reflects the assumption that the combined effect of changes in relative incomes and deprivation should be to reduce the extent of what is regarded as exclusion at a point in time. The third reflects the assumption that in the long term, people will not be able to participate in what comes to be regarded as ordinary living standards if their incomes fall too far below the average: a sustained reduction in poverty can then be achieved only by bringing them closer to average incomes.

Together with appropriate indicators and targets for other aspects of social exclusion such as health, education, unemployment/joblessness and housing, this would provide a basis for assessing progress in tackling poverty in Ireland which both reflects domestic concerns and specificities and links directly with the agreed indicators in use at EU level.

Conclusions

The set of EU common indicators for social inclusion, as agreed at Laeken and subsequently refined, represents a major step forward in the development of EU social policy. Common indicators have the potential to bring about a significant change in the way policy is developed, providing policy-makers with a basis on which the starting positions and progress over time in the different Member States in terms of key areas of social concern can be reliably compared. The scope for policy learning should be considerably enhanced by the focus on agreed and harmonised outcome measures, and this has the potential to transform the framework within which Member States develop their national policies to tackle poverty and social exclusion. Some gaps in the indicators remain to be filled, and the evolution of their role is still at a relatively early stage. Even at this stage the framing of targets is moving centre-stage. Ireland was a pioneer in setting explicit quantified outcome targets for reducing poverty: the next challenge is to align the national use of indicators and targets with the common EU indicators.

References

Atkinson T., Cantillon B., Marlier E. and Nolan B. (2002), *Social Indicators: The EU and Social Inclusion*, Oxford University Press, Oxford.

Atkinson T., Marlier, E. and Nolan. B. (2004), "Indicators and Targets for Social Inclusion in the European Union", *Journal of Common Market Studies*, 42 (1), pp. 47-75.

European Commission (2002), *Joint Report on Social Inclusion*, Office for Official Publications of the European Communities, Luxembourg.

European Commission (2003), *Strengthening the social dimension of the Lisbon strategy: Streamlining open coordination in the field of social protection*, Communication from the Commission, COM (2003) 261 final, Brussels.

European Commission (2004a), *Joint Report on Social Inclusion*, Office for Official Publications of the European Communities, Luxembourg.

European Commission, (2004b), "Delivering Lisbon: Reforms for the enlarged Union", Communication from the Commission, COM (2004) 29 final, Brussels.

European Commission (2006a). *Joint Report on Social Protection and Social Inclusion*, European Commission: Brussels.

European Commission (2006b). *Technical Annex to the Joint Report on Social Protection and Social Inclusion*, European Commission: Brussels.

Layte, R., Maitre, B., Nolan, B. and Whelan (2000), "Targeting Poverty: Lessons from Monitoring Ireland's National Anti Poverty Strategy", *Journal of Social Policy*, 29(4), pp. 553-575.

Maitre, B., Nolan, B. and Whelan, C.T. (2005), *Reconfiguring the Measurement of Deprivation and Consistent Poverty in Ireland,* Policy Research Series Paper No. 58, Dublin: Economic and Social Research Institute.

Nolan, B. and Whelan, C.T. (1996) *Resources, Deprivation, and Poverty*, Oxford: Clarendon Press.

Nolan, B., Gannon, B., Layte, R., Watson, D., Whelan, C.T. and Williams, J. (2002), *Monitoring Poverty Trends in Ireland: Results from the 2000 Living In*

Ireland Survey, Policy Research Series Paper No. 45, Dublin: Economic and Social Research Institute.

Social Protection Committee (2001), *Report on indicators in the field of poverty and social exclusion*, Brussels.

Social Protection Committee. (2003), *Common Outline for the 2003/2005 NAPs/inclusion,* European Commission: Brussels.

Whelan, C.T., Layte, R., Maitre, B., Gannon, B., Nolan, B., Watson, D. and Williams, J. (2003). *Monitoring Poverty Trends in Ireland: Results from the 2001 Living in Ireland Survey*, Policy Research Series Paper No. 51, Dublin: Economic and Social Research Institute.

Notes

[1] In November 2004 a High-Level Group chaired by Wim Kok reported on progress towards the Lisbon objectives and recommended that overriding priority be given to economic and employment growth policies (European Communities, 2004), arguing that fulfilment of the social objectives would result from progress in these areas.

[2] For detailed definitions, see (Indicators Sub-Group, 2006). Updated figures for all commonly agreed indicators and context statistics are given as they become available on Eurostat's web site, http://eurostat.cec.eu.int.

[3] The median is the value above and below which half the distribution fall; it is more satisfactory than average income in this context because the average is strongly influenced by very high or very low incomes that may not be reliably measured.

[4] See, for example, Nolan and Whelan (1996).

Chapter 10

BASIC INCOME: RECENT ANALYSES FOR IRELAND

Sean Ward

In its simplest or purest form basic income is a substantial, uncondi-
tional and tax-free payment from the exchequer to all citizens on an
individual basis and it is financed by a flat tax on all income. It replaces
tax credits and tax allowances for those in paid employment and it replaces welfare payments for those who are not in paid employment.
There are many variants of basic income, including:

- *Universal full basic income*: a substantial income, which is usually
  set at a social welfare rate. It may be topped up by conditional payments for particular groups.

- *Conditional full basic income*: a substantial payment which is conditional. This conditionality can be defined in different ways. For example, it may depend on being usefully engaged, i.e. being in paid
  employment, having a caring role, engaging in voluntary work, attending classes, engaging in work search activity, etc.

- *Universal partial basic income*: a universal but less than full payment, which may be topped up by conditional payments in respect of
  unemployment, disability, non-market work, etc.

- *Conditional partial basic income*: a less than full conditional payment, which may be topped up by further conditional payments in
  respect of unemployment, disability, non-market work, etc.

The administration of basic income can also vary. Thus Child Benefit (which is a basic income for children) is paid directly to the parent or guardian. However, for those at work, a Refundable Tax Credit[1] would be another way of administering basic income.

When assessing basic income or any other tax/welfare model, it is important to set out the principles or criteria against which any model or proposal will be assessed. According to CORI (Healy and Reynolds, 1995), the following principles are relevant:

1. Nature and its resources are for the benefit of all

2. Income adequacy

3. Adequacy must be guaranteed

4. Penalty-free

5. Equity

6. Efficiency

7. Simplicity and transparency

8. Freedom.

These authors went on to assess their basic income proposal against these criteria (Healy and Reynolds, 1995).

In an earlier essay (Ward, 1998), I examined the development of the idea of basic income in Ireland from the 1970s to the late 1990s. This essay consists of a summary of key themes which have been developed since then, notably by Clark (2002) and in the work carried out by the ESRI and the Department of Finance for the government Green Paper on Basic Income (Department of the Taoiseach, 2002). These themes are:

•   Financial aspects

•   Gainers and losers

•   Implications for paid work

•   Some broader implications.

The essay goes on to consider the role of basic income and areas of contest and consensus and, finally, some conclusions are attempted.

Financial Aspects

Whatever about the apparent attractions of a basic income system, vastly differing estimates had been put forward regarding the personal tax rate that would be required to fund a basic income system in Ireland. Estimates had ranged from 48 per cent (Clark and Healy, 1997) to 68 per cent or more (Callan, O'Donoghue and O'Neill, 1994). If the higher estimates were necessary, then basic income would not be viable.

One of the aims of the government Green Paper was to revisit these varying estimates in the light of a fully specified model of a basic income system. For the Green Paper, a full basic income model was developed with the following characteristics:

- Basic income payments were paid unconditionally and payment amounts were aligned with social welfare rates, which they replaced

- All tax expenditures were abolished

- All farm income supports remained

- DIRT was set at 24 per cent

- A Social Responsibility Tax (replacing Employers' PRSI) was set at 8 per cent; this money was used to provide "top up" payments to certain low income individuals.

The basic income model was established for 1998 using projected budgetary data from February of that year. Both the basic income system and the "conventional" system were projected to 2001, using "harmonised" data: this means that both the basic income system and the "conventional" system had access to the same resources in 2001. It became apparent during the course of the Green Paper studies that these projections for 2001 were conservative. According to the Green Paper:

> The additional resources which were calculated to be available for this updated estimate were not included in the income distribution analyses of basic income that were carried out by the two sets of consultants. The reason for this is that the additional resources could be used not just to enhance basic income but equally they could be used to enhance the conventional options. Hence, by using tax rates

which they calculated based on the original study parameters, the consultants achieved "like with like" comparisons.

Based on the agreed parameters, the two consultants engaged in the Green Paper process produced estimates of the required tax rate for the basic income model of 47.3 per cent (Clark, 1999) and 53 per cent (Callan et al., 2000) – plus an (agreed) Social Responsibility Tax of 8 per cent.

In 1999, the Department of Finance was asked by the Green Paper Steering Group to provide an estimate of the required tax rate for 2001, taking account of the faster than expected economic growth that had occurred. According to the Department of Finance, a single tax rate of 48 per cent and a Social Responsibility Tax of 8 per cent would be required to fund this scheme. According to Clark (2002), "these income tax rates are within the realm of Ireland's recent experience".

The Green Paper reported some uncertainty around the tax rate required to fund basic income in that the data used in the Department of Finance analysis did not fully capture the economic growth that occurred between 1999 and 2001: according to the Green Paper, the use of updated (2001) data would reduce the required income tax rate below 48 per cent in 2001. Further uncertainty arose, however, from the dynamic effects to which basic income could give rise, for these could be either positive or negative.

One result of the Green Paper analysis of the required tax rate is that the earlier, very high, estimates are no longer applicable. As the actual estimate, which was reported in the Green Paper, was calculated by the Department of Finance using administrative sources, it would be relatively straightforward for this work to be replicated to provide an up-to-date estimate.

Gainers and Losers

Ireland has less equality of opportunity than other European countries and this has changed little over the last decade despite a huge expansion in education and economic growth. We now have a wealthier but a more unequal society with the richest 20 per cent of our working age population earning 12 times as much as the poorest 20 per cent – one of the highest levels of market income inequality

among OECD countries. Nearly 14 per cent of households in poverty
are now headed by those with a job, a rise from 7 per cent in 1994 –
an indication that employment is not always, on its own, a route out
of poverty (NESF, 2006).

Some of the reasons for this outcome have been outlined by the Combat
Poverty Agency:

> The level of income poverty is likely to be due to a number of fac-
> tors. First, social welfare increases have not kept pace with consider-
> able wage growth over the past decade. Second, very significant and
> dramatic economic growth has resulted in a large increase in high
> paid jobs stretching the upper tail of the income distribution higher.
> Third, successive income tax cuts have benefited high-income indi-
> viduals more (in real terms) than those on low incomes over the past
> decade. Thus, the taxation system in Ireland needs to work better at
> redistributing resources (Combat Poverty Agency, 2006).

It has been proposed that a key advantage of basic income would be that
it could facilitate greater equity and a reduction in income poverty
(Healy and Reynolds, 2005).

Valuable work was undertaken under the aegis of the Green Paper by
the ESRI, who carried out a distributional analysis using micro data in
their SWITCH model (Callan et al., 2000a). The analysis was very rigorous in that both the existing tax/welfare system and basic income were
allocated identical resources for distribution. Accordingly, any gains accruing to individuals under basic income versus a conventional alternative must be counterbalanced by equal losses accruing to other individuals under basic income versus the same conventional alternative.

According to the analysis, the combined effect of the full basic income payments and the conditional top-up payments would be very significant for the distribution of incomes. With regard to income poverty,
the analysis showed that:

- 70 per cent of households in the bottom four deciles would gain from
  basic income, while 16 per cent would lose out

- Half of the individuals who would be below the 40 per cent poverty
  line under conventional options would be brought over this poverty
  line by basic income.

Counter balancing these gains, basic income would bring about many "losers" compared with the current system: this arises inevitably from the equality of resources for both systems referred to above. Thus, only 15 per cent of individuals in the top four deciles would gain under basic income, whereas 84 per cent would lose compared with the current system.

According to the proponents of basic income, the alleviation of income poverty and the promotion of equity would be major advantages of the introduction of basic income; this contention was largely borne out in the Green Paper analysis.

Implications for Paid Work

This remains a contested area. The Green Paper acknowledges that analysis of this issue is necessarily tentative. Typically, two statistics are employed in discussing the implications for labour supply: the Replacement Rate and the Marginal Tax Rate.

The Replacement Rate (RR) is calculated as "out of work family income" divided by "in work family disposable income". The RR statistic is relevant for those facing the choice between (low) paid employment and no work – the lower the value of RR, the greater the incentive to take up paid employment.

Under basic income, the RR is lower for those out of work and for many in work on low wages; the main reason for this is that basic income is not withdrawn on taking up paid employment (Green Paper, 2002).

However, the availability of basic income to those who are not in paid employment also means that for many other people their RR rises. For example, the percentage of women engaged in home duties facing an RR of more than 70 per cent would increase from 36 per cent to almost 50 per cent.

It has been argued that the reduction in RR (consequent on basic income) for those out of work and those on low pay is the relevant statistic and that RR is largely irrelevant for those on higher wages as they are generally not facing a choice between paid work and no-work (Clark, 2002).

With regard to the rise in RR (consequent on basic income) for women in home duties, it has been argued that this diminution in the incentive to take up paid employment could lead to a reduction in participation in the paid workforce by this group (Callan et al., 2000b). On the other hand, it has been argued that:

> Those in home duties have chosen to carry out these important and necessary activities, and thus have chosen not to be in the labour force as conceived by economists. Clearly, the only reason to calculate the replacement ratio of adults in home duties is to figure out what price signals would force these persons into paid employment. Here a basic income is clearly contrary to this view, as it gives adults in home duties the financial support to make a decision on how they will contribute to society based on what they feel is best for their families, and not forcing them into taking up a low-paying job because of economic need (Clark, 2002).

Another statistic, which is relevant for the supply of labour (the number of hours worked) is the Marginal Tax Rate (MTR). According to the Green Paper:

> The main impact of a change to a basic income scheme was found to be on taxpayers with marginal tax rates less than 30 per cent under the conventional system, whose marginal tax rates would rise to 50 per cent, or more in certain circumstances, under a basic income system. This increase could apply to 57 per cent of taxpayers. Changes in marginal tax rates can affect decisions regarding hours of work, decisions to work overtime, to take on extra hours or to opt for part time work. It should be noted that in a basic income system each person receives a tax-free payment from the State. This means that their average tax rate could, and in many cases would, be lower while their marginal tax rate would be higher.

It has also been argued that tax rates and benefit levels have very limited impact on adult males and single females and that, in general, income effects overwhelm the substitution of leisure for income in these situations. However, it is agreed that an increase in the marginal tax rate could influence the number of hours worked by married females (Clark, 2002).

Arising from the divergent arguments about Replacement Rates and Marginal Tax Rates, there are two alternative "forecasts" of the effect of basic income on labour supply. According to one view, married women would be less active in the labour force and this would be the main channel for a forecast fall in labour supply. According to another view, by enabling greater flexibility for individuals who are freer to make choices that suit their personal circumstances, basic income may reduce the supply of labour for full-time work patterns, but still would result in an overall increase of labour supply in a more flexible market (Green Paper, 2002).

Some Broader Implications

Basic income does not merely present individuals with the choice of paid work or cash transfers that are contingent on behaviour and/or a means test. Rather, it facilitates paid work, but also caring, education, personal development, etc.

Regarding *participation in tertiary and continuing education*, Callan et al. (2000b) posit two distinct and opposing influences of basic income:

> On the one hand, the guaranteed basic income may allow individuals who could not otherwise finance (a return to) further education and training to participate in such schemes. On the other hand, the financial incentive to forego current earnings in the anticipation of future increases in income may be seriously affected for those individuals (a majority of current employees) who see their marginal tax rates rise by about 20 percentage points. The net impact for any one individual will depend on a range of factors including the level of earnings and the discount rate applied to future earnings. We can expect that for some individuals the lower cost of financing a spell in education or full time training will dominate, so that they will be able to choose a higher level of education under the basic income system, while for others the reduced returns to investment in education and training will induce them to choose a lower level of education than under the conventional system. The net impact on the skill level of the workforce is unclear.

The view of Clark (2002) is more about freedom and possibilities than forecasts:

> The new model (for the new economy) is for moving between paid employment and further education. Workers who want to be retrained, either in their present field, or changing fields, would have the basic income payment to live on while they are earning less or no income. Furthermore, a basic income makes it easier for low-income households to send their children to tertiary education, as they will

not need the income these teenagers and young adults would have contributed to the households.

Regarding the *financial independence of women*, Callan et al. (2000b) state that:

> One of the claims made about basic income is that it increases the financial independence of women. There are two major features of the basic income system which support this claim. First, women who are currently treated as "qualified adults" in the social welfare system would receive a higher payment than at present, and receive it directly in their own right. While the current system allows for split payments, this is somewhat unusual. The change could be seen as increasing the financial resources of many such women, and potentially increasing the women's control over those resources. Second, for married women described as "engaged in home duties", whose husbands are in employment, the change in system would bring about a direct cash payment instead of a transferable cash allowance reducing the husband's tax bill. The impact on the net financial resources of the couple may be positive or negative.

> There are, however, other perspectives on the financial independence of women which would stress the role of employment in providing women with longer-term economic independence. The combined effect of the basic benefit and the basic benefit tax rate is to raise the replacement rate for a substantial number of women in employment. A likely consequence is that fewer women will choose to participate in the paid labour market. This may have negative long-term consequences for women's financial independence. Those wishing to re-enter the labour market at a later date would tend to find the wage which they could command would be adversely affected, with the size of the impact depending on the length of the period of withdrawal.

Clark's view, again, is more about freedom and possibilities:

> Participation in the paid workforce should be based on a voluntary choice, not by the force of material deprivation…A basic income allows both men and women more freedom in making the choices of how they wish to participate in society, using the criteria of where they feel they can make a contribution and where they feel the need is greatest, and not merely avoiding destitution (Clark, 2002).

Regarding *crime and social problems*, Clark (2002) states that:

> As a basic income system reduces some of the barriers to social par-
> ticipation (poverty and employment traps) it will have a positive ef-
> fect on crime and social problems. But, more importantly, a basic in-
> come system has the potential of ending material poverty.

Finally, according to Wilkinson (2002), quoted in Clark (2002), countries with the best health are the ones that have the smallest income differentials between rich and poor. Egalitarian societies have stronger
community life, stronger social fabric, lower crime rates, less stress and
other corrosive effects of inequality.

Roles of Basic Income

There are two broad roles which can be played by basic income. Firstly,
basic income can be viewed as *destination*. As there are many variants of
basic income, so there can be many destinations. These may be ranked as
shown in the following chart:

Figure 10.1: Typology of Basic Income

	Universal	Conditional
Full	1 Universal full basic income	2 Conditional full basic income
Partial	3 Universal partial basic income	4 Conditional partial basic income

Some work in Ireland was concerned with the third variant, viz. universal partial basic income (Ward, 1994). Since then, however, the focus of
subsequent analyses has been on the first variant, viz. universal full basic
income (Clark and Healy, 1997; Green Paper, 2000; Clark, 2002; Healy
and Reynolds, 2005).

Secondly, basic income can be viewed as a *discriminating concept*, which can help in understanding the nature of existing or proposed components of a tax/welfare system.

One of the main aims of basic income is to reduce inequality. We have seen above that it can make an effective contribution in this regard. Accordingly, proposals for reform can be assessed in relation to basic income as a guide to their redistributive effects. Thus, a proposal to reduce the top rate of tax or to widen the standard tax band would widen income differentials compared to the narrowing of income differentials that would accompany basic income. On the other hand, a proposal to abolish or to standard rate tax expenditures or to make tax credits refundable would be consistent with basic income and promote greater tax equity.

Main Areas of Contest and Consensus

Contests

The early objections to basic income centred on its cost (Honohan, 1987; Callan et al., 1994). However, it has been shown in several studies that tax rates, including employee PRSI, of 45-50 per cent could fund a full basic income system (Clark and Healy, 1997; Green Paper, 2000; Clark, 2002).

It has been argued that the effects of basic income on labour supply would be negative (Expert Working Group on the Integration of the Tax and Social Welfare Systems, 1996; Callan et al., 2000b), primarily due to the negative effect on labour market participation by women in home duties. On the other hand, Clark and Kavanagh (1995) and Clark (2002) have argued that basic income supports an entrepreneurial, risk-taking culture which includes learning, atypical working and business formation.

Consensus

There is consensus that basic income would involve a significant transfer of income. This would result in less income for most households in the upper deciles and higher incomes for most households in lower deciles (Green Paper, 2002). It has been argued that in periods of economic growth the adverse effects on "losers" can be mitigated so that their incomes may not actually fall but simply not rise as quickly as those of the "gainers" under basic income (Healy and Reynolds, 2005).

Conclusions

Paid employment is a good antidote to income poverty for many people. However, paid employment is not an option for everyone. In addition, one-third of those below 60 per cent of median income are either employed, self-employed or a farmer (Whelan et al., 2003).

Figure 10.2: Composition of Those below 60 per cent of Median Income in 2001

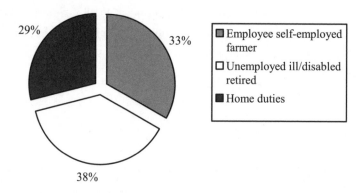

At present, across Europe, many people would like greater flexibility regarding the number of hours that they work and easy movement into and out of education and caring roles. While some workplaces have become more flexible in recent years, many people feel that the balance between paid work and other activities is not optimal (Anxo et al., 2006).

As shown in the Green Paper (2002) and Clark (2002), basic income can be effective in helping to meet both of these challenges: optimising income adequacy and optimising time, including working time.

Adjusting tax and welfare systems is a complicated process. Perhaps unconsciously, elements of basic income have already emerged in current practice and thinking. Thus, basic income is present in the current systems in the form of Child Benefit, which is a universal partial basic income for children. Financial supports for older people (Old Age Contributory and Non-Contributory Pensions) are two parallel conditional basic income systems. If tax credits were made refundable, they would constitute a conditional basic income system for those in paid employment.

An interesting perspective was provided by a senior civil servant interviewed by Jordan et al. (2000):

> A refundable tax credit would now be technically much easier to administer . . . (On basic income) a technical, incremental stumbling backwards into it is more likely than a full-blown conversion.

References

Anxo Dominique, J. Boulin, C. Fagan, I. Cebrian, S. Keuzenkamp, U. Klammer, C. Klenner, G. Moreno, L. Toharia (2006), *Working Time Options over the Life Course: New Work Patterns and Company Strategies,* Luxembourg: European Foundation for the Improvement of Living and Working Conditions.

Callan, Tim, C. O'Donoghue, C. O'Neill (1994), *Analysis of Basic Income Schemes for Ireland*, Dublin: ESRI.

Callan, Tim, B. Nolan, J. Walsh, J. McBride, R. Nestor (2000a), *Basic Income in Ireland: A Study for the Working Group on Basic Income,* Dublin: Department of the Taoiseach.

Callan, Tim, G. Boyle, T. McCarthy, B. Nolan, J. Walsh, R. Nestor, D. van de Gaer (2000b), *Dynamic Effects of a Basic Income: Phase 2 of a Study for the Working Group on Basic Income*, Dublin: Department of the Taoiseach.

Clark, Charles M.A. and C. Kavanagh (1995), "Basic Income and the Irish Worker" in S. Healy and B. Reynolds (eds.), *An Adequate Income Guarantee for All*, Dublin: CORI.

Clark, Charles M.A. and J. Healy (1997), *Pathways to a Basic Income*, Dublin: CORI.

Clark, Charles M.A. (1999), *Report for Working Group on Basic Income,* Dublin: Department of the Taoiseach

Clark, Charles M.A. (2002), *The Basic Income Guarantee: Ensuring Progress and Prosperity in the 21st Century*, Dublin: The Liffey Press.

Combat Poverty Agency (2006), *Policy Statement: Promoting Equity in Ireland's Tax System*, Combat Poverty Agency: Dublin.

Department of the Taoiseach (2002), *Basic Income: A Green Paper*, Dublin: Department of the Taoiseach.

Expert Working Group on the Integration of the Tax and Social Welfare Systems (1996), *Report of the Expert Group on the Integration of Tax and Social Welfare*, Dublin: Stationery Office.

Healy, Seán and B. Reynolds (1995), "An Adequate Income Guarantee for All" in B. Reynolds and S. Healy (eds.), *Towards an Adequate Income for All*, Dublin: CORI.

Healy, Seán and B. Reynolds (2005), *Socio-Economic Review 2005: Pathways to Inclusion*, Dublin: CORI.

Honohan, Patrick (1987), "A Radical Reform of Social Welfare and Income Tax Evaluated", *Administration*, Vol. 35, No.1.

Jordan, Bill, P. Agulnk, D. Burbridge, S. Duffin (2000), *Stumbling Towards Basic Income*, London: Citizen's Income Study Centre.

National Economic and Social Forum (2006), *Report 33: Creating a More Inclusive Labour Market*, Dublin: NESF.

Ward, Seán (1994), "A Basic Income System for Ireland" in B. Reynolds and S. Healy (eds.), *Towards an Adequate Income for All*, Dublin: CORI.

Ward, Seán (1998), "Basic Income" in S. Healy and B. Reynolds (eds.) *Social Policy in Ireland*, Dublin: Oak Tree Press.

Whelan, C.T., R. Layte, B. Maitre, B. Gannon, B. Nolan, W. Watson, J. Williams (2003), *Monitoring Poverty Trends in Ireland: Results from the 2001 Living in Ireland Survey, Policy Research Series No. 51*, Dublin: ESRI.

Wilkinson, R.G. (1996), *Unhealthy Societies: The Afflictions of Inequality*, London: Routledge.

Notes

---

[1] Some employees do not earn enough to use up the full tax credit and therefore they do not benefit from increases in the tax credit, which are implemented in the annual budget. A Refundable Tax Credit would mean that the "unused" part of the tax credit would be refunded to the employee.

Chapter 11

TAXATION POLICY AND REFORM

Francis O'Toole and Noel Cahill

This chapter explores various features of taxation policy in the Republic of Ireland ("Ireland"), concentrating on the period since the publication of the first edition of this book, i.e. 1998, and on taxation issues and policy decisions that are likely to arise in the near-future. This chapter places taxation decisions against the appropriate policy backdrop of expenditure decisions.

The first section places taxation policy in its international context and highlights the likely need for policy choices with respect to the future development of the composition, and scale, of tax revenue in Ireland. The next section focuses on the area of income tax and social insurance contributions. Notwithstanding significant changes in this area in the period 1987 to 1998 (as outlined in the first edition of this book) and significant further changes in the period since 1998 (e.g. the replacement of basic tax allowances with tax credits), the scope for, and importance of, domestic policy-making in this area remains very significant from both an efficiency and equity perspective. This section also discusses tax expenditures, particularly with respect to the private provision of pensions, and the issue of a minimum tax rate. The final section examines various policy reform options and highlights the potential role of alternative revenue-raising sources.

Irish Taxation: Composition and Scale

This section addresses two international aspects of taxation: the evolving composition and scale of Irish taxation revenue relative to other EU countries. The need for policy decisions in both cases is highlighted.

The Composition of Taxation Revenue

The figures in Table 11.1 demonstrate that Ireland has continued the process of becoming more European in terms of the composition of tax revenue. For example, Ireland's reliance on excise taxes has continued its recent historical decline, although Ireland's dependence on revenue from value added taxes has increased significantly relative to the EU15 benchmark. In turn, the EU15 appears to be reducing its emphasis on social insurance contributions, which represents movement towards the Irish composition of tax.

Table 11.1: Composition (%) of Tax Revenue, 1997 and 2004

	Ireland 1997	EU15 1997	Ireland 2003	EU15 2003
Taxes on Personal Income	30.7	26.4	26.5	25.0
Corporation Tax	8.5	6.9	12.9	8.1
Employee Soc. Sec. Contribution	4.8	10.4	4.7	8.7
Employer Soc. Sec. Contribution	8.9	16.3	9.2	15.3
Taxes on Property	4.5	4.2	6.5	5.2
Taxes on goods and services of which:	40.7	31.0	38.4	30.4
value added taxes	*21.2*	*17.7*	*24.5*	*18.9*
taxes on specific goods and services	*17.5*	*11.8*	*12.1*	*10.1*

Source: OECD Revenue Statistics 1965-2004, OECD Publications, Paris, 2005.

However, in at least two important respects, the composition of taxation in Ireland remains relatively unique. First, notwithstanding its very low rate of corporation tax (12.5 per cent, with respect to all trading activities, compared to, say 30 per cent in the UK), revenue from corporation tax is proportionally much more important to Ireland than to the rest of the EU15. The combination of low tax rate, wide tax base and high corporation tax revenue, however, leaves the Irish economy particularly vulnerable to an economic shock as a significant proportion of the corporation tax base is in the foreign-owned multinational sector. Lane and Ruane (2006, p. 20) note that approximately 9.4 per cent of total taxation revenue in Ireland in 2002 came from corporation tax revenue from the foreign-owned multinational sector. The ESRI (Medium Term Review 2005-2012) also highlight the significance of the likely knock-on effects associated with an eventual US economic "adjustment" on the Irish economy. In addition, EU member states may refrain from attempts to change the Irish corporation tax system and instead simply copy the system. Already some of the newer member states (e.g. Hungary and Poland) have adopted a low corporation tax policy. Finally, the Enterprise Strategy Group (2004, pp. 31-2) notes the increased restrictions on State aid (e.g. regional aid) that are likely to be imposed on Ireland after 2006. Although these restrictions won't affect the corporation tax rate itself, they will affect the additional supports that are often offered to the foreign-owned multinational sector.

Second, and notwithstanding some signs of convergence between Ireland and the EU15 with respect to the contribution of revenue from social insurance contributions, it is clear that Ireland still places much less reliance on both employee and employer social insurance contributions. Although tax policy towards pensions is discussed below, it is clear that both demographics and lower real-valued state pension payments in Ireland contribute to this continued significant difference between Ireland and the EU.

In summary, the current composition of Irish tax revenue, and in particular the peculiar case of corporation tax, is rather vulnerable to both internal and external shocks. Revenues from stamp duties associated with the property boom also seem very vulnerable. In addition, it is possible that Ireland (as well as a number of other EU member states) will eventually be forced to move away from the use of the vehicle registration tax (VRT) as a source of revenue; VRT in Ireland accounts for approximately €1 billion in revenue annually, equivalent to approximately 2 per cent of total tax revenue. As such, it would seem sensible to make at least some preparations for a shift in emphasis on the revenue side of the country's budgetary accounts.

Scale of Taxation Revenue

The significant improvement in the Irish public finances that occurred in the late 1980s and early 1990s involved a large reduction in the share of public expenditure in total output produced in Ireland, independently of whether the latter concept is defined with respect to gross domestic output (GDP) or gross national output (GNP). Because the initial position of the public finances in 1987 was one of unsustainable deficit, a reduction in the share of public expenditure as a share of output did not allow for a corresponding reduction in the so-called tax "burden" – total taxation revenue as a proportion of the value of total output.

The figures in Table 11.2 chart the evolution of Ireland's total tax burden over the period 1987 to 2003 and the evolution of the equivalent EU15 figure. The standard comparison is with respect to GDP and in this respect it is clear that Ireland's tax burden has fallen fairly steadily from approximately 35 per cent to approximately 30 per cent over the period in question, while the equivalent figure for the EU15 has remained fairly constant at approximately 40 per cent. However, and as pointed out by many commentators, GNP, by excluding foreign-owned multinationals' repatriated profits, provides a more appropriate measure of the value of economic output available for residents in Ireland; in contrast, in most EU15/OECD countries, there is little distinction in value between GDP and GNP. In addition, it should be noted that the percentage gap between Irish GDP and Irish GNP has also increased gradually over time from approximately 10 per cent in 1987 to approximately 15 per cent by 1997 to approximately 20 per cent in 2004.

Table 11.2: Total Tax as a Percentage of GDP, 1987–2003

	1987	1989	1991	1993	1995	1997	1999	2001	2003
Ireland	36.0	33.9	34.1	34.4	32.8	32.2	31.9	30.0	29.7
EU15	39.6	39.1	39.4	39.9	40.1	40.9	41.5	41.0	40.5
Ireland (GNP)	39.6	38.3	38.8	38.6	37.0	36.8	37.5	35.8	35.5

Source: OECD Revenue Statistics 1965-2004, OECD Publications, 2005 (Table 3, p.68).

When taken as a percentage of GNP, Ireland's taxation burden is seen to decrease from approximately 40 per cent in 1987, when it was very similar to the equivalent EU15 figure, to approximately 36 per cent by 2003.

De Buitleir and McArdle (2003), albeit in the direct context of an examination of spending as opposed to taxation, demonstrate that if adjustments are made for Ireland's low debt service costs, beneficial demographics, low unemployment rate and low defence expenditures, Ireland's tax burden, even allowing for significant public capital deficiencies in Ireland, is broadly similar to the EU15 average. However, and following O'Reardon (2004), if GNP as opposed to GDP is being utilised as the appropriate measure of national output then tax payments made by the foreign-owned multinationals should also be excluded from the measure of taxation revenue. This adjustment is appropriate when tax burdens, as opposed to expenditures shares, are being compared across countries. Given the significant scale of this source of taxation revenue in Ireland (see above), it is clear that Ireland's appropriately adjusted tax burden would once again be significantly below the EU15 average.

Developmental Welfare State

Given the generally negative efficiency effects as well as administrative complexities associated with the imposition of taxation, it is appropriate to consider the reasons for the existence of taxation. Apart from the need to impose taxation for the purposes of correcting for market failures (e.g. environmental taxes), taxation is imposed to finance the provision of social expenditures (e.g. education and health) as well as for the purpose of redistribution (e.g. social protection). In 2005 the National Economic and Social Council (NESC) published a comprehensive document on the development of Irish social policy, the *Developmental Welfare State*. This report outlines an approach, agreed in broad terms by the social partners, to the evolution of the Irish welfare state. A distinctive feature of the approach is the emphasis on the possibility that enhanced social protection can be structured in such a way as to be supportive of first-rate national economic performance.

The report identified a series of challenges in regard to social protection in Ireland that are not being adequately addressed. These include the deep-rooted social disadvantage of a section of the population showing little mobility off (means-tested) social assistance, educational disadvantage and severe barriers to people with disabilities. The report noted that the rate of child poverty in Ireland is among the highest in the EU, notwithstanding relatively generous cash transfers on behalf of children. The relatively high rates of child poverty in Ireland reflect low levels of market income in the most disadvantaged families (NESC, 2005, pp. 132-3).

The report affirmed that adequate money income is an essential condition for participation in society and highlighted the importance of improving social welfare payments to meet current commitments of government as well as the need to continually improve policies that enable money incomes to continue rising. However, the report also argued that improvements in social welfare incomes are not sufficient to address the current challenges of social protection and that the principal requirements for widening participation are of a nature which increases in social welfare alone are inadequate to address. These requirements include access to childcare by lone parents; education and training for people with low skills; affordable and available health services and housing; secure and attractive housing areas; the return to education of early school leavers (both young and old); and public services and public places that are accessible to people with disabilities.

The logic of this report points to a need for increased spending on certain services to address the challenges of social protection. As such, it may well be necessary to consider increased levels of taxation to finance such policy decisions. However, the report also points out that increased social spending is not sufficient and hence the report also makes wide ranging recommendations for reform in the formulation and implementation of social policy.

Personal Income Taxation and Social Insurance Contributions

The figures in Table 11.3 confirm that the standard rate of income tax fell from 27 per cent at the start of 1997 to 20 per cent by 2001, and that the higher rate of income tax fell from 48 per cent at the start of 1998 to 42 per cent by 2001. Given that inefficiency and the associated inequities in the tax system and in the interactions that occurs between the tax and social welfare systems are generally caused and/or exasperated by high marginal tax rates, it is clear that the basic efficiency of the Irish personal income tax system has improved considerably over time. In addition, it should be noted that the pay-related social insurance (PRSI) contribution rates have also fallen, especially the employee PRSI rate.

Table 11.3: Distribution (%) of Tax Units in Tax Bands (Rates), 1994–2002

	0	Marginal Relief	Standard Rate	Higher Rate
1994-1995	25.7	8.0	38.1 (27%)	28.3 (48%)
1995-1996	24.1	7.6	37.1 (27%)	31.3 (48%)
1996-1997	24.3	8.0	39.1 (27%)	28.6 (48%)
1997-1998	25.2	5.9	40.8 (26%)	28.1 (48%)
1998-1999	24.9	3.7	41.4 (24%)	30.0 (46%)
1999-2000	28.4	1.0	37.6 (24%)	32.9 (46%)
2000-2001	28.2	0.6	38.1 (22%)	33.1 (44%)
2001	30.4	0.2	45.5 (20%)	23.9 (42%)
2002	33.6	0.7	39.7 (20%)	26.0 (42%)

Source: Statistical Report, Office of the Revenue Commissioners, Various Years.

The figures also suggest that there has been a significant level of consistency with respect to the distribution of tax units – either an individual or a married couple – across the various tax rates with one notable exemption, namely, the almost complete removal of tax units facing the marginal relief rate of 40 per cent. More specifically, most of these units have moved to the 0 per cent tax rate, i.e. they have effectively been removed from the tax net. Notwithstanding some significant year-on-year changes, the proportions of tax units paying tax at the standard rate and at the higher rate have remained fairly constant at 40 per cent and a little below 30 per cent, respectively.

Although much focus is placed on the proportion of tax units that face the higher rate of income tax (see below for further discussion), the fact that approximately one-third of tax units pay no income tax also appears noteworthy. The conversion of basic tax allowances to tax credits and, in particular, the subsequent significant increases in the PAYE tax credit facilitated this transition, as did moves towards individualisation of the tax code. In addition, there appears to have been a particular political push, primarily through the social partnership process, to increase the minimum wage (€7.65 per hour since 1 May 2005) and to ensure that those receiving the minimum wage pay no income tax.

Individualisation

There has been a significant move towards individualisation of the income tax code in recent years. The Budget of December 1999 ended the practice of automatically allowing a married couple with one income to have the same tax treatment in terms of the width of the standard rate tax band as a married couple with two incomes. Notwithstanding the introduction of a partially off-setting Home Carer Tax Credit (which is available where on-going care is being provided to a dependent, e.g. child) in the subsequent Finance Act, the individualisation trend has continued. The value of the standard single tax allowance (€32,000) is now almost 80 per cent of the value of the married couple with one income tax allowance (€41,000), as opposed to being just 50 per cent before Budget 2000 and approximately 60 per cent after Budget 2000. In addition, the Home Carer Tax Credit (€770) has hardly increased since its introduction and the PAYE tax credit (which by its design was never transferable between spouses) has gone from being approximate one-third of the Home Carer Tax Credit in 2000 to now almost being twice.

Ireland and OECD

Almost all are likely aware of the significant changes that have taken place with respect to the Irish personal tax system (e.g. reduced rates as outlined above). However, it is likely that at least some are unaware of the extent of the similar changes that have occurred in many other OECD countries. The OECD Tax Database (annual) allows for comparison between the effects of the various tax changes that have occurred within these countries, and in particular facilitates a comparison between Ireland and other OECD countries with respect to the structure of the personal tax and social security system(s).

The effective (i.e. average) personal tax rate (incorporating employee PRSI and levies) confronted by Irish taxpayers is without doubt very low by international standards. When attention is restricted to the admittedly rather nebulous concept of "the single worker on the average wage", the

Irish figure of 17.7 per cent is very low compared to other OECD countries; for example, the equivalent figures for the UK and the US are 26.5 per cent and 23.6 per cent, respectively. When the single worker marries (a partner with no market earnings) and has two children, the effective tax rate declines to 8.7 per cent, again significantly below almost all other OECD countries (e.g. 24.6 per cent and 5.0 per cent in the UK and US, respectively). Indeed, only Korea and Mexico, and to a lesser extent the US, have lower effective personal tax rates. When attention moves to the average tax wedge, which brings employer PRSI contributions into the comparison, matters do not change significantly. Indeed, it is the rates of PRSI, as opposed to income tax rates, that seem primarily responsible for the relatively low Irish rates. For example, in France the employee rate is well over 10 per cent while the employer rate is approximately 30 per cent.

However, the single worker at average earnings in Ireland faces rather high marginal personal tax rates and high marginal tax wedges by OECD standards. For example, the (hypothetical) average Irish worker confronts a 42 per cent marginal income tax (although it should be noted that the average Irish wage is very close to being in the 20 per cent tax band), a 6 per cent employee PRSI and levy contributions and a 10.8 per cent employer PRSI contribution. In contrast, for example, France's top marginal income tax rate is 37 per cent.

This paradox of very low average tax rates and wedges but rather high marginal tax rates and wedges, at least for the hypothetical "average" workers, is at least partly explained by the small number of income tax rates in Ireland. By international standards, it is rather unusual to reply on only two (positive) income tax bands, namely 20 per cent and 42 per cent. Although other countries have followed Ireland in reducing both their rates of income tax and the number of income tax bands, almost none have moved to having just two income tax rates; even the UK has three tax rates (10 per cent, 20 per cent and 40 per cent). Inefficiencies caused by the existence of high marginal tax rates and wedges, as well as fundamental inequities in the Irish tax system, could be addressed by the introduction of an extra income tax rate and/or the alteration, or elimination, of particular tax expenditures.

Tax Expenditures

Tax expenditures is the term used in economic analysis to encompass tax exemptions, which exclude certain categories of income from the tax base, and tax allowances or credits, which reduce the tax base or tax payment, respectively. In addition, a distinction is usually drawn between discretionary and non-discretionary tax expenditures with the former being available to only certain categories of activities (e.g. health expenses) and the latter being available to all tax units (e.g. the standard personal tax credits); this sub-section is primarily concerned with discretionary tax expenditures. Tax expenditures give rise to concerns from the perspective of equity (they are of greater value to higher income taxpayers) and efficiency (they may encourage excessive expenditure in particular areas).

Table 11.4 contains estimates on the "expenditures" associated with a small number of the most prominent tax expenditures in Ireland. It must be emphasised that estimates of tax revenue forgone are generally very tentative, both in the sense that the data collected on tax expenditures are often rather inexact (e.g. some categories of tax expenditures can be combined by taxpayers when filing tax returns) and in the sense that should a tax expenditure be removed it is very likely that at least some of the underlying income would be redirected, i.e. revenue forgone tends to overestimate the revenue implications associated with removing a single tax expenditure.

There have been some potentially very positive recent reforms with respect to tax expenditures in Ireland. There has been a move towards the standard-rating of tax expenditures, both with respect to discretionary expenditures (e.g. trade union subscriptions) and non-discretionary expenditures (e.g. PAYE allowance). Standard-rating ensures that all tax units receive the same absolute level of financial benefit from a given tax expenditure; without standard-rating higher income taxpayers would receive 42 per cent, as opposed to 20 per cent, of the relevant amount. Indeed, some of the more well-known standard-rated tax expenditures (e.g. mortgage interest relief and health insurance premiums) are now payable at source and have, in effect, become refundable tax credits in that all tax units receive equivalent treatment. The Department of Finance has recently completed its review of tax expenditures (Review of Tax Relief and Exemptions for High Earners, 2005) and the government is in the process of implementing some potentially very significant changes.

Table 11.4: Estimated Cost of Certain Tax Expenditures (€m), 1993–1994 and 2002

	1993-1994	2004	2004 (# of tax units)
Employees' Contributions to Approved Superannuation Schemes	73.7	563.3	709,300
Employers' Contributions to Approved Superannuation Schemes	180.3	623.1	N/A
Exemption of Net Income of Approved Superannuation Funds (assuming standard rate)	311.4	1,271.6	N/A
Mortgage Interest Tax Relief	≈254	192.8	430,000
Rent Paid in Private Tenancies	1.5	26.4	97,400
Urban Renewal/Rented Residential Accommodation (Section 23/Section 27 Reliefs)	N/A	N/A	N/A

Source: Statistical Report, Office of the Revenue Commissioners, Various Years.

However, some tax expenditures have still not been standard-rated. For example, expenditures associated with health expenses which "cost" €63.2 million in 2002, and which benefited over 140,000 tax units, are worth significantly more to a higher rate taxpayer than to a standard-rated taxpayer. Notwithstanding questions as to the merits or otherwise of whether there should be certain tax expenditures available in the first place, it seems clear that in the interests of equity, all available/justifiable tax expenditures should, to the greatest extent possible, be standard-rated.

In the context of a property boom, both property-based and area-based tax incentives schemes seem very difficult to defend, particularly as the (non standard-rated) benefits appear to accrue to a relatively small number of higher-income taxpayers (see Department of Finance, 2006, Volumes I and II). The continued existence of mortgage interest tax relief and relief on rent paid in private tenancies (which arguably was introduced so as to level the playing-field between owner-occupiers and renters) also appears very difficult to justify, apart perhaps from relief to first time buyers. Although the real value of these reliefs to the individual tax unit has gone down significantly in real terms, the cost in terms of revenue forgone is approximately €200 million.

Tax Expenditures and Pensions

Tax expenditures on pensions are larger than any other element of tax expenditures. The Revenue Commissioners estimate the total level of tax relief on pensions at approximately €1.5 billion or roughly 1.5 per cent of GNP in 2002. Somewhat different estimates were derived in an OECD study (Yoo and de Serres, 2004) which utilised a more comprehensive methodology. The study estimated the net present value of tax relief on pensions. One advantage of this method is that it takes full account of the tax paid on pensions when they are drawn upon. The OECD study estimated that the value of tax expenditures on pensions in Ireland was around 1.9 per cent of GDP in 2003, approximately 2.3 per cent of GNP. This was the highest of the 16 OECD countries included in the study. One reason why the OECD estimate is higher than the Revenue Commissioners' estimate is that in the OECD study employer contributions were viewed as deductions from personal income (and hence incurring a tax saving at personal tax rates) while the Revenue Commissioners view employer contributions as a deduction from corporate profits (and hence a saving at the lower corporate tax rate). In 2003 the combined level of expenditure on social insurance and means-tested social assistance pensions was around €2.4 billion or 2.15 per cent of GNP. Hence, using the comprehensive OECD figures, the level of tax expenditures on private pensions at 2.3 per cent of GNP was actually in excess of direct social welfare expenditure on pensions.

Hughes (2005) and Stewart (2005a) question both efficiency and equity aspects of the current tax-supported pensions model. From an efficiency perspective, arguably the model fails as Ireland has a high rate of relative income poverty among older people, reflecting the historic pattern of pensions coverage. Notwithstanding some recent increase, pension coverage remains low in the Irish work-force and is often inadequate; in 2004 just over half (52 per cent) of all those at work had an occupational or personal pensions (up from 46 per cent in 1995). In addition, occupational pensions make a modest contribution to the incomes of the current older population. From an equity perspective, the distribution of tax expenditures is highly uneven. Ranked by income, around two-thirds of tax relief for employees in 2000 went to the top 20 per cent of employees while just 1 per cent went to the lowest 20 per cent (Hughes 2005, pp. 143-5). It is widely agreed that reform of the current pension system in Ireland is required.

Tax Expenditures and Minimum Tax Rate

At least some of the controversy generated by tax expenditures is caused not by the appropriateness, or otherwise, of the "expenditures" themselves but by the cumulative effect that their existence has on the effective tax rate paid by individual high income earners. For example, CORI Justice Commission (2005, pp. 3-4) in quoting Revenue Commissioners' figures (also available via www.finance.gov.ie), notes that of the top 400 income earners in Ireland in 1999/00, 73 paid less than 15 per cent of their income in tax. By 2001, this figure had fallen to 58 people. However, in 2001, it was also the case that 41 people earning over €500,000 paid no income tax, while a further 242 people earning over €100,000 also paid no income tax.

Some observers (e.g. Combat Poverty Agency, 2005) suggest a direct response to this inequality, namely, the introduction of a minimum tax rate into Ireland's income tax code. In effect, the minimum tax rate would limit the extent to which any tax unit could benefit from any combination of tax expenditures (be they appropriate or inappropriate) within a given tax year. The major disadvantage associated with the introduction of a second income tax system running parallel to the original system is administrative, primarily from the taxpayer's perspective. By its very nature, any initially simple income tax system, e.g. a 15 or 20 per cent minimum tax rate system, tends to gather its own exemptions, deductions and inefficiencies. For example, an income floor of, say, €100,000 implies the existence of very high marginal tax rates at income levels just above €100,000. The US experience may be instructive in regard to this debate. The US's Alternative Minimum Tax (AMT) system was introduced in 1970 as a result of high income earners paying little or no income tax. The AMT appears somewhat unpopular at present (e.g. see Report of the President's Panel on Federal Tax Reform, 2005), perhaps primarily as a result of the non-indexation of the AMT system and its likely future impact on those on middle incomes; this latter effect is being accentuated by significant tax cuts with respect to the standard income tax system. However, appropriate indexation of the AMT would appear to address many of its deficiencies.

Taxation Reform: Issues and Proposals

It is possible to consider taxation reform under two headings: structure of taxation and sources of taxation. The former focuses on reform proposals that take the underlying tax structure as effectively given, while the latter focuses on possible changes with respect to the introduction of new sources of tax revenue.

Structure of Taxation

Expenditure Taxes and Income Taxes. From an equity perspective, there is a strong argument for reducing the emphasis placed on value added taxes (VAT) as a source of revenue in Ireland. Aside from the Nordic countries, Ireland's standard rate of 21 per cent is very high by OECD standards. Any reduction in the standard rate of VAT comes at a high price in terms of tax revenue forgone and would have to be offset by an increased reliance on other taxes, and in particular on income taxes and/or social insurance contributions.

Greater reliance on income tax could result in higher marginal tax rates. In view of this and the arguments made above, there is a strong argument towards the introduction of a third income tax rate. For example, the 0 per cent, 20 per cent, 42 per cent system could be replaced by a, say, 0 per cent, 20 per cent, 35 per cent and 45 per cent system that could be designed to raise more revenue. Increased revenue from income taxes would also stem from the base-broadening measures associated with the introduction of further restrictions (e.g. standard-rating) on tax expenditures.

Tax Expenditures and Pensions. The issue of tax expenditures on pensions needs to be considered in the wider context of reform of the pensions system itself. Whatever policy option is finally adopted, there is a case for reduced reliance on tax expenditures in view both of effectiveness and equity considerations. Hughes' (2005) proposed reduction in the earnings limit that can be used for the purposes of eligibility for tax relief (currently €254,000) to a more moderate level seems very reasonable. In addition, the maximum allowable size of a pension fund for tax purposes (currently €5 million) should also be reduced. The standardrating of pension contributions would also seem appropriate.

Minimum Tax Rate. Within an Irish context, there appears to be a trade-off with respect to the introduction of a minimum tax rate. Its introduction would certainly directly address serious equity issues but at the cost of a significantly increased administrative burden. Perhaps the following three-stage process with respect to policy towards minimum tax rate and tax expenditures would be appropriate in Ireland? First, significant changes have been recently announced with respect to tax expenditures, e.g. certain limits have been placed on the value of specific reliefs to individual tax units and it seems reasonable to await the preliminary results of the cumulative effect of these changes. Second, further changes could and should be introduced to the current arrangements with respect to tax expenditures, e.g. standard-rating. Third, and subsequent to the previous two stages, if it is found that a significant number of high earners could still pay little or no income tax as a result of combining tax expenditures, a minimum tax rate regime should be introduced. Indeed, a credible commitment with respect to the implementation of the third stage if and when appropriate would likely facilitate implementation of the second stage, perhaps even to the extent that the third stage would not need to be implemented.

Individualisation. Individualisation of the tax code has the effect of lowering the marginal tax rate on a spouse entering, or re-entering, the paid labour market and hence has a positive efficiency aspect. The equity aspects of tax individualisation are probably less clear-cut but it is noteworthy that the policy debate with respect to the individualisation of the standard rate tax band appears to be over. It will be interesting to see whether or not individualisation arises in other aspects of the tax and social welfare codes.

Sources of Taxation

Given the previously mentioned vulnerability associated with certain significant tax revenue categories in Ireland, e.g. corporation tax, stamp duties (on properties) and VRT, some further consideration should be given to property and environmental taxes.

Property Tax. The case for a residential property tax has been stated on many occasions including in the previous edition of this book. Had a property tax been in place in the past few years, it almost certainly would have made a contribution to moderating demand and reducing the risk of a property bubble developing in the housing market.

Property tax-related issues also arise in the approach taken to the arrangements for bringing new land into development and the allocation of the increase in the value of such land. The overall process of zoning and developing land gives rise to a very significant increase in the value of land. The large increase in land values leads to pressures for developer-led planning and has been a significant source of corruption in Ireland. There are a number of options, including the use of taxation instruments, that potentially can make the development process more effective and equitable. Taxation instruments that could be used include a higher rate of capital gains tax could be applied to sales of development land; a planning gains levy (PLG) would involve payment of a new levy at the time that planning permission is granted; extension of development levies to cover a wider range of social amenities including schools; and, a site value tax. A detailed assessment of the possibilities is presented in a background paper (NESC, 2004a) to the NESC housing study (NESC, 2004b).

Environmental Taxation. Environmental taxation and related economic instruments have considerable potential in addressing the very considerable environmental challenges that Ireland faces, e.g. the successful introduction of the tax on plastic bags. While major investment in public infrastructure is required in Ireland there is scope for road pricing to reduce the level of traffic congestion and improve traffic flows; the congestion charge in London, which levies a charge on vehicles entering inner London, has proved to be both an economic and political success.

One major environmental policy challenge is the commitment under the Kyoto Protocol to limit greenhouse gas emissions. A key instrument that is being used to achieve the reductions is a scheme of tradable emissions permits. However, this will not be sufficient, in itself, to achieve the required reductions in greenhouse gases; in the most recent ESRI Medium Term Review, it is assumed that a carbon tax will be introduced by 2010 for the sectors not covered by the emissions trading system.

Conclusion

The tax burden in Ireland continues to be relatively low. The basic efficiency of the tax system has improved over time and it is noteworthy that approximately one-third of tax units are now exempt from income tax. The authors' main recommendations are as follows. First, in terms of tax structure, there is a case on equity grounds for reducing the emphasis on VAT as a revenue source in Ireland. Second, it would be desirable to introduce a third intermediate income tax rate in order to reduce marginal tax rates for people on around average earnings. Third, building on progress to date, a phased approach should to taken to further reform of tax expenditures as described above, including if necessary the introduction of a minimum tax rate. Finally, there is a strong case for the greater use of taxation and related instruments to achieve environmental policy objectives.

References

Combat Poverty Agency (2005), "Review of Tax Reliefs and Exemptions for High Earners", Submission to the Department of Finance, March.

CORI Justice Commission (2005), "Submission to Department of Finance Consultation Process on the Review of Tax Reliefs and High Earners 2005".

de Buitleir, D. and P. McArdle (2003), "Tax and Spend: A Look to the Future with an Eye on the Past". Paper presented to Kenmare Economics Conference, 11 October.

Department of Finance (2006), Budget 2006: Review of Tax Schemes (Vol. I: Indecon review of Property-based Tax Incentives Schemes; Vol. II: Goodbody

Review of Area-Based Tax Incentive Renewal Schemes; Vol. III: Internal Review of Certain, Tax Schemes), February.

Economic and Social Research Institute (ESRI) (2005), *Medium Term Review 2005-2012*, No.10.

Enterprise Strategy Group (2004), *Ahead of the Curve: Ireland's Place in the Global Economy*, Dublin: Forfás.

Hughes, G. (2005), "Pensions Tax Relief and Equity", in J. Stewart (2005b).

Lane, P. and F. Ruane (2006), "Globalisation and the Irish Economy", IIIS Occasional Paper, No.01/March, Institute for International Integration Studies.

National Economic and Social Council (2004a), "Approaches to Land Management, Value and Betterment", Background Paper 7 to NESC (2004b), (www.nesc.ie/dynamic/docs/Background%20Paper%207.pdf).

National Economic and Social Council (2004b), *Housing in Ireland: Performance and Policy*, NESC Report No. 112, Dublin: National Economic and Social Council

National Economic and Social Council (2005), *The Developmental Welfare State*, NESC Report No. 113, Dublin: National Economic and Social Council.

OECD (2006), *Economic Surveys: Ireland*, Paris: OECD Publications.

OECD Tax Database.

OECD (2005), *OECD Revenue Statistics 1965-2004*, Paris: OECD Publications.

O'Reardon, C. (2004), "Improving Irish Public Services", *Irish Banking Review*, July.

Report of the President's Advisory Panel on Federal Tax Reform (2005), "Simple, Fair, and Pro-Growth: Proposals to Fix America's Tax System", November.

Revenue Commissioners, Various Years, Statistical Report, Office of the Revenue Commissioners.

Stewart, J. (2005a), "Issues in Pension Provision", in J. Stewart (2005b).

Stewart, J. (2005b), (ed.), *For Richer, For Poorer: An Investigation into the Irish Pension System*, Dublin: Tasc at New Island.

Yoo, K-Y. and A. de Serres (2004), "Tax Treatment of Private Pension Savings in OECD Countries and the Net Cost Per Unit of Contribution to Tax-Favoured Schemes", OECD Working Paper No. 406.

Chapter 12

WORK, EMPLOYMENT
AND UNEMPLOYMENT

Seán Healy *and* **Micheál L. Collins**

Nowhere has the transformation of Ireland been more visible than in the labour market. The once dominant societal phenomenon of unemployment has faded – though not entirely. New jobs have been created in record numbers, achieving levels in excess of 90,000 per annum in some years. Instead of people leaving to find work, immigrants now come to Ireland to join its ranks of workers. The change has been truly dramatic.

This chapter considers that change and a number of the consequences, questions and problems that it has thrown up. We commence by briefly reviewing how the labour market is measured before moving to assess trends in employment and unemployment over recent years. The chapter also considers the need for society to see work as being broader than paid employment. Before concluding, we offer some policy suggestions.

Measuring the Labour Market

Throughout the world, definitions set out by the International Labour Office (ILO, 2005) dictate approaches to measurement in the labour market. They define the labour force as all those in the population who are economically active (aged between 16 and 65 years). The labour force is therefore the sum of the employed plus the unemployed. The proportion of the overall population who are in the labour force is measured by comparing both and calculating a labour force participation rate (LFPR). The numbers of young people and the elderly will influence the LFPR, as will the number of people of working age who are engaged in activities outside the labour market (e.g. education/training).

The ILO also offers definitions for the terms employment and unemployment. A person is considered to be employed if they are working for payment, profit or in the family business (including work on the family farm) for one hour or more each week. Where a person is working for more than an hour but less than they would wish, they are considered to be underemployed. To be counted as unemployed, a person must be without work but looking for work and available to commence work within the next two weeks (CSO, 2006a, p. 28). Those without work who are not seeking employment are not counted as unemployed but as economically inactive. Therefore, where a country is recording a 10 per cent unemployment rate this implies that one in every ten of its economically active labour force is without work but is looking for work.

Using these ILO definitions data on Ireland's labour force is collected by the Central Statistics Office (CSO) four times a year in the Quarterly National Household Survey (QNHS). These figures are taken to be the most accurate indicator of the labour market and as such are the primary data sources cited throughout this chapter. However, there are two other sources of labour market data available. The official record of those collecting unemployment payments from the state, the live register, also provides figures. It generally indicates that there is a higher number of unemployed people as among those "signing on" are part-time employees (those who work up to three days a week), seasonal workers, casual employees entitled to unemployment assistance or benefit and those disaffected workers who are without work and are not interested in returning to employment. Census returns also provide information on the number of people who indicate in their census forms that their principal economic status is unemployed. Again, this figure tends to record higher unemployment rates that the QNHS as the underemployed, part-time workers and disaffected workers are all classified into the unemployment category.

Employment

One of the most remarkable changes in Ireland over recent years has been the dramatic rise in both the labour force and the numbers employed. As Figure 12.1 shows, in 1991 there were 1,354,000 people in the Irish labour force of whom 1,155,900 people were employed. Since then the labour force has grown by over 700,000 to exceed two million people in 2005. Simultaneously the numbers employed have climbed by over 800,000 to reach a figure of almost 1,990,000 employed people in Ireland in 2005. The rate at which new jobs have been created in Ireland over recent years is also remarkable. The last two years of the 1990s saw employment increases of approximately 90,000 per annum. The net increase in employment between 2003 and 2004 was 57,000, while the corresponding figure for 2004-05 was 96,000. During 2006, the overall employment figure is projected to exceed two million.[1]

Figure 12.1: The Numbers of People in the Labour Force and Employed in Ireland, 1991-2005

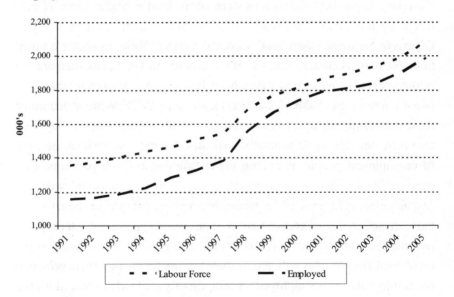

Source: CSO, QNHS various editions.

An indication of the location of these new jobs is presented in Table 12.1. Gains have primarily occurred in the service sector which grew its employees by 85 per cent between 1994 and 2005. Within that broadly defined sector the main drivers of this growth have been the wholesale and retail trade, financial services and the public sector (administrative, health and education). The industry sector also experienced an increase in employees, albeit less pronounced. Breaking down this sector, the increase is entirely driven by expansions in the number of construction employees with traditional industries recording a marginal decline in employees during the period. Over the twelve years examined the numbers employed in the agricultural sector declined by 18.6 per cent.

Table 12.1: Employment by Broad Economic Sector 1994-2005 (000s)

Year	Agriculture	Industry	Services	All
1994	146.9	343.6	730.0	1,220.6
1998	136.0	428.4	929.6	1,494.0
2000	132.9	475.7	1,062.8	1,671.4
2005	119.6	546.7	1,353.5	1,989.8

Source: CSO (2005a:35; 2006a:8) and CSO online labour force Excel files.

The gains in employment have primarily flowed to two groups: women and migrants. As the labour market expanded in the 1990s the primary gainers of the newly created jobs were Irish women who returned to the labour force. As Table 12.2 shows female participation rates have climbed steadily in recent years, surpassing 50 per cent labour force participation in 2005. The proportion of males participating in the labour force also grew, though from a higher base and at a slower pace.

Table 12.2: Labour Force Participation Rates, 1998-2005

Year	Males (%)	Females (%)	All (%)
1998	69.5	44.0	56.5
2000	71.2	47.1	59.0
2005	73.7	52.9	63.2

Source: CSO (2005a, p. 34; 2006a, p. 7)

During the 1980s net emigration from Ireland reached almost 40,000 in some years. From the start of the 1990s onwards this trend reversed and from the mid-1990s Ireland began to experience net immigration (more people coming into the country than leaving it) (CSO, 2005a, p. 8). Data for the years 2000-05 in Table 12.3 show that this trend continued at some pace. Immigrants, including many returning Irish, arrived to fill available jobs. Table 12.3's data suggests that almost 350,000 immigrants arrived over six years. Following the expansion of the EU in mid-2004 a large inflow of workers from the ten accession states occurred. As these immigrants were initially not entitled to welfare benefits, we can assume that all became employed. Given the limited availability of Irish workers, as jobs continue to be created further increases in immigrants can be expected.

Table 12.3: Estimated Immigration classified by Nationality, 2000-2005 (000s)

Nationality	2000	2001	2002	2003*	2004*	2005*
Irish	24.8	26.3	27.0	17.5	16.9	19.0
UK	8.4	9.0	7.4	6.9	5.9	6.9
Rest of EU-15	8.2	6.5	8.1	6.9	10.6	7.1
EU Accession 10	–	–	–	–	–	26.4
USA	2.5	3.7	2.7	1.6	1.8	1.6
Rest of World	8.6	13.6	21.7	17.7	14.9	9.0
Total	**52.6**	**59.0**	**66.9**	**50.5**	**50.1**	**70.0**

Source: CSO (2005b:8)

Notes: * Preliminary data; Rest of the EU-15 are Austria, Belgium, Denmark, Finland, France, Germany, Greece, Italy, Luxembourg, Netherlands, Spain, Sweden and Portugal; EU accession 10 are those countries that joined the EU on 1 May 2004, namely, Cyprus, Czech Republic, Estonia, Hungary, Latvia, Lithuania, Malta, Poland, Slovakia and Slovenia.

Unemployment

As an issue, unemployment dominated the social and political landscape of Ireland for much of the State's existence. The failure to create sufficient jobs for our own people drove the aforementioned tradition of emigration. In 1986 Ireland had an unemployment rate of 17.1 per cent, however in recent years unemployment has dramatically decreased. In 1990 the unemployment rate was 13.4 per cent and by 2000 it had fallen to 4.3 per cent (OECD, 2006, p. 247). Leddin and Walsh (2003, p. 430) note that it was only in 1999 that the Irish unemployment rate fell below that of the UK for the first time. Since 2000, unemployment rates have remained reasonably static.

Figure 12.2: The Numbers of Unemployed and Long-Term Unemployed in Ireland, 1991-2005

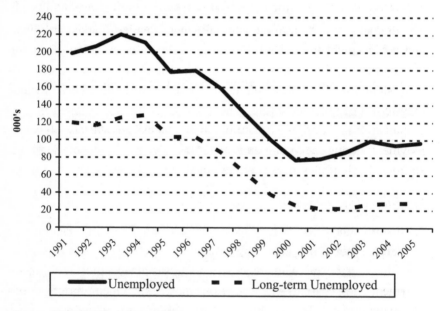

Source: CSO, QNHS various editions.

Figure 12.2 and Table 12.4 trace the numbers unemployed. Of the 96,700 people classified as unemployed in 2005, 58,000 were men and 38,800 were women. The corresponding unemployment rates for men and women are 4.8 per cent and 4.4 per cent respectively. Overall, some 80,200 of the unemployed are recorded as searching for full-time work, while 16,500 are seeking part-time employment. The latter group is primarily comprised of unemployed females (12,000 women) (CSO, 2006a, p. 7).

Table 12.4: The Irish Labour Force, 1998-2005 (000s)

	1998	2000	2005
Labour Force	1,620.4	1,745.9	2,086.5
In Employment	1,494.0	1,671.4	1,989.8
Unemployed	126.4	74.5	96.7
of whom LT Unemployed	63.6	27.7	28.1
Unemployment Rate	7.8	4.3	4.6
LT Unemployment Rate	3.9	1.6	1.3

Source: CSO (2005a, pp. 34, 38; 2006a, pp. 7, 18)

The dramatic reduction in the unemployment rate has marked an important achievement for Ireland. However, a closer examination of the unemployment statistics suggests that from a social policy perspective, society should remain concerned about a number of issues. These include long-term unemployment, the concentration of the unemployed in geographical areas known as unemployment blackspots, levels of unemployment among the young and unemployment among people with disabilities. Each of these issues is examined in turn below.

Long-term Unemployment

A person is classified as long-term unemployed if they are unemployed (as defined by the ILO) for twelve months or more. Thus, this classification identifies people who are experiencing sustained exposure to unemployment and separates them out from those experiencing brief periods of unemployment. In recognition of the seriousness of those in such a position, the 2002 National Anti-Poverty Strategy review committed "to eliminating long-term unemployment as soon as circumstances permit but in any event not later than 2007" (2002, p. 11).

Alongside the decline in the overall unemployment numbers, Figure 12.2 shows that since 1994 the numbers classified as long-term unemployed have decreased. However, there has been limited change in the proportion of the labour force in this category since 2000. In 2005, a total of 28,100 people were unemployed for 12 months or more, representing a long-term unemployment rate of 1.3 per cent.

Unemployment Blackspots

Like many forms of disadvantage, unemployment is often found clustered in particular areas. Due to the statistical sampling approach adopted by the CSO, the QNHS is unable to provide a small area breakdown of the distribution of unemployment. However, to gain some insight into this phenomenon we can use data from the census which provides information on unemployment for every electoral division (ED) in the country.[2] According to the 2002 census, there were a total of 88 EDs where more than 20 per cent of the labour force indicated that they were unemployed. Table 12.5 outlines the geographic distribution of these areas. The census found that these areas recorded unemployment rates ranging between 22 and 30 per cent. The census results also noted these blackspots were not just urban-based as many were located in rural areas (CSO, 2003a, p. 15).

Table 12.5: Unemployment Blackspots at Electoral Division Level by County, 2002

County	Number of Locations	Average Unemployment (%)
Cork City	11	24.7
Dublin City	15	24.0
Donegal	18	25.2
Galway County	6	27.6
Limerick City	11	24.8
Louth	4	22.1
Mayo	5	29.9
Waterford City	6	24.5
Other Counties	12	22.6
Total	**88**	**24.0**

Source: CSO (2003a, p. 15)

Youth Unemployment

An examination of the age structure of the unemployed indicates a sustained problem of youth unemployment. As Table 12.6 shows, this is particularly of concern among those aged 15-19. Similarly, those aged

20-24 years record unemployment levels well above the national average. Given the projections for further increases in unemployment in the years ahead, the fate of any low-skilled individuals who have become unemployed is a concern, a point also made by National Economic and Social Forum in their document entitled *Creating a More Inclusive Labour Market* (NESF, 2006). Depending on the extent of an economic slowdown, the potential for these individuals to become trapped in unemployment should be monitored. Another factor relevant to any assessment of youth unemployment is its association with other societal problems and in particular suicide. When considering the results of an eight-year study of suicides in County Kildare (1995-2002) McGovern and Cusack (2004) found that unemployed males under the age of 30 were the group most likely to commit suicide.

Table 12.6: Unemployment Rates across the Age Groups, Sep-Nov 2004 and 2005

Age Group	Sep-Nov 2004	Sep-Nov 2005	Change
15-19	13.4	12.2	-1.2%
20-24	7.1	7.6	+0.5%
25-34	4.0	4.3	+0.3%
35-44	3.4	3.2	-0.2%
45-54	3.4	3.5	+0.1%
55-59	2.8	3.1	+0.3%
60-64	1.9	1.8	-0.1%
65+	0.3	0.9	+0.6%

Source: CSO (2006b:17)

People with a Disability

The results of a 2004 QNHS special module on disability revealed that of all persons aged between 15 and 64, 10.9 per cent indicated that they had a longstanding health problem or disability (CSO, 2004). This equates to 298,300 people in Ireland, of whom 155,800 were male and 142,500 were female. Of those individuals only 37 per cent were in employment. This is a figure considerably below the participation rate of the overall population in 2004 which stood at 61 per cent. Furthermore, of those employed approximately one-quarter worked part-time while the remaining three-quarters were in full-time employment. Relative to the rest of the labour force, this low rate of employment among people with a disability is of concern. Apart from restricting their participation in society it also ties them into state dependent low-income situations.

Work Outside the Labour Market

A major question raised by the current labour-market situation concerns assumptions underpinning culture and policy making in this area. One such assumption concerns the priority given to paid employment over other forms of work. Most people recognise that a person can work very hard even though they do not have a conventional job. Much of the work carried out in the community and in the voluntary sector fits under this heading. So too does much of the work done in the home.

The need to recognise voluntary work has been acknowledged in the Government White Paper, *Supporting Voluntary Activity* (Department of Social, Community and Family Affairs, 2000) and by Taoiseach Mr Bertie Ahern TD, who has stated that "voluntary activity forms the very core of all vibrant and inclusive societies". The report was prepared to mark the UN International Year of the Volunteer 2001 by Government and representatives of numerous voluntary organisations in Ireland. The report made a series of recommendations to assist in the future development and recognition of voluntary activity throughout Ireland. The national social partnership agreement *Towards 2016* (Department of the Taoiseach, 2006) also contains commitments in this area. In that agreement the Government undertakes to:

> . . . continue to develop policies on volunteering arising from the package of measures initiated in February 2005. A key principle underlying the Government's approach is that volunteering finds meaning and expression at a local level and that supports and funding should seek, as far as possible, to recognise this reality. The Government remains committed to further developing policy to support volunteering, drawing on the experience in delivering these measured and informed by the recommendations of the Task Force on active Citizenship.

The decision in the same national agreement to investigate the feasibility of introducing national "shadow" or "satellite" accounts also offers some potential to address this deficit. These accounts seek to redress the failure of our present national accounts which miss fundamentals such as the value of unpaid work. That failure has resulted in policy decisions being made without full realisation of the consequences of these decisions on other aspects of societal life. The focus on maximising participation in paid employment did not pay sufficient to the impact of such an approach on issues such as caring which is provided on an unpaid basis for large numbers of children, older people, those who are ill and people with a disability.

An insight into this issue was provided by a report presented to the Joint Oireachtas Committee on Arts, Sport, Tourism, Community, Rural and Gaeltacht Affairs. It established that the cost to the state of replacing the 475,000 volunteers working for charitable organisations would be a minimum of €205 million and could cost up to €485 million per year. Similarly, research on the work of carers has shed some light on the scale of the non-labour market work they carry out. Results from the 2002 census found that 4.8 per cent of the population aged over 15 provided some care for sick or disabled family members or friends on an unpaid basis (CSO, 2003b, pp. 25-26). This figure equates to almost 149,000 people of whom 61 per cent (91,000) are women. The dominant caring role played by women was further highlighted by the fact that one in every ten women in Ireland in their 40s and 50s is a carer. When assessed by length of time, the census found that some 40,000 people provide unpaid help to ill or disabled family members and friends for 43 hours a week or more, a working week considerably in excess of the standard working week for paid workers. According to the Carers Association, people caring full-time for the elderly and people with disabilities are saving the state approximately €2 billion a year in costs which it would otherwise have to bear.

Policy

To conclude this chapter, we consider some policy implications that arise from the above analysis. These concern job creation, the segmentation of the labour market, the provision of active labour market programmes, retraining, incorporating older workers into the labour market and developing policies that recognise all forms of work.

Job Creation

As we have shown above, there has been a remarkable and sustained increase in employment in Ireland. Furthermore, as Table 12.1 displayed there has been a definite shift in employment towards services. The new situation created by the huge growth in available jobs raises major questions concerning the focus of policy in this area. Should Ireland continue to expend resources to increase further the number of jobs available? Given the problems being experienced in trying to increase the labour supply (by recruiting women, older people and people from abroad), should more emphasis be placed on improving the quality of jobs available, and the education, training and life-long learning capacity of people in the labour force? The latter approach seems more sensible.

The changing context and the need for balance mean that Ireland's approach to job creation must also change. The National Economic and Social Council (NESC) captures this reality very neatly in its Strategy Report when it states:

> . . . the goal of national prosperity and well-being, based on a dynamic economy, is no longer neatly reflected in the proximate goal of employment creation, in and of itself. This has implications in a range of economic and social policy areas. It is far from clear that aiding all employment creation in private business – for example, through granting work permits to employers to employ migrants in low-skilled work in cost-based export industries – adds to national economic and social development. . . . The rationale for active policies to strengthen indigenous enterprise and attract inward investment is changing, as the focus switches from job creation and boosting recorded national exports to building and finding firms that enhance Ireland's position and capabilities in key high-value sectors (NESC, 2005, pp. 87-88).

The NESC approach suggests a need for some change in the way we as a society approach economic growth and job creation. Moving to accept and adopt the implications of that approach is a challenge for the years ahead.

Segmentation of the Labour Market and the Minimum Wage

The dramatic growth of the labour market, coupled with large-scale immigration and an expanding services sector, suggests that the Irish labour market is likely to experience some segmentation. In its simplest form, a segmented labour market implies a division between well-paid skilled workers and low-paid unskilled workers – a feature generally reflected by a broadening earnings distribution. At the lower end of that distribution the need for a reasonable minimum wage remains an important policy priority. In a situation where unemployment re-appears as a problem, and where there is increased competition for employment among the lower paid, the prospect of low wages falling is unacceptable. Policy should continue to support a reasonable minimum wage, one benchmarked against average wages, and one which provides enough income for a low-paid worker to live on.

Active Labour Market Programmes

Active labour market programmes (ALMPs) have played an important role in labour market policy in Ireland over the years and continue to do so. In common with the experience in most other EU member states, they were developed gradually to combat high and persistent unemployment. The share of total public expenditure on unemployment support on active programmes increased throughout the 1990s but has been decreasing in real terms as Ireland's unemployment rate fell dramatically and the numbers long-term unemployed fell. Today there is a strong emphasis on active labour participation measures as opposed to passive income transfers.

An additional issue emerged for the community and voluntary (C&V) sector as the number of people on active labour market programmes declined. These programmes had started off in periods of high unemployment and were essentially designed to progress unemployed people to the open labour market. They were also used to provide valuable human resources to providers of essential social services, especially in disadvantaged areas. The decline in the number of participants produced a negative knock-on effect in the social services provided by those working in these active labour market programmes. The C&V pillar of social partners argued that reform would best be undertaken by separating out what was being provided by ALMPs and associated initiatives into three strands, as follows: (a) An active labour market programme providing experience and training for people seeking employment in the labour market. (b) A local services support programme to finance the services being provided to local communities by the community and voluntary sector. These services should not be forced to depend on financing being made available solely through the employment of long-term unemployed people. (c) A programme that provides "supported" employment for a number of people who would not benefit from places on an ALMP. Reforming ALMPs along these lines remains a challenge for policy makers and practitioners in the years to come.

Retraining

In their 2004 Lifelong Learning study, the OECD reported that there is widespread agreement across OECD countries on the need for increased investment in training and education of the adult population (OECD, 2004). Such increases are required in response to the changes in employment and the need for ongoing upskilling of the labour force if the needs of a competitive economy are to be met. New skills are constantly required and increasingly these skills have to be made available among existing workers. Individuals who lose their jobs or are at risk of losing them also require upskilling if they are to take up available positions. Consequently, there is an ongoing need to prioritise ongoing education and retraining among the adult population.

Older Workers

As the Irish economy continues to grow, demand for workers will continue to occur. It is expected that by 2011, almost 1.2 million workers in Ireland will be aged between 45 and 69 years. As a consequence the NESF report entitled *Labour Market Issues for Older Workers* (2003) highlighted the need to facilitate older people in accessing and retaining employment. Among the recommendations suggested by that report are the following:

- More actively explore avenues to promote the benefits of in-work training and retraining for older workers.

- Enhance the provision of supports to older workers, particularly in relation to flexible working, reduced working hours and retraining.

- Put in place a strategy as a matter of priority to implement the recommendations of the Task Force on Lifelong Learning.

- Broaden the remit of the National Training Advisory Committee to include the design and development of a work-based training package that takes account of the specific needs of older workers.

- Examine how best to undertake a regular company-level survey of the training needs of older workers.

- Give greater consideration to the specific educational needs of older workers, including opportunities for progression and the recognition of prior experiential learning. This should apply to programmes like the Vocational Training Opportunities Scheme, which provide education opportunities for the unemployed.

- Develop a series of guidelines for employers in relation to older workers and IT and build on the success of the Fast Track to IT scheme.

- Extend the Employment Action Plan re-engagement process to those aged over 55 and to those not on the Live Register but currently out of work, such as older women returning to the labour force (NESF, 2003, pp. 14-16).

It is important that these recommendations are implemented and that in the years to come Ireland's older people are given every chance to achieve and retain a productive role in society. At the same time it is important that the element of choice be retained and that older people are not compelled to take up paid employment if they do not wish to do so.

Policies to Recognise All Forms of Work

Likewise it is important to put in place policies that recognise all forms of work. As well as recognising the value of unpaid work through the development of "satellite" national accounts already referred to, there is a need to ensure that the income distribution system recognises the value of unpaid work in the home, in the community and in the wider society.

Paid employment is important and valuable. But so too are other forms of work. These too need to be recognised and remunerated.

Conclusion

The transformation of the Irish labour market during the late 1990s stands as one of the most important achievements by the Irish State. In particular, it marked a signal that as a country Ireland was capable of supplying employment for its own people. Since then the success of the labour market to create more jobs, accommodate an influx of migrants and control unemployment has been remarkable.

In the context of that success, this chapter notes that there are a number of challenges that lie ahead. Long-term unemployment remains stubbornly present, youth unemployment is notably high, people with disabilities remain unable to access employment and in both urban and rural areas there are unemployment blackspots. As well as addressing these remaining problems, we also highlight the need for Irish society to begin to recognise the role played by those who engage in work outside the labour market. Addressing all these issues poses challenges for the years ahead.

References

Central Statistics Office (2003a), *Census 2002 – Principal Socio-Economic Results*, Dublin: Stationery Office.

Central Statistics Office (2003b), *Census 2002: Volume 2 – Ages and Marital Status*, Dublin: Stationery Office.

Central Statistics Office (2004), *Quarterly National Household Survey – Disability,* Dublin: Stationery Office.

Central Statistics Office (2005a), *Statistical Yearbook of Ireland, 2005*, Dublin: Stationery Office.

Central Statistics Office (2005b), *Population and Migration Estimates*, Dublin: Stationery Office.

Central Statistics Office (2006a), *Quarterly National Household Survey – Quarter 1 2006*, Dublin: Stationery Office.

Central Statistics Office (2006b), *Quarterly National Household Survey – Quarter 4 2005*, Dublin: Stationery Office.

Department of Social, Community and Family Affairs (2000), *Supporting Voluntary Activity*, Dublin: Stationery Office.

Department of Social, Community and Family Affairs (2000), *Supporting Voluntary Activity*, Dublin: Stationery Office.

Department of the Taoiseach (2006), *Towards 2016 - Ten-Year Framework Social Partnership Agreement 2006-2015,* Dublin: Stationery Office.

Drudy, P.J. (2004), "Dublin and the Regions: Economic and Social Trends Compared" in Drudy, P.J and A. McLaren (eds.) *Dublin Economic and Social Trends-Vol 4*, Dublin: Centre for Urban and Regional Studies.

International Labour Office (2005), *World Employment Report 2004-05: Employment, productivity and poverty reduction,* Geneva: ILO.

Leddin, A. J. and Walsh, B.M. (2003), *The Macroeconomy of the Eurozone: An Irish perspective*, Dublin: Gill and Macmillan.

McGovern, C. and Cusack, D.A. (2004), "A Study of Suicides in Kildare, 1995-2002", *Journal of Clinical Forensic Medicine,* Vol. 11, Issue 6, pp. 289-298.

National Anti-Poverty Strategy Review (2002), *Building an Inclusive Society* Dublin: Stationery Office.

National Economic and Social Council (2005), *NESC Strategy 2006: People, Productivity and Purpose*, Dublin: NESC.

National Economic and Social Forum (2003), *Labour Market Issues for Older Workers,* Dublin, NESF.

National Economic and Social Forum (2006), *Creating a More Inclusive Labour Market*, Dublin: NESF.

OECD (2004), *Co-financing Lifelong Learning: Towards a Systemic Approach,* Paris: OECD.

OECD (2006), *Employment Outlook – Boosting Jobs and Income,* Paris: OECD.

Notes

---

[1] The QNHS for the first quarter of 2006 recorded an employment figure of 1,998,100 (CSO, 2006a, p. 7).

[2] See Drudy (2004, p. 12) for a discussion on comparisons between QNHS and census unemployment data.

Chapter 13

HOUSING IN IRELAND: PHILOSOPHY, PROBLEMS AND POLICIES

P.J. Drudy

A secure affordable home appropriate to needs is one of the most basic human requirements. Yet even in the relatively developed countries many thousands have unsuitable accommodation or none at all. Worse still, in the developing countries in Africa, Asia and South America, millions of people are without basic shelter. The provision of housing is thus of universal concern.

In Ireland, housing has long been a matter of concern and a range of policies have been put in place by successive governments both before and after independence to improve standards and provision. Over the last few decades, in particular, significant progress has been made. Coinciding with improved employment opportunities, especially during the last decade, large numbers of homes and apartments have been built for sale or for rent – over recent years more than 70,000 units per annum by private developers and over 5,000 by Local Authorities and housing associations. Basic facilities such as clean water and sanitation, lacking in many homes in the past, are now available to most. A high proportion of the population own their homes without a mortgage and many own second homes either in Ireland or in other countries. Some individuals and companies own multiple properties. The construction industry is a significant employer. The Government receives significant revenue from stamp duty and Value Added Tax on building materials. The number of housing units in the private rental sector, in decline for many years, has increased.

In view of such apparent progress, it may seem surprising that many people in Ireland are still faced with a housing problem – indeed for some it is a "housing crisis". This problem has been particularly obvious since the mid-1990s and, ironically, it has coincided with the period when Ireland's economy has been most successful. This chapter first examines a number of philosophical approaches to housing. It then outlines the way housing provision and tenure have changed in recent decades, and the nature and causes of the current "housing problem". Finally, a number of policy changes are suggested.

Housing Philosophy: A Market Commodity or a Home?

There are a number of philosophical approaches to housing. These approaches derive from a particular "paradigm" of core beliefs and assumptions. As Healy and Reynolds explain in the first chapter of this book, paradigms underpin decisions concerning what constitutes a problem, how it should be approached and what action, if any, should be taken (Healy and Reynolds, 2006). The particular paradigm or philosophy which is dominant at a point in time has a critical influence on the kinds of policies pursued by central and local government and the type of housing system which emerges as a result. For convenience, a distinction is drawn here between an approach which views housing primarily as a market commodity or, alternatively, as a home. The first approach views "the market" as the ideal provider of housing and as a determinant of the price purchasers and renters must pay. This approach seeks to minimise the direct provision of housing by the state. Rather, it asserts that the state's role is to facilitate such provision by private developers, to fast-track planning permissions and re-zonings and to encourage private provision with tax and other incentives, while carrying the cost of essential services such as water, sewage, roads and amenities. While public housing would still be provided by Local Authorities and other non-profit organisations, it would be a "residual" sector for low-income groups and the market approach to provision would be the dominant one.

In a pure market system, the market forces of supply and demand (where ability to pay is the critical factor) determine who gets housing as well as its price or rent. If there is excess supply (inadequate demand), developers, builders, landlords and estate agents will have empty houses for sale or rent and prices are likely to fall as a result. Those capable of purchasing or renting homes will benefit from an increased choice and lower prices. On the other hand, inadequate supply (excess demand) will tend to push up prices and rents and put purchasers under pressure. In this market system prices will, it is argued, tend to stabilise (or reach "equilibrium") when supply equals demand. In theory, this is the way the "housing market" should operate. In reality, there are often extended periods when the supply of housing is insufficient to meet demand and therefore prices and rents fail to stabilize. Instead, they continue to increase at rates far greater than the rate of general inflation. This is the well-known problem of market failure (Drudy and Punch, 2005).

There is a further fundamental problem with the market as a mechanism to allocate housing – that is, that the market completely excludes those who do not have the ability to pay. Those involved in the production or sale of housing do so in order to earn incomes or profits. Housing will simply not be provided to those who cannot pay the market price. In the case of housing for purchase, this normally means the ability to borrow a substantial sum of money from a building society or bank. The ability to borrow depends on such factors as well-paid and steady employment, the ownership of other property, or access to relations who are prepared to protect the lender by acting as guarantor or by contributing to deposits or other costs. In effect, those on low incomes invariably fail to fulfil these "requirements" and are therefore excluded from purchasing housing on the market. Therefore, those on relatively high incomes tend to be the main house purchasers. In this philosophical approach, therefore, housing is "commodified" – it becomes another "commodity" or "product" like televisions, motor cars, race horses or stocks and shares to be bought and sold "on the market" by those who can afford to do so. Unlike the stock market, however, those buying are invariably advised that a house is a "good investment", that it will "appreciate in value" and when sold in due course the seller can expect to make a profit. With this approach the contribution of housing is measured mainly in *quantitative* terms – the level of profit, return on investment and capital gain (Drudy and Punch, 2002).

This "market approach" to housing inevitably encourages the "segregation" of housing types and particular social groups. Housing is invariably sold on the advice that, apart from being a home, it is a secure investment and an appreciating asset which can be "traded up" or from which "profit-taking" can occur at any time. In order to protect these suggested attributes, it becomes important therefore to avoid dilution of the "commodity" with low-priced homes or those from lower socioeconomic groups. Such a philosophy can play a central role in such segregation. Thus, those from the lower social classes are excluded or displaced from the highly-priced areas through the prohibitive cost of housing and such areas are, in effect, "ring-fenced" from invasion by the poor or other "undesirable" social groups who must then seek accommodation elsewhere. In effect, therefore, a market-driven housing system tends to perpetuate inequality and segregation (Lee et al. 1995; Lee and Murie, 1997; Drudy and Punch, 2001; Fitzgerald and Winston, 2005). Despite this, and the fundamental inadequacies outlined above, the market is commonly applauded as an "ideal" or "natural" mechanism to allocate housing by many economists, developers, estate agents, landlords and those representing the building industry.

One alternative approach, in stark contrast to the above view, is to place the emphasis on housing as a home – shelter, a place to stay, to feel secure, to build a base, find an identity, participate in a community and society. In this approach, housing would be treated primarily as a fundamental "social" requirement like education or public health, and would be produced mainly in response to need as well as the ability to pay. As with education and health, serious efforts would be made to ensure that the cost of housing did not escalate in an unreasonable manner. In line with this perspective, housing has been given the status of a "right" in the Constitutions or in legislation in various countries – a position strongly supported by a range of individual experts and agencies (Connolly, 1998; CPSU and SIPTU, 1998; Kenna, 2002; Threshold, 2002; CORI, 2005).

The right to housing is long-established in a wide range of international human rights instruments. First stated in the United Nations' *Universal Declaration of Human Rights* in 1948, the right to housing has been explicitly restated and amplified in a series of subsequent international human rights conventions, including the *International Covenant on*

Economic, Social and Cultural Rights, adopted by the United Nations General Assembly in 1966. These conventions set out internationally accepted standards and illustrate the sustained global support given to the right to adequate housing by the international community. Ireland is a party both to the *Universal Declaration* and to several other conventions.

Article 25 of the *Universal Declaration* states that:

> Everyone has the right to a standard of living adequate for the health and well-being of himself (herself) and his (her) family, including food, clothing, housing, medical care and necessary social services...

Article 11 of the International Covenant on Economic, Cultural and Social Rights is as follows:

> The States Parties to the present Covenant recognise the right of everyone to an *adequate* standard of living for himself/herself and his/her family, including adequate food, clothing and housing and to the continuous improvement of living conditions. The States Parties will take appropriate steps to ensure the realisation of this right.

The UN Committee on Economic, Social and Cultural Rights, the body responsible for monitoring States parties' compliance with the obligations they have assumed under the Covenant on Economic, Social and Cultural Rights, has spelled out in some detail what is meant by the term "adequate housing". This must be affordable, habitable and accessible to disadvantaged groups. It should include security of tenure, availability of services, materials, facilities and infrastructure. Its location must allow access to employment, health care, schools, child care centres and other social facilities (United Nations Office of the High Commissioner for Human Rights, 1991).

Because provision is not for speculative profit in such non-market or rights-based approaches, housing is normally allocated by central or local government or by voluntary and charitable bodies. In some countries, there is also an important tradition of individual or community self-build models, and co-operative housing. In this way, the provision of housing also becomes a central element of a more holistic "development" process, not simply a contributor to economic growth, but containing positive actions to improve the broader quality of life and well-being for all (Todaro and Smith, 2005).

This approach does not of course rule out profit. The provision of homes would still be dominated by builders who make a "construction profit" but the speculative gains characteristic of a commodified system would be reduced or even eliminated (Barlow and Duncan, 1994). The question arises therefore as to whether housing policy should emphasise the concept of housing as a home and a right as opposed to a market commodity solely for profit, investment, speculation and wealth creation for an elite group.

In addition to this, however, it can be argued that we should place housing in a broader "development" framework. Obviously, people need homes, but their needs (and their demands) will not be met by the provision of housing alone. A better quality of life and well-being for all are the real measures of whether or not real development takes place in any society. These will be achieved only when, in addition to secure affordable dwellings appropriate to needs, a more comprehensive set of related needs and requirements are satisfied. These include access to appropriate employment opportunities, better education and lifelong learning, a high standard of health and nutrition, less poverty, greater equality, a cleaner environment as well as sufficient social and cultural amenities (Todaro and Smith, 2005). This broader development perspective is a prerequisite for good housing policy. It places the emphasis on "human development", "human rights", inclusiveness and sustainability.

Table 13.1 attempts to illustrate the implications of the above two opposing philosophies – one which sees housing as yet another market commodity and one which views housing as a home. Obviously, the different perspectives would lead to significantly different policy approaches.

Table 13.1: Housing as a Commodity or as a Home

Housing as a Commodity	Housing as a Home
• Market provision	• Non-market provision
• Commodity for sale	• Housing as a right for shelter
• Housing as an economic good	• Housing as a merit good
• Housing linked to ability to pay	• Housing linked to needs
• Developer/speculator profits	• Non profit or construction profit only
• Personal investment/ profit taking, wealth generation	• Home, community, shelter, etc.
• Speculative acquisition of land and capital gains; monopolies	• Public land banking for building and provision
• Segregation	• Integration

In the following section we examine the way in which housing provision in Ireland has changed from one with a strong emphasis on public (non-market) housing to one that is almost exclusively provided by the private (market) sector.

Housing Provision and Tenure

Market provision of housing – for profit by the private sector – has been afforded an increasingly dominant role in Ireland in recent decades, while public (non-market) provision has been greatly reduced. In the past, public provision had played a much more central role, including a substantial public intervention in rural housing from the end of the nineteenth century. At that time Ireland had one of the most significant state-subsidised housing programmes in Europe (Fraser, 1996; Fahey, 1998 and 1999). Moreover, after independence Local Authorities became increasingly important providers of housing in Dublin and other urban centres, producing good-quality residential environments (MacLaran, 1993; McManus, 2002). From 1932 to 1942 Local Authorities provided 49,000 units, representing 60 per cent of total housing output. During the Second World War period public provision represented 65 per cent of the housing total and was as high as 70 per cent in the year 1945/46 (Finnerty, 2002). Even during the early to the mid-1950s public provision always exceeded 50 per cent of the total new build. Most public housing schemes were built to a consistently high standard and quality.

Since the late 1950s, however, private provision, normally with state assistance, increased significantly, and by 1975 it represented 67 per cent of the total. Private provision increased further to 93 per cent in 2005 (See Table 13.2), leaving public provision at a mere 7 per cent of the total. This includes a minor role played by housing associations and voluntary bodies, whose contribution on a national basis dropped from 917 in 1996 to a mere 485 units in 1998, and only recovered to an annual average of 1,500 over the last three years (Department of Environment, Heritage and Local Government, 2006). In effect, non-market provision has been "residualised" over many years (Fahey, 1999; Galligan, 1999).

Table 13.2: Provision of Housing in Ireland

	"Market"	"Non-Market"
1975	18,000	8,800
	(67%)	(33%)
2005	75,398	5,559
	(93%)	(7%)

Source: Annual Housing Statistics Bulletins

Alongside the above movement towards a market-dominated system of provision, housing tenure has changed in a significant way in Ireland over the past few decades. Owning a home has been a long-held aspiration in Ireland and as far back as 1946 almost 53 per cent of households owned a home. As Table 13.3 shows, by 2002 this proportion had risen to 77 per cent – one of the highest rates of home ownership in Western Europe (Norris and Redmond, 2005). While this pre-occupation with home ownership may result to some extent from difficult historical experiences and a corresponding high regard for the security attached to property ownership, one of the main factors influencing the current high rate of owner-occupation has been a range of government incentives aimed almost exclusively at homeowners over the last four decades.

Table 13.3: Housing Tenure in Ireland, 1961-2002

	1961	1971	1981	1991	2002
			000's		
LA	124.6	112.6	111.8	98.9	88.2
PRS	116.3	96.7	90.3	81.4	141.5
O/O	404.6	499.7	667.0	808.4	990.7
Other	30.9	17.4	27.0	31.0	59.2
Total	676.4	726.4	896.1	1,019.7	1,279.6
			Per Cent		
LA	18.4	15.5	12.5	9.7	6.9
PRS	17.2	13.3	10.1	8.0	11.1
O/O	59.8	68.8	74.4	79.3	77.4
Other	4.6	2.4	3.0	3.0	4.6
Total	100.0	100.0	100.0	100.0	100.0

Source: Census of Population, 1961–2002

During most of this period, the proportion of accommodation provided for rent by private landlords declined significantly. The privately rented sector, which stood at 26 per cent of the total in 1946, had declined to only 8 per cent by 1991. This form of housing tenure expanded to almost 142,000 households by 2002 (an increase of 60,000 in a ten-year period), and now represents 11 per cent of the total. However, even if we take into account this recent growth, the Irish figure for privately rented accommodation is quite small compared to most countries in Western Europe or Scandinavia. For example, France, Portugal, and Sweden all have rates of 20 per cent or more, while Austria and Germany have 40 per cent and 51 per cent respectively.

The number of dwellings rented from Local Authorities in Ireland steadily increased up to 1961 but since then it has dropped consistently – from 125,000 in that year to 88,000 units in 2002. Consequently the local authority rental sector now represents a mere 7 per cent of total housing. The situation with public housing also varies considerably throughout Europe – from less than 3 per cent in Greece, Austria, Spain and Luxembourg to in excess of 20 per cent in the U.K., Denmark and Sweden, with a high of 35 per cent in the Netherlands (Norris and Shiels, 2004).

Owning a Home: The Problem of Affordability

As outlined earlier in the chapter, the price of housing in a market-oriented system is determined by the market forces of supply and demand. If there is excess demand (inadequate supply), such a system can create significant problems of affordability, especially for first time buyers. New house prices rose fairly consistently since 1974 with the major escalation only commencing after 1994/95. Second-hand house prices showed similar increases since then. The average new house price for which loans were approved for the country as a whole increased from €72,732 in 1994 to €276,221 in 2005 – an increase of 280 per cent. Over the same period, the average new house price in Dublin increased from €81,493 to €350,891 or 331 per cent. The average second-hand house price for the country as a whole increased from €69,877 in 1994 to €330,399 in 2005 – an increase of 373 per cent. Over the same period, the average second hand house price in Dublin increased from €82,772 to €438,790 or 430 per cent (see Tables 13.4 and 13.5). Most other urban centres throughout the country have also experienced significant increases, but the price gap between Dublin and other centres persists, making it particularly difficult to purchase a home in Dublin.

It is instructive to compare these house price increases with other commonly-used price indices. Up to 1994, new house prices increased broadly in line with the Consumer Price Index, house building costs (comprising labour and material costs) and average industrial earnings. Since 1994, however, house prices have diverged significantly from these other indices. Using a base of 1991 = 100, house building costs (labour and materials) increased from 111 in 1994 to 186 in 2005 or 68 per cent. The Consumer Price Index increased from 108 to 150 or 39 per cent. Over the same period, the index for new house prices for the country as a whole increased from 109 to 412, or 278 per cent. In other words, new house prices have increased about four times faster than house building costs and more than seven times faster than the consumer price index since 1994.

Table 13.4: New House Prices by Area, 1994-2005 (€)

	State	Dublin	Cork	Galway	Lim.	Waterf.	Other
1994	72,732	81,993	71,378	77,375	68,238	69,185	66,829
1995	77,994	86,671	76,608	87,783	73,348	69,950	71,829
1996	87,202	97,058	85,351	93,050	83,281	79,784	82,091
1997	102,222	122,036	96,046	109,905	91,077	91,608	94,664
1998	125,302	160,699	112,133	118,738	104,248	107,954	116,589
1999	148,521	193,526	141,007	138,928	121,880	132,050	136,970
2000	169,191	221,724	166,557	163,824	145,834	145,713	154,050
2001	182,863	243,095	174,550	171,161	152,205	155,488	166,834
2002	198,087	256,109	184,369	187,607	168,574	167,272	179,936
2003	224,567	291,646	211,980	223,388	197,672	195,173	203,125
2004	249,191	322,628	237,858	242,218	210,868	220,286	228,057
2005	276,221	350,891	265,644	274,905	226,393	246,914	254,006

Source: Housing Statistics Bulletin, various editions

Table 13.5: Second-Hand House Prices by Area, 1994-2005 (€)

	State	Dublin	Cork	Galway	Lim.	Waterf.	Other
1994	69,877	82,772	63,883	69,258	58,405	55,347	61,567
1995	74,313	88,939	70,796	78,370	61,099	59,409	64,170
1996	85,629	104,431	77,152	88,020	71,066	62,956	74,254
1997	102,712	131,258	88,535	100,791	78,256	73,308	86,347
1998	134,529	176,420	110,432	126,914	96,791	93,948	111,878
1999	163,316	210,610	139,473	147,152	119,072	115,768	135,096
2000	190,550	247,039	169,064	166,145	142,188	141,662	158,442
2001	206,117	267,939	179,687	189,713	157,176	155,242	177,203
2002	227,799	297,424	200,155	206,571	172,273	170,342	192,301
2003	264,898	355,451	240,444	249,404	201,477	201,871	218,061
2004	294,667	389,791	276,605	278,813	218,869	220,029	235,829
2005	330,399	438,790	307,007	317,811	232,271	252,765	263,653

Source: Housing Statistics Bulletin, various editions

How do these price increases compare with the situation in other countries? Drawing on an index of house prices drawn up by the *Economist* magazine in June 2005 we find that over the period 1997-2005, Ireland had the highest rate of price increase (192 per cent) of all the relatively developed countries examined. It was followed by Britain (154 per cent), Spain (145 per cent) and Australia (114 per cent). Most countries were well below these figures. For example, the United States, New Zealand and Canada increased by 73 per cent, 66 per cent and 47 per cent respectively. A number of countries even registered negative rates – house prices in Hong Kong fell by 43 per cent during the period examined, Japan by 28 per cent and Germany by 0.2 per cent. In the light of this survey, the *Economist* argued that Irish housing was significantly "overvalued" and it predicted a drop in house prices over the next few years. There is certainly little doubt that Irish house prices are out of line with normal inflationary tendencies as shown above.

Are the house prices described above affordable? One commonly-used measure is the ratio of average earnings to house prices. In 1984, the average price of a new home was €45,427, while the average industrial wage was €10,641, a ratio of 4.3 to 1. By 1994, the ratio had decreased slightly: average new house prices for the country as a whole (€72,732) were 4.2 times the size of the average industrial wage (€17,292). In Dublin, the ratio was 4.8. By 2005, however, the ratio of average new house prices to average industrial earnings (€30,020) had deteriorated to 9.2 to 1 for the country as a whole and 11.7 to 1 in Dublin.

A further indication of affordability can be gained from an examination of the incomes of borrowers. Official estimates show that those with a combined incomes of less than €30,000 account for a decreasing proportion of total lending – from 9.9 per cent in 1998 to 0.9 per cent in 2005. Even borrowers with incomes up to €50,000 have fallen from 66.3 per cent to 17.3 per cent of the total during this period. The typical borrowers have a combined income of more than €50,000, 36.9 per cent having between €50,000 and €70,000 and 43.8 per cent having incomes over €70,000 (Department of Environment, Heritage and Local Government, 2006). It is clear therefore that the vast majority of house purchasers are now in the higher income categories. Even these are increasingly taking on long-term mortgages of 35 years and more – a practice unheard of 20 years ago. Those on low incomes simply cannot enter this market at all.

The affordability problem is also illustrated by the growing extent of long-distance commuting. This is particularly obvious in the Dublin area where prices are highest, but it is also a problem in the other main urban centres. For example, large numbers of those working in the Dublin region who aspire to own a home at an affordable price have little option but to live within what estate agents loosely call "commuting distance of the capital". Therefore, the Dublin commuting zones now include adjoining counties of Meath, Wicklow and Kildare, but also counties further afield such as Wexford, Carlow, Kilkenny, Tipperary, Laois, Offaly, Westmeath, Longford, Cavan and Louth.

Long-distance commuting brings with it a range of serious economic and social implications. One of the most obvious is the increased direct costs of petrol and wear and tear, often involving two cars and several hours travel each day. A further direct cost is the extra time spent in travelling, often in excess of two hours each way. This extra time is rarely taken into consideration by those building and selling homes in outlying counties but it is a very real extra cost for those involved. Apart from such "private" costs accruing to individuals, a huge "social" cost is imposed on other road users in terms of increased traffic congestion, increased fuel consumption, pollution and frustration. Long-distance commuting is especially problematic for young working couples with children. It is now commonplace for couples to leave children in a local crèche, if available, from early morning until late evening. Alternatively, they must transport the children at an early hour to childcare facilities in or near their place of employment. If children are of school-going age, another challenge arises as population growth in such areas has invariably out-paced the provision of schools, recreational facilities and amenities. Until such schools and other facilities are provided (and this may take many years) parents must transport their children to schools in the city. Whichever option is chosen, the parents are denied access to, and enjoyment of, their children for long periods. The children are similarly without their parents during these periods. Without a doubt this situation represents a serious reduction in the quality of family life for all.

Perhaps the most critical measure of affordability is the inability to purchase a home at all. The officially accepted measure in recent years is a home whose loan repayments are no greater than 35 per cent of after-tax income (Government of Ireland, 2000a). Recent estimates carried out by the Local Authorities indicate that 33 per cent of new households (about 14,000 households each year) over the period 2001-2006 would not be able to afford to purchase a home. This figure rises to 42 per cent in urban areas and is as high as 51 per cent in Fingal County, 55 per cent in Dun Laoghaire/Rathdown and 65 per cent in Waterford City (Local Authorities, 2001/2002 and Punch et al., 2002).

The Causes of House Price Inflation

As pointed out earlier, Ireland's housing system has changed from one where not-for-profit provision by the state, based on the need for homes, was significant to one in which the market, influenced by demand (as opposed to need) has become the predominant influence on supply. Demand for housing, implying the ability to pay with one's own resources or through borrowing from lending institutions, is influenced by a range of factors. First, there are few alternatives to house purchase. The private rented sector, which we examine later, offers an expensive, insecure and often sub-standard alternative. As regards social housing, many individuals and families are above the relevant threshold and thus ineligible for such housing and, in any case, waiting lists are very long. The end result is excess demand for homes for sale, even by those who have considerable difficulty in purchasing.

Other factors influencing demand include the significant growth of population over recent decades, coupled with increased employment opportunities and incomes (see, for example, the work of Bacon et al. 1998; Roche, 2003; McQuinn, 2003). Demand has also been influenced by low interest rates over an extended period and the ready willingness of the lending institutions to make significant funding available to borrowers. Such flexible lending policies obviously push up demand and contribute significantly to house price increases. It has also resulted in a dramatic increase in housing indebtedness (a total of €57 billion over the period 1999-2003 alone) on the part of the Irish.

Lending institutions have also been prepared to give substantial loans for investment in housing to considerable numbers of people who view housing as an investment or speculative opportunity, even on a short-term basis. These groups have also been encouraged by a range of tax incentives over several decades, by the reduction in capital-gains tax to 20 per cent in 1997 and the rapid escalation in prices illustrated earlier. This has placed further upward pressure on house prices and has resulted in a significant displacement of aspiring first-time buyers in recent years. In a short period between 2001 and 2005, the proportion of first-time buyers of new homes fell from 63 per cent to 45 per cent for the country as a whole, with an even greater fall in the Dublin area (Department of Environment, Heritage and Local Government, 2006). In contrast, investors and holiday home owners increased from 37 per cent to 55 per cent for the country as a whole.

Government policies have, over many years, shown a heavy bias towards market provision of housing and to home owners, thus contributing to the escalation in house prices. The availability of mortgage interest tax relief, stamp duty remission and first-time buyer grants were intended to reduce the cost of housing for owner-occupiers and as such they proved popular political initiatives. In reality, however, with very few alternatives to house purchase, they ultimately contributed to increasing demand for market-driven housing and thus to higher house prices, creating an affordability problem even for relatively well-off purchasers (O'Connell and Quinn, 1999). The abolition of residential rates in 1978 and a property tax in 1997 (in force over the period since 1984) means that, apart from stamp duty which falls on purchasers, housing in Ireland, in contrast to many other European countries, is virtually free from taxation.

Despite the significant increase in housing provision in recent years, the supply has been inadequate to meet the sustained level of demand, leaving developers and builders in a strong position to charge "what the market will bear" and in many cases to secure "super-normal" profits achievable in monopoly-type situations. This is, in effect, what has happened over the last decade – the market has failed to supply sufficient housing to meet demand and to stabilise prices. From a consumer viewpoint, this is a fundamental flaw in the market mechanism.

What are these supply-side problems? One factor of central importance is the supply and availability, as well as the price, of land suitable
for housing (see, for example, McNulty, 2003; Roche, 2003). With a relatively fixed supply of land and excess demand, even for land zoned for
agricultural or amenity purposes and without planning permission, it is
inevitable that there will be an upward pressure on land prices. When
land is rezoned for housing and planning permission thus seems possible,
the price of land will rise further. Recent land sales indicate that the average proportion of a house price taken up by the price of land could be as
high as 40-50 per cent (Casey, 2003). These exceptional increases in the
price of land are invariably passed on to house purchasers in the form of
higher house prices.

There is evidence to suggest that land suitable for housing in some
parts of the country, and especially in the Dublin area, is controlled by a
relatively small number of landowners and developers. It has been shown
that over recent years about 25 major developers (many of them companies) have gained control over 50 per cent of land suitable for housing in
the Fingal County in the Dublin region (Casey, 2003). This small group
can effectively operate a monopoly-type influence on the availability and
price of land and, as a result, the price of housing. Of even greater concern is the part the Local Authorities play, often under duress, in further
enriching such landowners when, every five years or more often in some
cases, "in the interests of the common good", they re-zone agricultural
land for residential purposes – a further critical factor affecting supply.
The price of such land can multiply a hundred–fold overnight even
though the owners have carried out no productive activity whatsoever.
Over 30 years ago, a Committee under the Chairmanship of Mr Justice
Kenny made various proposals for policy change in order to deal with the
high cost of land (Kenny, 1973). More recently, an all-party Oireachtas
Committee again recommended similar policy changes (Government of
Ireland, 2004). No action has been taken to date.

A range of reports have made recommendations for change over the
past decade (e.g. Bacon, 1998; Downey, 1998; Drudy et al., 1999;
O'Sullivan, 1999; NESF, 2000; NESC, 2004). Since 1998 the Government has placed a considerable emphasis on increasing the supply of private housing (Government of Ireland, 1999 and 2000). It also accepted

the need to move more rapidly on the provision of serviced land for housing and agreed to increase the number of planning graduates with a view to reducing delays with planning permission. Mortgage interest relief was eliminated for investors for a short period, but under pressure from property interests was re-instated. A proposed anti-speculative tax was never introduced.

Since 1999, the government has also introduced various affordable housing schemes designed to provide housing for sale to low-income groups at a discount below the prices which could be obtained on the market. In 2005 a total of 2,800 homes were completed in the "affordable" for-sale category (Department of Environment, Heritage and Local government, 2006). The 2000 Planning Act also introduced the concept of Special Development Zones, the first of these which was subsequently designated at Adamstown in the Dublin region in order to "fast-track" the supply of housing. As a result of the same Act, the planning authorities produced a range of housing strategies over the period 2001-02 in which they proposed major rezoning of land for housing. As part of the *Sustaining Progress* agreement in 2002, the government also committed itself to providing an extra 10,000 "affordable" houses over the period to 2006. However, due to the slow progress with this proposal, the Government announced in August 2005 the establishment of an "Affordable Homes Partnership" in order to bring forward land and to speed up the provision of affordable housing for sale. A similar commitment was made to encourage the provision of "affordable" housing in the most recent Social Partnership Agreement, *Towards 2016*, in June 2006 (Department of the Taoiseach, 2006).

Private Rented Housing

For many years, there has been a generally negative image of renting from private landlords due to a perception of high rents, poor standards and insecurity of tenure. Private renting has therefore long been regarded by many as a short-term option before either purchasing a home or renting a less expensive one with greater security from a Local Authority. Despite the sector's negative image, there are many landlords who continue to provide good accommodation at reasonable rents and who offer secure homes for long periods to satisfied tenants. Furthermore, this sector can play a most important role in any housing system by providing accommodation for those who are either unwilling or unable to purchase and who cannot gain access to Local Authority housing, as well as for workers on short employment contracts and for students attending third level institutions. In recent years, it has also arguably fulfilled a useful role in providing accommodation for low-income groups eligible for government rent supplement.

Now a total of 141,500 units of accommodation, the private rented sector in Ireland had been in decline for many years. For example, in 1961 there were 116,000 units; this had declined to 81,000 by 1991. However, it showed a remarkable increase of 60,000 units by 2002, largely due to the availability of generous tax incentives (see Table 13.3). The vast majority of the units (115,600 units) are now furnished, with most still in detached, semi-detached or terraced housing. Almost 43 per cent of the accommodation is in flats/apartments and in the light of recent construction patterns, especially in the main urban centres, this is likely to be a more important element in the years ahead. The private rented sector accommodates a total of 343,000 people, two-thirds living in traditional housing and the remainder in flats/apartments. The largest concentration of private rented accommodation is in the Dublin area (38.8 per cent), followed by Cork, Galway and Limerick. A total of 60,500 units were built since 1980, while slightly more (62,000) were built prior to that date. Almost 44,000 units pre-date 1960 (Drudy and Punch, 2005).

At one level, the private rented sector has high-grade accommodation occupied in the main by high-income households (about 25 per cent of the total), including employees of multinational companies. A further section of accommodation is occupied by middle-class, relatively advantaged and educated salaried workers (about 56 per cent). These include a high proportion of younger households who cannot now purchase a home due to the significant price escalation described earlier. One unfortunate result of this trend is the "crowding-out" of disadvantaged households (Downey, 2003).

One of the most serious difficulties in the private rental sector, at least from the tenant viewpoint, have been the high level of rents and the uncertainty regarding future rent increases. Attempts to control or regulate rents have always met with opposition from landlord interests, while being applauded by tenants. It can be argued that any form of rent regulation will tend to put pressure on landlords who either neglect their rented properties or possibly dispose of them, thus reducing the supply of accommodation. This argument had a great deal of validity with regard to a rigid form of "first generation" rent control which existed in Ireland and throughout Europe and the United States for an extended period since 1915. However, since the 1970s rent regulation has taken the interests of both landlords and tenants into consideration and there is no evidence that such regulation has adverse effects (Arnott, 1995).

While rent regulation is now almost non-existent in Ireland, and the rights of property owners are given priority in the Irish Constitution, it is nevertheless important to note that Article 43.2.1 of the Constitution states that private property rights "ought to be regulated by the principles of social justice" and may be delimited by law in the interests of the "common good". The Constitution Review Group reporting in 1996 also argued that "the state must have a general capacity to regulate (and even in some cases extinguish) property rights" (Constitution Review Group, 1996).

An earlier study by O'Brien and Dillon (1982) identified the high level of rents and regular rent increases as causes of major concern to tenants. Security of tenure and the ease of eviction, as well as the poor standard of accommodation, were also primary concerns. In the absence of a lease or written agreement, the landlord at that time and until recently could take action for possession with only 28 days' notice irrespective of whether or not a breach of agreement took place.

Similar problems persist in recent times? For example, over the period 1998-2001, average rents in Dublin (the main location for private renting) increased by 53 per cent – far in excess of the consumer price index. A comparative study by the European Central Bank showed that the highest level of rent increases over the 1997-2001 period across the European Union was recorded in Ireland (European Central Bank, 2003). Rents fell over the period 2002 to 2004 but have been increasing again since 2005 (DAFT, 2005). One recent study suggested that one in five in the private rented sector exceeded the affordability limit (Fahey, Nolan and Maitre, 2004). Many tenants therefore regard the private rented sector as a "tenure of last resort" (McCashin, 2000) and are encouraged to get into home ownership or Local Authority and Housing Association accommodation if at all possible.

Under legislation since the early 1990s, landlords are obliged to ensure that rented houses or apartments comply with health and safety legislation and with a range of "minimum standards" relating to such items as structural repair, sanitary facilities, heating, electrical and gas fittings and equipment. However, in 1998, five years after the enactment of legislation on standards, 2,710 units or 53 per cent of those inspected, did not meet minimum standards. The most recent available data for 2005 showed that 2,048 units (30 per cent of those inspected) were in breach of regulations (Department of Environment, Heritage and Local Government, 2006). If this sample is representative, it would imply that (assuming the 60,000 units built since 1991 are in compliance) over 24,000 units in the private rental system do not meet the minimum standards. Furthermore, Local Authorities have been slow in enforcing the legislation. In 1998, no case was taken although 2,710 units were in breach of regulations. Even by the end of 2005 only 11 cases of enforcement were initiated.

Apart from safety considerations, much of the private rental accommodation – even the new units – can be regarded as unsatisfactory in terms of size, overall quality and suitability for families and children. Kelly and MacLaran (2004) show that 91 per cent of apartments contained only one or two bedrooms and were lacking in terms of storage space and play areas for children.

The Commission on Private Rental and New Legislation

In view of widespread concern over many years regarding the difficulties in the private rented sector, the government established a Commission in 1999 to examine concerns regarding security of tenure of tenants, the rights and obligations of landlords and tenants, and to make recommendations on how the sector might be developed further (Commission on the Private Rented Residential Sector, 2000). The Commission report offers an interesting view of the different philosophies of landlords and tenants. Core issues such as giving a right to tenants to continue in occupation for an extended period, with some certainty regarding rent levels, proved most difficult. The report of the Commission was, therefore, "the result of much compromise between the various interests".

The Residential Tenancies Act, 2004 largely reflected the majority view of the Commission. The Act specifies that a landlord can terminate a tenancy without giving a reason, during the first six months. After this a tenant can normally remain in occupation for a further three and a half years. However, a landlord can terminate a tenancy during this latter period for a range of specified grounds such as failure by the tenant to comply with their obligations under the tenancy, proposed sale of the dwelling, occupation by the landlord or a member of their family or substantial refurbishment. While an improvement on the existing situation, these loopholes would seem to provide relatively easy methods to secure an eviction if a landlord so wishes, so that security of tenure is more apparent than real.

The Act specifies that the rent payable by a tenant shall be the "market rent" agreed between landlord and tenant, and rent shall be reviewed no more than once per annum, unless a substantial refurbishment has occurred (2004 Act, Sections 19-20). There is thus virtually no rent regulation and, with an inadequate supply, this puts landlords in a strong negotiating position. Furthermore, there is no formal provision for regulating the extent of rent increases which is a central element of modern "second generation" rent regulation in Europe and the United States. The typical rental contract in the EU includes an indexation clause linked to the consumer price index. Germany, for example, only allows increases in rents of sitting tenants up to a maximum of 20 per cent over three years (European Central Bank, 2003).

One of the most important initiatives in the 2004 Act was the establishment of the Private Rental Tenancies Board recommended by the Commission. Although the Board only commenced its work in 2005, its potential is enormous in relation to resolving disputes regarding the so-called "market rents", standards of accommodation, security of tenure and return of deposits. Whether the Board has the resources and determination to deal with the undoubted challenges in the private rented sector remains to be seen.

In recent years the private rental sector has become an alternative form of public housing with the widespread use of a rent supplement paid by the Department of Social and Family Affairs. Originally, rent supplement was meant to be a means of income support to provide immediate and short-term assistance with unmet needs. However, it has become, almost by default, a mainstream housing income support for low income families. The cost of accommodation being subsidised under the scheme has also increased considerably over the years from €7.8 million in 1989 to €370 million in 2005 (Department of Social and Family Affairs, 2005). Rent supplement is now being phased out and is being replaced by a new Residential Accommodation Scheme. This is an attempt to secure more long-term accommodation in the private rented sector for those on low incomes, but the question arises as to whether such an arrangement represents good value for money in comparison with the provision of more public housing.

Housing Need: The Poor Relation?

In view of the difficulties outlined above it is inevitable that many people are in "housing need". These people lack the resources to purchase or rent homes on the market. Assessments of housing need are carried out by Local Authorities every three years. In 1993 it was estimated that the total number of households in housing need was 28,624. By 2002 this figure had risen to 48,413 but in 2005 had fallen to 43,700. There is much debate regarding whether real housing need is greater or less than these estimates. There are, however, a number of reasons why the most recent (2005) official figure of 43,700 families in housing need (which includes the "homeless" category) may under-estimate the number who actually require housing but are not in a position to either purchase or rent at an affordable price. In addition to this official estimate, there are two further important categories of need which must be taken into account. First, Local Authority estimates show that, in the case of one-third of new households formed in Ireland each year housing is, in effect, "unaffordable". This amounts to about 14,000 new households each year. Second, about 58,000 households were receiving rent supplement for accommodation in the private rented sector in 2004 and 43,500 of these were not on the official waiting list. This latter number of households can therefore also be defined as being in "housing need". Putting the three categories together, we get a total of 101,200 households or about 236,000 people.

A number of groups in housing need face particular difficulties. For example, the number of homeless doubled between 1993 and 2005 despite a range of initiatives designed to tackle this problem. Similarly, in 2003 over 1,600 Traveller families (38 per cent of the total) were in unsatisfactory accommodation, 788 of these on unauthorized sites without washing or sanitary facilities. People with intellectual disabilities also fare badly. Large numbers still live at home with elderly parents, almost 400 are inappropriately accommodated in psychiatric hospitals and there is a requirement for over 2,000 extra accommodation places by 2010.

In response to this need, the record of public provision over the period since 1994 has been rather weak. Local Authority provision is made up of newly-built houses and those acquired at market prices. The gross gain in the Local Authority stock (built and bought at market prices) over the last eleven years was 48,380 homes or an average of 4,031 each year. However, this gain was counteracted by the sales of 19,547 (1,629 each year) Local Authority houses to sitting tenants at a significant discount. The net gain was thus only 28,833 homes or an average of 2,403 each year since 1994.

A range of philanthropic bodies and housing associations, acting in co-operation with the Local Authorities and with government funding, have been active for some years in building houses for rent. For most of the period above they provided less than 1,000 homes each year, but with increased support from government this rose to an average of 1,500 over the past three years. In summary, Local Authorities and housing associations between them have provided an average net increase of 3,400 homes per annum over the last decade – a modest performance in view of the large housing need illustrated earlier. It seems clear that a low priority has been given over recent years to non-market housing provision, and some Local Authorities increasingly see themselves as "enablers" or "facilitators" of provision by the market rather than direct providers.

The Problem of Segregation

Over many years Local Authority housing has been heavily concentrated in particular geographical areas. This is particularly obvious in the main urban centres and on the periphery where some estates contain up to 90 per cent Local Authority mainly low-income tenants. Furthermore, such areas often suffer very high rates of unemployment, low levels of educational achievement, drug abuse, poor physical infrastructure and facilities and insufficient attention to estate management and tenant involvement. The "surrender grant" of the 1980s (designed to encourage tenants to purchase homes elsewhere) had the adverse effect of denuding Local Authority estates of those who were employed on relatively high incomes and their replacement with low-income families, thus contributing further to residualisation and segregation.

Such segregation is inevitable since access to this tenure is confined to the most marginalised families. As argued earlier, it is also apparent that segregation is an integral element in a market-driven housing system. In this market model, access and housing choice depend on ability to pay. As a result, the poorest groups have the least choice and end up in the least desirable locations, while the richest can access the more exclusive areas, where house prices are highest and there is strong expectation of steady future increases.

Part V of the Planning and Development Act (Government of Ireland, 2000) was an attempt to deal with this problem. The aim of the legislation was to provide for the future housing requirements of the population and to avoid "undue segregation". The Act required that Local Authorities could require the provision of up to 20 per cent of any residential development for "social and affordable housing" as a condition of planning permission. It may be noted that this was, in fact, a market-oriented mechanism, insofar as it depended largely on the co-operation of private developers. This meant that, rather than direct provision by the Local Authorities, the provision of social and affordable housing remained dependent on reaching agreement with private developers. Under pressure from building interests, the provisions were significantly diluted by the Minister for the Environment, Heritage and Local Government in late 2002. The amendments meant that developers could, in effect, avoid implementing the 20 per cent requirement in a variety of ways.

In any case, the operation of Part V to date has been disappointing, producing only 217 social housing units (for rent) and 374 affordable ones (for sale at a discount) over the period 2000 to 2004 (Department of the Environment, Heritage and Local Government, 2005). This policy may be more successful in the future. However, it is hardly surprising that an attempt to deal with segregation with the co-operation of profit-driven private developers would have a weak impact. A housing paradigm which relies heavily on market-driven mechanisms to achieve social policy aims must inevitably face such difficulties.

Conclusions

While much progress has been made in Ireland in relation to the provision and standard of housing in recent years, a number of difficulties and challenges remain. In particular, housing policy in Ireland over recent years has been under-pinned by a dominant paradigm, which has placed enormous emphasis on market provision and downgraded the role of the state. In effect, this has led to the commodification of what should be treated as an important social good, like health or education. The almost exclusive reliance on "the market" as a provider has influenced many to see housing as a means of speculation and wealth creation rather than as a shelter, a home and a fundamental human right. It has also resulted in escalating house prices and rents, a high level of personal debt and a poor record in dealing with housing need.

There is a strong case therefore for a fundamental change of direction to ensure that every person has affordable, secure, good quality accommodation appropriate to their needs. In concluding, I would suggest a number of key principles if this is to be achieved:

- Housing should be treated as a social good, rather than as a commodity for trading or wealth generation. Housing policies should clearly reflect this principle.

- Housing is a fundamental economic and social need; everyone should have a right to housing which is affordable and appropriate to needs. The right to housing should be established in legislation in line with signed international covenants and agreements.

- Since land is a fundamental requirement in relation to housing provision and co-ordinated planning, the state should have a long-term strategy of land acquisition in order to meet at a reasonable price the needs of both market and non-market providers, and to ensure that the necessary social infrastructure and amenities are made available without delay.

Arising from these principles, a range of policy changes would be necessary to deal with the difficulties facing those attempting to purchase or rent homes on the market.

There is also a particularly urgent need for an expanded construction programme of public housing by all non-profit providers – including Local Authorities, housing associations, co-operatives and other voluntary and community development organizations. Furthermore, there is a strong case for broadening the base of public housing provision as has happened in other European countries in order to give it the status it deserves, to place it in competition with the private market and to address the problem of segregation. This would involve a new role for public/ social housing in providing "general needs" housing for the large numbers who cannot afford the current house prices as well as for its traditional clients. The financial surplus generated from renting to middle-income residents could cross-subsidise the costs of providing housing for poorer households.

References

Arnott, P. (1995) "Time for Revisionism on Rent Control?" *The Journal of Economic Perspectives* 9 (1), pp. 99-120.

Bacon, P. and Associates (1998) *An Economic Assessment of Recent House Price Developments* Dublin: Report to the Minister for Housing and Urban Renewal.

Barlow, J., and Duncan, S. (1994) *Success and Failure in Housing Provision: European Systems Compared*, Oxford: Pergamon Press.

Casey, J. (2003) "An Analysis of Economic and Marketing Influences on the Construction Industry", *Building Industry Bulletin*, Dublin

Commission on the Private Rented Residential Sector (2000) *Report of the Commission on the Private Rented Residential Sector,* Dublin: Stationery Office.

Connolly, Jerome (1998) *Re-Righting the Constitution: The Case for New Social and Economic Rights,* Dublin: Irish Commission for Justice and Peace.

Constitution Review Group (1996) *Report*, Dublin: Stationery Office.

CORI (2005), *Policy Briefing: Housing and Accommodation*, Dublin: CORI Justice Commission.

CPSU and SIPTU (1998) *Affordable Accommodation: A Trade Union Issue and Human Right,* Dublin: CPSU and SIPTU.

DAFT (2005), see report at www.daft.ie

Department of An Taoiseach (2006), *Towards 2016: Ten Year Framework Social Partnership Agreement,* Dublin: Stationery Office.

Department of Social, Community and Family Affairs (2005) *Statistical Report on Social Welfare Services,* Dublin: Stationery Office.

Department of the Environment & Local Government (2006) *Annual Housing Statistics Bulletin 2005* (Dublin: Stationery Office).

Downey, D. (1998) *New Realities in Irish Housing,* (Dublin, CRUBE, Dublin Institute of Technology).

Downey, D. (2003), "Affordability and Access to Irish Housing", *Journal of Irish Urban Studies,* Vol. 2, No. 1, pp. 1-24.

Drudy, P.J. et al. (1999) *Housing: A New Approach, Report of the Housing Commission,* Dublin: Irish Labour Party.

Drudy, P.J. and Punch, M. (2001) "Housing and Inequality in Ireland", in: S. Cantillon, C. Corrigan, P. Kirby and J. O'Flynn (Eds) *Rich and Poor: Perspectives on Inequality in Ireland*, Dublin: Oak Tree Press.

Drudy, P.J. and Punch, M (2002) "Housing Models and Inequality: Perspectives on Recent Irish Experience", *Housing Studies*, 17 (4), pp. 657-672.

Drudy, P.J. and Punch, M. (2005), *Out of Reach: Inequalities in the Irish Housing System*, Dublin: TASC at New Island.

European Central Bank (2003) *Structural Factors in EU Housing Markets*, Brussels: ECB.

Fahey, T., (1998) "Housing and Social Exclusion" in Healy, S. and Reynolds, B. (Eds), *Social Policy in Ireland*, Dublin: Oak Tree Press, pp. 285-302.

Fahey, T. (Ed.) (1999) *Social Housing in Ireland: A Study of Success, Failure and Lessons Learned*, Dublin: Oak Tree Press.

Fahey, T., Nolan, B. and Maitre, B. (2004), *Housing, Poverty and Wealth in Ireland*, Dublin: Institute of Public Administration.

Finnerty J., (2002) "Homes for the Working Class? Irish Public House-building Cycles, 1945-2001", *Saothar: Journal of Irish Labour History*, Vol. 27, pp. 65-71.

Fitzgerald, E. and Winston, N. (2005), "Housing, Equality and Inequality", in Norris M. and Redmond, D. (Eds) *Housing Contemporary Ireland,* Dublin: Institute of Public Administration.

Fraser, M. (1996) *John Bull's Other Homes: State Housing and British Policy in Ireland, 1883-1922,* Liverpool: Liverpool University Press.

Galligan, Y. (1999) "Housing policy in Ireland: Continuity and change in the 1990's", in: N. Collins (Ed.) *Issues in Irish Politics,* Manchester: Manchester University Press.

Government of Ireland (1999) *Action on House Prices*, Dublin: Government Information Office.

Government of Ireland (2000) *Action on Housing*, Dublin: Government Information Office.

Government of Ireland (2000a) *Planning and Development Act, 2000,* Dublin: Stationery Office.

Government of Ireland (2004), *Ninth Progress Report: Private Property*, Dublin: Stationery Office.

Healy, S. and Reynolds, B. (2006), "Progress and Policy: The Need for a New Paradigm", in Healy, S., Reynolds, B. and Collins, M.L. (eds.), *Social Policy in Ireland*, Dublin: The Liffey Press (Chapter 1, present volume).

Kenny, Justice (1973) *Report of the Committee on the Price of Building Land,* Dublin: Stationery Office.

Kelly, S. and MacLaran, A. (2004) "The Residential Transformation of Inner Dublin", in: Drudy, P.J. and MacLaran, A. (Eds) *Dublin: Economic and Social Trends, Volume 4,* Dublin: Centre for Urban and Regional Studies.

Kenna, P. (2002) "A Right to Housing: Is It More than a Mere Right to Shelter in Market Societies like Ireland?", in: Punch, M. and Buchanan, L. (Eds) *Housing Rights: A New Agenda?* Dublin: Threshold and the Centre for Urban and Regional Studies.

Lee, P., and Murie, A. (1997) *Poverty, Housing Tenure and Social Exclusion,* Bristol: The Policy Press.

Lee, P., et al. (1995) *The Price of Social Exclusion,* London: National Federation of Housing Associations.

Local Authorities (2001/02), *Housing Strategies.*

MacLaran, A. (1993) *Dublin: The Shaping of a Capital,* London: Belhaven Press.

McCashin, A. (2000) *The Private Rented Sector in the 21st Century: Policy Choices,* Dublin: Threshold & St. Pancras Housing Association

McQuinn, K. (2004), *A Model of the Irish Housing Sector*, Dublin: Central Bank of Ireland

McManus, R. (2002) *Dublin, 1910-1940: Shaping the City and Suburbs*, Dublin: Four Courts Press.

McNulty, P (2003), "The Emergence of a Housing Affordability Gap", *Journal of Irish Urban Studies,* Vol. 2, No. 1, pp. 83-90.

National Economic and Social Council (2004), *Housing in Ireland: Performance and Policy,* Dublin: National Economic and Social Council.

National Economic and Social Forum, (2000), *Social and Affordable Housing and Accommodation*, Dublin: NESF.

Norris, M. and Shiels, P. (2004) *Regular National Report on Housing Developments in European Countries: Synthesis Report,* Dublin: Department of the Environment, Heritage and Local Government.

Norris, M. and Redmond, D. (Eds) (2005), *Housing Contemporary Ireland*, Dublin: Institute of Public Administration.

O'Brien, L. M. and Dillon, B. (1982) *Private Rented – The Forgotten Sector*, Dublin: Threshold.

O'Connell, T. and Quinn, T. (1999) "Recent Property Price Developments: An Assessment", *Central Bank of Ireland, Bulletin*, Dublin: Central Bank of Ireland.

O'Sullivan, E. (1999) *National Report on Housing in Ireland,* Brussels: FEANTSA.

Punch, M., Hickey, C., Buchanan, L, and Bergin, E. (2002), *Housing Access for All? An Analysis of Housing Strategies and Homeless Action Plans,* Dublin: Focus Ireland, Simon Communities of Ireland, St. Vincent de Paul, Threshold.

Roche, M. (2003) "Will there be a Crash in House Prices"?, *ESRI Quarterly Economic Commentary,* pp. 57-72.

Threshold (2002), *Strategic Plan,* Dublin: Threshold.

Todaro, Michael and Smith, Stephen (2005), *Economic Development*, London: Pearson Education

United Nations Office of the High Commissioner for Human Rights (1991) *The Right to Adequate Housing*, General Comment No. 4, Geneva: United Nations.

Chapter 14

HEALTH POLICY IN IRELAND

Eamon O'Shea *and* **Patrick Gillespie**

This chapter explores the nature and production of health in Ireland and sets out a potential framework for health policy decision making in the future. We reframe the definition of health from that of a simple state of well-being to a dynamic variable which can have a major impact on the economy, but only if, in return, the influence of the economy on health is also recognised. This influence occurs on both the supply side and the demand side of the economy. At present, health care is seen as the primary determinant of health with vast resources dedicated to advancing technological responses to individual health problems. There is much less emphasis on the economic and social determinants of health which, if addressed, could lead to an overall increase in aggregate health and a reduction in health inequalities across socio-economic groups. The latter is the most serious health issue facing the country today but rarely features in current policy debates which, instead, have focused on access to hospital beds as the most pressing problem in the health sector. This is so only if one considers illness as the goal of health policy, which is, of course, ludicrous and the opposite of what a credible health policy is about.

The chapter is organised as follows. The first section outlines the basic theoretical model, a framework which is used to organise our analysis. Health is examined as both an input and an output of economic and social development. In the second section the effectiveness and efficiency of the health care system are considered. This is followed by a discussion of equity in its many forms. Health policy in Ireland is then briefly considered. In the final section we outline a potentially new approach for Ireland focusing on equality of opportunity for health. We argue for the reorientation of Irish health policy away from the current health care dominated technological approach to an integrated intersectoral health determinants model.

Conceptual Framework

Health as defined by the World Health Organisation (WHO) is "a complete state of physical, mental and social well-being and not simply the absence of disease or infirmity" (WHO, 1946). The remit of health policy is surely to ensure that every individual in society has the opportunity to achieve this broad state of health, their most basic human right. To explore how this might be achieved we adopt a theoretical model which charts the role of health in society and incorporates the various socio-economic factors that determine health. The model can be viewed as a production function, an economic concept, within which health is an important input and output. Health, in various forms, enters on both sides of this equation. First, health plays an important role in the production of goods and services, economic growth and social progress. Second, many interacting factors combine to produce a level of health within society.

The model, which is incorporated from work by Suhrcke et al. (2005), is outlined in Figure 14.1. We argue that this is an appropriate framework for public policy decisions which involve a health dimension. The underlying components of the model are evident from the diagram. The right-hand side describes the role of health as an input in the production of important individual and macroeconomic outcomes. The left-hand side of the model describes the various interacting factors which combine to produce individual and population health, only one of which is health care.

Figure 14.1: An Economic Model of Health Production

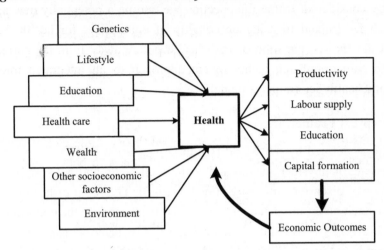

Source: Suhrcke et al (2005)

Health as an Input

The 2001 *Health Strategy: Quality and Fairness – A Health System for You* emphasised the need to view health expenditure as an investment which not only has the potential to contribute to societal well-being but also to overall economic development (Department of Health and Children, 2001). Suhrcke et al. (2005) identify four "channels of influence" in which health can potentially generate such economic outcomes. An individual's level of health can influence each of the following.

- **Productivity**. Healthier individuals could reasonably be expected to produce more per hour worked. On the one hand, productivity could increase directly due to enhanced physical and mental activity. On the other hand, more physically and mentally active individuals could also make better and more efficient use of technology, machinery or equipment.

- **Labour Supply**. The impact of health on labour supply is theoretically ambiguous. Good health obviously reduces the number of individual sick days, which results in an increase in the number of healthy days available for either work or leisure. The decision to dedicate these additional healthy days to work or leisure activities depends on the individual. The individual's preferences for additional wages will compete for their preferences for leisure and free time. If good health changes neither preferences nor wages, but raises life expectancy, lifetime consumption would increase, thereby leading to an increase in the supply of goods and services to meet additional demand.

- **Education**. According to human capital theory, more educated individuals are more productive. Since children with better health and nutrition tend to achieve higher educational attainment and suffer less from school absenteeism and early drop-out, improved health in early ages indirectly contributes to future productivity.

- **Capital Formation — Savings and Investment**. The state of health of an individual or a population is likely to impact not only upon the level of income but also the distribution of this income between savings and consumption and the willingness to undertake investment. Individuals in good health are likely to have a longer time horizon and therefore a higher savings ratio than that of individuals in poor health. Higher levels of savings provide funds for investment in physical or intellectual capital.

The net result of these individual impacts will ultimately produce economic outcomes at the aggregate or macroeconomic level. This conceptual framework is based on sound theoretical and empirical evidence. Economic growth refers to the steady process by which the productive capacity of the economy is increased over time to bring about rising levels of national output and income (Todaro, 2000). It is a desirable objective as it can potentially improve the welfare of society as a whole. According to neoclassical economic theory, economic growth depends on three factors: the stock of capital, the stock of labour and productivity which, in turn, depends on technological progress.

Much debate has centred on how public policy can generate economic growth. Becker (1964) formalised the theory that investments in human capital or skilled labour, through education, training and health, have merit as they can potentially raise productivity levels. There is much empirical evidence to support the importance of human capital for economic growth with education singled out as the key component of human capital (Denison, 1985; Griffin and McKinley, 1992; Fogel, 1994).

The integral role that health plays in human capital formation was first addressed by Michael Grossman (1972) when he developed a model for the demand for health. Health is distinguished into two categories: health as a consumption good and health as a capital good. As a consumption good, health enters directly into the utility function of the individual, as people enjoy being healthy. As a capital good, health reduces the number of days spent ill, and therefore increases the number of days available for both market and non-market activities. It follows, therefore, that if health is an important component of human capital, then health will matter for economic outcomes. The empirical evidence confirms the positive relationship between health and economic outcomes. Health, measured as life expectancy, has been shown to be a sizeable predictor of subsequent economic growth in virtually all studies that have examined growth differences between poor and rich countries (Barro, 1996; Sachs and Warner, 1997; Bloom and Williamson, 1998). Disability days lost and years of potential life lost damages both the economy and society.

This analysis provides important implications for public policy. Specifically, policy-makers interested in improving economic outcomes would have good reason to consider health investment as one of their options by which to meet their economic objectives. Furthermore, public policy decisions which influence population health should attempt to incorporate the value of the potential economic impact. The debate on health care in Ireland has focused almost exclusively on the consumption benefits of health care, with little or no reference to the investment effects in terms of increased output.

Health as an Output

As illustrated in the left-hand side of Figure 14.1, health is produced by many factors including genetic endowments, lifestyle, living and working conditions and more general socioeconomic, cultural and environmental conditions (Suhrcke et al., 2005). The significance of economic factors for health is reflected by the arrow from "economic outcomes" back to "health". Economic outcomes can influence health in two ways: firstly, through the direct effect on the material conditions of people's lives that have a positive impact on survival and health, and secondly, through an effect on social participation, the opportunity to control life circumstances and the feeling of security (Marmot, 2002). Ultimately, individual and population health depends on the interaction of these factors. It follows that the scope of health policy should extend across all of the important determinants of health. In order to develop an effective health system, the determinants of health, that is, the social, environmental and cultural factors which influence health, must be taken into account.

Material and structural conditions matter for health. The effect of income inequality on health reflects a combination of negative exposures and lack of resources held by individuals, along with systematic under-investment across a wide range of physical, health and social infrastructure (Lynch, Due, Muntaner and Davey Smith, 2000; Black Report, 1980). Societies that tolerate a more unequal distribution of income are likely to care less about public investment in human, physical, health and social infrastructure. As the rich get richer they use their own money to invest in human capital formation. At the same time, they become increasingly reluctant to support public spending, health care expenditure and welfare provision that benefits the whole of society. This under-investment adversely affects individual and aggregate health by reducing the economic and social resources available to individuals as well as undermining the health care system.

Income inequality may not only affect an individual's economic and social environment, but may also affect the individual directly, bringing with it feelings of hopelessness, lack of control and loss of respect. These emotions are thought to influence health through their effect on stress levels. Wilkinson (1996) argued that income inequality affects health through perceptions of place in the social hierarchy based on relative position according to income. Such perceptions are thought to produce negative emotions such as shame and distrust that are translated "inside" the body into poorer health via psycho-neuroendocrine mechanisms and stress-induced behaviours such as smoking. This argument is often supported by recourse to evolutionary theory. For most of our evolutionary history, humans lived in societies that were egalitarian. Assuming that human health is maximised when we live under the conditions that have been beneficial to our evolution, inequalities, when and where they arise, are likely to be a hazard for our health (Deaton, 2001).

Increased income inequality may also reduce social cohesion, which in turn negatively impacts on health. As the distance between the rich and the poor widens, social cohesion begins to breakdown. The extent and form of social capital within communities may also be adversely affected by income inequality. Social capital has been defined as those features of social organisation – such as the extent of interpersonal trust between citizens, norms of reciprocity and voluntary group membership – that facilitate co-operation for mutual benefit. Inequality is a barrier to the development of health-inducing social relations and for that reason investment in appropriate social capital should be a key strategy for public health (Wilkinson, 2000). Social networks furnish tangible assistance, such as money and informal care, and may also encourage health-improving behaviour (Putnam, 2000, p. 327). The difficulty for researchers is generating cross-country measures of social capital that incorporate these various effects. Individual-level studies may be much better at generating this data than are population-based cross-country studies (Kennelly et al., 2003).

There is a growing appreciation in the public policy arena of the role that non-health care factors play in the determination of health. The National Anti-Poverty Strategy highlights the important link between poverty and health. Poverty limits access to affordable health care and reduces the opportunity for those living in poverty to adopt healthy lifestyles (WHO, 2002). However, while there is good evidence that income and health are strongly associated in any cross-section analysis (see Deaton, 2003, for a recent review of the economic literature), the causal mechanisms are far from understood and detailed life-cycle exploration and institutional analysis are required to establish the precise relationships. For example, Van Doorslaer and Koolman (2004) have found significant health and health care utilisation inequalities in all European countries with the scale and scope of inequality associated with the way each society treats its non-active portion of the working age population, in terms of both income protection and health protection.

The Irish Health Care System

Although it is clear that many health-enhancing factors can be influenced by public policy, Ireland has focused almost exclusively on health care services as the solution to health problems in the country. This raises the general question as to the contribution of health care systems to health. The impact of "curative medical measures" is said to have had little effect on mortality decline prior to the mid-twentieth century (Colgrove, 2002). Since then, however, the scope and quality of health care have changed almost beyond recognition. Nolte and McKee (2004) found that improvements in access to effective health care had a measurable impact on mortality decline in many countries during the 1980s and 1990s and confirm the potential for investment in health care services to improve population health outcomes, particularly when existing provision is weak.

There is less agreement that spending more and more on health care leads to better overall population health, including longer life expectancy and reduced overall mortality. The United States, with higher health care spending than any other country, is closer to "flat of the curve" medicine than other countries, in the sense that additional spending on health care is less likely to produce increases in health outcomes (Phelps, 2003). International data show far more association between life expectancy, mortality and the income level of countries than with health system categorisation and health care expenditure (McPake et al., 2002), Not surprisingly, therefore, in many developed countries, the health policy debate is no longer concerned with the amount of money being invested in health care each year, but instead by the manner in which this money is being invested and for whom. A major problem with health care expenditure in Ireland is the almost complete absence of evaluation of outcomes, making it difficult to determine which programmes should be funded and for whom.

Total expenditure on health care in Ireland amounted to 8.1 per cent of Gross Domestic Product (GDP) in 2002; 6.6 per cent of which is accounted for by public expenditure (Gross-Tebbe and Figueras, 2004). This is low in a comparative context, but such comparisons may be misleading due to the strong economic performance of the Irish economy in recent years. For example, when per capita health care expenditure is estimated, Ireland rank eighth of fifteen OECD countries (Table 14.1).

Table 14.1: Total Expenditure on Health per Capita US $ PPP (Public and Private)

Country	2002 ($)	Rank
Austria	2,220	9
Belgium	2,515	7
Denmark	2,580	5
Finland	1,943	12
France	2,736	3
Germany	2,817	2
Greece	1,814	13
Ireland	**2,367**	**8**
Italy	2,166	10
Luxembourg	3,065	1
Netherlands	2,643	4
Portugal	1,702	14
Spain	1,646	15
Sweden	2,517	6
UK	2,160	11

Source: OECD Health Data 2004

Expenditure on health care services in Ireland increased significantly throughout the 1990s. The most recent OECD estimate indicates that Irish health care spending per capita in 2002 measured at 102 per cent of the EU 15 per capita average, which is in contrast with the situation in 1990 when Irish per capita health expenditure was about 60 per cent of the EU average. Reviewing the Department of Health and Children Statistics provides further insight into increases in expenditure levels. Between 1990 and 2000, health expenditure increased by 180 per cent in current terms and by 79 per cent in real terms (1995 prices). While there was a steady increase in health expenditure through the early 1990s, it is from 1996 onwards that the rate of health expenditure began to rise sharply. Health expenditure in current terms increased by 59 per cent between 1990 and 1996 compared to an increase of 157 per cent from 1996 and 2002. Similarly, health expenditure in real terms increased by 23 per cent in the period 1990-1996 compared with an increase of 86 per cent from 1996 to 2002.

The general hospitals programme is the largest single programme accounting for approximately half of total health care expenditure. While spending on this programme declined as a share of total health care expenditure between 1990 and 2002, hospital expenditure actually increased in real terms by 285 per cent during this period (Nolan, 2005). The remaining components are, in order of expenditure, the community health services programme (which includes expenditure on primary care services), the programme for the handicapped, the community welfare programme (which mainly includes cash grants for those incapacitated for work), the psychiatric programme, the general support programme and the community protection programme (which mainly includes expenditure on the prevention of infectious diseases, food hygiene standards and health promotion). There is evidence of a small change in the distribution of expenditure away from in-patient care (general, long-stay and psychiatric hospitals) into community-based services (Nolan, 2005). However, pay and technology in the acute sector remain two of the key elements of overall expenditure in the health care system.

Effectiveness

Given the significant investment in health care in Ireland in recent years, particularly in respect of spending on hospitals, it is pertinent to examine the effect of this spending on individual and aggregate health. How has this spending impacted on life expectancy, infant mortality and perinatal mortality in Ireland? Life expectancy for males in Ireland was 75.2 years in 2002, up from 70.1 years in 1980-82. For females, life expectancy at birth increased from 75.6 years in 1980-82 to 80.3 years in 2002. Infant mortality rates declined by one-third during the period 1980 to 2001, while perinatal mortality also declined during the same period, but only by 2.2 per cent (Department of Health and Children, 2003).

Despite these improvements, Irish people have one of the lowest life expectancies of all the EU 15 countries for both males and females. Similarly, at age 65, life expectancy of 14.3 years for men is below the EU 15 average of 15.8 years, while for women the EU average of 19.8 years at the age of 65 is also higher than the 17.9 years estimated for Irish women (Department of Health and Children, 2003). Ireland has the third highest infant mortality rate in the EU-15 (Eurostat, 2003). Mortality rates in Ireland are worse than the EU average for a range of illnesses, particularly diseases of the circulatory system, breast cancer and death from smoking-related illnesses (Balanda et al., 2001). A WHO report in 2000, utilising a broad approach in assessing health sector performance covering life expectancy, infant mortality and other variables such as the responsiveness of the systems and fairness of financial contribution, provides sober reading. In comparison to the EU-15 countries, Australia, Canada, Japan, New Zealand and the US, Ireland fared poorly, coming close to the bottom of the rankings in 18th place.

Efficiency

Efficiency is a concept that is closely related to effectiveness. Not only should health expenditure generate positive effects, but it should do so efficiently. The decision to commit resources to tackling a health problem denies society use of these resources to tackle other health problems. In economics, the gains foregone are called opportunity costs. The objective within any health care system should be to maximise benefits and minimise costs (Donaldson et al., 2005). To deploy resources inefficiently means that these resources could be reallocated to increase output elsewhere thereby enhancing social welfare. Achieving efficiency is therefore about comparing the costs (or resources spent) and benefits (or well-being produced) of competing health care interventions and ensuring that resources are allocated in such a way as to maximise health gains to society. The importance of efficiency objectives has only recently entered the realm of health care decision-making in Ireland. The 2001 Health Strategy highlights the need to ensure "that the most modern appropriate care and treatments are used, in a way that maximises health gain and achieves value for money" (Department of Health and Children, 2001).

The case-mix adjustment to hospital budgets has been the major innovation in respect of promoting more efficient use of resources in health care in Ireland in recent years. The case-mix measure assigns all in-patient cases to one of 500 diagnosis-related groups (DRGs). Each DRG represents a class or category of cases which may be expected to have the same clinical characteristics, receive similar treatment and use a similar amount of hospital resources. A case-mix adjusted cost is estimated for each hospital and each diagnostic group. Hospitals performing

poorly relative to others in the group lose funding, whereas those performing better receive extra funding. In 2002, the rate of adjustment to
hospital budgets was 20 per cent of the in-patient budget and 10 per cent
for the day cases, with the remainder of the budget allocated on historical
grounds (Wiley, 2001). The objective of this approach is to entice hospital managers to manage their resources more efficiently. The new system
will help reduce previously unexplained differences in length of stay and
resource use across hospitals treating similar patients.

This commitment to moving toward a more effective and efficient
service in Ireland is also reflected in the establishment of the Health Information and Quality Authority (HIQA) in 2005. The objective of the
HIQA is to promote delivery of health and personal social services based
on practices that evidence has shown produce high quality, effective and
efficient outcomes. The functions of the HIQA include the development
of health information, the promotion of and implementation of quality
assurance programmes nationally and overseeing health technology assessment. Information is the key to better decision-making, but it has
largely been ignored in the Irish health care system, even where it exists,
as evident by the poor use made of the Hospital In-Patient Enquiry
(HIPE) data. Health Technology Assessment (HTA) is also conspicuous
by its absence in Ireland. There is no consistent technology assessment
yet in place and economic and social evaluation of health care programmes remains the exception rather than the rule.

Two independently commissioned reports have highlighted structural
efficiency concerns within the health care system, related to the impact
of the common contract for hospital consultants (Deloitte and Touche,
2001; Brennan Commission, 2003). Specifically, private patients treated
by consultants in public hospitals are not charged the full economic cost
of care and treatment so that the state effectively subsidises their treatment. This gives insurers an incentive to encourage the treatment of private patients in public rather than private hospitals, and public hospital
managers an incentive to encourage the treatment of private patients as
they represent an additional income stream for the hospital. This goes
against an often-cited rationale for the private insurance system in Ireland – that it relieves pressure on the public hospital system. Furthermore, it represents an inefficient use of resources which could be made

available to other areas of the health service such as Accident and Emergency (A&E) services. Indeed, a recent report on the A&E crisis in Irish health care suggests that the solution may well depend as much on more efficient use of current resources within and outside hospitals than any investment of further resources. In respect of the former, A&E is sometimes used to fast-track access to inpatient care thereby bypassing waiting lists. A&E has also become the first point of call of some patients unwilling to pay GP charges, or in circumstances where GPs are difficult to access during "out-of-hours".

Equity

Equity is a concept that is closely related to equality. Within most societies there exists, in some form or another, a concern that health care resources and benefits should be distributed in some fair way. Equality is a particular interpretation of equity. Whereas equality is concerned with equal shares, equity is concerned with fairness, and it may be judged fair to be unequal. There has been much written on which equity objective is appropriate for a health care system (Culyer et al., 1991; Donaldson et al, 2005). Specifically, should the equity objective be to achieve fair health or fair health care? In theory, both objectives seem reasonable, but have very different implications for resource allocation.

Equity in health is the absence of systematic differences in one or more aspects of health status across socially, demographically or geographically defined populations (Donaldson et al., 2005). In recent reports the Public Health Alliance Ireland and the Institute of Public Health provide a detailed account of the serious range of health inequalities by socio-economic groups in Ireland (Burke et al., 2004; Balanda et al., 2001). The evidence suggests that people who are poor and excluded get sick more and die younger than people who are better off. There was more than a three-fold difference in the age-standardised death rates between men in the lowest and the highest socio-economic groupings during the period 1989-1998. This impact of occupational class on mortality rates was also evident for nearly all of the major causes of death in Ireland. The death rates for all cancers among the lowest occupational class is over twice as high for the highest class, it is nearly three times higher for strokes, four times higher for lung cancer and six times for accidents

(Nolan and Callan, 1994). Perinatal mortality is three times higher for children of unskilled manual workers than the higher professional category (Cullen, 2002).

Health inequalities are also evident in many measures of morbidity, self-reported health status and health lifestyle. Adults in the lowest socio-economic group were twice as likely to report a long-standing illness as those in the highest socio-economic group (Nolan and Callan, 1994). Women in the poorest socio-economic groups are more than twice as likely to give birth to low birth weight children than women in the higher professional group (Cullen, 2002). The 1998 and 2002 National Health and Lifestyle Surveys (SLAN) found that poorer people are more likely to smoke cigarettes, drink alcohol excessively, take less exercise, and eat less fruit and vegetables than richer people. Poorer people's lifestyle and behavioural choices are directly limited by their economic and social circumstances (Kelleher et al., 2003).

Most of the focus in Ireland has been on inequalities in health care. Equalising access to health care (for equal need) within the Irish health care system is seen as means of dealing with the latter. However, the process of measuring and monitoring "access" and "need" has proved to be conceptually difficult in any attempt to explore the effectiveness of this policy target as a means of reducing health inequalities. Layte and Nolan (2004) found that inpatient hospital services, GPs, outpatient hospital services and filled prescriptions were used substantially more by those at the lower end of the income distribution, while dental and optician services were used substantially more by those higher up the income distribution. After standardising for health status, they found that large differences in usage between different income groups could largely be accounted for in terms of "need" factors, though for GP services lower income groups made greater use of these services than might be predicted from measured health need. Having said that, the proportion of the population considered eligible for a medical card has fallen from 35.7 per cent in 1981 to 29.6 per cent in 2002 (General Medical Services Payments Board, 2003). This is indicative both of an overall rise in income levels and also of the failure of income guidelines used to determine eligibility to keep pace with the change in income levels. The concern is that those on the margins of medical card entitlement are denied access to important health care services.

The 2001 Health Strategy acknowledged that there is a "two-tier" element to hospital treatment where public patients frequently do not have fair access to elective treatments (Department of Health and Children, 2001). This is supported by evidence for 2001 which suggested that 25 per cent of medical cardholders had waited for 12 months or longer for in-patient admission to a public hospital, while only 12 per cent of those with private insurance cover had been waiting 12 months or longer (CSO, 2002). Furthermore, a consultancy report commissioned by the Department of Health and Children suggests that hospital consultants may spend more time on private health care than appropriate to their contracts (Deloitte and Touche, 2001). Statistics for bed occupancy in public hospitals has raised further concern that access to public hospitals for elective procedures is not always distributed by need but by ability to pay. There is evidence that the rate of discharges for private patients in certain public hospitals is greater than that for public patients for elective and emergency in-patient services and day procedures (HIPE, 2002).

Health Policy in Ireland

The emphasis on health care as the primary determinant of health in this country is at odds with the evidence. It is also hard to reconcile with the rhetoric of successive governments' support for a more holistic and comprehensive approach to the generation of both individual and population level health. An analysis of recent health policy documents in Ireland reveals a paradox. The support in public health policy documents for a multi-faceted approach to the production of health as far back as the 1980s has not translated into structural reforms or a willingness to commit resources to finance a broader model of health production (O'Shea and Kelleher, 2001). In 1986, a document entitled *Health – The Wider Dimensions* was published, in which the broad determinants of health were discussed for the first time. The document conceptualised equality in health in the following terms suggesting that a broader definition of health was envisaged:

> Equality in health is a step beyond guaranteeing an equitable distri-
> bution of available health services, however. It implies that each in-
> dividual is offered the same opportunity to enjoy good health. Given
> that health is multi-faceted, i.e. it may be as dependent on the aggre-
> gate effect of income level, living environment, working environ-
> ment, employment status etc., as on health care.

The intention seemed to be that all of the factors which impact upon health and are amenable to public policy were to be addressed. The document recognised the need for an inter-sectoral action in tackling inequalities in health. The document sees the role of the health sector in addressing inequalities as ". . . drawing attention to the problem, leading the debate on possible solutions and ultimately co-ordinating an inter-sectoral response to particular health problems". For that reason, the discussion document is an important landmark if only to illustrate that policy-makers were capable of thinking comprehensively about health inequalities, if not acting upon the implications of their musings. The health care system was only part of the solution. An understanding of economic and social processes would likely tell us much more about the production of health than would an examination of the medical care system. However, little was seen of this new approach in the years following the publication of *Health – The Wider Dimensions*, as the focus turned to cutting back expenditure on health care; however, this was in response to the effect of cumulative fiscal crises at the time rather than as part of any new model of health production.

The next major policy document was published in 1994 titled *Shaping a Healthier Future* (Department of Health, 1994). By then the emphasis had shifted back again to seeing health care as the key determinant of health in the country. While the 1986 discussion document saw the Department of Health leading an inter-sectoral approach to reducing health inequalities, the 1994 document envisages a more stand-alone role for the Department in addressing inequalities. While consideration of equity imposes a particular obligation upon the health services to pay special attention to geographic areas or population groups where the indicators of health status are below average, most of the causal factors, such as poverty and unemployment, were considered to be outside the direct control of the health services. The health services could improve the health status of disadvantaged groups through tailoring and organising the delivery of health education programmes and community services, but it could not address the underlying economic and social causes of existing health inequalities. The health care equity target *equal access for equal need* underpinned the 1994 health strategy. However, it was possible to take a number of possible meanings from this target which were compatible with an infinite number of expenditure distributions. In short, the target was introduced without any clear thinking about what it might mean in practice for health care reform. But it was clear that health care was the only game in town in relation to dealing with health problems.

Specific strategies on cancer and heart disease were formulated in the second half of the 1990s. The Cancer Strategy (Department of Health, 1996) and the Cardiovascular Strategy (Department of Health and Children, 1999) both highlighted the need to tackle disadvantage as part of any reform process. However, the main focus of both strategies was on reducing the overall incidence of cancer and heart disease. Reducing incidence took priority over reducing the differentials that exist among different socio-economic groups and different regions. The bulk of the additional resources that came on-stream as a result of these strategies went on funding in-patient technological care rather than supporting multi-faceted, community-based models of health enhancement. Despite the fact that class differentials are known to exist (and that health promotion strategies have demonstrated a graduated pattern of effectiveness), there has been little concerted effort to address why these differentials exist. Nor has there been any consistent attempt to shift the focus of public policy to increase the material and structural resources of the less advantaged. Health care remains the focus.

The most recent health strategy, *Quality and Fairness: A Health System for You* (Department of Health and Children, 2001), marked a return to a multi-faceted approach to dealing with health issues in Ireland. The strategy recognises that social, environmental and economic factors, including deprivation, education, housing and nutrition, affect an individual's health status. The health strategy acknowledges that there is a need for more radical methods to tackle health inequalities than has been used in the past. In that regard, a number of targets were set for the reduction in inequalities. The problem is that most of the measures proposed to

meet these targets continue to be focused on overcoming access problems to health care. Those that are not directly concerned with access, for
example integrating an equality dimension into health and social services, are very general in content and are difficult to both monitor and
implement in the absence of specific targets. There is no comprehensive
approach for dealing with health inequalities and no model of how various state agencies might combine to reduce social variation in health in
Ireland. Once again, rhetoric has triumphed over reform when it comes
to implementing strategies to deliver on a broad social determinants
model of health production that is not dominated by health care delivery
and access, however important both of these are for individual health.

Equal Opportunity for Health – An Alternative Approach

There is an alternative approach, whose origins can be traced back to the
consultative document *Health – The Wider Dimensions* in 1986. Equal
opportunity for health reflects the ideal that everyone should have a fair
opportunity to attain their full health potential and, more pragmatically,
that no one should be disadvantaged from achieving this potential, if it
can be avoided. Equality of opportunity goes beyond equality in health
care. It involves all factors that potentially impact upon health and which
are amenable to public policy intervention, including income, working
conditions and educational attainment. Such an approach requires multi-
sectoral action. Policies aimed at equal opportunities are concerned with
providing resources and removing barriers in ways that enable individuals to achieve their full health potential. Equalising opportunities is a
supply-side phenomena concerning the constraints on individuals'
choices for better health in terms of both resources and social structures
(Birch, 1994). Equality of opportunity for health enables individuals to
make the choices to achieve their optimal health, but, of course, this does
not mean that they will make these choices.

According to Le Grand (1991), equality of opportunity involves
compensating people for any disadvantages they suffer through no fault
of their own, but not for disadvantages they suffer as a result of their
own free choice. Williams and Cookson (2000) interpret this as meaning
that everyone should have the same opportunity to obtain good things in
life, but it should be then up to them to choose how they exercise that

opportunity. Any theory of equality of opportunity requires a theory of free choice to determine what counts as being freely chosen and what counts as being beyond one's own voluntary control. The aim of public policy for equity in health is not, therefore, to achieve equality of health, but rather to reduce or eliminate differences in health that result from factors which are considered to both avoidable and unfair. The target of equal opportunity for health treats health status as a valuable resource to society, and its maintenance is at least an equivalent consideration to other outputs and objectives in determining policy generally.

Equality of opportunity for health should become the new focus for public policy in health in Ireland in the coming decades. Because the causes of ill health are so varied, they cannot be dealt with by focusing on health care alone. Equality of opportunity for health requires inter-sectoral action at central and local government level. This approach condemns discriminatory barriers and requires robust measures aimed at mitigating the effects of socio-economic inequalities and other contingencies on opportunity. This requires an understanding of, and consensus on, what is avoidable and unfair and what should be tackled by government. At present we do not fully understand why people in manual socio-economic groups have higher morbidity and mortality than those in non-manual groups, or what the precise transmission mechanisms are from socio-economic variables to health. However, we do know that a broad range of factors including income, education, housing, work, working conditions and lifestyle are likely to play an important role in promoting better health. More action is required on each of these if the health of the nation is to be improved.

The introduction of a health-proofing framework, together with explicit equality of opportunity targets for health attainment, would be an important response to the problem of the social gradient in health. Health-proofing would ensure that all relevant government departments and agencies would have to demonstrate the impact of their policies and programmes on equalising opportunity for health among citizens. The first recommendation of the Independent Inquiry into Health Inequalities (Achenson, 1998) in England was that all policies likely to have a direct or indirect effect on health should be evaluated in terms of their impact on health inequalities, and should be formulated in such a way that by favouring the less well off they will, wherever possible, reduce such inequalities. However, the development of a similar inter-sectoral, health-proofing approach in Ireland faces many challenges. Policy-makers are not always aware of the health implications of their policies. Information is poor and economic evaluation is rarely available. Moreover, there is nearly always competition for limited resources among government departments and programmes, which may inhibit co-operation.

The improvement of living and working conditions is an important area where equality of opportunity for health might be immediately enhanced. Because living and working conditions determine many inequities in health, attempts to reduce the latter need to focus on these root causes, with the aim of preventing problems developing. This is potentially a more efficient approach than relying solely on the health care sector to patch up the morbidity and mortality that arise from housing conditions or work practices. Examples of policies in this area include those designed to provide adequate and safe housing, to control pollution and to raise the standard of occupational health and safety. The importance of improving working conditions in an attempt to tackle health inequalities has been highlighted by a number of authors (Whitehead and Dahlgren, 1991; Mackenbach, 1994; Achenson, 1999). Other preventive policies related to living and working conditions include job creation for disadvantaged groups and raising the absolute and relative income of poorer socio-economic groups through more generous welfare and disability payments.

Equality of opportunity should also be concerned with enabling disadvantaged people to adopt healthier lifestyles. The process of enabling people to adopt healthier lifestyles involves the recognition that some social groups may come under greater pressure to adopt health-damaging behaviour (Whitehead, 1992). Health education and disease prevention policies need reorientation. Beneficial changes in health behaviour have occurred to a greater extent in the more affluent and the better educated. The decline in tobacco consumption in Ireland has been relatively greater in the professional and managerial social classes (Department of Health and Children, 1999). Targeted programmes reach those in greatest need more effectively than general information dissemination.

Conclusion

In this chapter we presented a framework to evaluate future public policies which in some way influence or are influenced by population health. Health is an important variable in generating economic and social development. Investment in health contributes to future economic growth and development through its influence on human capital. Therefore, policymakers interested in improving economic outcomes have good reason to consider investment in health as a key strategy in meeting economic objectives. Any investment in health requires an integrated approach across government departments and agencies to tackle the main determinants of health. The solution to health problems does not lie solely within the health care system. Economic, social, environmental and cultural factors are equally, if not more, important in determining the level and distribution of health outcomes within a country. Consequently, a national health strategy must embody both an investment and holistic model of health production. The implication for policymakers is that investment in health must extend beyond the realm of traditional health care policy. The focus should be on equal opportunity for health, which involves positive discrimination and the provision of material and structural support for individuals and groups whose choices in relation to health are currently compromised by their economic and social circumstances.

References

Achenson D. (1998) *Independent inquiry into inequalities in health report*, London: Stationery Office.

Balanda, K. and Wilde, J. (2001), *Inequalities in Perceived Health: A report on the All Ireland Mortality Data*, Dublin: The Institute of Public Health.

Barry, J., Sinclair, H., Kelly, A., O'Loughlin, R., Handy, D. and O'Dowd, T. (2001), *Inequalities in Health in Ireland – Hard Facts*, Dublin: Department of Community Health & General Practice.

Barro, R. (1996), *Health and Economic Growth*, Programme on Public Policy and Health, Pan American Health Organisation, World Health Organization

Becker, G.S. (1964), *Human Capital: A theoretical and empirical analysis with special reference to education,* Third Edition, Chicago and London: University of Chicago Press.

Birch, S. (1994). "Nurturing health and equitable health policy: Never give up on a dream". Paper presented at the Health Economics Study Group meeting, University of Newcastle-Upon-Tyne, England.

Black Report (1980), *Inequalities in Health*, Report of a Research Working Group chaired by Sir Douglas Black, London: HMSO.

Bloom, D. and Williamson, J. (1998), "Demographic transitions and economic miracles in emerging Asia", *World Bank Economic Review,* 12(3), pp. 419–55.

Burke. S., Keenaghan, C., O'Donovan, D., Quirke, B. (2004), *Health in Ireland – An Unequal State*, Dublin: Public Health Alliance Ireland.

Cardiovascular Health Strategy Group: Building Healthier Hearts (1999), Dublin: Stationery Office.

Colgrove, J. (2002), "The McKeown thesis: A historical controversy and its enduring influence", *American Journal of Public Health,* 92, pp. 725–29.

Commission on Financial Management and Control Systems in the Health Service ("Brennan Commission") (2003), Report, Dublin: Stationery Office.

Central Statistics Office (2002), *Quarterly Household Survey – Health (First Quarter 2001)*, Dublin: Stationery Office.

Cullen, G. (2002), Perinatal *Statistics for 1999*, Dublin: ESRI, HIPE and NPRS Unit.

Culyer, A., Van Doorslaer, E., Wagstaff, A., (1992), "Comment on Utilisation as a Measure of Equity", *Journal of Health Economics*, May; 11(1), pp. 93-8.

Dahlgren, G. and Whitehead, M. (1991), *Policies and Strategies to Promote Social Equity in Health*, Stockholm: Institute of Futures Studies.

Dahlgren, G. and Whitehead, M. (1992), *Policies and Strategies to Promote Equity in Health*, Copenhagen, World Health Organisation.

Deaton, A. (2001), *Relative deprivation, inequality and mortality*. NBER Working Paper No. 8099.

Deaton, A. (2003). "Health, inequality and economic development". *Journal of Economic Literature*. Vol XL1, pp 111-158.

Deloitte and Touche (2001), *Value for Money Audit of the Irish Health System, Report to the Department of Health and Children.*

Denison, E. (1985), *Trends in American economic growth, 1929–1982*, Washington DC: Brookings Institution.

Department of Health and Children (2001), *Quality and Fairness: A Health System for You, Health Strategy*, Dublin: Stationery Office.

Department of Health and Children (2003), *Health Statistics 2002*, Dublin: Stationery Office.

Department of Health (1986), *Health – The Wider Dimensions (A consultative statement on health policy)*, Dublin: Stationery Office.

Department of Health (1994), *Shaping a Healthier Future: A Strategy for Effective Healthcare in the 1990s*, Dublin: Stationery Office.

Department of Health (1986), National Cancer Strategy, Dublin: Stationery Office.

Donaldson, C., Gerard, K., Mitton, C., Jan, S. and Wiseman, V. (2004), *Economics of health care financing: The visible hand. 2nd edition*, Basingstoke: Palgrave Macmillan.

Eurostat (2003), *Key figures on Health Pocketbook – 2003*. Luxembourg: Office of Official Publications of the European Communities.

Fogel, R. W. (1994), "Economic growth, population theory, and physiology: The bearing of long-term process on the making of economic policy", *The American Economic Review*, 84(3), pp. 369–395.

General Medical Services Payments Board (2003), *Annual Report and Financial Statements 2002*, Dublin: GMSPB.

Griffin, K. and McKinley, T. (1992), *Towards a Human Development Strategy*, Occasional Paper No 6, Human Development Report Office.

Grossman, M. (1972), "On the concept of health capital and the demand for health", *Journal of Political Economy,* 80(2), pp. 223–255.

Gross-Tebbe, S. and Figueras, J. (2004), *Snapshots of Health Systems: The state of affairs in 16 countries in Summer 2004*. Copenhagen: World Health Organisation Regional Office for Europe.

HIPE & NPRS Unit (2002), *Activity in Acute Public Hospitals in Ireland 1990*, Dublin: The Economic and Social Research Institute.

Kelleher, C., Friel, S., NicGabhain, S. and Tay J, B. (2003), "Sociodemographic predictors of self rated health in the Republic of Ireland: Findings from the National Survey on Lifestyle, Attitudes and Nutrition (SLAN)". *Soc Sci Med.* Aug; 57 (3), pp. 477-86.

Kennelly, B., O'Shea, E. and Garvey, E. (2003), "Social capital, life expectancy and mortality: A cross-national examination". *Social Science and Medicine*, 56, pp. 2367-2377

Layte, R. and Nolan, B. (2004), "Equity in the Utilisation of Health Care in Ireland", *Economic and Social Review*; 35(2), pp. 111-134

Lynch, J.W., Due, P., Muntaner, C. and Davey Smith, G. (2000), "Social capital-Is it a good investment strategy for public health?", *Journal of Epidemiology and Community Health*, Vol. 54, pp. 404-408.

Mackenbach, J.P. (1994). "Socio-economics inequalities in health in the Netherlands: Impact of a five-year research programme". *British Medical Journal* 309, pp. 1487-1491.

Marmot, M. (2002), "The Influence of Income on Health: Views of an epidemiologist", Health *Affairs,* 21(2), pp. 31-46.

Nolte, E. and McKee, M. (2004), *Does Health Care Save Lives? Avoidable mortality revisited,* London: The Nuffield Trust.

Nolan, A. (2005), "Health: Funding, Access and Efficiency" in O'Hagan J (ed), *The Economy of Ireland: Policy and Performance of a European Region,* Dublin: Gill and Macmillan.

Nolan, B, and Callan, T (eds.), (1994), *Poverty and Policy in Ireland.* Dublin: Economic and Social Research Institute, Dublin.

OECD, *Health Data 2004,* OECD, Paris 2004, 1st edition.

O'Shea, E and Kelleher, C. (2001). "Health Inequalities in Ireland" in Cantillon, S., Corrigan, C., Kirby, P. & O'Flynn, J. (eds). *Rich and Poor: Perspectives on Tackling Iinequality in Ireland.* Dublin: Oak Tree Press in association with the Combat Poverty Agency.

McPake, B., Kumaranayake, L., and C. Normand (2002). *Health Economics: An International Perspective,* London: Routledge.

Phelps, C. (2003), *Health Economics.* Boston: Pearson Education.

Putnam, R.D. (2000). *Bowling Alone: The Collapse and Revival of American Community,* New York: Simon and Schuster.

Suhrcke, M., McKee, M., Arce, R.S., Tsolova, S. and Mortensen, J. (2005), *The Contribution of Health to the Economy in the European Union,* Luxembourg: Office for Official Publications of the European Communities.

Sachs, J. D. and Warner, A. M. (1997), "Sources of slow growth in African economies", *Journal of African Economies,* 6(3), pp. 335–376.

Todaro, M. P. (2000), *Economic Development,* New York: Addison-Wesley.

Van Doorslaer, E, and Koolman, X. (2004), "Explaining the differences in income-related health inequalities across European countries", *Health Economics*; 13(7), pp. 609-628.

Wagstaff, A., and Van Doordlaer, E. (2000), "Equity in Health Care Finance and Delivery" in A. Culyer and J Newhouse (editors), *Handbook of Health Economics, Volume 1B*, Oxford: Elsevier.

Wiley, M.M. (2001), "Case-Mix in Ireland: Budgeting Basis for Acute Hospital Services", in France, F.H. Roger, Mertens, I., Closon, M.M., Hofdijk, J. (eds) *Case-Mix: Global Views, Local Actions – Evolution in Twenty Countries,* Amsterdam: IOS Press.

World Health Organisation (WHO) (2000), *World Health Report 2000: Health Systems: Improving Performance*, Washington DC: World Health Organisation.

World Health Organisation (WHO) (2002), *Dying for Change – Poor People's Experience of Health and Ill Health*, Copenhagen: World Health Organisation.

World Health Organisation (WHO), (1946): Preamble to the Constitution of the World Health Organization as adopted by the International Health Conference, New York, 19-22 June, 1946; signed on 22 July 1946 by the representatives of 61 States (Official Records of the World Health Organization, no. 2, p. 100) and entered into force on 7 April 1948.

Whitehead, M. (1992). "The concepts and principles of equity and health". *International Journal of Health Services* 22, pp. 429-445.

Williams, A. and Cookson, R. (2000) "Equity in Health", pp. 1863–1910, in Culyer, A.J. and Newhouse, J.P. (Eds.), *Handbook of Health Economics*, Amsterdam: Elsevier.

Wilkinson, R.G. (1996), *Unhealthy Societies: The Afflictions of Inequalities,* London: Routledge.

Wilkinson, R.G. (2000), "Inequality and the social environment: A reply to Lynch et al.", *Journal of Epidemiology and Community Health*, Vol. 54, No. 6, pp. 411-2.

Chapter 15

NEO-LIBERALISM AND EDUCATION

Kathleen Lynch

Publicly funded and regulated education has produced universal benefits for humanity wherever it has been provided. This is very evident in Ireland where investment in education has produced enormous dividends, not only economically but also socially and culturally. To maintain the level of social and economic development that derives from high quality publicly available education requires continual substantial Sate investment however. And there are at least six major reasons why education at all levels needs to be provided within a system of democratic control and why it should be freely available:

1. Education is *a right*. People's rights to education are enshrined in Article 26 of the Universal Declaration of Human Rights and Article 13 of the International Covenant on Economic, Social and Cultural Rights.

2. Education is *indispensable* for realising other rights. Education credentials play a crucial *role in mediating access to other goods*, including employment, cultural goods and political participation. Making any form of education available on a fee-paying or commercial basis severely comprises not only the right to education for those who cannot pay but also the realisation of other rights to which education mediates access.

3. Education enables one to *overcome other social disadvantages*. It has many unforeseen and unintended benefits. In a market-driven system attending to the educational needs of the disadvantaged (be it in terms of disability, age, gender, ethnicity, family status, etc.) becomes a secondary objective as the incentive is to educate those who can pay.

4. Education has an *intrinsic value* for the development of the individual – for the exercise of capabilities, choices and freedoms regardless of its economic or political utility. In a commercially-oriented system the intrinsic value of education for the individual cannot be protected as it may not be viable in market terms.

5. Education has *a care function* as well as a development function. The care dimension cannot be guaranteed in a commercialised system as care has costs.

6. Education is a *public good* as well as a personal good. It enriches cultural, social, political and economic life locally and globally. In a commercially-driven system the public good dimension is not always visible in the short term and is not likely to be prioritised.

With the rise of the new-right, neo-liberal agenda, there is an attempt to offload the cost of education, and indeed other public services such as housing, transport and care services for older people, on to the individual. There is an increasing attempt to privatise public services, including education, so that citizens will have to buy them at market value rather than have them provided by the state. This development is recognised by scholars across a range of fields, including those working within bodies such as the World Bank (Angus, 2004; Bok, 2003; Bullen et al., 2004; Dill, 2003; Henkel, 1997; Steier, 2003; Stevenson, 1999).

Irish education is no exception to this trend. The OECD report on higher education in Ireland (2004) concentrates strongly on the role of education in servicing the economy to the neglect of its social and developmental responsibilities. The view that education is simply another market commodity has become normalised in policy and public discourses while schools run as businesses (the so-called "grind schools") have grown a pace in the last 20 years (Lynch and Moran, 2006; Sugrue, 2004).

Schools operating as businesses are a growing phenomenon within and without Europe and there is an increasing expectation in several countries that schools will supplement their income from private sources, even though they are within the State sector. In Ireland the use of "voluntary contributions" from parents to fund primary and second-level schooling represents a privatisation of the cost of compulsory education.[1]

In this chapter I present a critique of the neo-liberal model of marketised education and a challenge to educators to work as public intellectuals both individually and with civil society organisations to develop a counter-hegemonic discourse to neo-liberalism. The chapter focuses on the impact of neo-liberalism on the higher education sector, particularly on the universities, as neo-liberal ideology has taken hold most strongly, both at the level of rhetoric and practice, within this field.

Neo-Liberalism: History and Implications

The corporatisation and marketisation of education has its origins in neo-liberal politics that is premised on the assumption that the market can replace the democratic state as the primary producer of cultural logic and value.[2] Neo-liberalism offers a market view of citizenship that is generally antithetical to rights, especially to state-guaranteed rights in education, welfare, health and other public goods (Chubb and Moe, 1990; Tooley, 1996, 2000). The citizen is defined as an economic maximiser, governed by self-interest. There is a glorification of the "consumer citizen" construed as willing, resourced and capable of making market-led choices. In this new market state, the individual is held entirely responsible for their own well-being. The state's role is one of facilitator and enabler of the consumer and market-led citizen (Rutherford, 2005). This neo-liberal position is fundamentally Hobbesian in character, focusing on creating privatised citizens who care primarily for themselves. The privatised, consumer-led citizenry of the neo-liberal model are reared on a culture of insecurity that induces anxiety, competition and indifference to those more vulnerable than themselves.

When transposed to education the neo-liberal model of citizenship has very serious implications (Giroux, 2002). It treats education as just another service to be delivered on the market to those who can afford to buy it. The rationalisation that is offered is that it provides people with choice. Choice is the carrot with which people are duped into believing that they will have freedom to buy what education (or other services) they like is some brave new market. This drive to increase "choice" and shift control from the school or university to the sovereign consumer is indicative of a broader political shift towards the right. A distinctive neo-liberal interpretation of fairness and efficiency based on the moral might and supremacy of the market has taken root across the public sector (Apple, 2001; Bonal, 2003; Loxley and Thomas; 2001; Thrupp, 2001). And small countries like Ireland are no exception to this trend (Allen, 1999; Kirby, 2002; Lynch and Moran, 2006).

Yet the evidence is overwhelming that in economically unequal societies only those with sufficient resources can make choices and those who are poor have no choices at all (Archer, Hutchings and Ross, 2002; Ball, 2003, Gewirtz et al., 1995, Lauder et al., 1999; Lyons, et al., 2003; Reay and Lucey, 2003, Whitty et al., 1998). What is ignored is the fact that what people may want is not a choice of school or college (or public service) but access to an affordable, accessible and available education of high standard (Tight, 2000). For those with limited resources, choice is a secondary rather than primary value, taking its place behind quality, affordability and access (Lynch and O'Riordan, 1998).

The Liberal Inheritance

Neo-liberalism has inherited the core values of liberalism in both its humanistic and economic forms. It shares with classical liberalism a humanist tradition that defines the person as an autonomous and rational being, a Cartesian man *sic* whose humanity is encapsulated in the phrase *Cogito ergo sum*.[3] As such, it carries through into the twenty-first century a deep indifference to the inevitable dependencies and interdependencies that are endemic to the human condition (Noddings, 2003; Nussbaum, 1995a, 1995b). It is disregarding of the role that emotions play in our relationships and our learning, and correlatively indifferent to the central role of care and love relations in defining who we are (Kittay, 1999; Baker, Lynch, Cantillon and Walsh, 2004; Lynch and Baker, 2005). In line with classical economic views of education, it also defines the person to be educated in economic terms as *homo economicus*, a labour market actor whose life and purposes are determined by their economic status. These twin sets of values are reinforced with a third set of educational purposes, namely, the conceptualisation of the person to be educated as a highly individualised, self-regarding and consuming economic actor. Competitive individualism is no longer seen as an amoral necessity but rather as a desirable and necessary attribute for a constantly reinventing entrepreneur (Apple, 2001; Ball, 2003). What neo-liberalism has succeeded in doing, however, which classical liberalism did not do, is to subordinate and trivialise education that has no market value.

The moral opprobrium that has been accorded to the definition of the educated person as one who is autonomous, rational, market-oriented, consuming and self-interested has profound implications for the operation of education as a social practice. It is indifferent to the fact that the majority of citizens in society at any given time are not actively earning consumers (children, older people, unpaid carers, etc.). Many are in no position to make active consumer choices due to the poverty of their resources, time and/or capacities. In line with its classical origins, the neo-liberal perspective also jettisons from educational formation much of the work and living concerns of humanity. It is disregarding of the fact that while we are undoubtedly economic actors, consumers and rational actors, neither our rationality nor our economic and consumer choices can be presumed to be devoid of relationality Gilligan, 1982, 1995). For most of humanity, much of life is lived in a state of profound and deep interdependency and for some prolonged dependency (Kittay, 1999). Humanity may be characterised as homo sapiens or homo economicus but we are also undoubtedly homo interdependicus and at times homo dependicus.

The neo-liberal model is also indifferent to the fact that the state is an in-eliminable agent in matters of justice. It ignores the reality that only the state can guarantee to individual persons the right to education. If the state absolves itself of the responsibility to educate, rights become more contingent – contingent on the ability to pay. What is at issue here is the difference between democratic accountability and market accountability. In a market-led system access to educational services will be contingent on market capacity or the ability to pay, whereas in a democratic, publicly controlled system, one's right to education is protected (however minimally at times) by the state.

Making Markets in Education: Ranking and League Tables

With the decline in the value of manufacturing industry in terms of investment returns, and the rise of the value of the services sector in both scale and profitability, there is an ongoing movement to define education as a tradable service worldwide. This policy direction is most evident in higher education, although the marketising of formerly public primary and second-level schools, especially in the more profitable (namely middle class and upper middle class) sectors, is well advanced in a number of South American and Asian countries (Hill, 2005). The pressure to move education from a public service to a tradable service is very much part of the ideology of the World Trade Organisation (WTO) General Agreement on Trade and Services (GATS), the purpose of which is to liberalise all services in all sectors of the economy globally (Robertson, Bonal and Dale, 2002). So far the EU has resisted the opening up of sectors such as health and education to such trading in the manner envisaged in the planned Bolkestein Directive, although it is likely to return to the political agenda in Europe over time.

The reasons for wanting to make education a tradable service are quite simple. In year 2000 UNESCO estimated that education was a $2 trillion global "industry". There is definite potential for profitable returns if such a service can be traded, especially among those sectors of society that can afford to pay for it. This possibility is recognised by the international investment bankers Merrill Lynch.[4] In its publication *The Book of Knowledge,* Merrill Lynch defines education as a service that presents one of the major new opportunities for investors in profit terms (Moe et al., 1999). The rise of influential and financially endowed social movements in the United States to promote for-profit higher education (as an example, see www.ecs.org and Callahan (2001) and Covington (2001) for a critique of this trend), and the fact that there are 650 for-profit colleges and universities, is a clear indication that for-profit trading in higher education is well under way (Morey, 2004). The largest of the for-profit universities, the University of Phoenix in Arizona, is trading for several years and now has 174,900 students. Interestingly, and perhaps not surprisingly given the profit-orientation of its operations, it has very few tenured faculty staff – there are only 285 full-time academic staff – but a sizeable and easily dispensable body (17,000) of adjunct or part-time staff (ibid.). The casualisation of the academic and teaching staff is an inevitable correlate of for-profit education (Hill, 2005).

The move to create markets in education is not limited to the for-profit sector of higher education. There are many ways in which academic capitalism is fostered through the funding of research (patenting) and in ancillary services associated with college entry such as tutoring (grinds) and test preparation (Slaughter and Leslie, 2001; Lynch and Moran, 2006). There are also school chains operating as businesses not only in the US but also in Europe (including Ireland) and in a number of South American countries (Hill, 2006; Lynch and Moran, 2006). Commercial sponsorship of school services in return for the guaranteed use of commercially sponsored materials is widespread in the US (Brighouse, 2005); it also operates subtly in Ireland but is rarely problematised or discussed.[5] The privatising of support services in schools and colleges, and the creation of internal markets, is a coterminous development in many countries. The move to allow schools to become mini-companies and to take over other schools (permitted under the UK Education Act, 2002) is another manifestation of the influence of the market practices in education.

While Ireland has not succumbed to the pressure from the media in particular to create league tables for second-level schools as has happened in the UK, the whole ideology of league tabling is strongly sponsored in higher education in particular. The move to create global league tables for universities is symbolically the most powerful indicator that market values have been incorporated into the university sector. What is significant is that this ranking has been undertaken by commercial operations (newspapers in a number of cases) and universities themselves have little control over their operation. There are commercial rankings for a number of years in the US, Australia, Canada and the UK (Dill and Soo, 2005). While some ranking systems can and do take into account official evaluations such as the Research Assessment Exercise (RAE) and the Teaching Quality Assurance (TQA) rating in the UK, the rankings are far from systematic and scientific (Tight, 2000).

One of the most frequently cited of these global rankings is that undertaken by Shanghai Jiao Tong University (a technological university focused heavily on engineering sciences). In 2003 and again in 2004, Shanghai Jiao Tong developed a ranking system for evaluating universi-

ties world-wide in terms of their relevance to their postgraduate and research needs. The criteria by which they evaluated the top 500 universities are listed below. What is remarkable about this evaluation scheme is
the clear bias against the arts, humanities and social sciences (AHSS)
that is built into the measurement schema; not only does it explicitly exclude journal articles in the arts and humanities, it also excludes many of
those in the social sciences. In addition, it is disregarding of the fact that
50 per cent of what is published in the AHSS is not in journal form, nor
does it advert to the reality of policy-related published work in any field.

Shanghai Jiao Tong (China) World Ranking of Universities, 2004

Five criteria were used. Only published articles are included, all books are
excluded. Publications in literature, the arts and humanities are excluded

- 10% for Nobel laureates among graduates (chemistry, physics, medicine,
  economics and Fields Medals in maths) five subjects only

- 20% for Nobel laureates awarded to current staff in above five areas

- 20% for Articles in two science-related journals, *Science* and *Nature*

- 20% for listing on the Highly Cited Index (HCI*) (all 21 subject areas bar
  one, and part of another, are in science or technology.

- 20% for Articles in Science Citation Index-expanded and Social Science
  Citation Index (many prestigious journals in the social sciences are not
  listed. All arts/humanities are excluded)

- 10% for scores on the above divided by full-time staff members

- Total 100%

Despite the narrowness and selectivity of the Jiao Tong ranking scheme,
in particular its neglect of student learning experiences and its blatant
bias against the arts and humanities and most of the social sciences, it

---

* The basis on which the HCI index works within the social sciences and education fields is
difficult to establish. I have checked to see if a number of well-known European social science
and educational scholars were on the HCI index and none were listed as highly cited.

has been widely cited as providing a legitimate evaluation of universities.[6] The Times Higher Education Supplement (THES) has initiated a similar index in 2004/5.

League tables direct us away from many of the core values that are central to university work, including quality teaching at undergraduate level, research which is of public value, outreach work and the inclusion of students from diverse backgrounds. They focus higher education attention on a narrow set of internal market considerations, particularly on what can be measured (Taylor, 2001). None of the so-called league tables focus on the quality of student experiences and none assess universities in terms of their inclusivity and respect for diversity. They strongly discourage us from focusing on access as they are fundamentally about ensuring that universities become even more elite in their orientation (Tight, 2000; Dill and Soo, 2005).

To date, the formation of the evaluation scheme for the appraisal of universities has been generally outside of the control of European universities. It has been especially outside the control of those working in the arts, humanities and social sciences, as their work is clearly not defined as central to the national development agenda by agencies such as the OECD. The attitude of the OECD to the arts, humanities and social sciences in Ireland is evident from the OECD review of higher education in 2004 (OECD, 2004). Throughout the report on Irish higher education the focus is on developing a *skilled work force for the economy*. There is no reference in the body of the report to the role of the universities in developing the civil, political, social or cultural institutions of society, either locally or globally. Interestingly, the terms of reference for the OECD group do make reference to the importance of identifying strategies for developing skills and research needs "for economic and social development" but there is no reference to these objectives in the published report.

School League Tables and the Myths of Choice

At school level, the international educational landscape has been increasingly characterised politically, ideologically and often structurally by the neo-liberal rhetoric of choice. The inter-related drive to increase choice, raise standards and shift control from the "bureaucratic school" to the "sovereign consumer" may be regarded as representative of a broader political shift towards the right, where a distinctive neo-liberal interpretation of fairness and efficiency based on the moral might and supremacy of the market has taken root (Apple, 2001; Bonal, 2003; Thrupp, 2001).

Yet, there is an extensive literature outlining the limitations of the ideology and practice of "choice" and league tables within an educational context, especially in the UK (Ball, 2003; Gewirtz et al., 1995; Lubienski, 2003; Reay and Lucey, 2003; Whitty et al., 1998). This research has highlighted the adverse effects of choice on working class (and other low income) parents and their children in particular, while also highlighting how middle class choices operate as acts of exclusion, and class reproduction. It demonstrates how, despite league tables, few choices exist for low-income households. What choices exist are generally between equally limiting educational options. Low income families cannot afford to prepare their children for the types of examinations that will enable them to out-compete others to enter the more selective school or universities. Neither can they simply choose to live in catchment areas where they can access the more academically-oriented and/or selective schools. Overall, the options promising significant class mobility are alien, risky and potentially costly socially, psychologically and financially (Archer and Yamashita, 2002; Lucey and Reay; 2002; Munns and McFadden, 2000; Taylor and Woollard, 2003).

It is clear from the research literature also that choice ideology legitimates class reproduction and silences class dissent by fostering illusions of opportunity. It is, in many respects, a logical extension of meritocratic individualism that underpinned the liberal equal opportunities projects of an earlier era, assuming that those who have the "talent" and who "*choose* to make the effort" should and would be meritorious (Young, 1958). Both choice and meritocratic ideologies blind us to the fact that there needs to be equality of condition to promote substantive as opposed to formal equality of opportunity in education (Baker et al., 2004; Lynch, 1987; Tawney, 1964). Thus choice functions not only mechanistically at the level of practice to exclude those who do not possess sufficient economic, social or cultural capital to avail of and benefit from the array of choices, but also ideologically, as it hides the disjuncture between the will and the means to choose behind a façade of equal opportunities rhetoric. If the ultimate objective of our analytical concern is to eliminate inequalities in education, focusing so much attention on "school choice" and league tables as a tool of discernment for choice creates an illusion that choice exists for all, and even if it did exist it would improve educational attainment for those who are disadvantaged. Inequality is relational and those with significantly greater resources will retain advantage as they can supplement school services with private resources whether school choice exists or not. Economic inequality and the global capitalism underpinning it remain at the root of inequality in education. The ideology of choice is a mere political distraction from confronting the foundational cause of educational inequality (Lynch and Baker, 2005; Lynch and Moran, 2006).

As the marketisation of education has taken hold most strongly in Ireland in the university sector in recent years, the remaining part of the paper will focus on the implications of marketisation for higher education in particular. Many of the issues that arise from the commercialisation of higher education also arise for other sectors of education however.

The Implications of Marketisation

Changing Cultures

That there is a major global movement to change the nature of the university's role in society is beyond doubt (Angus, 2004; Bullen, Robb and Kenway, 2004; Rutherford, 2005). It is a movement that was heralded in the early 1990s when the World Bank published its report titled *Higher Education: The Lessons of Experience* (1994) that promoted the idea of developing private universities, private funding for higher education, and public funding for universities subject to performance. While many working in Western and Northern universities took little notice of such a proposal, assuming it to apply to African and other poorer countries, it was a portent of what was to come for all universities.

What is notable about the change is that the university is being pressurised to change from being "a centre of learning to being a business organisation with productivity targets . . . to transfer its allegiance from the *academic* to the *operational*" *(my italics)* (Doring, 2002, p. 140 citing McNair, 1997). The move from the academic to the operational is not framed publicly in terms of serving commercial interests or values in all countries or at all times (although it seems to have happened in this way in the UK; see Rutherford, 2005). It may be explicit, as in the development of joint ventures and conferences between business and the universities[7] but other times it comes in the name of efficiency, productivity and excellence. The Report of the Interdepartmental Committee on Science, Technology and Innovation (2004) on *Building Ireland's Knowledge Economy* exemplifies such a trend. In the section on "Realising the Vision", the report outlines the actions for the Public Research System (effectively the universities and other higher educational institutions) as being to:

> (v) Develop a national plan to increase the performance, productivity and efficiency in the higher education and public sectors and (vi) to sustain Ireland's commitment to building an international reputation for research excellence.

Throughout the report the development of society is equated with economic development and the latter is focused primarily on science and technology. In my own university, the Inaugural Foundation address of the new President outlining his vision for the university demonstrates a similar tendency to define excellence and performance as values in and of themselves, regardless as to for what purposes excellence is achieved or how it is achieved.[8]

There is a relatively silent colonisation of the hearts and minds of academics and students happening in universities. Such a colonisation is made possible by the seemingly apolitical nature of the neo-liberal agenda; it depoliticises debates about education by hiding its ideological underpinnings in a language of economic efficiency (Giroux, 2002). The changes are significant not only in terms of how they refocus research and teaching efforts in the university but also in terms of how they change the cultural life of the university. Not only is constant auditing and measuring a recipe for self-display and the fabrication of image over substance (Ball, 2003), it also leads to a type of Orwellian surveillance of one's everyday work by the university institution that is paralleled in one's person life with a reflexive surveillance of the self. One is always measuring oneself up or down (Leathwood, 2005). Everything one does must be measured and counted and only the measurable matters. Trust in professional integrity and peer regulation has been replaced with performance indicators. Yet, there is a deep alienation in the experience of constantly living to perform. It leads to feelings of personal inauthenticity and a culture of compliance, as externally-controlled performance indicators become the constant point of reference for one's work regardless of how meaningless they might be (Cooper, 2000 cited in Rutherford, 2005). Rewarding staff on a measurable item-by-item performance basis will inevitably lead to a situation where personal career interests will entirely govern academic life. It will mean that the measure of educational and research worth is increasingly one's ability to serve what is counted on the academic market.

While many can and do resist the aforesaid changes through personal and collective actions, the power and speed of change can make resistances seem futile and ritualistic.[9] The allegations against those who resist change are also inevitable; they are accused of blocking progress or being anti-reform, of being university luddites who do not realise what the brave new world of the market has to offer. As there are opportunities in the market for commercialised professionals and academics (Hanlon, 2000) internal division between staff in the universities are inevitable and open to exploitation by management. Fear of being labelled as anti-innovation or change (a cardinal sin where change is made to be a virtue regardless of its educational or academic merit) means that the important difference between the positively innovative (in our own university opening up to undergraduates the opportunity to take options each year outside their main degree programme is an obvious case in point), the genuinely destructive (only rewarding staff for what can be easily measured) and the purely self-serving (refusing to disclose information about large salaries to senior staff on the grounds of commercial sensitivity) is never made public. The conflict becomes polarised and the loss of what has been of value in the university is hidden behind the loss of the inessential.

But the culture shift does not apply only to staff. Students' lives are also directed increasingly to economic self-interest and credential acquisition. Student and staff idealism to work in the service of humanity is seriously diminished as universities operate as entrepreneurial, purely competitive business-oriented corporations (Elton, 2000).

> When universities openly and increasingly pursue commercialisation, it powerfully legitimises and reinforces the pursuit of economic

> self-interest by students and contributes to the widespread sense
> among them that they are in college solely to gain career skills and
> credentials. (Harkavy, 2005, p. 15)

In other words, when the commercialisation of life is normalised in educational bodies, its values are encoded in the educational system, generally without reflection. Colleges of higher and further education become producers of commercially-oriented professionals and skilled workers rather than public interest professionals (Hanlon, 2000). While this may seem like merely a change in form rather than substance, the danger with this advancing marketised individualism is that it will further weaken public interest values among those who are college educated. Yet a welfare-oriented democratic state depends on the realisation of such values to provide services on a universal basis. Without adhesion to such values, the only basis on which services will be provided is on the ability to pay.

A further consequence of uninterrogated marketisation is the gradual elision of the divide between the commercial and the scholarly in the research field. The merging of commerce and research is presented as both desirable and necessary and university policies are increasingly directed towards rewarding such links. The rhetoric of accelerating costs is used to drive the industry-university links agenda as the neo-liberal state attempts to extricate itself from the cost of publicly funded higher education. What is often forgotten in these discussions is that the claim by the state of inability to pay for education is not new. In the Irish case, it has been part of the history of all public education from the mid-nineteenth century when the cost of primary education was regarded as too great for the rate payers (Coolahan, 1981). More recently, when free public secondary education was introduced in the 1960s there was an outcry that Ireland could not afford free secondary education for all students (ibid). The same arguments are merely repeated now about higher education.

While the colleges of higher education have both a need and a responsibility to work with a wide range of public and private sector interests, as a public institution the interests and values of the for-profit sector cannot drive their research. University scholarship is of its nature critical and reflexive. It is founded on the assumptions of independence and autonomy. Quite understandably, the ethical principles and priorities of the business sector are not synonymous with those of a public interest body such as a university (Eisenberg, 1987). If universities become too reliant on industry-funded research, or too beholden to the business-driven agenda of the government of today (even if it comes coded in the guise of advancing science), there is a danger that the interests of the university become synonymous with powerful vested interests. This will undermine the purposes of the university as an enlightenment institution serving the good of humanity in its entirety. It will also undermine the very independence of thought that is the trademark of university research (Blumenthal, 2002; Lieberwitz, 2004). It will compromise public trust in the scholarly integrity of university research and teaching. The university will become, and be seen to become, the handmaiden of a set of power-ful sectoral interests. There is evidence that this is happening already in sensitive areas such as food production, genetics, biotechnology and en-vironmental protection (Monbiot, 2000).

Marketisation and the Threat to Critical Voices

Another issue that must be addressed with moves towards the market is the threat marketisation poses to the very existence of critique and crea-tivity itself. If universities are dependent increasingly on contract re-search, this will leave little time to develop the critical and creative con-ceptual frameworks that are developed outside of the contract research world or that follow after contracts are finished. Contract research work is also deeply exploitative at times although this is matter is rarely the subject of debate in Ireland.[10]

Making the universities market-oriented also greatly weakens the po-sition of the arts, humanities and critical social sciences as most research and teaching in these fields does not service the business sector directly; their remit is to educate for the public sphere, for civil society and not for profit. Research in East Germany shows that when universities were re-structured after unification, the departments that were most often closed in the technical universities were those involving critical social scientific dis-ciplines, multidisciplinary programmes and women's studies programmes (Bultmann, 1996, cited in Stevenson, 1999). The closure of the highly suc-cessful but also strongly critical Centre for Contemporary Cultural Studies and Sociology Department in the University of Birmingham in 2002 is further proof of the fact that there is a serious threat to critical thought in a more marketised higher educational system (Webster, 2004).

While the social sciences and critical programmes are not being closed down in a planned way, they are gradually losing status and influence as the state does not invest in the arts, humanities and social sciences at a rate that is remotely comparable to the physical sciences.[11] Without state investments such fields cannot flourish, as there is no serious alternative to government funding. Profit-oriented businesses have no short-term stake in funding fields such as Critical Theory, Literary Theory, Feminist Philosophy, Equality Studies, Community Development, Critical Social Policy, Cultural Studies, etc., not least because such fields of scholarship are often critical of the values and operational systems of profit-driven interests. So if the state recedes from higher education investment in new professorships and academic posts in the arts and human sciences, or invests at a very low level in critical disciplines, there is a gradual shrinking of these sectors of higher education by default if not by design.[12]

Making the universities strongly market-oriented can and will over time lead also to a concentration of resources in universities outside of public control. In the US this is already happening as public universities are finding it increasingly difficult to attract successful researchers and academics; they cannot offer the same salaries as private institutions (Smallwood, 2001). And there is increasing evidence also that elitism does not produce better learning or scholars. A distinction has been drawn between the "prestige" status of a university and what Dill (2003) and others (Brewer et al., 2002) call the "reputation" status. While prestige colleges may emphasise the highly selective profile of their student and staff intake this does not necessarily translate into quality education. A study of 26 private and public universities and college in the US by Rand (Brewer et al., 2002) suggests that competition for prestige does not seem to improve the quality of educational delivery, while it can lead to investment in building research facilities with high maintenance and matching funds costs without clear benefits for students or society more generally.

What Counts: Undermining the Democratisation of Learning

One of the other serious challenges we face in the university is the regulation of our publications, lectures and engagements according to a narrowly defined set of market principles. While it is self-evident that peer review is vital for scholarly advancement, confining the academic voice to peer review alone has serious consequences for the democratisation of learning and for the dissemination of research in more publicly accessible forums. Once academics are only assessed and rewarded for communicating with other academics that is all they will do. In a research assessment system where one is rewarded for publishing in peer-reviewed books and journals, there is little incentive to invest in teaching, even the teaching that is part of one's job (Taylor, 2001). The incentive to teach or disseminate findings in the public sphere through public lectures, dialogues or partnerships with relevant civil society or statutory bodies (including professional bodies representing teachers and other educational workers) is negligible. There is a strange irony in the fact that a lecture given to a professional body such as teachers or school principals involving several hundred people, or a publication of one's lecture for that body, is not counted as a serious academic event, whereas a seminar to one's peers where ten or fifteen people attend does count as a significant academic exercise, and the subsequent paper is counted, no matter how specialised, small or self-selecting the peer audience may be for the journal/conference proceedings in question.

There are growing disincentives therefore to being a public intellectual, to share ideas with publics in one's own society, outside the universities, to engage in public debate in newspapers, popular books or the media. While this may be the norm from the perspective of the academy, it shows how the universities systemically devalue dialogue with persons and bodies other than academics. It effectively privatises learning among those who are paid-up members of the academic community, be it as students or academics. The lack of dialogue with publics, apart from one's peers, not only privatises knowledge to closed groups, it also forecloses the opportunity to have hypotheses tested or challenged from an experiential standpoint. It limits the opportunities for learning that occur when there is a dialogue between experiential and theoretical knowledge.

The penalising of academics for publishing in their own language or in their own country journals is another way in which the current peer review system is deeply problematic and undermining of nationally relevant scholarship. The system in the University of Oslo is an interesting example. Academics are given 1,000 Norwegians kroner for publishing an article in a Norwegian journal (i.e. in Norwegian in Norway); they are given 7,000 kroner for publishing an article in English outside of Norway. This not only threatens the scholarly vibrancy of the Norwegian language, it also strongly encourages academics to dialogue primarily with specialist academics outside their own country (Brock Utne, 2005). In Irish universities a similar practice is in operation in the assessment of staff publications. Publishing in Irish journals is accorded a lower status than publishing in "international" journals, although journals that are defined as international are English language US- and UK-based journals for the greater part. While it is clear that US journals have wider circulation than Irish journals given the population base of that country, if public interests are to be served, academics need to publish in their own countries and in their own languages (as well as in other country journals), especially in fields like the humanities and social sciences where so much of what needs to be understood is local as well as global. This will not happen unless such work is rewarded and recognised.

When there is no "peer review" value in engaging in public debate, there is no incentive to engage in the public sphere, to challenge ill-informed absolutisms and orthodoxies. In effect there is no incentive to publicly dissent or engage within the very institutions that are charged with the task of dissent and engagement. The reward system of academic life means that the "good" academic is encouraged to become a locally silent academic in their own country, silent in the public sphere and silent by virtue of dialoguing only with academic peers outside one's own country.

The response to any challenge to the limitations of over-reliance on the conventional peer-review system is that Finnish, Latvian, Danish, Slovenian, Maltese, Irish (or other similar small country) academics will become global players and that their global profile will indirectly lead to the dissemination of their ideas in the public sphere through internationalisation (Ramusson, 2005). To make this kind of impact, scholars, would need to be competing in a system where there is equality of condition as there can be no *equality of competition* without *equality of condition* (Baker, Lynch, Cantillon and Walsh, 2004). Such is not the case in the higher education sector. The control of global commercial publishing is centred in the major cities of the powerful capitalist states in the world.

It is naive to expect the majority of academics from minority cultures and languages to dominate the higher education market where they are minnows in competitive terms. While there are isolated exceptions, at the corporate level, powerful universities with big budgets can and do provide the best opportunities for globalisation of ideas, not least because of their massive financial reserves (reportedly several billion in the case of Harvard; see Lieberwitz, 2004) and their central location within the global publishing markets (Smallwood, 2001). This is not to say that scholars from other countries do not produce excellent research or publish successfully, rather it is to face the competitive global reality that those who have most resources and access to global capitalist publication networks are likely to be able to globalise their ideas.

One of the unforeseen negative consequences of relying on narrowly-defined, peer-reviewed systems to disseminate research knowledge is that academics will become increasingly invisible to the people who pay their salaries, and that is the taxpayers for those who work in predominantly state-funded university systems. Even if one has no interest in democratising research relations, or in being public intellectuals, there is a simple political reality that taxpayers are unlikely to fund universities if they cease to engage in a visible and accessible way with the big public issues of our time. Maintaining an ongoing engagement with both professional and community partners in education is an ongoing remit not only for education departments but also for faculties and schools whose research and teaching has immediate relevance outside of the university setting. If academics cease to engage they will cease to inform; they will also engender their own demise by their invisibility in the non-academic public sphere.

Finding a Voice: Sites of Resistance

In most European countries there is a long history of democratic struggle over education, including university education. Consequently the discourses on university education are not singular. While the neo-liberal code is dominant, there are alternative narratives – narratives of equality and inclusion that challenge the prevailing orthodoxies. These narratives are part of the official EU rhetoric and are given expression in various treaties and directives. Albeit subordinated, such discourses provide opportunities for challenging the market-driven agenda. They provide spaces for resistances and opportunities for redefining the purposes of the university.

In Ireland, for example, there is a growing political demand to promote diversity in the university body, not only in terms of the socio-economic profile of students, but also in terms of their age, ethnicity, disability and citizenship status (Higher Education Authority, 2005). The Irish Universities Association recognises the importance of being inclusive and lists "widening participation" as one of its core objectives. The European University Association, representing 30 National Rectors' Conferences and 537 individual European universities, in the Gratz Declaration signed in Leuven in July 2003, has strongly stated its objections and concerns regarding the operation of the GATS (General Agreement in Trade and Services) in relation to higher education. It outlines as a basic principle the fact that

> Higher Education exists to serve the public interest and is not a "commodity", a fact which WTO Member States recognized through UNESCO and other international and multilateral bodies, conventions and declarations.

It goes on endorse UNESCO's 1998 World Declaration on Higher Education for the Twenty-First Century and states that

> The mission of higher education is to contribute to the sustainable development and improvement of society as a whole by: educating highly qualified graduates able to meet the needs of all sectors of human activity; advancing, creating and disseminating knowledge through research; interpreting, preserving and promoting cultures in the context of cultural pluralism and diversity; providing opportunities for higher learning throughout life; contributing to the development and improvement of education at all levels; and protecting and enhancing civil society by training young people in values which form the basis of democratic citizenship and by providing critical and detached perspectives in the discussion of strategic choices facing societies (www.eua.be/en/policy/global_GATS).

There is a growing recognition too that there is a contradiction between pursuing a business-oriented and privatised approach to university education and promoting access for disadvantaged students. This is most clearly seen in the former socialist states of Eastern Europe and the former Soviet Republics where there were no private third-level institutions in the early 1990s but now there are several hundred. The evidence from Eastern Europe, including Russia, is that privatisation has a negative impact on equality in terms of student intake, not least because of the absence of an adequate system of financial supports (Steier, 2003). As noted by Steier (writing within a World Bank context), "increased institutional choice for students is meaningful only for those who can afford to pay tuition at private institutions or for those with access to financial aid" (Ibid, p. 163).

It is clear from the above that maintaining diversity in intake is a key policy objective if universities are to implement the Gratz Declaration and the UNESCO Declaration that they have signed up to. They cannot adopt market norms that will undermine their duty to educate all sectors of society. It is our duty and our opportunity to hold our universities to account in terms of these agreements.

Rather than being bewildered and overwhelmed by neo-liberal rhetoric, we need to build a counter-hegemonic discourse, a discourse that is grounded in the principles of democracy and equality that are at the heart of the public education tradition. We need to reinvigorate our vision of the university as a place for universal learning and for challenging received orthodoxies. The work of Paulo Freire (1972, 1973, 1976), the great Brazilian educator, offers such a challenge even though it would move us far from whence we came in terms of university education as it would require us to recognise the importance of mutuality in learning, the importance of creating a dialogue between student and teacher, between researchers and those being researched. It is a challenge to democratise the social relations of teaching, learning and research production and exchange, a challenge that many traditional university educators may well not feel comfortable with. Yet the question is, do we have much choice if we are to create new visions for our universities? If we have regard for the public service purposes of the university, for our responsibility to educate all members of society and educate them for all activities in society, including non-commercial activities be it in the arts, in caring work or in public service work, then we must radically alter the ways in which we define university education. We need to create allies for public education in civil society and in the public sector so that the public interest values of the universities can be preserved. As noted elsewhere, such a move would radically alter the way we educate and the way we do research (Lynch, 1999).

Conclusion

> If the university do not take seriously and rigorously its role as guardian of wider civic freedoms, as interrogator of more and more complex ethical problems, as servant and preserver of deeper democratic practices, then some other regime or ménage of regimes will do it for us, in spite of us, and without us (Toni Morrison, 2001 cited in Giroux, 2002, fn, p. 121).

Public universities were established to promote independence of intellectual thought, to enable scholars to work outside the control of powerful vested interest groups. Scholars are artists of the intellect, granted the freedom from necessity to write and research on the presumption that they do so in a manner that is disinterested in the purest sense of that term. It is widely understood and assumed that academic independence and objectivity is the guarantor of the public interests; it is expected that university scientists and scholars equate their self-interest, in research terms, with the public interest. While the public know that research conducted by profit-driven operations and powerful interests within the government and the state can and often is subject to political interpretation, in line with the interests of the funders, it is assumed, rightly, that this does not happen in the university.

There is therefore a widespread public trust and belief that the university employs scholars whose task it is to undertake research and teach for the public good. There is a hope and expectation that those who are given the freedom to think, research and write will work for the good of humanity in its entirety. Consequently, university research has been funded by the public purse for the greater part, even in countries such as the US where it is estimated that between 70 and 80 per cent of funding for university life sciences research comes from public sources (Blumenthal, 2002).

Because higher education is designed to serve the weakest and most vulnerable in society as well as powerful economic interests, it has a major responsibility to inform and vivify the work of the public sector, and the voluntary, community and care sectors, both locally and globally. It cannot simply serve commercial and professional interests. The civil, public and care infrastructure of society is the lifeblood that courses through the veins of economic development. It is the civil, public and care institutions that drive the heart of the body public. They ensure that the services, resources and understandings that are vital for change and development are renewed and reinvigorated on an ongoing basis. Unless higher education plays a central role in building the civil infrastructures of society by advancing thinking in cognate fields, not only social but also economic development will be in jeopardy.

Instead of yielding to the pressures to simply service the market, and to import its values and methods unquestioningly into higher education, universities both collectively and individually are in a powerful position to challenge the new neo-liberal orthodoxies. Academics have the space and the capability to work collaboratively to create strong alliances and networks not only among themselves but also with the entire civil society sector whose interests are so central to the public interest, and whom the universities have a duty to serve.

There is a sense in which the university's intellectual independence is always at risk, given its reliance on external funding from many sources, and yet its history grants it the capability to reclaim its own independence (Delanty, 2001). To maintain independence, the university needs to declare its distance from powerful interest groups, be these statutory, professional or commercial. It must maintain a critical distance from the institutions of power not only rhetorically but also constitutionally and practically.

As Ireland, and Europe generally, has become increasingly dependent on education to drive its social, political, cultural and economic infrastructure, access to higher education is increasingly becoming a prerequisite for survival. We need to challenge the neo-liberal commercialising agenda in education, not least because higher education is increasingly a necessity for the majority rather than a privilege for the few.

References

Allen, K. (2003) "Neither Boston nor Berlin: Class polarization and neo-liberalism in the Irish Republic" in: C. Coulter and S. Coleman (Eds.) *The End of Irish History? Critical Reflections on Celtic Tiger Ireland*. Manchester: Manchester University Press.

Angus, L. (2004) "Globalization and Educational Change; bringing about the reshaping and re-norming of practice", *Journal of Education Policy,* Vol. 19, No. 1, pp. 23-41.

Apple, M. W. (2001) *Educating the "Right" Way: Markets, Standards, God and Inequality* (New York: Routledge Falmer).

Archer, L., Gilchrist, R. Hutchings, M., Leathwood, C., Phillips D. and Ross, A. (2002) *Higher Education and Social Class: Issues of Inclusion and Exclusion* London: Falmer Press.

Archer, L. and Yamashita, H. (2003) "Knowing their limits"? Identities, inequalities and inner city school leavers" post-16 aspirations, *Journal of Education Policy*, 18(1), pp. 53-69.

Baker, J., Lynch, K., Cantillon, S. and Walsh, J. (2004) *Equality: From Theory to Action.* London: Palgrave Macmillan.

Ball, S. (2003) "The Teacher's Soul and the Terrors of Performativity", *Journal of Education Policy,* Vol. 18, No. 2, pp. 215-228.

Blumenthal, D. (2002) "Biotech in North East Ontario Conference: Conflicts of Interest in Biomedical research". *Health Matrix,* 12, p. 380.

Bok, D. (2003) *Universities in the Marketplace: The Commercialization of Higher Education.* Princeton: Princeton University Press.

Bonal, X. (2003) "The neoliberal educational agenda and the legitimation crisis: old and new state strategies", *British Journal of Sociology of Education*, 24(2), pp. 159-175.

Bourdieu, P. (1984) *Distinction: A Social Critique of the Judgement of Taste,* tr. Richard Nice, London: Routledge and Kegan Paul.

Bourdieu, P. and Passeron, J.C. (1977) *Reproduction in Education, Society and Culture,* Beverly Hills, CA: Sage.

Brewer, D, Gates, S., et al., (2002*) In Pursuit of Prestige: Strategy and Competition in US Higher Education*. New Brunswick, NJ: Transaction Press.

Brighouse, H. (2005) "Channel One, the Anti-Commercial Principle and the Discontinuous Ethos", *Educational Policy,* Vol. 19, No. 3, pp. 528-549.

Brock-Utne, B. (2005) "In Whose Language is Whose Knowledge Presented in Africa and in Europe? Paper presented to the *GENIE (Globalisation and Europeanisation Network in Education) Summer Institute,* Aalborg, Denmark, 5-7 July.

Bullen, E., Robb, S. and Kenway, J. (2004) "Creative Destruction: Knowledge economy policy and the future of the arts and humanities in the academy", *Journal of Education Policy,* Vol. 19, No. 1, pp. 1-22.

Bultmann, T., (1996) Die Standorgerechte Dienstleistungshochschule [The Location Appropriate Service College] [64 paragraphs] [On line serial 104. Available: http://staff-www.univ-marburg.de/~rillingr/wpl/texte/1bultman.htm.

Callahan, D. (2001) Report for the National Committee for Responsive Philanthropy *$1 Billion for Ideas*: Washington, National Committee for Responsive Philanthropy.

Chubb, J., and Moe, T. (1990) *Politics, Markets and America's Schools.* Washington: Brookings Institute.

Coolahan, J. (1981) *Irish Education: History and structure.* Dublin: Institute of Public Administration.

Covington, S. (2001) *Moving a Public Policy Agenda.* Report for the National Committee for Responsive Philanthropy: Washington

Delanty, G. (2001) "The University in the Knowledge Society", *Organization,* Vol. 8, No. 2, pp. 149-153.

Dill, D. D. (2003) "Allowing the Market to Rule: The Case of the United States", *Higher Education Quarterly,* Vol. 57, No. 2, pp. 136-157.

Dill, D.D. and Soo, M. (2005) "Academic Quality, League Tables and Public Policy: A Cross-National Analysis of University Ranking Systems" *Higher Education,* Vol. 49, pp. 495-533.

Doring, A. (2002) "Challenges to the Academic Role of Change Agent", *Journal of Further and Higher Education*, Vol. 26, No. 2, pp. 139-148.

Eisenberg, R.S. (1987) "Propriety Rights and the Norms of Science in Biotechnology Research", *Yale Law Journal,* Vol. 97, pp. 181-184.

Elton, Lewis (2000) "The UK Research Assessment Exercise: Unintended Consequences", *Higher Education Quarterly,* Vol. 54, No. 3, pp. 274-283.

Forfás (2004) *Building Ireland's Knowledge Economy.* Dublin: Forfás.

Freire, P. (1972, reprinted in 1996) *Pedagogy of the Oppressed.* London: Penguin.

Freire, P. (1973) *Education for Critical Consciousness.* London: Sheed and Ward.

Freire, P. (1976) *Cultural Action for Freedom.* Cambridge. Mass: Harvard Educational Review, Monograph Series, No. 1.

Gewirtz, S. Ball, S. J. and Bowe, R. (1995) *Markets, Choice and Equity in Education*, Buckingham: Open University Press.

Gilligan, C., (1982) *In a Different Voice.* Cambridge, Mass: Harvard University Press.

Gilligan, C. (1995). "Hearing the difference: Theorizing connection." _Hypatia_ 10 (2 Spring), pp. 120-127.

Giroux, H. (2002) "Neoliberalism, Corporate Culture and the Promise of Higher Education: The University as a Democratic Public Sphere", *Harvard Educational Review*, Vol. 72, No. 4, pp. 1-31.

Gouldner, Alvin V. (1970) *The Coming Crisis of Western Sociology,* London: Heinemann.

Gurin, P., Dey, E., Hurtado, S. and Gurin, G. (2002) "Diversity and Higher Education: Theory and Impact on Educational Outcomes" *Harvard Educational Review,* Vol. 72, No. 3, pp. 330-366.

Hanlon, G., (2000) "Sacking the New Jerusalem? The New Right, Social Democracy and Professional Identities" *Sociological Research Online,* Vol 5, No. 1. http://www.socresonline.org.uk/5/1/hanlon.html

Harkavy, I. (2005) "The Role of the Universities in Advancing Citizenship and Social Justice in the 21st Century", Paper delivered to the *Citizenship Education and Social Justice* Conference, Queen's University Belfast, 25 May 2005.

HEA (Higher Education Authority) (2005) "Achieving Equity of Access to Higher Education: Setting an Agenda for Ireland". 6-7 December 2004 Conference Proceedings. Dublin: HEA.

Henkel, M. (1997) "Academic Values and the University as Corporate Enterprise", *Higher Education Quarterly,* Vol. 51, No. 2, pp. 134-143.

Hey, V. (2001) "The Construction of Academic Time: Sub/contracting academic labour in research", *Journal of Education Policy*, Vol. 16, No. 1, pp. 67-84.

Hill, D. (2005?) "Globalisation and its educational discontents: Neoliberalism and its impacts on education workers" rights, pay and conditions. *International Studies in Sociology of Education,* Vol. 15 pp. 257-288.

Hutchings, M. (2002) "Financial Barriers to Participation" in Louise Archer et al., *Higher Education and Social Class: Issues of Inclusion and Exclusion* London: Falmer Press.

Kittay , E. (1999) *Love's Labor: Essays on Women, Equality and Dependency.* New York: Routledge

Kirby P. (2002) *The Celtic Tiger in Distress: Growth with inequality in Ireland.* Basingstoke: Palgrave.

Lauder, H., Hughes, D., et al. 1999. *Trading in Futures: Why markets in education don't work.* Buckingham: Open University Press.

Lieberwitz, R. L. (2004) "University Science Research Funding: Privatizing Policy and Practice", in Ronald G. Ehrenberg and Paula E. Stephan (eds.) *Science and the University.* Wisconsin: University of Wisconsin Press.

Loxley, A. and Thomas, Gary. (2001) "Neo-conservatives, neo-liberals, the New Left inclusion: stirring the pot", *Cambridge Journal of Education*, 31(3), pp. 291-293.

Lubienski, C. (2003) "Innovation in education markets: theory and evidence on the impact of competition and choice in charter schools", *American Educational Research Journal*, 40(2), pp. 395-443.

Lucey, H. and Reay, D. (2002) "Carrying the beacon of excellence: Social class differentiation and anxiety at a time of transition", *Journal of Education Policy*, 17(3), pp. 321-336.

Lyons, Maureen, Lynch, K., Close, Seán, Sheerin, Emer & Boland, Philip. (2003) *Inside Classrooms: The teaching and learning of mathematics in social context* Dublin: IPA

Lynch, K. (1987) "Dominant Ideologies in Irish Educational Thought: Consensualism, Essentialism and Meritocratic Individualism", *Economic and Social Review,* Vol. 18, No. 2, pp. 101-122.

Lynch, K. (1999a) *Equality in Education,* Dublin: Gill and Macmillan.

Lynch, K. (1999b) "Equality studies, the academy and the role of research in emancipatory social change", *The Economic and Social Review* 30, 1, pp. 41-69.

Lynch, K. and Baker, J. (2005) "Equality in Education: The Importance of Equality of Condition", *Theory and Research in Education,* Vol. 3, No.2, pp. 131-164

Lynch, K. and Moran, M. (2006) "Markets, Schools and the Convertibility of Economic Capital: The complex dynamics of class choice", *British Journal of Sociology of Education,* Vol. 27, No. 2.

Lynch, K. and O'Riordan, C. (1998) "Inequality in Higher Education: A Study of Class Barriers", *British Journal of Sociology of Education* 19, pp. 445-478.

McLaren, P. and Leonard, P. (1993) *Freire: A Critical Encounter.* London: Routledge.

McNair, S. (1997) "Is there a crisis? Does it matter?" in R. Barnett and A. Griffin (Eds.) *The End of Knowledge in Higher Education.* London: Cassell.

Moe, M. T., Bailey, K. and Lau, R. (1999) *The Book of Knowledge: Investing in the Education and Training Industry.* Merrill Lynch, Delaware.

Monbiot, G. (2000) *Captive State.* London: Macmillan.

Morey, A.L. (2004) "Globalization and the Emergence of For-Profit Higher Education", *Higher Education* Vol. 48, No.1, pp. 131-150.

Morrison, T. (2001) "How Can Values be Taught in this University" *Michigan Quarterly Review,* 278.

Munns, G. and McFadden, M. (2000) "First chance, second chance or last chance? Resistance and response to education", *British Journal of Sociology of Education*, 21(1), p. 59.

Noddings, N. (2003, 2nd edition) *Caring: A Feminine Approach to Ethics and Moral Education.* London; Berkeley: University of California Press.

Nussbaum, M. (1995a) "Emotions and Women's Capabilities" in Martha Nussbaum and Jonathan Glover (eds), *Women, Culture and Development: A study of human capabilities* Oxford: Oxford University Press, pp. 360-395.

Nussbaum, M. (1995b) "Human Capabilities, Female Human Beings" in Martha Nussbaum and Jonathan Glover (eds), *Women, Culture and Development*

Nussbaum, M. C. (1997) *Cultivating Humanity: A classical defence of reform in liberal education.* Cambridge MA and London: Harvard University Press.

OECD (Organisation for Economic Co-operation and Development) Review of (2004) *National Policies for Education: Review of Higher Education in Ireland,* *EDU/EC* (2004) 14. Paris: OECD.

Rasmussen, P. (2005) "Globalisation and Education: Current Discourses" Paper presented to the *GENIE (Globalisation and Europeanisation Network in Education) Summer Institute,* Aalborg, Denmark, 5-7 July.

Reay, D. and Lucey, H. (2003) "The limits of 'choice': Children and inner city schooling", *Sociology,* 37(1), pp. 121.

Reay, D. (2004) "Cultural Capitalists and Academic Habitus: Classed and Gendered Labour in Higher Education, *Women's Studies International Fo*rum, Vol. 27, No. 1, pp. 31-39.

Robertson, S.L., Bonal, X., and Dale, R. (2002) "GATS and the Education Service Industry: The Politics of Scale and Global Restructuring", *Comparative Education Review,* Vol. 46: No. 4, pp. 272-296.

Rutherford, J. (2005) "Cultural Studies in the Corporate University", *Cultural Studies*, Vol. 19, No. 3, pp. 297-317.

Slaughter, S. and Leslie, L.L. (2001) "Expanding and Elaborating the Concept of Academic Capitalism", *Organization,* Vol. 8, No. 2, pp. 154-161.

Smallwood, S. (2001) "The price professors pay for teaching at public universities", *Chronicle of Higher Education* (April 20)

Steier, F. S. (2003) "The Changing Nexus: Tertiary education institutions, the marketplace and the state", *Higher Education Quarterly*, Vo. 57, No. 2, pp. 158-180.

Stevenson, M. A., (1999) "Flexible Education and the Discipline of the Market" *Qualitative Studies in Education,* Vol. 12, No. 3, pp. 311-323.

Sugrue, C. (Ed.) (2004) *Curriculum and Ideology: Irish Experiences, International Perspectives,* Dublin: The Liffey Press.

Tawney, R.H. (1964) *Equality,* London: George Allen & Unwin.

Taylor, A. and Woollard, L. (2003) "The risky business of choosing a high school", *Journal of Education Policy*, 18(6), pp. 617-635.

Thrupp, M. (2001) "Education Policy and social class in England and New Zealand: An instructive comparison", *Journal of Education Policy*, 16(4), pp. 297-314.

Tight, M. (2000) "Do League Tables Contribute to the Development of a Quality Culture? Football and Higher Education Compared", *Higher Education Quarterly,* Vol. 54, No. 1, pp. 22-42.

Tooley, J. (1996*) Education without the State*. London: IEA Education and Training Unit.

Tooley, J. (2000) *Reclaiming Education,* London: Cassell.

Turner, D. (2005) "Benchmarking in Universities: League tables revisited" *Oxford Review of Education,* Vol. 31, No. 3, pp. 353-371.

UNDP (United Nations Development Programme) (2004) *Human Development Report 2003:* New York: Oxford University Press

Webster, F. (2004) "Cultural Studies and Sociology at and after the closure of the Birmingham School", *Cultural Studies,* Vol. 18, No. 6, pp. 847-862.

Whitty, G., Power, S. and Halpin, D. (1998) *Devolution and Choice in Education: The school, the state and the market,* Buckingham: Open University Press.

World Bank (1994) *Higher Education: The lessons of experience.* Washington: World Bank.

Young, M. (1958) *The Rise of the Meritocracy, 1870–2033: An essay on education and equality,* London: Thames & Hudson.

Notes

---

[1] According to the National Parents Council, "The practice of 'voluntary contributions' is proving to be very problematic because of the pressure being put on parents, the average amount requested by schools is €60 the Max is €180. Some schools are now asking for a registration fee and in some cases this is non refundable...." (www.npc.ie/17 August 2005)

[2] To say that the neo-liberal perspective glorifies the market and denigrates the State is not to deny the need that markets have for strong legislative and regulatory protections to protect commercial interests and legitimate market practices (Olssen, 1996; Apple, 2001). However, if international institutions (such as the European Union) and agreements (such as the General Agreement on Trade and Services) can override state actors in determining the regulatory environment for capitalist interests then the role of the nation-state is compromised in terms of its regulatory powers. While major capitalist states can and do exercise influence over the international regulatory environment for capitalism, the role of small states is severely limited. The observation by economists that Ireland is one of the most "open economies" in thre world is merely a euphemism for stating that, as a nation state, Ireland (and similarly small states) has very little control over the global trading environment in which it has to operate.

[3] "I think therefore I am".

[4] Merrill Lynch is a US-based global financial management company with offices in 36 countries.

[5] The most visible example is the "day out" sponsored by Coca Cola in a wide range of primary schools in particular. This is a basic marketing strategy for recruiting young children to Coca Cola products. In second-level schools the lack of funding has meant that some schools have relied on commercial operations (such as Proctor and Gamble producers of sanitary towels named "Al-

ways") to offer education on menstruation to young teenage girls. Needless to say the companies use these events to market their own products.

[6] *The Irish Times* (widely regarded as the most prestigious daily newspaper in Ireland) cited the rankings of the Jiao Tong league tables on multiple occasions throughout 2004, especially after the publication of the OECD Report on Higher Education in Ireland in that year. The ranking of Irish universities was treated unproblematically and the limitations of the ranking system were not analysed in any depth. It also cited the rankings of the Times Higher Education Supplement rankings, again very unquestioningly.

[7] The joint conference of the Irish Universities Association (IUA) and the Irish Business and Employers Confederation (IBEC), "Careering Towards the Knowledge Society: Are business & academia geared up to provide a future for high level researchers in Ireland?" 30 November 2005, is an example of the new kind of alliance the universities are developing with business interests. In the research field the links are well established and the Intel, 4th Level Ventures and the CRANN project are an example of this trend. Science Foundation Ireland (funded by the Irish taxpayer) has contributed €10 million to a new Centre for Science, Engineering and Technology (CSET) entitled the Centre for Research on Adaptive Nanostructures and Nanodevices (CRANN) in TCD, with partners in UCD and UCC (announced Jan 2004). Intel Ireland is CRANN's main industry partner; it located four Intel staff members to CRANN where they have a five-year contract as researchers-in-residence at a cost of €2.9 million to Intel. While the collaboration is identified by TCD Provost John Hegarty as one which will help push TCD to the forefront of worldwide innovative research (Trinity Online Gazette), Intel is quite explicit about the corporate interests served by the partnership: "By building technical leadership and research capability in Intel Ireland staff, CRANN allows Intel Ireland to add value to its existing operations while also demonstrating strategic value to Intel Corporation. CRANN enables Intel Ireland to explore niche scientific research in Ireland, which will allow the company to look towards Ireland for future Intel research initiatives." From the Intel website, 17/05/04 http://www.intel.com/ireland/about/ pressroom/2004/january/011204ir.htm

[8] "A research-intensive university where bold and imaginative educational programmes and excellence in teaching go hand-in-glove with a commitment to the discovery process, research and innovation; A university that is shaping agendas nationally – supporting where appropriate and challenging where warranted; A university that is truly international and truly Irish; A university where excellence is the benchmark for everything that we do, whether it be teaching, research or administration." (Dr. Hugh Brady, UCD President, Inaugural Foundation Day Address, Friday, 4 November 2004, UCD O'Reilly Hall.

[9] Throughout 2004 and early 2005 UCD went through a wide range of changes in its statutes and structures. The number of Faculties were reduced from eleven to five (now called Colleges) while Departments were reduced in number from over ninety to thirty five. Statute 6, governing the day-to-day operations of the university, was radically altered centralising power increasingly in the President and his close associates. Staff challenged and resisted many of these changes, particularly those that appear to erode the limited democratic controls that they had in the university. They held meetings with and without their trade unions, organised lectures and directly challenged the plans at Faculties, Academic Council and the Governing Authority. However, as time wore on it was clear that changes the so-called "President's Team" proposed were going to be passed regardless of protests and concerns. Consultations with staff increasingly developed a meaningless ritualistic character as changes in structures were pushed through (with some very minor concessions) regardless of dissent.

[10] Reay (2004) notes that the "research team" is a euphemism that operates to conceal the true hierarchical and often exploitative relations within the so-called teams. It operates to ensure compliance by concealing the true hierarchies of power, status, income and control that operate within it. Contract researchers are often out of contract by the time papers are written, often leaving them with no publication record in return for their work (Hey, 2001).

[11] The budget for Science Foundation Ireland (SFI), that funds the physical sciences, engineering and related mathematical areas, has increased dramatically in the last 5 years. SFI is now a multimillion euro operation with individual research programmes over €10 million being strongly promoted. The funding for research in Humanities, Arts and Social Sciences has remained relatively static with the entire budget for research in the Irish Research Council for the Humanities and Social Sciences (IRCHSS) being less than that available for single projects in the sciences and engineering areas. (Source: direct communications with SFI and the IRCHSS and published materials from both).

[12.] There is ample anecdotal evidence that this is happening already in Irish universities. In UCD the Chair of Equality Studies and the Chair of Disability Studies are the only two endowed professorships in the College of Humanities to be funded from outside sources (funded by philanthropic bodies and a statutory agency) in the last five years. There has been no endowments for professorships in the arts and humanities in that period while there has been a large number of endowed chairs in the College of Life Sciences and the College of Physical Sciences and Mathematics most of which are commercially funded.

Chapter 16

RURAL DEVELOPMENT:
POLICY THEMES AND MEASURES
OF THE EARLY TWENTY-FIRST CENTURY

Patricia O'Hara *and* **Patrick Commins**

Rural development policy and practice, which ultimately aims to improve the standard of living, life choices, quality of life and general well-being of rural citizens, has undergone very significant changes since our review in the last edition of this book (O'Hara and Commins, 1998). Given the spatial impact of Ireland's relatively sudden and sustained economic growth and prosperity from the mid-1990s, this is not surprising. Rapid economic progress has been associated with changes in the sectoral and occupational mix in rural areas, population increases, urbanisation, and related changes in the relationships between rural and urban space. Concerns about the environment, about planning issues, about access to land, as well as escalating land prices, are among the issues that have come to the fore since the turn of the century. Rapid urbanisation and rising property values have also altered popular perceptions of the rural from a "backwater" to a desirable place of retreat from congested urban centres.

In the earlier chapter, we noted that there were two models of rural development then in operation. One with a narrow agricultural focus and associated with payments to farmers through the Common Agricultural Policy (CAP) of the European Union (EU) and linked to farm development, diversification and support to farm incomes. The second we characterised as "area-based" and "bottom-up", supported by a combination of EU and exchequer funds and delivered by LEADER groups and local partnerships to a much wider rural constituency.

Since then, while CAP-supported rural programmes have remained primarily targeted at farmers, rural development policy has extended its scope more widely and now encompasses a broad range of interests and concerns. EU policies are still a dominant influence, but other EU funding, such as the Structural and Cohesion Funds, have become relevant to rural development. Ireland's recent and rapid prosperity has stimulated a shift in national policy from concern with rural decline and bottom-up development, to regional development and to the task of managing spatial development. Policy has had to respond to an increasing array of spatial issues, including new infrastructural needs, environmental management and demands for improved services. These are articulated by diverse interests involved in the policy development process through the various structures of participation that have emerged in civil society.

Rural development discourse and policy are therefore shaped by many influences: international economic and technological forces; EU regulations; national interests; and the way these are responded to at national level and articulated locally. We have already documented the forces that influenced Irish rural development policy priorities and practice before and after entry to the then Common Market in the 1970s and pointed out the dominant influence of European policies and support measures through the various reforms up to the mid-1990s (Commins and O'Hara, 1991; O'Hara and Commins, 1998).

In this chapter we consider rural development policy trends since the late 1990s. We feel it is important to make a distinction between policy discourses and actual policy measures. A discourse is a specific language of terminology, viewpoints, sets of ideas and assumptions that is manifest in sustained critiques of existing policies, arguments for asserting the legitimacy of new approaches and in rhetoric which supports some policy directions as more appropriate than others (Haughton et al., 2003). Thus, in the first section of the paper we review some of the main themes of the discourse which has influenced the shaping of rural policy in Ireland over the past decade. The second section summarises the actual policy measures in place over the period, and those planned under the new

EU programming period (2007-2013). This period will also see the implementation of a new National Development Plan and the loss of EU Objective 1 status for the Border, Midlands and West (BMW) Region. Some concluding comments are provided in Part Three.

Policy Discourse — Themes and Influences

International and European Influences

Globalisation, Competitiveness and Knowledge. In a world economy dominated by transnational corporations, the strength of regional economies is linked to their capacity to attract or retain footloose international capital and to grow indigenous companies that can trade successfully in a global context. As a small, open, trade-intensive economy Ireland's economic progress is very much influenced by global trends. Globalisation has led to an emphasis on competitiveness and productivity as the drivers of economic growth in EU and national policies.

This is highlighted in the Lisbon Strategy which aims to position the European Union to become the most dynamic and competitive economy in the world, and is also reflected in the prominence of the competitiveness agenda in national policies. Globalisation and associated competition impact on rural economies, so that their capacity to attract, or to retain, inward investment and to grow indigenous businesses that can trade successfully in the international global economy, are seen as major challenges.

Competitiveness is driven by research and innovation, i.e. the production of knowledge aimed at the creation of new products and processes and at inventing new forms of organisation for the geographical distribution of economic activities. The production and distribution of knowledge on an unprecedented scale is one of the characteristics of globalisation. Its impacts on finance, trade, business, economic growth and social affairs have been so pervasive as to give rise to the concept of the "knowledge economy". Knowledge economies have a high level of economic activity based on knowledge as a factor of production, or incorporated into production through capital investment. They have significant proportions of their workforce employed in "high-tech" firms which both produce and utilise sophisticated information and communications technology (ICT). Creativity and expertise of workers is a critical element of the knowledge economy and the continual enhancement of skills is essential to maintain competitiveness.

ICT can revolutionise access to knowledge and lessen the constraints of location thus providing unprecedented opportunities to do business from relatively remote rural locations, once the necessary communications infrastructure is available. However, the stronger tendency is for knowledge-intensive firms to "cluster" around urban centres, because of proximity to an education and scientific infrastructure; this poses significant challenges for rural economies.

It is also evident that the forces of globalisation have been paralleled to some extent by a reaffirmation of the local – whether given expression in locally-based food production and consumption networks (e.g. farmers' markets) or in the revival of local cultural practices and communications systems (e.g. for local tourism and in community radio stations). The diversification of the rural economy and the increasing significance of the rural landscape as a "public good" (freely available to all) have very significant implications for rural development policy and practice.

Influences on EU Policies

In broad terms, the EU, primarily through the CAP but also to a lesser extent through the Structural Funds, continues to be a major influence on rural development policy. Although, the proportion of the total EU budget accounted for by the CAP has dropped dramatically as a result of the budgetary reform of the past two decades, it remains a very significant source of support to rural regions. This is particularly so in the Border, Midlands and West Region (BMW) which loses Objective 1 (priority) status after 2006 so that monies from the Structural Funds will decline dramatically. Reforms have also altered the form of support given to farmers which impacts on both farm and rural development.

Among the key drivers of CAP reform have been world trade liberalisation and EU enlargement. International trade liberalisation is overseen by the World Trade Organisation (WTO) which aims to free up world markets by lessening state involvement and regulation. The Uruguay Round of the World Trade Negotiations 1995-2000 covered agriculture and food for the first time, and the EU participated as a single entity. The Uruguay agreement, which remains in place until a successor is negotiated under the forthcoming Doha Round, required significant reductions in the system of supports and subsidies to agriculture and food products.

The enlargement of the EU to 25 member states in 2004 meant a major increase in the Union's rural population. In the EU-25, 56 per cent of inhabitants live in rural regions which generate 45 per cent of Gross Value Added (GVA), and provide for 53 per cent of employment, but these tend to lag behind in terms of per capita incomes and other socio-economic indicators. Agriculture is much more significant in the enlarged Union, both in terms of GDP and employment, with new member states having three times the percentages in the combined EU-15. The size and diversity of regions in the new member states and the potential budgetary impact on the CAP caused a major rethink of policy.

CAP Reform

CAP reform happened in three phases, beginning in the mid-1980s. The European Commission's 1988 document *The Future of Rural Society* recognised that farmers were a decreasing minority in many of Europe's rural areas (due in large measure to the restructuring associated with the operation of the CAP), and that rural development needed to encompass the non-farm sector. Three different "types" of rural regions were set out, defined largely by their spatial relationship to large conurbations. At this time also, the move toward European Union brought into focus the need to support peripheral regions. This led to the designation of "less-developed" regions (Objective 1) for priority support from Structural and Cohesion Funds, and an emphasis on concepts such as integrated, multi-sectoral development, partnership, participation and subsidiarity. At the same time locally-based "bottom-up development was supported through successive LEADER programmes. Nevertheless, while some supply controls were introduced (e.g. milk quotas), the CAP continued to be the main EU support for rural areas and this was delivered through subsidising farm incomes.

The second phase of reform began with the so-called McSharry reforms of 1992, which emphasised the diversity of farming and the protection of the rural environment. This was given effect in a major change in the form of support to farmers by shifting the emphasis from price subsidies to direct (non-price-related) payments and introducing schemes whereby farmers could be compensated for conserving aspects of environment and landscape. In Ireland this agri-environmental dimension was implemented as the Rural Environment Protection Scheme (REPS). The European Model of Agriculture (EMA) became the cornerstone of EU policy on rural issues in Agenda 2000. According to the EMA, the multifunctional character of European agriculture rests on three main functions, namely: food, feed and fibre production; preservation of the rural environment and landscape; and contributing to the viability of rural areas and balanced territorial development. Agriculture's role in the provision of what are termed "public goods" (e.g. landscape, cultural heritage features, and biodiversity) provide an important rationale for continuing support to agriculture. The EMA is the model that the EU seeks to protect in WTO negotiations.

New EU Rural Development Policy

The "new rural development policy" of the EU is encapsulated in Agenda 2000 and in a third phase of CAP reforms (the "Fischler" reforms in 2002/03), in which rural development has been (re)integrated into the CAP and labelled as the "second pillar". The first, or market, pillar involves a full decoupling of income support from agricultural production. Farmers are now given a single payment in return for maintaining their farms in good condition and are free to produce otherwise for the market but without payments made specifically to boost market prices (see further below under "Sectoral Policies"). Future changes in EU policy are likely to continue the trend by which market realities, and not subsidies, will drive the production decisions of farmers and government. These realities are predicted to accentuate the spatial concentration of farm production (Commins et al., 2005).

The "second pillar" of the CAP provides support for rural development to underpin the EMA. EU rural policy for the period 2007-2013 will involve a new strategic approach with a focus on the agri-food economy, the environment and the broader rural economy and population. The Goteborg Guiding Principles for Sustainable Development and the renewed Lisbon strategy for growth and jobs, which call for matching strong economic performance with the sustainable use of natural resources, are to be the guiding principles of the new policy. The EU Commission has set out broad strategic guidelines as a framework and member states are expected to formulate their own national development strategies.

The measures to be supported will be based on four axes: competitiveness in agri-food and forestry; land management and the environment; quality of life/diversification; and innovation in governance based on locally-based "bottom-up" approaches to rural development.

Axis 1 prioritises knowledge transfer, modernisation, innovation and quality in the agri-food and forestry sectors. It includes support for farm training, establishing new entrants in farming, early farmer retirement, food quality and downstream food and forestry activities. Axis 2 aims to promote biodiversity and preservation and conservation of landscapes and natural resources. It provides for payments to farmers in disadvantaged areas and for preservation of the environment and countryside. Environmental regulations generally will be increasingly important in agriculture along with the directives already in place on waste management and pollution control.

Axis 3 measures are aimed at diversification of the rural economy and include support for tourism, crafts, micro-businesses, take up of ICT, village renewal, local heritage, training and capacity-building. Axis 4 is aimed at animating local capacity to meet the goals of competitiveness, environment and quality of life, and is effectively a mainstreaming of the LEADER approach. The Commission stipulates that a minimum of 10 per cent of the funding must be spent on Axes 1 and 3 and 25 per cent on Axis 2.

The overall orientation is, to an extent, a return to nationalisation, i.e. the guiding principles are devolution of responsibility with some flexibility at the point of implementation. Member states are required to produce a national rural development strategy which provides a rationale for the measures to be supported and this has required a close engagement with rural policy issues (see second section below).

Regional and Spatial Perspectives

As CAP reform proceeded to bring about a widening of the agri-centred model of rural development, both EU and national policies over the past decade or so have increasingly linked rural development with regional development. This shift began in Europe with the emphasis on territory, space and the mapping of rural regions in *The Future of Rural Society*. It continued with the designation of territories as the targets of particular measures (and associated concentration of support) in the reform of the Structural Funds.

The European Spatial Development Perspective (ESDP), published in 1999, set out the broad strategic framework for the development of Europe's regions. Based on a rationale of achieving greater economic competitiveness, its main objectives are: a balanced and polycentric city system and associated new urban rural partnerships; parity of access to infrastructure and knowledge; and sustainable development, prudent management and protection of culture. Balanced regional development is the goal but not at the expense of global competitiveness. The region emerges as an increasingly important focus of rurality in Europe, and cities are seen as the driving forces of regional economic development within an increasingly competition oriented space economy. These trends had a strong influence on Irish policy, as we shall see in the next section.

The White Paper on Rural Development 1999

The first ever white paper on rural development was launched in 1999, just months before the publication of the National Development Plan (NDP) 2000-2006. *Ensuring the Future – A Strategy for Rural Development in Ireland* identified the challenges facing rural areas as growing urbanisation; continuing population loss in remote areas; decline in agriculture; relative disadvantage of rural areas in attracting and sustaining jobs; social exclusion in rural areas; and the need for protection of the rural environment. The overall objective was to identify and implement a strategy which would:

- Provide sufficient employment opportunities to compensate for the loss of employment in agriculture

- Counter out-migration and depopulation in many areas

- Meet the needs for public service delivery in terms of access to the range of services which are required to sustain viable rural communities.

According to the White Paper:

> If rural communities, and especially people leaving agriculture, can be integrated into the wider economy without geographic displacement, the central goals of rural development will be achieved (p. 9).

Strong market forces will favour urban areas at the expense of the rural. However, the White Paper considers rural development as a public good, that is, an issue not to be left to the dictates of the market. It identified six elements of an overall strategy for rural development: a dedicated focus on rural development through appropriate institutional mechanisms, particularly a "lead department"; a regional approach to development; service and infrastructure provision; sustainable economic development; human resources development; and a focus on poverty and social exclusion. The commitment to "rural proofing" whereby national policies are analysed for impact on the well-being of rural communities was also reiterated.

Of particular significance, in light of the discussion above on the convergence between rural and regional policy, is the explicit statement about the scope of the rural development policy agenda as follows:

> . . . all Government policies and interventions which are directed towards improving the physical, economic and social conditions of people living in the open countryside, in coastal areas, in towns and villages and in smaller urban centres outside of the five major urban areas. The agenda will, at the same time, facilitate balanced and sustainable regional development while tackling issues of poverty and social exclusion (p. 20).

The publication of the White Paper was a milestone in the evolution of Irish rural development policy. Not only was it the first comprehensive articulation of Irish government policy strategy in regard to rural development, but it widened the compass of policy to the needs of those living in all areas outside of the major urban centres. It also fused the policy agendas for rural and regional development. This regional approach and the objective of balanced regional development anticipated the National Development Plan 2000-2006, published a few months later, which is discussed further in the second section below.

The National Spatial Strategy 2002

The dominant trends in European regional policy strongly influenced the evolution of Irish policy towards a regional model in the 1990s. The requirements of Objective 1 status,[1] initially for the entire country, and more latterly for the BMW Region, led to the creation of regional authorities which, despite their relatively limited powers, put the regional issue on the policy agenda. The effects of the very rapid economic growth of the 1990s were spatially uneven and made the disparities between the urbanised East and South and the rural West and North West more apparent. These spatial imbalances are associated with differences in incomes, output, and productivity as well as demographic imbalances and the incidence and risk of poverty.

The commitment to "balanced regional development" is one of the key objectives of the NDP 2000-2006 and a strategic framework for spatial development was set out in the National Spatial Strategy (NSS) published in 2002. The NSS was closely modelled on the ESDP, based as it is on a hierarchy of urban centres – gateways and hubs – and identifying them as the focus for growth and development in the regions because of their attractiveness to high-tech foreign-owned firms and to skilled workers, and their capacity to provide a range of services and facilities. Urban-generated development was expected to have beneficial spill-over effects on rural areas.

The NSS identified five broad rural area types which face very different rural development challenges, and the most appropriate policy responses in each case. These are set out in Table 16.1. Strong areas are predominantly in the South and East (S&E) while weak and remote areas are located in the West, Midlands and Border Regions (BMW).

Table 14.1: Rural Area Types and Policy Responses

Rural Area Type and Description	Rural Area Policy Responses
1. Strong Mainly in the South and East where agriculture will remain strong, but where pressure for development is high and some rural settlements are under stress	• Support agriculture by maintaining the integrity of viable farming areas • Strengthen rural villages and small towns by making them attractive to residential and employment-related development • Reduce urban sprawl through a renewal emphasis on appropriate in-fill development
2. Changing Including many parts of the Midlands, the Border, the South and West where population and agricultural employment have started to decline and where replacement employment is required	• Support communities where the viability of agriculture is under stress through promoting diversification in enterprise, local services and tourism
3. Weak Including more western parts of the Midlands, certain parts of the Border and mainly inland areas in the West, where population decline has been significant	• Build up rural communities through spatially targeted and integrated measures • Develop new rural tourism resources such as inland waterways
4. Remote Including parts of the west coast and the islands	• Promote marine and natural resource-based development • Overcome distance barriers with the support of technology
5. Culturally Distinct Including parts of the west coast and the Gaeltacht which have a distinctive cultural heritage	• Enhance accessibility • Strengthen existing settlements • Conserve cultural identity

Source: National Spatial Strategy 2002-2020

Priorities for rural areas identified in the NSS include: strengthening the rural economy based on natural resources and environmental quality; strengthening communities through settlement policies; and enhancing accessibility and supporting cultural heritage and identity. The NSS itself is not very specific on how these might be addressed and they have been taken up in practice to varying extents. However, the idea of linking gateways to provide a "counter pole" to the national dominance of the Greater Dublin Region has been the point of strongest impact on policy discourse. Regional planning guidelines have been drawn up which are intended to give effect to the NSS and provide a framework for local planning, but not a detailed strategy for local development.

The Agri-Food Sector – Envisaging the Future

Two recently published policy documents are of interest because, while they focus on the future of the agri-food sector, they advert to the role of rural development in countering the adverse demographic consequences that are foreseen to accompany the anticipated economic rationalisation and restructuring in this sector.

The Agri-Food 2010 Committee, a "think tank" set up to assess the future for the industry, reporting in 2000, identified the main challenges as follows:(a) further trade liberalisation; (b) more restrictive EU policies following enlargement of the Community and budgetary pressures; (c) new trends in food markets driven by consumer lifestyles and concerns for food safety, as well as by globalisation and concentration at retail level. These changes will have the effect of squeezing the profit margins of producers and processors, thus placing much greater emphasis on the need for innovation, marketing and food safety assurance. The Committee's recommendations centred on rationalising farm structures, increasing the scale of the individual farm business, achieving greater efficiencies in farm production, meeting the requirements of consumers in regard to food quality and safety, and having greater competitiveness in the food industry. Its report recognised that an agri-food economy, driven by a sustained quest for economic competitiveness, would result in serious decline in the numbers of full-time farms.

Taking up this last point, the later Agri Vision 2015 Committee (set up to devise strategy in the light of developments since 2000), reporting in 2004, projected that by 2015 the numbers of economically viable full-time farms would drop to less than half the number in 2002 and that part-time farms would predominate. As a result of the increase in part-time farming and the likely reduced intensity of farming activity on part-time farms, full-time farms will account for an increasing proportion of Irish agricultural output. These will be overwhelmingly concentrated in the southern half of the country.

Although little attention is paid to the consequences of the predicted changes in the agri-food economy for the less developed rural regions, the Agri 2015 Committee stressed the importance of addressing what it termed "substantial regional differences in economic development" (p. 40), arguing that rural development, as well as broader regional development and planning policy, should address the diversity in economic performance.

The Rural Economy – A Look Towards 2025

Other future-oriented perspectives were outlined in the report of the Rural Foresight Project, published in 2005 as *Rural Ireland 2025* (NUI Maynooth, University College Dublin, and Teagasc). This report concluded that, although the aggregate "headline indicators" in the national economy are currently positive, they mask underlying weaknesses that will be to the detriment of the longer-run prospects for the rural economy. If these persist or worsen, there will not be an acceptable regional balance in Ireland's economy. Population, commercial agriculture and modern enterprises will be even more concentrated than at present. It is likely also that a large part of manufacturing activity will move to lower cost economies. Employment in building and construction will not continue at currently high levels, while "new economy" types of employment will not be located in the many rural communities outside of commuting zones.

The Foresight Project stated that a more desirable scenario could be achieved by:

- A greater policy commitment to regional and rural development

- A recognition that rural development requires a strong focus on coordinated multisectoral development, tailored to the circumstances of different regions and extending beyond agricultural policy measures

- Positioning the Irish rural economy in the evolving global context, with a special emphasis on applying research and new knowledge in the transition to a services-based economy

- Constructing an effective institutional framework for implementing multisectoral rural development, and changing the prevailing mode of public policy-making such that (a) the rhetoric of stated policy is followed through with clear operational programmes (e.g. in relation to the 1999 White Paper, or the National Spatial Strategy), and (b) public programmes are initiated proactively without undue dependence on directives from Brussels.

Having considered some of the international, European and domestic influences on rural development policy in Ireland, we now turn to some of the key policy measures in operation in 2006 and anticipated for the period 2007-2013. We also consider briefly the main institutional structures for policy delivery in rural areas.

Policy Measures and Policy Implementation

In the broadest sense development policy measures for rural areas are effectively all those relating to infrastructure, to the productive sectors and to human resources. It is not possible to review all of these here so we concentrate on key rural-related policies or policy proposals which have evolved over the past decade.

Agriculture – Farm Level

Since the early 1990s the most important policy measures for Irish farms have been the range of direct non-market payments based on a landholder's herd of different categories of livestock and on arable land farmed. Over the years these payments assumed increasing significance as a proportion of farm income. Between 1995 and 2003, in the BMW Region, their contribution to the "operating surplus in farming" rose from 41 per cent to 83 per cent; the corresponding increase in the S & E region was from 28 per cent to 58 per cent. Nationally, in 2004, they accounted for 74 per cent of aggregate farm income. Clearly, direct payments prevented widespread poverty among farming households.

Since the introduction of the "single farm payment" in the most recent reform of the CAP, all livestock and arable crop subsidies are paid without regard to what a farm produces, as we have already noted. The scale of these payments to a farm, which will run to at least 2012, is generally referenced to the payments made under the old system during 2000 to 2002. They are linked to compliance with statutory management requirements, and to a stipulation to keep all farmland in good environmental and agricultural condition.

The Rural Environmental Protection Scheme (REPS) provides for payment to farmers in return for undertakings to farm and maintain their land in a way which protects the landscape and environment. Participants wishing to enter the scheme must comply with 11 basic compulsory measures, as well as two out of a further 16 options – one of which is organic farming. REPS has proved attractive to small to medium-sized landholders in the more disadvantaged farming areas of the west and north-west. Approximately one-third of all agricultural land (some 43,000 landholders) is now farmed in accordance with its specifications.

Capital grants are also available for managing farm waste, as are investment aids for enterprises not in surplus (e.g. deer, sport horses). Special financial aid is provided to encourage private forestry development. Again, the response has been greater in the BMW Region where the farms are smaller and the land of more marginal quality.

Enterprise Support

Rural areas generally contain a large number of relatively small firms and businesses that are engaged in providing mainly locally-based services and small-scale manufacturing. The White Paper on Rural Development noted the importance of strengthening rural enterprises. Support for such businesses comes through national agencies (e.g. Enterprise Ireland, FAS), regionally based agencies (e.g. Údarás na Gaeltachta , the Western Development Commission), sectoral agencies like Bórd Bia and Fáilte Ireland and Regional Tourism Authorities (RTAs), as well as the locally-based agencies which are LEADER companies, County Enterprise Boards (CEBs) and Partnerships. However, with the exception of LEADER, none of these agencies has specifically-defined measures or polices for rural enterprises.

In a Review of Enterprise Support in Rural Areas, undertaken for the Department of Community, Rural and Gaeltacht Affairs, Fitzpatrick Associates (2004) noted that 15 enterprise agency systems provided direct support to rural enterprises. Pointing out that this situation is unsatisfactory because of the potential for overlap and duplication,[2] as well as its unwieldiness, Fitzpatricks concluded that to be effective, modification would require a holistic approach across a range of government departments. Among their recommendations from a detailed study of enterprise supports were:

- CEBs should be the first "port of call" for enterprise supports

- LEADER companies should engage in animation and capacity-building in order to maximise any latent enterprise potential in rural areas

- Specialist sectoral expertise should be accessible to smaller firms in rural areas

- Sectoral targeting which builds on the natural competitive advantages of rural regions would be an effective approach and could be coordinated by the CEBs. This is particularly appropriate in the tourism industry.

These recommendations have been taken up to a relatively limited extent to date.

The lack of adequate and up-to-date information on small business is a major barrier to effective policy development for this sector. This was one of the key issues raised by the Small Business Forum, set up to advise on the adequacy and appropriateness of policy for small businesses in Ireland, which published its report in 2006.

Tourism Development

Tourism is an important element of rural economies, particularly in peripheral regions where other business options may be limited. This was acknowledged in the White Paper which concluded that a carefully planned strategy is needed to achieve its potential.

The NSS also identified the potential of tourism for regional development, particularly for so-called "weak rural" areas:

> Tourism is characterised by the fact that consumption takes place where the service is provided. Also significant is the fact that tourism activity is focused in some cases on areas with an otherwise weak

economic base. As a result it can have a positive influence on regional development (p. 99).

A number of strategic tourism opportunities for rural regions were identified in the NSS and based on developing existing natural attractions and
investment in new facilities to create critical mass and "package" tourism
products.

However, despite recognition of the importance of tourism for rural
development, the policy response has been weak, and Ireland has experienced a trend of increasing spatial concentration of tourist numbers.
Apart from Dublin, all regions have seen a decline in overseas tourist
numbers since the peak year of 2000. The loss of momentum brought
about by the virtual closure of rural areas to tourists during the outbreak
of foot and mouth disease in 2001 has not been easy to recover. Numbers
have grown since then but have not reached the 2000 levels, demonstrating how hard it is to regain visitor numbers from overseas.

Global trends in tourism markets, such as the growing tendency for
short breaks to easy to reach destinations, competition from other European countries and cheap airfares to cities pose real challenges for tourism development in rural regions. There is a recognised need for product
development but where monies have been committed to this, as in the
NDP 2000-2006, they have not been spent. Budgeted expenditure under
the NDP was only 1 per cent of forecast by June 2005. Promotion of innovative product development, better air access and improved services
are among the issues that need to be addressed by policy.

A new strategy for sustainable development of tourism was agreed in
2003,[3] but it pays relatively little attention to how tourism is to be dis-
persed to rural regions. The strategy sets out a single regional target related to the doubling of the numbers of overseas visitors staying at least
one night in the BMW region by 2012. In addition, policies in other sectors such as planning, culture, heritage, infrastructure and even signpost-
ing are often not very well aligned with tourism needs.

Since much rural tourism is activity-based, access to the countryside
is an important tourism issue. Comhairle na Tuaithe, comprising representatives of the farming organisations, recreational users of the countryside and state bodies with an interest in the countryside, was set up in
2004 to address this and to develop a Countryside Code and a National

Countryside Recreation Strategy. Comhairle na Tuaithe has agreed a set of countryside access parameters, to serve as a basis for preventing conflicts among users of the countryside and integrating a variety of needs and responsibilities. This body has also agreed the key features necessary for countryside code development.

Transport and Communications Infrastructure

Rapid economic growth has brought the need to address inadequacies in Ireland's transport and communications infrastructure to the forefront of national policy. Upgrading of road and public transport infrastructure has been a particular focus of policy attention and support. Rural areas experience particular disadvantages with poor quality roads and very limited public transport services. Consequently, delivery of new investment to upgrade national and regional routes and improve rail services, including opening of new lines (such as commuter routes and the western rail corridor), are regarded as crucial if rural areas are to attract and retain both people and businesses. These have been provided for under the investment programmes in the NDP 2000-2006 and in the Transport 21 programme. Additional support for rural areas is also available under the CLÁR Programme (see below).

The deregulation of the telecommunications market has favoured urban areas where population concentration gives private companies a better return on investment in broadband infrastructure. Public investment in the provision of broadband infrastructure via metropolitan networks and a County and Group Broadband Scheme has had limited impact, so far, on availability in rural Ireland.

Area-based Policy Measures

Apart from sectoral polices, there are a range of policy measures which are targeted more specifically at rural areas either because they are tailored to the needs of particular regions, or directed at rural areas in particular. The most significant of these are discussed below.

The National Development Plan (NDP) 2000-2006. We have already referred to the NDP which, while having a national focus does have a spatial dimension in the form of two regional programmes. Balanced regional development is one of the key aims of the NDP 2000-2006. Actions to achieve this have involved a combination of: investment in infrastructure particularly roads, public transport, and environmental services; the promotion of regional gateways to be identified in the NSS; positive discrimination in relation to attracting foreign investment into the BMW Region and support for new enterprise; investment in education and training; and the inclusion of two Regional Operational Programmes (for the Objective 1 BMW Region and the remaining S & E region) targeted at local infrastructure, the local productive sector and the promotion of social inclusion.

A rural development measure was included in each of the two regional operational programmes. This provided for investment under the Western Development Commission's Investment Fund (a loan and equity fund for businesses and social enterprises) in the seven western counties; support for policy research, rural services and rural development programmes including rural tourism; and support for diversification and development of non-surplus products and alternative enterprises. Apart from this specific measure, the priorities and measures to support balanced regional development were largely as set out in the White Paper published a few months previously. Effectively, rural and regional development becomes synonymous in the NDP.

The new NDP 2007-2013 is now (mid-2006) in preparation and is expected to be less detailed than its predecessor. It will be funded entirely from the national exchequer, and is expected to be built around strategic priorities and some flagship projects rather than detailed operational measures.

The CLÁR Programme. The CLÁR programme (Ceantair Laga Árd-Riachtanais), launched in October 2001, is a targeted investment programme in selected rural areas. CLÁR provides funding and co-funding to Government departments, state agencies and Local Authorities to accelerate investment in selected priority developments. These investments support physical, community and social infrastructure across a variety of measures. The 16 areas originally selected for inclusion in the CLÁR programme were those that suffered the greatest population decline from 1926 to 1996. The average population loss in these regions was 50 per cent.

Following an analysis of the 2002 Population Census data, the CLÁR areas were extended. The areas were again expanded in 2006 following a further analysis of the 2002 population. Areas now eligible for inclusion in CLÁR are based on an average population fall of 35 per cent per county between 1926 and 2002. Towns of 3,000 and over and their peri-urban areas have been excluded, irrespective of county decline in population. The new areas are either contiguous to existing CLÁR areas or have a minimum population of 1,000. Infrastructure investments supported under the CLÁR Programme include roads; water and sewerage; area enhancement; sports and community facilities; health; needs of islands; telecommunications and electricity infrastructure.

LEADER. LEADER is the EU Community Initiative for Rural Development that provides approved Local Action Groups with public funding (EU and national) to implement multi-sectoral plans for the development of their own areas. Over the period 2000-2006 LEADER was delivered via two programmes known as LEADER+ and the LEADER National Rural Development Programme.

The aim of LEADER+ is to encourage the emergence and testing of new approaches to integrated and sustainable development in 22 rural communities throughout the country. The LEADER National Rural Development Programme forms part of the Regional Operational Programmes under the National Development Plan 2000-2006. The Programme complements the LEADER+ Programme and ensures the availability of funding in the 13 areas that were not appointed to deliver the LEADER+ Programme.

Under both LEADER+ and National LEADER, groups provide supports to "innovative small firms, craft enterprises and local services", including tourism, based on the following guidelines:

- Support, guidance, and the provision of an advisory service

- Provision of a range of assistance types for start-up enterprises

- Expansion of existing enterprises including the adoption of new technologies

- Development of innovative products and local services

- Provision of a range of assistance types for adding value to local products including support for business networks, collective marketing, local branding initiatives, improved quality and development of processing facilities.

The LEADER model is to be mainstreamed as part of the new EU Rural Development Programme 2007-2013 outlined below.

Local Development Partnerships

There are 38 Local Area Partnerships and 33 Community Groups operating throughout Ireland. Their primary focus is to address the issue of social exclusion in the targeted urban and rural areas and they are funded as part of the NDP 2000-2006. These partnerships operate services for the unemployed which are specifically targeted at disadvantaged persons, and include proactive targeting and outreach to marginalised groups who require intensive support and interventions. This response includes helping individuals, groups and communities in accessing employment, and self-employment, through education, training, work experience, job placement, enterprise and the social economy, as well as supporting an enterprise culture the development of the social economy. A process of trying to align the work of Local Partnerships and LEADER companies to achieve greater coherence and efficiency in policy delivery, while retaining a local focus, is ongoing at the time of writing.

Rural Social Scheme

A Rural Social Scheme (RSS) was set up in 2004 to provide income support for farmers and fishermen who are currently in receipt of long-term Social Welfare payments, and to provide certain services of benefit to rural communities. It is managed at local level by LEADER companies. Participants work 19.5 hours per week on community projects such as environmental maintenance, social care, heritage and energy conservation.

EU Rural Development Programme 2007-2013

The new EU Rural Development Programme 2007-2013 was outlined above. The formal national strategy, setting out the framework within which it will be delivered, is being finalised (as of mid-2006) with the

European Commission. A detailed EU co-funded rural development programme containing specific measures will then be prepared and implemented by the Department of Agriculture and Food, and the Department of Community, Rural and Gaeltacht Affairs from early 2007.

Axis 3 measures, which are aimed at diversification of the rural economy, will be delivered on an area basis using the LEADER approach, and local action groups will be involved in the delivery of the programme. These measures are expected to address the following priorities:

- Creation of new micro-enterprises and jobs as well as sustaining and developing existing initiatives

- Development and upgrading of local infrastructure/services essential to community well-being

- Pursuit of environmentally friendly initiatives and conservation of areas of high natural and cultural value

- Support for alternative sustainable energy sources

- Heritage and crafts including restoration of ancient walkways and structures.

It is intended that local groups will have the freedom to take up and implement the most appropriate mix of measures for their own territory.

Institutional Arrangements

Establishment of a Department with Rural Development Responsibility. Giving effect to one of the key commitments in the White Paper, the Department of Community Rural and Gaeltacht Affairs (DCRAGA) was established in 2002, headed by a cabinet minister. This reinforced the separation of rural development from agriculture and positioned it as a distinct policy area in national government. This department's responsibilities include the CLÁR Programme (see above), and the administration of the NDP Rural Development Fund, as well as both LEADER programmes.

The Department issued "rural proofing" guidelines to government departments in 2002 and convenes an annual Rural Forum representing a broad range of rural interests. A Steering Committee on Cross-Border

Rural Development is also chaired jointly with the Department of Agriculture and Rural Development in Northern Ireland and this committee oversees EU funded rural development projects under the PEACE and INTERREG programmes.

The Western Development Commission (WDC). The WDC is a statutory body whose remit is to promote, foster and encourage economic and social development in the Western Region.[4] It operates under the aegis of DCRAGA. The Western Region is overwhelmingly rural and the WDC is involved in analysis of rural issues and development of policies for rural areas as well as in initiating a number of strategic projects in the tourism, organic agri-food and renewable energy sectors. The WDC operates the WDC Investment Fund, which provides venture capital and loans to businesses and social economy projects in the Western Region. The WDC Investment Fund is active in the rural economy with 61 per cent of the projects approved to the end of 2005 located in rural areas.

County Development Boards (CDBs). The Local Government Act of 2001 provided for the established of Development Boards in each local authority area, in response to an identified need for local authorities, state agencies and local development interests to work more in unison than in parallel. Each Board prepared a multisectoral and integrated strategy for its area, encompassing economic, social and cultural development to the year 2012. This is intended to be the mechanism by which improved coordination, strategic planning and better delivery of public services will be achieved at local level. Drafted on the basis of an intensive consultative process among all stakeholders, the strategies were set out in operational terms in which objectives, targets, timescales and responsibilities for different actions are detailed. The CDBs are formally responsible for ensuring that all public policies comply with, and reinforce the priorities of the strategy.

The CDB strategies were ambitious in content and expectation. Achieving the aims of the strategies is very much dependent on the individual agencies and organisations to carry out the actions they have agreed to, and to deliver the specified outputs. The strategies have since been reviewed and streamlined while the Boards attempt to develop effective methodologies for monitoring and coordination. Also, the activities of some locally-based development agencies and services are now formally endorsed by the CDBs.

Conclusions

Over the past decade there have been significant advances in the evolution of Irish rural development thinking and policy, especially if considered against its longer-term trajectory. In the 1970s a simplistic faith was placed in the CAP as a solution to rural problems; it provided relatively high commodity prices boosted by EU subsidies. Agricultural modernisation was the dominant developmental model; this emphasised technical innovation, intensive production and efficiency in farm management. As the limits and negative consequences of this model became apparent in the late 1980s (in commodity surpluses and budget problems, and skewed distribution of benefits), the EU policy discourse came to stress "rural development". However, the concept was interpreted narrowly; to an extent it was appropriated by the strong farming lobby which saw it as a means of maintaining income supports for conventional farming through the expansion of various types of non-market payments.

Since the mid-1990s a broader rural development agenda has emerged in Europe and this has been taken up in Irish discourse. The policy themes show a marked distance from models grounded mainly in conventional farming. There are two main elements: (a) multifunctional agriculture (or, more precisely, land use) which produces commodity and non-commodity outputs, the latter to include managed landscapes, amenity resources, greater bio-diversity, preserved archaeological features and environmental benefits; and (b) multisectoral and area-based development which shade into regional development and spatial strategies at the higher territorial scales. In Ireland also, the detachment of rural development from the conventional agricultural policy agenda – at least in part – is marked by the placing of responsibility for rural affairs in a separate government department.

This description of the evolution of policy agendas is not to suggest that there is less emphasis on farming as intrinsically important to rural areas. The reports of the 2010 and 2015 Committees assert the contrary. However, the pursuit of greater competitiveness and responsiveness to consumer demand in agri-food production, as well as the multifunctional agenda, has already resulted in increasing regional differentiation in land use – between the traditionally productive farming areas of the S & E and the BMW region – and it is likely that these differences will widen in coming years.

When considered from a regional and spatial perspective, the rural problem in Ireland has taken on a different character from that inherent in the agri-centred model. Both the association of the successful regional economies with the larger urban centres and the problems of congestion caused by very rapid growth in the Greater Dublin Area mean that urban centres have become the focal point – as "engines" of further growth and as priority spaces for policy and public resources. The rural problem has become more identified with the BMW Region, and with underdevelopment.

Urban centres will continue to be a primary focus for strategic public investment with some emphasis on the linkages between larger and smaller centres and their importance in realising the potential of rural areas. The tension between the need to create "critical mass" and respond to congestion in urban areas and the to invest in infrastructures in the rural regions to allow them to "catch up" will continue to be played out in the discourse of the various stakeholders, particularly in regard to investment priorities in transport, energy and communications infrastructure.

It is evident that rural problems are now well recognised in policy discourse and that there exists a range of rural development policy measures at both sectoral and spatial levels. However, the various measures do not amount to a coherent and purposeful strategy for the development of the rural economy, particularly as regards the smaller rural towns and the rural areas outside of commuting distance of larger towns, where population stabilisation may be difficult to achieve. Achievement of the goals set out in the 1999 White Paper requires a robust delivery mechanism to ensure a coordinated approach to policy at central level and maximise "value" from the various measures. The White Paper contained a commitment to establishing a Cabinet Sub-Committee and Interdepartmental Policy Committee to achieve this and it would seem opportune to establish such structures in place as Ireland enters the new programming period of 2007-2013.

References

Commins, P and O'Hara, P (1991) "Starts and Stops in Rural Development, An Overview of Problems and Policies", in Reynolds, B. and Healy, S. (eds.), *Rural Development Policy: What Future for Rural Ireland?* Dublin: CMRS, pp. 9-40.

Commins, P, Walsh, J.A. and Meredith, D. (2005) "Some Spatial Dimensions: Population and Settlement Patterns" in *Rural Ireland 2025: Foresight Perspectives*, Joint publication of National University of Ireland, Maynooth, University College Dublin and Teagasc, pp. 45-60.

Department of Agriculture and Food (1999) *Ensuring the Future – A Strategy for Rural Development in Ireland – a white paper on Rural Development*, Dublin: The Stationery Office.

Department of Agriculture and Food (2000) *Agri-Food 2010 Report*, Dublin: The Stationery Office.

Department of Agriculture and Food (2004) *Report of the Agri Vision 2015 Committee*, Dublin: The Stationery Office.

Department of Environment and Local Government (2002) *The National Spatial Strategy: People, Places and Potential*, Dublin: The Stationery Office.

Fitzpatrick Associates (2004) *Review of Enterprise Support in Rural Areas*, Dublin: Department of Community, Rural and Gaeltacht Affairs

Government of Ireland (1999) *National Development Plan 2000-2006*, Dublin: The Stationery Office.

Haughton, G., Beer, A. and Maude, A. (2003) "Understanding international divergence and convergence in local and regional economic development", in Beer, A., Haughton, G and Maude, A. (eds.) *Developing Locally,* Bristol: The Polity Press, pp. 15-35.

O'Hara, P and Commins, P (1998) "Rural Development: Towards the New Century", in Healy, S. and Reynolds, B. (eds.), *Social Policy in Ireland*, Dublin: Oak Tree Press. pp. 261-283.

Rural Ireland 2025: Foresight Perspectives (2005) Joint publication of National University of Ireland, Maynooth, University College Dublin, and Teagasc.

Small Business Forum (2006) *Small Business is Big Business,* Dublin: Forfás

Tourism Review Group (2003), *New Horizons for Irish Tourism: An Agenda for Action*, Dublin: Department of Arts, Sports and Tourism.

Notes

---

[1] Areas designated Objective 1 had priority funding form the EU Structural Funds, on the basis of the degree to which their Gross Value Added per capita diverged from the EU average.

[2] In practice, there was little evidence of outright overlap and duplication due to formal agreements between agencies and formal agreements on the ground.

[3] See Tourism Review Group (2003), *New Horizons for Irish Tourism: An Agenda for Action*

[4] Counties Donegal, Sligo, Leitrim, Roscommon, Mayo, Galway and Clare.

Chapter 17

MIGRATION IN IRELAND: A CHANGING REALITY

Piaras Mac Éinrí

Ten years or so since the phenomenon began, it has become a well-worn cliché to talk about the transformation of Irish life and society brought about by the demise of mass involuntary emigration and the arrival in this country of significant numbers of immigrants. In truth, more time will be needed before a definitive judgment can be offered about the period we are now living through, but certain changes stand out. Mass emigration has indeed largely come to an end; those who leave now are mainly those who wish to do so. This should not blind us to certain on-going realities – the benefits of the Celtic Tiger have not reached all parts of the nation in equal measure. There are people whose chances of work in Ireland are lessened if they left school early, have the "wrong" home address, live in one of those parts of rural Ireland where a rising tide has not carried all boats, or have the "wrong" sexual orientation. It is not easy, for instance, to be an openly gay or lesbian national or secondary teacher in these supposedly more liberal times. Such people may still be over-represented in the ranks of unwilling emigrants from Ireland, irrespective of the booming economy. Moreover, there are a number of worrying trends in the economy and labour market, not least of which is the relatively high percentage of young men involved in the building industry – more than one-eighth of the entire workforce (CSO, 2006a). A significant downturn in construction, for whatever reason, could see an overnight increase in unemployment and a possible rise in emigration, especially in the case of those who do not have the kinds of qualifications needed to participate in the knowledge economy. Even if this were to happen, however, the return of mass emigration on the lines of the 1980s or 1950s seems highly unlikely, for the simple reason that Irish fertility rates have plummeted in the past two decades and large families are no longer the norm. Above all, there is the undeniable fact that the number of people at work in the paid economy in Ireland has increased from a 1986 low of 1.0911 million to an estimated 1.998 million in the first quarter of 2006 (CSO, 2006a) – an increase of almost 82 per cent. While the Irish economy is doubly exposed because of its dependence on foreign direct investment and foreign exports, the fact remains that it has performed remarkably well and the medium outlook is relatively positive.

Meanwhile, Ireland has still largely failed to address the legacy of earlier waves of Irish emigration, the tens of thousands who left in more difficult times, with little more than a rudimentary education, to become for the most part the hewers of wood and drawers of water in more prosperous societies. Their remittances kept Ireland afloat, but to this day these emigrants are given insufficient recognition and support, especially if they wish to return to Ireland. We owe earlier emigrant generations a huge debt, but it seems as if we do not wish to acknowledge that debt. If the past is always a different country, for many Irish people it is also a place which has been consigned to oblivion by an act of collective willed amnesia.

Three Kinds of Migrants

What of immigrants? It may be useful to distinguish, in the first place, between three principal migration strands: economic migration, humanitarian migration and family reunification.

The first category, economic migration, is nearly always the dominant one. People move countries because they want to better their economic circumstances or at least to escape from a place where opportunities are few or non-existent. Economic migration falls into two main categories, at opposite ends of the labour market. On one hand, certain high skill professions are so much in demand around the world that a growing scarcity exists – examples can be found in the medical, para-medical and information technology areas. In such cases states are competing with each other to attract these migrants and will be prepared to offer relatively attractive conditions of entry and the possibility of prolonged or permanent residence. On the other hand, at the other end of the job market a post-industrial, wealthy modern society may have growing shortages of labour in less skilled, less well-paid and less attractive jobs – the "3d" (dirty, dangerous, degrading) categories. But unlike the high-skills posts, where demand is strong and supply is limited, such jobs are seen as attracting an almost unlimited supply of less-skilled migrant workers. In the absence of a strong commitment to equal treatment and human rights, states may be tempted to see such migrants as short-term and exploitable, as they can so easily be replaced by cheaper labour if it is needed.

The second kind of migration arises from certain of the many circumstances of a compelling kind – war, persecution, civil strife – which effectively force people to flee from their countries of origin and where international legislation and policy allows them to apply for refuge elsewhere as long as the asylum seeker can show that he or she, under article 1A(2) of the 1951 UN Convention on the Status of Refugees,

> . . . owing to a well-founded fear of being persecuted for reasons of race, religion, nationality, membership of a particular social group or political opinion, is outside the country of his nationality and is unable or, owing to such fear, is unwilling to avail himself of the protection of that country, or owing to such fear, is unwilling to return to it (UN Refugee Convention, 1951).

The Refugee Convention represents a unique commitment by states to protect those in need even though they are not citizens of those states. One of the reasons why such a relatively generous convention was adopted in the first place was that it reflected a post-WWII Cold War perspective which tended to see refugees in Europe (to which the Convention was originally confined) as heroic individuals fleeing from Communism. As time went on refugee numbers increased, aided in part by the growing perception that there was often no other way for desperate people to get from the impoverished South to the rich North, as states gradually imposed new barriers designed to make it administratively difficult, if not impossible, for many would-be refugees to apply for asylum. Moreover, poverty, famine and environmental disasters are not covered by the Convention. The victims of the nineteenth century Irish Famine had places to go to, however cold the welcome may have been, but no such solution is available to today's famine victims unless they can afford the high costs, in every sense, of forging new documents and new identities in order to try to get to countries which are likely to deny them legal entry. Those who do come and apply for asylum under the terms of the 1951 Convention are typically placed in quarantine until a decision on their case has been taken. They live in designated accommodation and do not have the right to work; official policy takes the position that integration does not arise until a person has been given refugee status or leave to remain. In practice, in Ireland and elsewhere, although many other states are more generous, the vast majority are refused and then become eligible for deportation. Some states such as Australia do not even allow would-be asylum seekers to arrive in the country and make their case, a right which is supposedly guaranteed under the UN Convention. Anyone who breaches the Australian regulations is automatically imprisoned.

The third category of migration reflects the fact that people are not merely atomised individuals or economic production units, but often have partners and children. To treat the migrant as an isolated individual, as migration legislation and policy does all too often, is to ignore this reality. If all migration was strictly temporary the question of admitting family members to live in the host country and, where appropriate, to work there, might not arise. However, many migrants stay in their host countries for significant periods and a minority become permanent and settled members of the new society. Yet family reunification is not guaranteed as a right, or codified in law. High-skills migrants may be treated in a relatively generous manner because their skills are much in demand, but for other labour migrants and for persons with refugee status or leave to remain,[1] family reunification is discretionary and must be applied for on an individual basis. Although Ireland enshrined the central role of the family in Article 41 of the Constitution, this centrality is not recognised and supported in the case of non-EU (strictly speaking, non EEA)[2] economic and humanitarian migrants, other than those in needed high-skills categories.

Finally, one should keep a sense of proportion about migration. Although it is the subject of much media coverage, often factually inaccurate and sometimes bordering on hysterical in tone, only about 3 per cent of the world's population are migrants (Global Commission on Migration, 2005). Most people prefer to stay in their own country and many of those who do migrate return there when and if this becomes possible for them.

Asylum Seekers and Refugees in Ireland

The first kinds of migrants to receive a notable degree of attention in 1990s Ireland, much of it negative, were asylum seekers and refugees. Compared to labour migrants their numbers were never large, peaking at about 1,000 persons per month in 2002 before falling to the present figure of approximately 400 persons a month (Irish Refugee Council, 2006). The arrival of asylum seekers in some numbers, although modest by international standards, led to varying public reactions. While official policy was slow and reactive, in many cities and towns across Ireland support groups were established and various statutory and voluntary organisations did their best to respond to the new communities. However, there were also virulently negative reactions on the part of individuals, including a small number of politicians, elements of the media and some sections of society. It was noticeable, for instance, that when a policy of "dispersal" and "direct provision" was introduced in early 2000, whereby asylum seekers were sent to live in accommodation leased by the Department of Justice Equality and Law Reform (D/JELR) and given a weekly pocket money allowance of just over €19 (not since raised to date) in lieu of normal social welfare allowances, the majority of such centres in Dublin and Cork cities were located in socially disadvantaged areas or outside the city, whereas three accommodation centres in middle class areas (Donnybrook in Dublin and Bishopstown and Rochestown in Cork) were among the very few projects not proceeded with, following vociferous opposition including political pressure and threats of legal action (e.g. Carolan, 2001). More recently, the abortive hunger strike by a number of Afghan asylum seekers in St Patrick's Cathedral in Dublin saw groups of adults and children as young as eight with posters saying "let them die" in the streets outside (Bracken, 2006).

A combination of factors has led to the reduction of asylum-seeking applications to Ireland since 2002. These include the world-wide fall in asylum-seeking numbers, the 2004 Citizenship Referendum,[3] the adoption of a "fast-track" system for the processing of asylum claims from so-called safe third countries, and the introduction of carrier sanctions (i.e. heavy fines on transport companies carrying people whose papers were not in order, which had the effect of making it much more difficult for would-be asylum seekers to reach Ireland).

Figure 17.1: Asylum Applications, 1992–2005

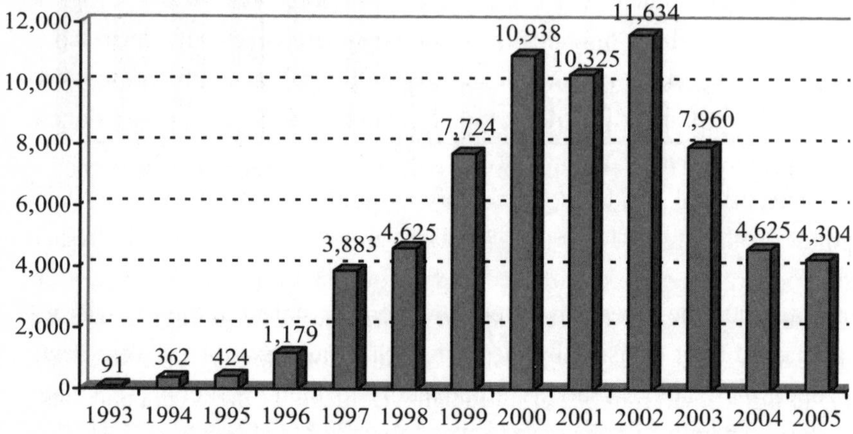

Source: Office of the Refugee Appeals Commissioner

Labour Migrants

The debate concerning asylum seekers and refugees overshadowed almost all other migration-related developments in the period of the late 1990s and early 2000s. Yet at the same time a quiet revolution was taking place in the Irish labour market. The late 1990s saw a dramatic rise in the number of non-EEA labour migrants, peaking at 47,551 in 2003 (Department of Enterprise, Trade and Employment, 2006); the number of EEA labour migrants also increased during the same period.

Figure 17.2: Work Permits, 1993–2005

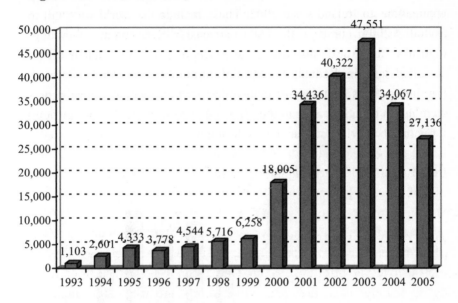

Source: Department of Enterprise, Trade and Employment

In May 2004 the accession of ten new member states[4] to the EU was accompanied by a decision by the Irish, British and Swedish governments to open their labour markets immediately to their workers.[5] The other twelve of the old EU-15 chose to assert their right to block access to their labour markets, something they had the right to do for up to seven years under the transitional arrangements, although there have been changes in some cases since that time.[6] Ireland's decision to open the labour market fully to migrants from the new accession states was accompanied by a sharp cutback in the categories of work for which a permit could be obtained for a non-EEA worker. Evidently the thinking is that there are sufficient numbers of available workers from the enlarged EEA not to require continuing access from outside except for high-skills migrants with specific qualifications in short supply. This explains the drop in work permits above, although a substantial number of people already present in 2004 had their permits renewed, and a further number of former work permit holders were from the new accession states and no longer required them to work in Ireland.

At present it seems likely that Ireland will not open its doors as widely for the next enlargement – Romania and Bulgaria – as it did for the new EU-10 in 2004. The argument that to do so would be unwise, while most of the old EU-15 still impose restrictions on the new EU-10, has merit, but one important point should be borne in mind. All previous processes of EU enlargement have led to improved economic conditions in the new member states, reflected in improved standards of living, increased inward investment and resulting increases in employment. Whereas it was once feared that Spanish and Portuguese accession in the 1980s, for instance, would lead to a further outpouring of migrant workers from those countries, the reverse happened over time, with net migration in the other direction. In short, most people, given a real choice, will choose to stay at home or to return there; half of those who left Ireland in the 1980s also returned. Mass migration is always partly, and usually largely, involuntary; Ireland itself is living proof of this maxim. One lesson to be learned from this is that over time, as conditions improve in new member states, migration from those states is likely to fall as it did in Spain, Portugal and Ireland. At that point Ireland may again need labour migrants from outside the EU. A related factor is that those who are most likely to return home relatively readily will be those from EU fellow states, while those for whom the "cultural distance" from Ireland is allegedly greater – refugees, for instance – having fewer incentives to return home, are more likely to stay.

Figure 17.3: PPSNs May 2004 to February 2006

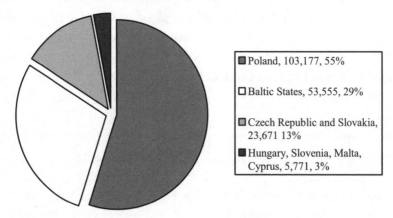

- Poland, 103,177, 55%
- Baltic States, 53,555, 29%
- Czech Republic and Slovakia, 23,671 13%
- Hungary, Slovenia, Malta, Cyprus, 5,771, 3%

Source: Doyle, Hughes, Wadensjö, 2006

Data Problems

The absence of data is a general problem. For example, if we wish to know the number of persons from the new accession states working in Ireland, the figures for PPSNs (personal public service numbers) are the only available data for intercensal periods. But while people are counted in when they register for PPSNs, they are not counted out again. The number of Eastern European migrant workers in Ireland may be high, but there is no way of knowing at this point how many will stay. Little or nothing is reliably known about their living and working conditions. It is clear, however, that many young migrants are over-qualified for the jobs they are doing. This may be indicative of a willingness on their part to accept hard work and relatively unattractive working conditions, but it is unlikely that they will remain in such employment in the long term. It is also a waste of skills from the point of view of the Irish economy and society if people are not doing work which is commensurate with their skills and qualifications.

The evidence available, through the forecasts of such bodies as the Expert Group on Future Skills Needs (EGFSN, 2005), Enterprise Strategy Group (Enterprise Strategy Group 2004), ESRI (ESRI, 2003) and the CSO (CSO, 2004), suggests that Ireland will continue to need substantial ongoing immigration for at least another decade if present rates of economic growth are to be sustained.

It is estimated by the CSO that Ireland requires net in-migration of approximately 30,000 migrants per annum over the period 2002-2006, and between 20,000 and 30,000 per annum in the years 2006-2011 (CSO, 2004).

Have States the Right to Control Immigration?

Nigel Harris' fascinating book *Thinking the Unthinkable* (Harris, 2002) makes the case for getting rid of all controls on immigration and argues that the floodgates would not open even if this were to happen. While his arguments are complex they can be summarised in a few key ideas:

- Migrants make rational decisions. In general they migrate to work and to better themselves. If work is not available they are likely to return home. People would rather be poor in their own countries, where at least they have other networks of sustenance, support and social capital, than somewhere else. Some Irish migrants came home from the US after the Great Depression even though Ireland was bitterly poor at the time. The operation of the EU's own internal open labour market is also living proof of this – people usually only move when there is work, although even then most people don't move anyway. Paradoxically, the imposition of tough immigration controls makes it less likely that people will follow this logical option because people will know that once they leave the host country they will not be able to return. Thus, the "immigration stop" imposed on labour migrants from outside the EEC (as it then was) in 1974 had the effect of ensuring that virtually all migrants already within the EEC stayed there and ultimately brought their families to join them.

- Mass global involuntary migration stems from conditions of economic inequality. In the short term the most effective way of fighting this is not foreign aid, but remittances, which dwarf foreign aid (even though one, private, transfer should never be seen as a simple substitute for the other, public one, and fundamental issues of social justice are involved). This point has been taken up more recently by the Global Commission on Migration (Global Commission on International Migration, 2005) and by the special UN delegate on migration, Peter Sutherland (Sutherland, 2006). In the longer term only a substantial re-balancing of economic and political power towards the majority world, in the context of a fairer and more equal world economy, will address chronic forced migration.

These arguments notwithstanding, governments are not going to abandon their current policies any time soon, not least because it would not be feasible for one country to implement such a policy on its own. Moreover, it would be pointless to deny that states have a legitimate interest in managing migration into their territories. Migration has implications for planning and infrastructure, for society and culture, for security and for the future of the economy. But this does not mean that states have an untrammelled degree of freedom in deciding how they should approach the issue. In the first place, Ireland has already signed up to a range of international commitments and obligations, including EU membership and the 1951 UN Refugee Convention. Many people already have the right to come and live and work here with their families, just as Irish people have benefited from the same rights and freedoms for many decades in a number of other countries. Domestic laws and policies have increasingly evolved to reflect a desire to build a just society based on human rights, respect for diversity and the rule of law. States such as Ireland are not free to approach immigration and integration in an arbitrary or purely discretionary manner, any more than they are free to discriminate against women, Irish speakers or Travellers. Yet in Ireland immigration policy is distinguished, compared to the other areas mentioned, by its unfinished and floating nature; much of it is not codified in legislation and thus not fully open to public and parliamentary debate and scrutiny. The involvement of civil society (i.e. voluntary organisations), even though the NGO sector is crucial to immigrants and their integration, has received minimal support.

A Displacement Effect?

One of the key questions which has arisen in the context of increased immigration is the putative impact of such immigration on indigenous workers. Is it leading to the displacement of Irish workers, or it is part of a process of underpinning continuing economic growth which itself is generating additional and better-quality jobs for Irish workers? Much of the debate about this issue has been somewhat simplistic.

As pointed out earlier, it is undeniable that there has been a dramatic increase in the numbers at work in the Irish economy in the past 20 years. Moreover, the increased immigration brought about by the opening of the Irish labour market to workers from the new accession states has not increased unemployment rates here, already the lowest in the EU – quite the contrary (European Commission, 2006). In other words, employment creation is not a "zero sum game" in which a finite number of jobs must be divided between Irish or migrant workers. The Irish economy in recent years has demonstrated a robust capacity to increase employment, although it is true that many of the new jobs are not highly paid or secure.

The proposal made by some labour unions, and rather more ineptly by the leader of the Labour Party, Pat Rabbitte TD, seems to be uncalled for.

The time may be coming when we will have to sit down and examine whether we would have to look at whether a work permits regime ought to be implemented in terms of some of this non-national labour, even for countries in the European Union (Collins, 2006)

There are, however, some grounds for concern. First, it may be true that unemployment, at least in the short term, has not been increased by the growing number of immigrants in Ireland. This is not to say, however, that wages and conditions of work have not been affected. There is some evidence that the rate of increase of wages at the lower end of the job market may be slower that that for other workers in the Irish economy.

Secondly, there is evidence of exploitation of foreign workers in parts of the Irish economy, although it has become fashionable for some employers and economists, as well as political defenders of Ireland's neo-liberal economic policies, to dismiss this as "anecdotal". The Gama and Irish Ferries cases are well documented (Doyle, Hughes, Wadensjö, 2006), but there are also persistent reports of everyday exploitation from trade union and NGO sources (e.g. Migrant Rights Centre Ireland, 2005; Jennings, 2006). A failure to pay the minimum wage or to provide PRSI and pension cover may only be part of the picture. Other common practices include arbitrary changes in duties and conditions of work, the failure to pay appropriate overtime rates, arbitrary dismissal or the threat of dismissal to prevent complaints being made and denial of training and promotional opportunities on the same basis as Irish workers to their foreign counterparts. While Irish legislation against discrimination in the workplace is excellent on paper, a shortage of labour market inspectors has militated against effective implementation of that legislation. This issue was to the fore in the national partnership negotiations of 2006 and a substantial improvement in the number of inspectors was agreed (Dooley, 2006).

Thirdly, in a small number of cases employment of Irish workers fell while that of foreign workers increased. These were in manufacturing, hotels and agriculture. The overall combined loss of Irish jobs in these three sectors in the year to the third quarter of 2005 was 20,700, and the employment of foreign nationals in the same period saw a growth of 16,300 (Beggs et al., 2006). It could, of course, be argued that what is happening here is that Irish workers are moving on to better jobs and being replaced in their old jobs by foreign workers. At this point the evidence is hardly definitive one way or another. What can be stated with some confidence is that a sector of employment where foreign workers are a substantial part of a relatively unskilled workforce is unlikely to revert to an Irish workforce, because the recruitment of such unskilled foreign workers is likely in many cases to lead to a once-for-all deterioration in wages and conditions, making the sector unattractive to indigenous workers from then on. At the very least, this does not bode well for the future, unless we make the rather complacent assumption that growth will either continue unimpeded or at least will adjust downwards gradually rather than seeing a sharp correction or worse.

Finally, as touched on earlier, it cannot be healthy for the Irish economy, and society more generally, that an assumption is made that, while "high-skills" workers may be needed as part of a long-term, strategic shift to a high-tech, high-added-value knowledge-based society, other migrant workers are somehow less necessary and more expendable. This is more than an assumption, as two employment schemes currently exist: a "work permit" scheme for most migrant workers, confined to a twelve monthly renewable system with few social rights, and a more attractive work visa or work authorisation scheme[7] for workers whose skills are in short supply. The reality is that workers are needed at nearly all levels and in nearly all sectors. Moreover, the policy outlined can only foster an ugly "them and us" mentality which sees the presence of such workers and their integration into Irish society as contingent and ultimately reversible. The knock-on effects of such an approach should not be underestimated either, such as the hidden discrimination arising from assumptions that "they" need not be offered promotion or other job opportunities on the same basis as Irish workers because "they" have not been in the country long enough or will be returning home in any event. Such a two-tier approach to economic and social integration amounts to a system of de facto apartheid which can only have the most negative effects in the long term for such migrants and for their children.

Immigration Policy

Immigration policy in Ireland needs to be understood in terms of the early twentieth century history of an impoverished state, an inward-looking and isolationist culture and an economy which up to the very recent past could not provide sufficient employment for Irish people, not to mention immigrants. With the obvious exceptional case of British people, immigrants to Ireland in the period before the 1960s were confined to very modest numbers, including a small Jewish community, mainly settled in Dublin and Cork, small Chinese and Italian communities and small number of other "aliens". Few as these incomers were, they were not always welcome, as Jews in Limerick found to their cost in 1904 when they were the target of a sectarian and anti-Semitic campaign by a local Redemptorist priest, Fr Creagh, and a number of families were forced out of the city (Keogh, 1998). Those Hungarians who arrived as refugees after the abortive revolt against the Communist regime there in 1956 found themselves to be literally guests of the state, held in detention in rural east Clare in conditions which were so trying that the majority of the camp went on hunger strike (Fanning, 2001).

Irish attitudes and policies subsequently changed, of course, starting with the economic reforms of the late 1950s, the opening up of the Irish society and economy, membership of the EEC (now EU), and the later, dramatic transformations of the period from 1986 to 2006. But it is worth bearing in mind, in the midst of all these changes, that the core legislation for non-EEA workers and residents in Ireland is still the *Aliens Act, 1935* and the *Aliens Order, 1946*. The reforms which have been made since 1946 mainly related to specific categories of foreigners and not to foreigners (or "aliens" or "non-nationals", to quote the repugnant terms still widely used by officialdom) in general. Thus, British people have never been treated in Irish policy and law as fully "foreign" (to have done so would have called the position of the Irish in Britain into question). Also, EEC membership led to free movement of workers from other member states, a situation which was reinforced by such legislation as the Treaties of Maastricht (1992) and Amsterdam (1997), and the UN Refugee Convention already referred to led to a modest number of refugees (e.g. from Chile and Vietnam) being given rights of residence and employment. Moreover, in the recent past a range of rights-based legislation and policy (e.g. the *Equal Employment Act, 1998*, *Equal Status Act, 2000* and *Equality Act, 2004*) has greatly improved conditions for all in terms of employment rights, the right to equality of treatment in service provision, and enhanced protection and redress against racism and discrimination (however, it must be regretted that the *Prohibition of Incitement of Hatred Act, 1989* has proved entirely toothless and that a promise made in 2002 to reform this legislation has not to date been honoured). But the fact remains that the majority of non-EEA migrants in Ireland, other than those married to Irish or EU citizens, are present in Ireland on terms and conditions which are usually temporary, conditional and discretionary.

The *Aliens Act, 1935* and *Aliens Order, 1946* (somewhat modified following a court challenge in 2004) are draconian provisions, reflecting their origins in First World War British legislation, adopted at a time when all foreigners were regarded with suspicion. Extraordinary, far-ranging and discretionary powers concerning immigration are conferred upon the minister of the day, who may take their decisions without explanation and without appeal. In the intervening years much of Irish immigration policy has been conducted by ad hoc ministerial orders, statutory instructions and confidential rules and procedures, with the unfortunate result that parliamentary scrutiny has only taken place on rare occasions and civil society has had little opportunity to develop an informed view of Irish immigration policy.

I do not intend to suggest that the original harsh measures provided for in the legislation have not been blunted over the years by some degree of emerging custom and practice, and a gradual opening of decision-making more generally to a greater degree of transparency and external scrutiny. But new legislation has been long overdue. It appears that this is on the way with the publication in 2004 of a discussion document on Immigration and Residence in Ireland (D/JELR, 2005a). Draft legislation is expected to be tabled by the Minister for Justice, Equality and Law Reform before the next election in mid-2007. At the same time, the Minister for Enterprise, Trade and Employment has also published a new Employment Permits Bill which will also probably become law by mid-2007. This Bill will be a step forward from the current situation whereby the employer and not the employee holds the work permit (a situation which has led to abuses). However the changes have been criticised by NGOs as essentially cosmetic (ICI, 2005) as the conditions under which a permit holder can change jobs will still be severely restricted and they will still not be allowed to offer their services freely on the open labour market. Moreover, as pointed out earlier, it would seem that while there will be an ongoing need to attract high-skills migrants from outside the EU, legislators believe a sufficient internal labour market will exist to supply the necessary demand for low-skills labour. This may indeed be the case in the short to medium term, particularly after Romania and Bulgaria join the EU. But most European countries have fertility rates well below that needed to replace the population, and so will not be future sources of labour migration. In the medium to long term it seems unlikely that internal EU labour movement alone will supply the needs of the labour economy once other member states open their labour markets and economic convergence, as I have argued, reduces the incentive to migrate in the first place. In the meantime the emerging distinction between an attractive regime for high-skills migrants and an unattractive one for low-skills migrants would seem to open the door to a new form of revolving-door *gastarbeiter* migration.

Integration Policy

Integration today is a highly contentious topic. Some countries, such as France, favour an assimilationist approach: that migrants should become "more French than the French themselves". Others, such as the UK and the Netherlands, have favoured a more "multicultural" approach, with recognition of cultural diversity. In the strict legal sense, multiculturalism has really only been applied in Canada and Australia.

Recent events, such as the riots in Britain in 2002 and the London bombings of 7 July 2005, the 2005 riots in France, and the murders of Pym Fortuyn in 2002 and Theo Van Gogh in 2004 in the Netherlands, as well as the backwash from 9/11 in the US, have suggested to some critics that all is not well with the multicultural model. Some oppose it on the grounds that certain minorities – many would instance fundamentalist Muslims – allegedly cannot be accommodated within the western liberal democratic model. Others argue against multiculturalism for an entirely different reason, holding that it encloses individuals within communities and ghettoises them, making integration more difficult by emphasising communal rights over individual ones. In this perspective, the 1998 Belfast Agreement exemplifies an approach where an emphasis on "parity of esteem" not only failed to attend to underlying issues of power and inequality, but arguably made the gulf between communities deeper than before by refusing to recognise the more complex and hybrid nature of many people's sense of identity, not easily pigeonholed into preconceived categories.

Whether one takes a pro- or anti-multicultural position, European countries have in general failed to deal with a deeper issue: a chronic underlying racism. In France a rhetoric of republican equality masks a reality of systematic discrimination in the workplace and society in general: mainstream French television station TF1's first black news presenter started work only in July 2006. In Britain, which has done much more than France to promote equality and integration, there remains a subtle and sometimes hidden problem of discrimination, most obvious when class and ethnicity intersect. Although many Commonwealth immigrants came to Britain with notions of the "mother country" and a strong desire to be integrated, the British educational system, notably, let down their children and their children's children, creating chronically marginalised black populations across the midlands and in other cities. This has led to a phenomenon of "parallel lives" where mutually alienated communities live side-by-side but have little interaction. Nowadays the UK uses the term "social cohesion" to imply a shift in emphasis from a commitment to diversity towards an approach stressing the necessity for communities to interact across the diversity boundary. Critics argue with justification that this can ignore the racialised nature of the state itself (e.g. MacPherson, 1999). Similar criticisms have been made of the Irish state's role (Lentin, 2004).

Behind much of the criticism of multiculturalism in Europe today lies a dangerously simple idea – dangerous, because in this field nearly all simple ideas are wrong. This is the neo-conservative notion that people can really only empathise with those "like us" – we will pay taxes, for instance, an expression of solidarity and a commitment to a social "safety net", only as long as we think that "the community" shares the same identity and attitudes as ourselves (Goodhart, 2004). This commitment to a primordial or tribal identity is of course deeply embedded in human history. But to erect it as a principle for the twenty-first century is to deny centuries of progress towards a civil society which embraces all, irrespective of origins, gender or belief. No one would argue for a return to a world where women were denied the vote or children had no rights, nor would we accept that misogyny, sectarianism or open racism were justifiable.

Irish Approaches to Integration?

In 1999 the Department of Justice Equality and Law Reform commissioned a report entitled *Integration: A two-way process* (DJELR, 1999). This is the only official report to date on the subject of integration and gives an indication of official thinking in this regard, even though it only applies to refugees and people with leave to remain and thus does not concern labour migrants and their families. The working definition of integration adopted by the report was as follows:

> Integration means the ability to participate to the extent that a person needs and wishes in all of the major components of society, without having to relinquish his or her own cultural identity (DJELR, 1999).

The report was produced at a time when Ireland's experience of immigration was new and relatively limited. It did not recommend "hard targets" in achieving the aims set out and no public review or evaluation mechanism was put in place to monitor implementation of the report. There was little appreciation of the need for a more fundamental shift in attitudes, structures and services. It is not simply a question of making public services more user-friendly for migrants, but of the whole nature of the relationship between the migrant and Irish society in general.

The initiatives in the area of refugees and persons with leave to remain are the only integration-related initiatives to date, with the significant exception of an antiracism publicity campaign and action against discrimination. However, there are signs that the government is moving towards developing a more wide-ranging approach to integration of all migrants, not just refugees. In March 2005 the Minister for Justice, Equality and Law Reform announced the establishment of the Irish Naturalisation and Immigration Service (INIS), which is intended to be a "one stop shop" for migrants in Ireland (D/JELR, 2005b). An integration policy will presumably be part of the INIS brief, although as yet the details of its mission have not been revealed.

National Action Plan against Racism (NPAR)

Matters advanced with the establishment in 1997 of the National Consultative Committee on Racism and Interculturalism (NCCRI) and the 2005 publication of the *National Action Plan against Racism* (DJELR, 2005c). Compared to *Integration: A two -ay process* this offers a more holistic and comprehensive approach to anti-racism and integration and details an agenda for action in every area of statutory activity, as well as the social domain more generally. However, it lacks a solid statutory basis for action, and the NCCRI lacks the status, budget or powers of its UK counterpart, the Commission for Racial Equality (CRE). Moreover, although there is a growing recognition that the role of the voluntary sector is crucial, it has yet to be spelled out how precisely it will be involved.

The intercultural framework underpinning the NPAR is based on the following elements:

- *Protection* – effective protection and redress against racism

- *Inclusion* – economic inclusion and equality of opportunity

- *Provision* – accommodating diversity in service provision

- *Recognition* – recognition and awareness of diversity

- *Participation* – full participation in Irish society.

The Future: Statistical Scaremongering

Forecasting immigration trends is not an exact science. A recent report by NCB stockbrokers makes the extraordinary estimate that immigrants could form one million, or 19 per cent of the population, by 2020 (NCB Stockbrokers, 2006):

> Our central population forecast assumes that the inflow of new migrants will hold for the period to 2010 at the 70,000 level recorded in the year to April 2005. Thereafter, we assume it will gradually diminish to around 43,000 by 2015 and hold at that level up to 2020. For emigration, we have assumed that the rate of outflow in 2005, i.e. around 4 per 1000 of the population, broadly holds over the forecast period.

> The result of these assumptions is that there is a net inward migration flow of around 53,000 annually in the years to 2010. From then until

2015, an inflow remains but it gradually falls to 25,000 where it sta-
bilises until 2020. After 2020, we assume zero net migration (NCB
Stockbrokers, 2006).

But the reasoning set out here is highly questionable. It does not take
account of the fact that some of those counted as immigrants are simply
returning *Irish* migrants and their foreign-born children. The gross figure
of 70,000 immigrants for the year to April 2005 is arguably a one-off
"spike", primarily caused by the fact that Ireland was one of only three
of the old EU-15 to open its labour market. Finally, it seems to assume
that virtually all immigrants to Ireland will remain in the country, or to
put it in more technical terms, that *flows* will inevitably become *stocks*.
If this were to happen it would fly in the face of virtually all immigration
patterns and trends elsewhere. It seems more likely that many of those
arriving in Ireland from the EU-10 will return as their own economic
circumstances improve, as in the past in Spain, Portugal and Ireland itself. Unless the Irish case is unique, it is therefore difficult to see how the
foreign-born population could jump to 19 per cent by 2020.

Needless to say, aspects of these forecasts were quickly taken up by
ill-informed commentators and sub-editors in the Irish media – both the
Irish Independent and the *Irish Daily Mail* used the "one million" tag as
a headline. Part of the problem is that statisticians and economists may
base their modelling too narrowly on the extrapolation of present trends,
rather than taking sufficient account of what we know from social research in other countries on migrant motivations and behaviour. It is not
helpful that, to date, the Irish media have no specialist correspondents in
the field and must therefore rely on somewhat superficial interpretations
of reports, done at second hand, rather than develop their own informed
analysis.

The above notwithstanding, immigrants are now a significant part of
the Irish population – 10 per cent according to the preliminary results of
the 2006 census (CSO, 2006b). Again, it should be borne in mind that
this figure is based in part on net inward migration since 2002 and includes inward migrants who are legally and ethnically Irish, such as returning migrants and their children. The 2002 census showed that 9.1 per
cent of the population at that time were not born in Ireland, but only
slightly over 7 per cent were "not Irish" (Mac Éinrí and Ní Laoire,

2006). A factor which is sometimes overlooked, however, is that a disproportionate number of women migrants are of child-bearing age. By definition, labour migrants tend to be young people and the migrant population will therefore contain far fewer older people than the population in general. It is not unreasonable to suppose that up to 15 per cent of all births in the state over the next 20 years may be to foreign-born mothers, virtually all of whom will be here legally and many of whose children will be entitled to Irish citizenship. The inevitable effect of this process will be that while in 20 years' time the proportion of migrants in the population as a whole will probably peak at a percentage a good deal lower than that being forecast by some commentators, such migrants *and their Irish-born children* will nonetheless constitute a significant range of ethnic minorities within the state, constituting up to 20 per cent of the overall population.

Conclusions

A number of challenges face us. In the first place, Ireland has, in common with other western European countries, developed various discourses concerning immigration, integration and diversity. Much of this debate has been highly polarised, ill-informed, divisive and counter-productive. Not all of the bitterness and divisiveness has been on one side only. A notorious example of an ill-thought out campaign (in this author's view) occurred in 2001 when Amnesty International's Irish branch attacked the Taoiseach, Tánaiste and then Minister for Justice, Equality and Law Reform with a billboard campaign featuring the tagline "some say they are racist; some say they are doing nothing about it" (Amnesty Ireland, 2001). This misconceived approach preached only to the converted and did much to alienate middle ground opinion from Amnesty's own aims. In fairness, it should also be said that Amnesty has undertaken much serious campaigning work and has commissioned groundbreaking research into racism in Ireland (e.g. Beirne and Jaichand, 2006).

It is up to those who are advocating change to make the case; in doing so, respect must be shown for those who fear it. Modern Ireland is often inaccurately called a post-modern or post-Christian society, with glib assertions about the Celtic Tiger and our supposed complete transformation. But the reality is more multi-layered – elements of past and present co-exist, something which presents dangers but also opportunities. Thus, the attempt by the present Government to promote voluntarism and community values (Ahern, 2006) and the Taoiseach's ongoing interest in the work of American sociologist Robert Putnam on the loss of social capital in modern society (Murphy, 2005), has been seen by some as an attempt to cover up for the withdrawal by a neo-liberal state from an over-arching and comprehensive social role. Moreover, many wish to progress beyond the frequent intolerance and patriarchal character of a traditional Ireland where there often seemed to be an exaggerated stress on community values, so that those who did not or could not conform were repressed and excluded. But it may also be possible to turn the question around and ask what we can learn from the traditional strengths of Irish society. To put it another way, state policies and interventions are a necessary but not sufficient basis for developing a new approach towards inclusion and diversity. Political leadership is needed and has all too often been largely rhetorical or lacking to date, but the emphasis on community values in Irish society can be beneficial if it is accompanied by a positive reappraisal of those values, including a thoroughgoing recognition of the ways in which some were excluded by their intolerant application. Bluntly, the question facing us is not merely how to deal with the "challenge of diversity" arising from immigration. If there were *no* immigrants, we would still need to broaden our approach to identity beyond the accepted "mainstream". Travellers, gays and lesbians, Jews, black Irish people, none of them migrants, have been excluded and marginalised in a myriad ways over the years. We should go beyond the "whisc" (white, heterosexual, Irish, settled, Catholic (Tracy, 2004)) model of identity, not only for migrants, but above all for ourselves. If we can do this, migrants will find their place as well in an enlarged identity. The work of the NCCRI and its National Action Plan against Racism is central to this project, but it must be embedded within a wider social and cultural context through the school system, the voluntary and community sector, faith communities and social partners.

Secondly, official political Ireland has, recently, rather smugly presented migration as being good for all of us, when it has in reality meant that it has been good for employers. The fact that this position has been accompanied by assertions of moral and ethical superiority for the Irish approach to immigration has not convinced those who see it as another attempt to force through an agenda of economic neo-liberalism under the banner of modernisation, including an allegedly liberal attitude to immigrants and the assertion that racism is not an issue in Ireland (much as in the past it used to be claimed that Ireland was a "classless" society). Social inclusion in Ireland represents an ongoing challenge, particularly when seen against a backdrop of some of the worst infrastructure, planning and public services in Europe. There is a great danger that those who are understandably cynical about the "you've never had it so good" rhetoric of the Government, when their own experiences tell them so much is wrong – for instance, with health, housing, and transport – may also reject the Government's message about immigration. They may also understandably see the message as an ongoing threat to their own wages and working conditions.

The NGO sector, for its part, needs to build better bridges with disadvantaged communities, their representatives and those working with them. NGOs working with migrants, for their part, are largely middle class and in some cases are still following an essentially charity-based model rather than one based on human rights. In far too many cases migrants themselves are the last to be consulted or heard.

Developing a fair immigration policy still requires much work, but will not be sufficient if Irish society does not also attend to the long-term integration of migrants and their children. Getting the balance right between respect for community values and for individual rights and liberties will be a challenging task. Respect for diversity does not mean an "anything goes" philosophy – on the contrary. Precisely because Irish society is diverse there is a need for a debate about what constitutes core values. Some, for example gender rights, are straightforward (implementing such values is another matter). Others, such as the requirement to learn the language(s) of the country or implement a citizenship programme, are not. If Irish society is to deal well with, and to encounter and manage positively, a change which is already upon us and already inevitable, it needs new definitions of membership and citizenship which extend the boundaries beyond place of birth and parental descent to a more active and flexible model.

References

Ahern, B. (2006), Speech by the Taoiseach, Mr Bertie Ahern, T.D., at the opening of the official exhibition of the Easter 1916 Rising at the National Museum, Collins Barracks. Dublin, Department of the Taoiseach, http://www.taoiseach.ie

Amnesty Ireland (2001), Anti-racism Campaign.

Beggs, J. et al. (2006), *Here to Stay: Non-national Workers in the Irish Economy,* Dublin: AIB Global Treasury Economic Research.

Beirne, L. and Jaichand, V. (2006), *Breaking down barriers: Tackling racism at the level of the State and its institutions.* Dublin: Amnesty Ireland.

Bozonnet, J.J. (2006). "L'Italie s'ouvre aux travailleurs de l'Est et regularise 517,000 clandestins". *Le Monde,* 23/24 Juillet.

Bracken, A. (2006), "Angry exchanges as Afghans are removed", *Irish Times,* 22 May.

Carolan, M. (2001), "Ballsbridge Reception Centre Challenged". *Irish Times* 13 February.

Collins, S. (2006), "Rabbitte calls for rethink of policy on immigrants", *Irish Times,* 3 January.

CSO (2004), *Population and Labour Force Projections 2006-2036.* Dublin: CSO.

CSO (2006a) *Quarterly National Household Survey Quarter 1 2006.* Dublin: CSO.

CSO (2006b), *Census 2006 Preliminary Report.* Dublin: CSO.

Department of Enterprise, Trade and Employment (2006), "Statistical Tables and Company Listings for the Work Permits Section". http://www.entemp.ie/labour/workpermits/statistics.htm, accessed 30/07/06.

Department of Justice, Equality and Law Reform (1999), *Integration: A two-way process. Report to the Minister for Justice, Equality and Law Reform by the Interdepartmental Working Group on the integration of refugees in Ireland.* Dublin: D/JELR.

Department of Justice, Equality and Law Reform (2005a). *Immigration and Residence in Ireland: Outline proposals for an immigration and residence bill.* Dublin: Department of Justice, Equality and Law Reform. www.justice.ie

Department of Justice, Equality and Law Reform (2005b). "Minister announces establishment of Irish Naturalisation and Immigration Service". Dublin: Department of Justice, Equality and Law Reform. www.justice.ie

Department of Justice, Equality and Law Reform (2005c). *National Action Plan against Racism.* Dublin: Department of Justice, Equality and Law Reform.

Dooley, C. (2006), "Partners agree on immigrants, job displacement". *Irish Times,* 26 April.

Doyle, N., Hughes, G., Wadensjö, E. (2006), *Freedom of Movement for Workers in Central and Eastern Europe. Experiences in Ireland and Sweden.* Stockholm: Swedish Institute for European Policy Studies, SIEPS 2006:5.

EGFSN (2005), *Skills needs in the Irish Economy: The role of migration.* Dublin: Expert Group on Future Skills Needs.

Enteprise Strategy Group (2004), *Ahead of the Curve: Ireland's Place in the Global Economy.* Dublin: Forfás.

ESRI (2003). *Medium Term Review 2003-2010.* Dublin: Economic and Social Research Institute.

European Commission (2006), *Report on the Functioning of the Transitional Arrangements set out in the 2003 Accession Treaty (period 1 May 2004-30 April 2006).* Brussels: European Commission.

Fanning, B. (2001) "Reluctant Hosts: Refugee Policy in Twentieth-century Ireland". *Administration,* Vol. 48, No. 4 (Winter 2000-01).

Global Commission on International Migration (2005), *Migration in an interconnected world: New directions for action. Report of the Global Commission on International Migration.* New York: United Nations.

Goodhart, D. (2004), "Discomfort of Strangers Prospect", February. Reproduced in *Guardian* 24/02/04. http://www.guardian.co.uk

Hand, C. and Shanahan, M. (2005), *Skills Needs of the Irish Economy: The Role of Migration. A Submission by the Expert Group on Future Skills Needs and Forfás to the Minister for Enterprise, Trade and Employment.* Dublin: Forfás.

Harris N. (2002), *Thinking the Unthinkable: The immigration myth exposed.* London: I.B. Taurus.

Immigrant Council of Ireland (2005), *Briefing Pack on Immigration and Residence Bill.* Dublin: ICI.

International Commission on Global Migration (2005). "Migration at a Glance". New York: United Nations.

Jennings, M. (2006), "Migrants and job 'displacment'". *Irish Times,* 24 February.

Irish Refugee Council (2006). "Irish asylum statistics". http://www. irishrefugeecouncil.ie/stats.html

Keogh, D. (1998), *Jews in twentieth-century Ireland: Refugees, anti-semitism and the Holocaust*. Cork: Cork University Press.

Lentin, R. (2004). "From racial state to racist state: Ireland on the eve of the citizenship referendum". *Variant*, vol. 2. number 20, summer 2004. www.variant.randomstate.org

Mac Éinri, P. and Ní Laoire, C. (2006). "The projected percentage of 'foreigners' in the Irish population in 2031 and a related issue concerning ethnicity". *Translocations, the Irish Migration, Race and Social Transformation Review*, vol. 1, issue 1 (available online at http://www.imrstr.dcu.ie)

MacPherson, W. (1999), *The Stephen Lawrence Inquiry: Report of an inquiry by Sir William Macpherson of Cluny*. Cmd 4262-I, London: HMSO.

McVeigh R. (1996). *The Racialisation of Irishness: Racism and Anti-Racism in Ireland*. Belfast: Centre for Research and Documentation.

Migrant Rights Centre (2005). *Private Homes: A public concern*. Dublin: Migrant Rights Centre.

Murphy, C. (2005), "Bowling for Bertie", *Village*, 9 September. http://www.villagemagazine.ie

NCB Stockbrokers (2006), 2020 Vision: Ireland's Demographic Dividend. Dublin: NCB.

Sutherland, P. (2006). Remarks by Peter Sutherland, UN Special Representative for Migration, at Dublin Conference sponsored by Institute for International Integration Studies, TCD, 7 July.

Tracy, M. (2000). "Racism and Immigration in Ireland: A comparative analysis". Dublin: TCD, unpublished MPhil Thesis.

United Nations (1951), *Convention relating to the Status of Refugees*. Geneva: Office of the High Commissioner for Human Rights.

Notes

[1] Persons with leave to remain are usually asylum seekers whose cases have, for one reason or another, been deemed not to have met the criteria set out in the 1951 UN refugee convention, but who have been allowed to remain in Ireland on humanitarian or related grounds.

[2] In fact, the EEA and Switzerland. The EEA (European Economic Area) consists of the EU member states plus Norway, Iceland and Liechtenstein; Switzerland has a separate but broadly similar arrangement with the EU/EEA.

[3] The 2004 referendum on citizenship replaced the automatic right of citizenship for all born in Ireland with a provision whereby the citizenship of children born to non-citizen parents will in future be dependent on legislation. The referendum closed an alleged loophole which in the Government's view created an incentive for women to have their children in Ireland and thus obtain long-term residency for themselves.

[4] Cyprus, Czech Republic, Estonia, Hungary, Latvia, Lithuania, Malta, Poland, Slovakia, Slovenia.

[5] While access to the labour market is unrestricted, a "habitual residence" clause means that access to the full range of social welfare benefits is only given, in Ireland and the UK, to persons who have been habitually resident in the state for at least two years.

[6] Finland, Greece, Portugal and Portugal opened their labour markets on 1 May 2006 and Italy has just announced that it will also do so (*Le Monde*, 2006) but there is no indication of any change yet in other member states. It should be noted that comparatively large numbers of new accession state workers are already present in Germany, for instance, but they are working there within a work permit style regime and cannot seek speculative work opportunities.

[7] The title varies depending on whether the holder is from a country for which a visa for entry to Ireland is required, but work visas and work authorisations are otherwise the same.

Chapter 18

FAMILY AND FAMILY POLICY

Tony Fahey

This chapter aims to outline some major recent developments in family policy and family behaviour in Ireland and offer some comments on the interaction between the two. The primary purpose is to provide some reflection on family policy – what the term means, what the field consists of and what its effects are – but a secondary purpose is to highlight some significant recent developments in family life in Ireland. The account begins with a brief discussion on the main components of family policy. It then turns to three major aspects of family life in Ireland, namely, family formation, marital dissolution and lone parenthood. It examines recent behavioural changes and policy developments in each, and comments briefly on what these three areas tell us about mutual influences between policy and behaviour in the family arena.

Components of Family Policy

The term "family policy" was little used in Ireland until the recent past. The state has long had an array of policies targeted on various aspects of family life but these are spread across a number of state agencies and government departments and until recently were rarely thought of as constituting a single policy domain. The work of the Commission on the Family, set up in 1995, marked a new departure in this regard since it represented a first effort to develop an integrated view of the treatment of the family in public policy (Commission of the Family, 1998). In 1997, the term "family" was included for the first time in the title of a government department, when the old Department of Social Welfare was renamed the Department of Social, Community and Family Affairs (the name was altered again to the Department of Social and Family Affairs in 2002). The Family Affairs Unit was set up in the Department in 1998 to coordinate the family-related aspects of its policy remit. The Family Support Agency was established in 2003 to provide a range of services to families, focusing especially on counselling and mediation related to marital difficulties. Institutional developments such as these do not of themselves produce an integrated approach to family policy, particularly since they do not bridge the gap between family law and family-related aspects of social policy that, as is outlined further below, is a major structural feature of this policy domain. However, they do indicate a greater awareness of the family as a policy target and of the diversity of policy areas that are relevant in this regard.

Family policy in the broadest sense has two main components – family law and family aspects of social policy. This is a distinction between the regulatory and distributive functions of policy. The regulatory function embodied in family law prescribes and enforces rules and norms of behaviour that govern the relationships of family and household members with each other (having to do, for example, with the formation and dissolution of marriage, parents' rights and duties in regard to children, children's rights and duties in regard to parents, domestic violence, inheritance, family property and so on). It is administered mainly through the courts and does not entail large public expenditures. The distributive function provides financial supports or services of various kinds to families, such as child benefit, payments for one-parent families, paid maternity (or parental) leave, state-funded childcare services, widows' pensions and so on (for a comparative review of Irish provisions in this area, see Daly and Clavero, 2002). This function is administered through a range of government departments and state agencies and gives rise to large expenditures by the state.

A comprehensive account of family policy would require an understanding of each of these components on their own and, equally important, of how they interact, shape each other and respond to common cultural and socio-economic influences (for a general overview, see Kennedy, 2001). In practice, the institutional distinction between the regulatory and distributive components of family policy – the former associated primarily with the family courts and the latter with executive branches of government – has tended to be echoed in academic study, where family law is normally dealt with in legal studies and family aspects of social policy are examined in a social science context. Some topics – for example, gender relations in the family – have often prompted a more integrated approach where the concern is with the joint effect of family law and social policy provision on family roles (the traditional focus on women in this context has recently expanded to include men – see, for example, the work by Ferguson and Hogan (2004) and McKeown et al. (1998) on the impact of family policy on the role of fathers in families). Further analytical complexity arises from the different levels at which family policy can exert its impact on behaviour. These levels range from concrete influences on the minutiae of day-to-day activity to broader normative or symbolic legitimation of certain family forms (the introduction of unmarried mother's allowances in 1973 is a good example of a policy development that had effects at both these levels, in that it provided both day-to-day material support for unmarried mothers and more diffuse symbolic acceptance of the idea of motherhood outside of marriage). In addition, there is the question as to how strong the effects of family policy may be in any instance, or even whether an intended or plausible influence turns out to have real impact at all. The issue here is that the state is only one of many possible sources of influence on family behaviour and may not always be a particularly important one.

In addition to the two major areas of family policy just outlined, a broad definition of the field could also include numerous indirect supports to families (that is, those which may benefit families but which are primarily directed towards broader purposes, such as housing provision, health services, education, etc.). However, since virtually all areas of government activity could be said to affect families indirectly, in order to have a meaningful concept of family policy it is necessary to limit its scope to policies in which the primary intention is have a direct effect on particular aspects of family life or particular kinds of family.

Family Formation

Of the many aspects of family behaviour that might be the concern of public policy, one relatively novel and challenging one arises from the recent collapse in fertility rates in many parts of the world. While the modern state has always regulated and supported family formation and reproduction, it usually did so on the assumption that the impulse to engage in these activities could be taken for granted and the question for policy was simply whether or in what directions it should be moulded or supported by the state. Today, that assumption has been thrown into question, as more and more societies around of the world have seen their fertility rates fall to critically low levels and the question has arisen as to whether the state can or ought to "do something" to reverse this trend. In the EU, for example, the total fertility rate[1] (TFR) had already fallen below population replacement level (that is, below 2.1) by the mid-1970s. Since the early 1990s it has been hovering around 1.5, which is less than three-quarters the replacement level (Figure 18.1). The TFR in a number of European countries – Italy, Spain, Bulgaria, the Czech Republic, the Ukraine and Latvia – dipped below the extremely low level of 1.2 at various points in the 1990s (Council of Europe 2000, p. 74). These developments caused the European Commission to express the worry that Europe has "lost its demographic motor" and badly needs to revitalize its demographic performance if its social and economic goals are to be met (European Commission, 2005).

Before looking at the Irish case in this context, it is worth noting that while sub-replacement fertility is now universal in the developed world, it is not nearly as low in some countries as in others and is less of a social concern in some as a result. The United States is a particularly important case in point. The TFR in the US dropped from close to 4 in the late 1950s, a very high level by developed world standards at the time, to 1.79 in 1978, similar to the level then found in Europe (Figure 18.1). In the 1980s, however, fertility in the US shifted slightly upwards, in contrast to continued decline in Europe, and since the early 1990s the TFR in the US has hovered around 2.0. At that, it has been the highest fertility rate among developed countries and, again in contrast to the situation in Europe, is sufficient when combined with a modest amount of inward migration to sustain population on a growth path for the foreseeable future. This suggests that whatever else may be said about the American as opposed to the European social model, the former has proved more effective than the latter as far as population reproduction is concerned.

Figure 18.1: Total Fertility Rates in Ireland, the EU15 and the USA, 1960-2004

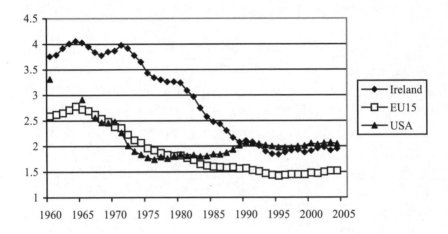

Source: CSO, Eurostat.

A striking feature of the Irish case is that its recent fertility performance has been closer to that of the US than of the rest of Europe, and in 2004 its TFR was 75 per cent above the EU average. The Irish TFR had been declining steadily since the 1970s but bottomed out in the early 1990s and then recovered slightly. By 2004 it was somewhat higher (at 1.95) than it had been in 1995 (when it was 1.84). This means that the women of childbearing age were slightly more likely on average to have children in the early years of this century than they had been a decade earlier. In addition, the number of women in the relevant age groups expanded, thus giving an additional substantial push to the annual number of births. As a result of this double positive effect, the number of births was 27 per cent higher in 2005 than in 1994 (61,042 compared to 47,900). The outcome for 2005 was still well below the 74,100 births that occurred in 1980, the peak year for births in the twentieth century, but as with the United States, it was a major factor in keeping Irish population on a strong growth path.

Certain other features of fertility trends in Ireland can be identified from official data. A surge in new family formation since the early 1990s, as evidenced by a rapid increase in the numbers of women having their first child, was the main proximate cause of the halt in fertility decline in the Ireland in that period. First births rose by 45 per cent between 1994 and 2005 (Figure 18.2). Their numbers in the early years of the present decade were the highest ever recorded in Ireland, despite the reduction in the total number of births since the 1970s. The large increase in first births between 1994 and 2005 carried forward into a slightly lesser increase in second births, which rose by 36 per cent over the same period. Third births showed a much smaller increase, but in the context of the trend towards very small families found elsewhere in Europe it is significant that there was any increase in third births at all. At the other extreme of family size, fifth and higher order births continued their long-term decline. In the past, higher order births were exceptionally common in Ireland. In 1960, for example, for every 100 first-born children, over 150 children were fifth-born or higher. By 2005, for every 100 firstborn children, only 8 children were fifth-born or higher. Thus, the very large family, which little more than a generation ago was very common, has now become rare. If we take the birth of a first child as a marker of new family formation, we can thus say that since the mid-1990s, Ireland has created new families at an unprecedented rate. These families are smaller than those of the past, but there still is a significant incidence of families with at least three children.

Figure 18.2: Number of Births by Birth Order in Ireland, 1960-2005

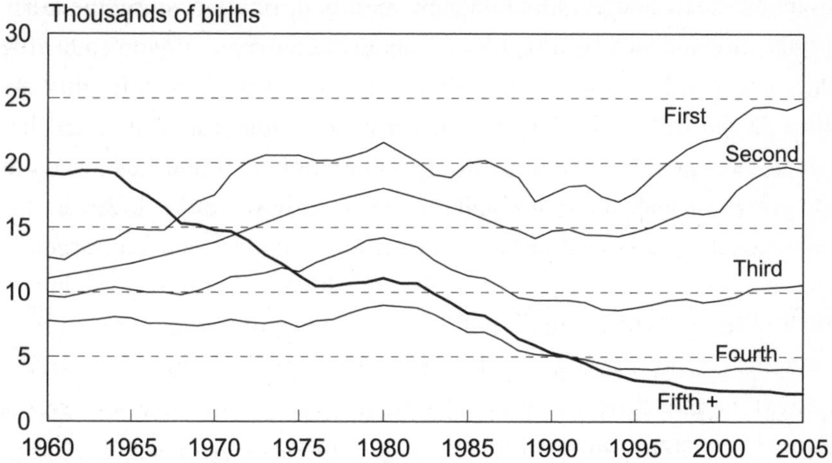

Thousands of births

Source: CSO Vital Statistics

The rise in family formation over the past decade has been accompanied to some degree by an increase in the incidence of marriage, though the large role played by childbearing outside of marriage means that family formation is no longer tied to marriage in the way it once was. A peak in the number of marriages in the 1970s was followed by two decades of decline, coupled with a rise in the age at which people married. By the early 1990s, the annual number of marriages was hovering around 16,000, a level that was only 70 per cent of the peak of 1974, and the average age of marriage had risen by two years for both men and women. As with births, however, the 1990s brought the period of decline to an end and turned it into recovery. In 2004, there were 20,600 marriages, 32 per cent more than in 1995. Some of this increase was simply a function of the growing size of the relevant age-cohorts, but there was also some rise in the propensity of people to marry. The marriage rate among those aged 16-49 rose from 17.7 per 1,000 persons in 1996 to 19.7 in 2002 in the case of males and from 17.8 to 20.2 in the case of females. At the same time, the average age of marriage rose sharply, in contrast to the growing youthfulness of marriage that occurred in the marriage boom of the 1960s and 1970s. Having risen by two years in the 1980s, average age at marriage jumped by a further four years between 1990 and 2002, rising to 32.5 years for men and 30 years for women –

high ages of marriage not seen since the 1940s. These age patterns suggest that the marriage surge of recent years is probably best interpreted in part as a consequence of catch-up among those who deferred marriage during the 1980s and early 1990s and then crowded into marriage from the mid-1990s onwards. The introduction of divorce in 1997 also contributed to both the higher incidence and older age of marriage, as it enabled those whose marriages had broken down to remarry. However, it is not possible to say what share of the upward trend was due to this factor.

Influence of Family Policy

These patterns taken together suggest that the past decade has witnessed a great deal of vitality in Irish patterns of family formation, not least in connection with fertility rates. The question arises as to what caused this vitality and in particular what contribution was made by developments in family policy. As far as fertility rates are concerned, a similar question applies to other countries with relatively high fertility rates (such as the United States), while the opposite question – why fertility rates have fallen so low – arises for much of Europe. One immediately evident aspect of cross-country differences in this regard is that they seem to be affected only to a limited degree by variations in the generosity or lack of it in state support for families with children. Those countries with the highest fertility rates (such as the United States, Ireland and New Zealand) tend to have *lower* levels of state support for families and children: state provision of pre-school childcare typically is slight, maternity leave is short, and tax-benefit supports for either two parent or lone parent families are ungenerous (D'Addio and Mira d'Ercole, 2005). Countries with strong state supports for families with children (France, the Nordic countries) perform moderately well as far as fertility is concerned but do not come up to the level of the top performing developed countries. Southern European countries have both family-unfriendly social policy regimes and low fertility, so their fertility behaviour is more in line with what one would expect in the light of their weak state supports for families with children. Nevertheless, it would appear that the states with the most generous provision for families with children do not have the highest rates of family formation.

The key to strong performance in this area seems to lie instead in general economic buoyancy, particularly where that gives rise to high levels of demand for female labour. A recent OECD analysis of fertility rates in developed countries in the period 1980-1999 identified four main influences on fertility rates, all of which related to women's employment (D'Addio and Mira d'Ercole, 2005). These were, first, the female employment rate (i.e. the proportion of women of working age who had jobs – a positive influence); second, the female unemployment rate (a negative influence); third, the share of women working in part-time jobs (a positive influence); and fourth, the degree of earnings equality between women and men. The last of these, surprisingly, the authors identified as a negative influence on fertility, with the reasoning that wage equality is associated with direct gender competition for jobs and puts women are under greater pressure to conform to male work practices, thereby making women less likely to have children. An equally striking finding of their analysis was that once aspects of demand for female labour were controlled for, family-friendly public policies seemed at most to have only small effects on birth rates. The level of net transfers to families with children and of wage replacement during maternity leave had small positive effects but extended parental leave had a small *negative* effect. The interpretation here is that extended maternity leave weakens labour market skills and makes it difficult for mothers to return to work.

The Irish experience is broadly consistent with these patterns, even though no detailed analysis has yet been provided to show why this might be so. The surge in new family formation since 1995 coincided with the boom in the economy that got underway at the same time and the rapid growth of employment, especially of married women's employment. In the high-job scenario that emerged in Ireland, disincentives to childbearing that are concentrated in early childhood (such as high direct costs of childcare and high costs of housing in the early stages of house purchase), coupled with weak state supports for families with children, may have had some deterrent effect on family formation and birth rates but they seem to have been counter-balanced by positive economic conditions, perhaps as these gave women confidence in their longer-term employment prospects. Poorly understood though these processes may be, they do seem to point to the cautionary conclusion that family policy on its own may provide only limited scope for affecting birth rates one way or the other, even where it is directed at creating family-friendly work practices. Broader economic policy may be more significant, especially where it contributes to a high demand for female labour, thus illustrating the indirect and diffuse nature of the social and economic influences that shape family life.

Marital Breakdown

A landmark development in regard to the family in Ireland in recent decades was the introduction of divorce in 1997. Intense public debate on this subject had been underway since the early 1980s, with both the pro- and anti-divorce lobbies portraying the issues in dramatic terms (Hug, 1999). A first referendum on the subject in 1986 produced a decisive vote in favour of retaining the existing bar to divorce in the Constitution. A second referendum held in November 1995 led to a different result, in that, by the narrowest of margins, the electorate voted to accept provisions for full legal dissolution of marriage. This was followed by the passage of the *Family Law (Divorce) Act, 1996*, which provided for no-fault divorce following four years of separation. This Act came into effect in February 1997.

In other western countries, the wave of liberalisation of divorce law that took place in the 1960s and 1970s was immediately followed by a spike in divorce rates, as the accumulated backlog of broken marriages was cleared, while in the longer term rates of marital breakdown trended upwards (Goode, 1993). The new provision for divorce in Ireland is on the somewhat restrictive end of the spectrum of what is now available in most western countries, in that it allows for divorce only after four years of marital breakdown. Yet it is a no-fault system which is part of the general western pattern of reasonably "easy" divorce. Consequently, echoing earlier patterns in other countries, one would have expected the arrival of divorce in 1997 to have been followed by a sharp surge in applications for divorce as pent-up demand was released, possibly within a longer trend of rising rates of marital breakdown. Did this happen?

As there was no system of registration of marital breakdowns prior to the advent of divorce, it is not possible to quantify long-term trends in rates of marital breakdown precisely. However, the available evidence suggests that marital breakdown had been increasing slowly in Ireland prior to the introduction of divorce, though on the eve of the advent of divorce those rates would appear to have been relatively low, similar to the levels found in the low-divorce countries of southern Europe (Fahey and Lyons, 1995). Census counts of those who are separated or divorced indicate that their numbers increased between 1996 and 2002 but not to a degree that would suggest that the introduction of divorce in 1997 had an immediate major impact on trends (Figure 18.3). The increase in *separated* persons between 1996 and 2002 was of a similar order to that which had occurred in the decade prior to the advent of divorce. The numbers *divorced* showed a bigger relative increase (from 10,000 in 1996 to 35,000 in 2002), but the increase was modest in view of the numbers who were already separated in 1996 (78,000) and would have qualified for divorce by 2002 under the four-year rule. Thus these figures give no evidence of a post-liberalisation spike in the incidence of divorce. The numbers who had remarried following a previous dissolution of marriage increased by 14,000 between 1996 and 2002, which amounted to an annual average of some 2,300 over the six-year period. This is a significant number, but again not enough to suggest that there was a major rush to re-marry as soon as the advent of domestic (as opposed to foreign) divorce made that option more accessible.

Expressed as a proportion of the ever-married population, the separated and divorced trebled between 1986 and 2002 – rising from 2.8 per cent in 1986 to 8.4 per cent in 2002 when the divorced who remarried are excluded from the count, and from 3 per cent to 9.8 per cent when the latter are included (Figure 18.4). Again, however, the rate of increase between 1996 and 2002 was more or less the same as it had been in the previous decade. It should be recalled that these data measure the *stock* of persons whose marriages had dissolved, not the *rate* of marital breakdown. Since the rate of exit from the stock was modest (as indicated by what appears to be a moderate rate of remarriage following divorce), much of the increase in the stock can be considered the consequence of an accumulation of people whose marriages had dissolved rather than of an increase in the rate of marital breakdown. Thus, while some increase in the rate of marital breakdown may have occurred, it is likely to have been far less than might thought in view of the tripling of the accumu-

lated stock of separated and divorced people that occurred over the period 1986-2002.

***Figure 18.3: Numbers of Divorced, Separated and Those Who
Re-married Following Dissolution of Marriage, 1986-2002***

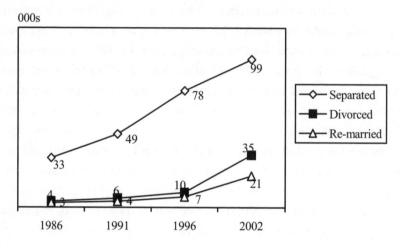

Source: Census of Population

***Figure 18.4: Separated/Divorced as a Percentage of the Ever-married
Population***

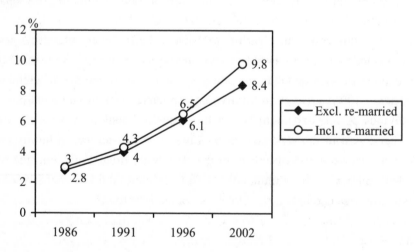

Source: Census of Population

A further indication of how the introduction of divorce had less of an impact than might have been expected was the lack of any dramatic shift towards divorce as a way of resolving broken marriages. In the pre-divorce era, judicial separation orders could be obtained from the Circuit Court by separating couples who were able to undertake the slow and costly procedures involved. However, the more common solution was to seek the simpler, quicker and cheaper remedies available in the District Court, such as orders for maintenance, child custody or access to children. There was also a heavy reliance on applications relating to domestic violence, which were the most heavily used family law proceedings of all (Fahey and Lyons, 1995).

If the advent of divorce were to have an impact on these patterns, the result would be evident in a shift in the distribution of family law cases towards the Circuit Court, since jurisdiction for divorce was accorded to the Circuit Court and not the District Court. However, as Table 18.1 shows, no such shift occurred: in 2003, as in 1994, family law applications in the District Court exceeded those in the Circuit court by four to one. In addition, applications relating to domestic violence continued to be numerically the largest element of the system, though at a somewhat lower percentage of all family law applications in 2003 (34 per cent) compared to 1994 (44 per cent). By 2003, in sum, divorce had acquired an important but in numerical terms still far from dominant place in the system.

These patterns suggest that, in the short term at least, the arrival in of divorce in Ireland in 1997 was not the transformational event that both its proponents and detractors had suggested in advance that it would be. There was no great surge in divorce applications in the immediate post-divorce period and there was a great deal of continuity with the pre-divorce era in the way that couples in conflict made use of family law. There was a long-term upward trend in marital breakdown, but this was well established before the advent of divorce and did not intensify when divorce was legalised.

Table 18.1: Family Law Applications in 1994 and 2003*

	1994	2003
District Court	14,274	23,316
Domestic violence**	7,548	9,881
Circuit Court		
Judicial separation	2,806	1,802
Divorce		3,733
Total	17,080	28,851

* Refers to legal years 1993-4 and 2002-3.

** Barring and protection orders in 1993, barring, protection and safety orders in 2003.

Source: Fahey and Lyons (1995); Courts Service (2004)

State Services and Social Welfare as Barriers to Joint Parenthood

As a final instance of the relationship between family policy and family behaviour, we can briefly consider the possible barriers or disincentives to joint parenthood that may be built into public services and welfare payments for lone parents. These effects have been pointed to especially in connection with the financial incentive to women to become lone parents which sometimes are alleged to be a feature of lone parent benefits (Department of Social and Family Affairs, 2006, pp. 80-83). (Distinct but related concerns arise in connection with the possible role of family support services and the family courts in preventing or discouraging fathers who are on the margins of family life from playing an active parenting role – see Ferguson and Hogan, 2004. However, space does not permit us to consider this issue here.)

In 1981, according to census data, lone parent families with children aged under 15 accounted for 7.2 per cent of all families with children of that age; by census 2002, that proportion had risen to 16.7 per cent. Entry routes to lone parenthood also changed, as the importance of widowhood declined and the role of unmarried parenthood and marital dissolution grew. According to micro-data from the Quarterly National Household Survey 2003 (Quarter 2), 59 per cent of lone parents with at least one child aged under 15 were unmarried, 35 per cent were separated, divorced or otherwise living apart from their spouses, and 6 per cent were widowed.

Because lone parent families have long been identified as a family type at high risk of poverty, they have been targeted for special social welfare payments (now in the form of the One-Parent Family Allowance), along with additional benefits regarding such things as access to local authority housing and extensive support under the scheme of Supplementary Welfare Allowances (for background, see McCashin, 2004, pp. 172-192). The level of combined benefit received by the majority of lone parent families is considerably higher than that received by couple families with children, particularly when the smaller household size of lone parent families is taken into account (Department of Social and Family Affairs, 2006, pp. 80-83). Furthermore, among families dependent on social welfare as their main income source, lone parent benefit might have the attraction to mothers that they would receive welfare benefits in their own name rather than as adult dependents of male partners. The possible incentive towards lone parenthood thus arises in the first instance from the higher levels of welfare support available to lone parents compared to couple parents and in the second instance from the independence from a partner's income that welfare benefits for lone parents entail.

In attempting to assess how significant these incentive effects might be, it is first necessary to recognise that there is a number of decision-points where they might operate. These include the decision to become pregnant in the first place, the decision whether or not to have an abortion, the decision whether or not to live with the other parent of the child, and, in cases where lone parenthood is the result of marriage breakdown, the decision whether to split up or not. (Other possible decisions that were important in the past, such as whether to put the baby up for adoption or to emigrate to have the baby abroad, have become less important in recent years and are not considered here.) The available evidence suggests that pregnancy outside of marriage is often unplanned and unexpected and arises from the non-use or ineffective use of contraception during sexual intercourse or takes place in the context of a ongoing relationship (Rundle et al., 2004; see also McCashin, 1996). Thus, the incentive effect of lone parent payments on the decision to become pregnant is unlikely to be large. The same is true in regard to the decision of married or cohabiting partners to split up, where conflict or dissatisfaction in the relationship is likely to be the main initiating cause of break-up. Furthermore, in many cases income and living standards for the parent who has custody of the children will fall when the couple separates.

It is in regard to the decision to abort or not abort and the decision to co-reside or not with the other parent that the incentive effects of lone parent supports may be most significant, though even here it is uncertain how decisive they are. These incentives, however, might be valued in opposite ways in the Irish policy context. Given the pro-life character of Irish policy on abortion, any incentive not to have an abortion that might arise from lone parent supports would have to be considered positive, even if it entailed an increase in the incidence of lone parenthood. The desire to attract women with crisis pregnancies away from the abortion option appears to have been a significant rationale for introducing welfare payments for unmarried mothers in the first instance (McCashin, 2004). An incentive to avoid co-residence with the other parent, on the other hand, would be considered negative, though again this is not to say that such a negative effect is strong or widespread. Since the vast majority – over 85 per cent – of parents of young children co-reside, it is evident that most families are not influenced by it. Even among women who give birth outside of marriage, the majority (possibly as many as two out of three) are either in an ongoing couple relationship when the child is born or enter one shortly thereafter. Nevertheless, this still leaves a small but significant minority for whom the incentive to live as a solo parent arising from lone parent supports could be important.

Recognising this possibility, the Department of Social and Family Affairs has recently proposed a reform of supports for lone parents (Department of Social and Family Affairs, 2006). The elements of the proposal that affect parenting incentives are to abolish benefits targeted on lone parents and introduce instead a Parental Allowance (PA) targeted on all low income families with children and to "individualise" the PA so that entitlement on the part of the recipient is independent of whether he or she is living with a spouse/partner or not. Whether on in what form the reforms will eventually be introduced and what effect they will have remains to be seen.

Conclusion

This chapter has sought to introduce what until recently in Ireland was the somewhat unfamiliar concept of family policy and to illustrate the questions and analytical difficulties that arise when trying to assess how its various components affect family behaviour. It identified the institutional divide between family law and family related aspects of social policy as an important structural feature of this policy domain and pointed to the need for research and commentary to take account of both sides of this divide. The chapter then considered three different aspects of family behaviour, namely, family formation (as evidenced especially by birth rates), marriage breakdown and lone parenthood, outlined recent developments in each and considered how they were moulded by family policy. The overall conclusion to emerge is that, while family policies can be an important part of the context of family life, their influence on family behaviour can easily be overstated. Trends in birth rates seemed to be more influenced by general social and economic conditions than by state provisions for families with children, the introduction of divorce in 1997 made only limited difference to the way couples in conflict made use of family law, and public provision for lone parents had uncertain effects on the levels and patterns of lone parenting. These instances are too limited to support any broader conclusions about the role of family policy in family life but they are sufficient to give rise to caution about how far interventions by the state shape the development of family behaviour in Ireland.

References

Commission on the Family (1998) Strengthening Families for Life. Final Report of the Commission on the Family to the Minister for Social, Community and Family Affairs. Dublin: Stationery Office.

Courts Service, 2004. Annual Report 2003. Dublin: Courts Service.

D'Addio, Anna Cristina and Marco Mira d'Ercole (2005) "Trends and Determinants of Fertility Rates". OECD Social, Employment and Migration Working Papers No. 27. Paris: Organisation for Economic Cooperation and Development.

Daly, Mary and Sara Clavero (2002) *Contemporary Family Policy. A comparative review of Ireland, France, Germany, Sweden and the UK*. Dublin: Institute of Public Administration.

Department of Social and Family Affairs (2006) Report of the Working Group on Lone Parents, Department of Social and Family Affairs. Reform of Income Supports for Lone Parents and Parents on Low Income: Proposals for Discussion. Published in Government Discussion Paper: Proposals for Supporting Lone Parents. Dublin: Family Affairs Unit, Department of Social and Family Affairs (February 2006)

Fahey, T. and H. Russell (2001) *Family Formation in Ireland. Trends, Data Needs and Implications*. Policy Research Series No. 43, Economic and Social Research Institute, Dublin.

Fahey, T. and M. Lyons (1995). *Marital Breakdown and Family Law in Ireland*. Dublin: Oak Tree Press.

Ferguson, H. and F. Hogan (2004). *Strengthening Families through Fathers*. Dublin: Family Support Agency.

Goode, William J. (1993) *World Changes in Divorce Patterns*. New Haven and London: Yale University Press.

Hug, Chrystel (1999) *The Politics of Sexual Morality in Ireland*. London: Macmillan

Kennedy, Finola (2001) *Cottage to Creche: Family Change in Ireland*. Dublin: Institute of Public Administration.

McCashin, A.. (1996). *Lone Parents: A local study*. Dublin: Combat Poverty Agency.

McCashin, A. (2004). *Social Security in Ireland*. Dublin: Gill and Macmillan.

McKeown, K., H. Ferguson and D. Rooney (1998). "Fathers: Irish experience in an international context – An abstract of a report the Commission on the Family", Chapter 18 in *Strengthening Families for Life*. Final Report of the Commission on the Family to the Minister for Social, Community and Family Affairs. Dublin: Stationery Office.

Rundle, K., C. Leigh, H. McGee and R. Layte (2004). *Irish Contraception and Crisis Pregnancy Study. A Survey of the General Population*. Dublin: Crisis Pregnancy Agency.

Notes

[1] The total fertility rate is the average number of births a woman would have during her reproductive life if she were exposed to the fertility rates characteristic of various childbearing age groups in a particular year.

Chapter 19

NEGOTIATING POWER AND POWERLESSNESS: COMMUNITY INTERESTS AND PARTNERSHIP IN RURAL IRELAND

Tony Varley

A mong social scientists there is wide acceptance that social "inclu-sion" and "exclusion" are ultimately to be viewed as phenomena of the distribution of power. Not alone are the poor, as Tovey et al. (1996, p. 321) remind us, relatively "powerless in society" but their persisting powerlessness is a reflection of how an ever more globalised established order operates in ways that "best suit the interests of the power-holders themselves".

Against such a backdrop the question explored in this chapter asks: how useful is it to study rural community development in terms of at-tempts by organised community interests to turn their collective action into forms of countervailing power? Such a question subsumes another that will be considered as well: how might "partnership" with the state contribute to community interests turning collective action into forms of countervailing power?

Both these questions will firstly be discussed conceptually by explor-ing some elements of "power" and "powerlessness" and how these might relate to each other. This discussion will be preliminary to considering two cases of rural community-centred collective action. The first of these, the community movement Muintir na Tíre, has long embraced partnership as central to its approach to community development. For our second case we will take the involvement of community interests in the Forum area partnership that has now been functioning for 16 years in the far west of Ireland. These two cases are chosen not just on account of their reliance on partnership, but also because their persistence allows us to look at how efforts at negotiating power realities within different contexts of "partnership" have fared over time.

Power and Powerlessness

Trying to characterise Irish community development is anything but easy (Ó Cinnéide and Walsh, 1990). Almost regardless of what dimension one takes, we seem to be surrounded by variety on all sides. We can see this in the way the aims, analysis, organisational forms, the tactics in use and the levels of achieved effectiveness can vary greatly between groups. Something else making for variety arises from the ways the state has taken an interest in stimulating community development.

To put some order on all this variety, one suggestion is that while groups and tendencies may be disparate they are often contiguous. Building on this insight, groups and tendencies have been arranged into "consensus" and "conflict" types on the basis of their characteristic analysis and choice of tactics (Curtin and Varley, 1995).

The approach to getting to grips with the variety of community action taken here is influenced by that strand of populism that sees rural interests in a structurally disadvantaged and relatively powerless position in urbanised societies, and that sees collective action on their part as a means of generating forms of countervailing power (Lipton, 1977; Kitching, 1989; Varley, 2003). Seen from this perspective, a "political" process of negotiating perceived oppositions between power and powerlessness becomes central to understanding the collective action of rural groups that project themselves as relatively powerless vis-à-vis relatively powerful forces in society.

To help us delve deeper into these perceived oppositions between power and powerlessness, the distinction between "power over" and "power to", familiar to students of power (see Morriss, 2002, pp. xiii-xiv), will now be introduced. Once recast in these terms the resort to collective action by groups that project themselves as relatively powerless can be seen as *beginning* a process of generating the "power to" assert themselves as organised interests and to control those dominating and exploiting forces that exert "power over" them.

While this use of the "power to" and "power over" distinction emphasises the negotiated or transactional nature of power relationships, it does not reveal the direction community interests might take or how far they might go in their attempts to turn collective action into forms of countervailing power. To explore this issue, with a view to providing "benchmarks" for the discussion of our empirical cases, two ideal-typical scenarios – the "radical" and the "pragmatic" – will now be briefly outlined. As these ideal-typical scenarios exaggerate and simplify realities they cannot be taken to be empirical descriptions in any strict sense; their use, instead, is to facilitate the interpretation and comparison of real world cases (see Burger, 1987, pp. 154-79).

Both our ideal-typical radicals and pragmatists would accept that the potential of collective action to become an effective form of countervailing power will depend on how well the "power to" possibilities of collective agency can be realised. Where they differ is in their conceptions of the powerless people, in what they take to be the desirable ends of collective action and in how they view the resources and opportunities relevant to turning collective action into forms of effective countervailing power.

The radical standard of effective collective action seeks an alternative to the established order that promises liberation from its characteristic "power over" forces for the most powerless groups of local society. In contrast, our pragmatists take the "whole community" as comprising the people and are prepared to settle for an accommodation that seeks to preserve the *status quo ante*.

The key resource for radicals is an analysis that not only tries to uncover the dynamics of structural inequality (both inside and outside the locality), but actively seeks an alternative to the established order built upon acceptance of equalitarian and communitarian ideals.[1] Other valued resources are a participative organisational culture built around the ideal of encouraging universal active involvement of "small man" and other relatively powerless local interests in collective action; and an approach to tactics that combines opposition to the state (seen as underpinning the

system of structural inequality) with building alliances with kindred disadvantaged groups. The radical view of opportunities is to see them
stemming from the ongoing and progressively more severe crisis conditions produced by processes of structural decline.

Given such a radical analysis (and view of the state), any suggestion
that state-inspired partnership-type initiatives might be genuinely interested in structural change, and that community partners might somehow
be equal with state partners in any strict sense, would tend to be dismissed. Even well-organised and radicalised rural interests would stand
little chance of being able to influence state-sponsored participative development initiatives to their own advantage.

Just as our radicals can view popular powerlessness as the product of
large-scale forces that work to the disadvantage of certain rural interests,
so too can our ideal-typical pragmatic populists accept that external
large-scale forces are able to inflict serious damage on disadvantaged
local communities, small-scale producers and other rural interests.
Where they differ is in their pragmatic acceptance that the immensely
powerful established order favours large-scale interests, and that the best
small-scale and local community interests can do is to accommodate
themselves to this reality. Searching for alternatives to the *status quo*
along radical lines is judged to be counter-productive and even utopian.
The crisis analysis pragmatic populists develop sees the pressure large-
scale forces can exert on disadvantaged local communities and small-
scale economic interests as a matter for most concern at those junctures
when some crisis occurs that unacceptably worsens the existing balance
(however unequal) between large- and small-scale interests.

As well as a reactive analysis that thinks in terms of restorative
change, other relevant resources for our pragmatists are a leadership-
centred organisational culture in which local notables are relied on to
lead the way and tactics that aim at cultivating close working relations
with the state. The pragmatic view of opportunities is to link them to the
sporadically occurring crisis conditions that threaten a fairly stable system (however unequally constructed), and prompts the state (as in the
area partnerships) to intervene so as to restore balance in a situation
where balance has been temporarily lost. In line with their preference for
working within the system, our ideal-typical pragmatic populist collec-

tive actors would optimistically see partnership with the state as offering both valuable opportunities and resources (such as funding and experience) to local community interests.

We have now sketched contrasting ideal-typical scenarios that portray how radicals and pragmatists might see the people, "power over" forces and how they might seek to turn collective action on the part of community interests into different forms of effective countervailing power. With these ideal-typical scenarios as our guides we are ready to turn to our two concrete cases. These cases will first be described individually and then compared with each other.

Muintir na Tíre and Partnership

Born out of the prolonged rural crisis of the inter-war period, Muintir na Tíre (People of the Land) aspired from the outset to be a movement capable of restoring power to a rural Ireland perceived to be sinking ever deeper into powerlessness. Its early analysis suggested that large-scale forces, finding expression in the post-war slump, the Great Depression and the Economic War (1933-8), had laid Irish agriculture low. Organising agricultural interests thus became the preoccupation of the early Muintir na Tíre (Muintir).

After an unpromising start and much agonising about how rural interests might best be organised (see Tierney, 2004), Muintir's founder, Fr John Hayes of Tipperary, eventually hit on the idea of building a rural movement around the Catholic parishes, conceived as whole communities and organised along vocationalist lines in the form of guilds and parish councils. In building "power to" capabilities, coming up with an organisation that would be at once popular and effective became the most critical of perceived resources.

Not alone did the early Muintir leadership tend to attribute people's economic and social difficulties to the manner powerful large-scale forces were operating to their disadvantage, but its analysis suggested that these destructive forces could be brought under popular control, if only rural interests were properly organised. For vocationalist collective action to function as a form of effective countervailing power, it would have to be organised on both the national and the local levels and it would have to make a significant difference.

How much of a resource did the Catholic Church, with its presence in every corner of the country and its large pool of parish clergy, provide to Muintir? Mark Tierney (2004, p. 35) reminds us how Fr Hayes had serious reservations at one point about his parish councils becoming "completely dominated" by the local clergy. What is certain, however, is that in Fr Hayes Muintir had a popular leader with an increasingly high public profile.

The movement was also well-positioned to ride the wave of interest in Catholic circles that ideas of vocational organisation aroused in the 1930s. While acceptance of the principle of subsidiarity meant that the early Muintir put much store on preserving its own autonomy, many of the opportunities that national and local Muintir would try to exploit stemmed from state campaigns to bring electricity and other services to the rural areas.

But how well did Muintir fare with its approach to local development? What quickly became clear was how a series of at times related oppositions would throw up many tensions. Prominent among these tensions were those between the local and the national levels of organisation, the pursuit of the common good as against sectional interests, the desire to represent everyone as against the underdog, the choice between having a Christian public persona as against a purely Catholic one, between amateurism and professionalism, between voluntarism and dependence on the state and between being representative and being effective.

Given Muintir's whole community approach, a particularly pressing opposition centred on the question of whether it was possible to represent everyone and the underdog at one and the same time? Being born in a Land League hut in County Limerick (his family had been evicted by Lord Cloncurry) had left Fr Hayes with a strong sense of social justice and an enduring identification with the underdog (see Tierney, 2004), especially the impoverished farm labourers. Yet his approach to community organising was the all-together one that sought to have the socially powerful and powerless of local society pull together in pursuit of the common good. Some accounts of local Muintir councils in operation suggest that, reflecting local power realities, they were very much leadership- rather than membership-led and that local notables (priests, teachers and big farmers especially) were heavily over-represented in the local leadership (see McNabb, 1964, p. 208; Eipper, 1986, p. 104; Silverman, 2001, p. 445).

How well then did Muintir succeed over time in creating a form of countervailing power out of collective action? At the national level the early movement established a high public profile for itself, though as vocationalism faded and circumstances changed some of its early analysis and organisation became somewhat outmoded. Most critically, Muintir may have succeeded in creating some local-level vocationalist organisation, and in stimulating and co-ordinating a considerable amount of local self-help improvement activity, but ultimately it failed to spread its local parish councils anything like evenly across the country.

This, in the longer term, was one reason why its national-level activists felt obliged to revisit the question of Muintir's relationship with the state. Other developments were also of importance. By the late 1960s Muintir had become a firm convert to the United Nations' view that effective "community development" required the building of partnership-type relations between organised community interests and the state. In 1970, the decision to replace the old parish councils with new representative community councils marked the formal end of vocationalism. Within a rapidly urbanising Ireland, Muintir's leadership was even keen to extend its approach to community development to the cities.

By the early 1970s national Muintir had come to see state funding as the key resource in the further development of its own "power to" capabilities. With sufficient state funding it was believed that the way would be cleared for Muintir to overcome its historic inability to spread its local organisation more comprehensively, and to nurture those councils at risk of disappearing for want of adequate back-up support.

What was contemplated amounted in effect to the state granting Muintir something akin to a monopoly in the organising and servicing of community councils. A professionally-staffed development unit was envisaged that, with proper state funding, would service the needs of an ever more numerous set of Muintir-affiliated community councils (Muintir na Tíre, 1971, pp. 36-37).

As things turned out, the sort of monopoly Muintir had in mind would never be conceded by the state. Muintir's strategic vision of building a supportive infrastructure for community councils would depend initially for its realisation on EC funding. Once this ended in 1979 the team of paid organisers Muintir had assembled and trained could not be kept together.

Despite this and other setbacks, restoring partnership-type relationships with the state/EC/EU has appeared to Muintir's national leadership to be its best chance of advancing its distinctive approach to community development. By far the most ambitious new partnership-type initiative Muintir has become involved in is Community Alert, a form of community policing that involves local groups working in association with the Gardaí.

Resonating with features of both our radical and pragmatic scenarios, two different interpretations of how Muintir has benefited from partnership are possible. The optimistic one – based on the experience with Community Alert – suggests that partnership has thrown Muintir a lifeline, supplying it with funding, with standing and with a foundation upon which to build a more secure future. The pessimistic view, on the other hand, suggests that Muintir has been impaired heavily in its work with organising community councils by its inability to secure an ongoing partnership-type funding commitment from official sources. The central thrust of its work – centred on the community councils – has in consequence tended to languish.

Partnership in the West

For almost two decades now organised local communities have been participating in area partnerships that take the combating of social exclusion and the promoting of local development as their aims. To consider the politics of negotiating power and powerlessness within the area partnerships, we will take as our example the Forum partnership of northwest Connemara, the Republic's only rural model action partnership of the third European anti-poverty programme (Poverty 3).[2] Originally built around one of Ireland's best known rural community groups, Connemara West plc (based in the village of Letterfrack) (O'Hara, 1998, pp. 60-8), it was Connemara West that had prepared the way for Forum, a process that involved selecting the target groups, recruiting the state partners and outlining a programme of work.

Building on a local tradition of "whole community" organising (at one time influenced by Muintir), Connemara West had built up its own organisation on a piecemeal basis as new activities were taken on. By the time of Forum's appearance it had its own formalised model of community organisation – based on specialisation, professionalisation and acquiring property for community purposes. Its achievements meant that it was in a strong position to set a standard for other local community interests to emulate. On top of this, as a participant in all three European anti-poverty programmes, Connemara West had built a track record of working within the system for the benefit of the locality.

Long before Forum's advent Connemara West activists had developed an analysis rooted in local circumstances that linked local economic disadvantages (and relative powerlessness) with the long-term structural decline of the remoter rural areas. The context here was one in which flight from the land had become locally endemic. For Connemara West the challenge of effective collective action has always been about confronting the developmental tendencies that produced such rural decline.

Identification with communitarian and "small man" ideals has allowed Connemara West to lend its support to local initiatives to resist the ongoing decline of small-scale agriculture. Its own efforts, however, have historically focused heavily on acquiring and managing community facilities, promoting tourism and providing training opportunities for young school-leavers.

How well did community interests in Forum get on in using the partnership to build their own "power to" capacities and to achieve some control over the tendencies making for rural decline? Here, no less than in Muintir's case, two rather different interpretations are possible. On the optimistic side, that Forum was largely conceived as a Connemara West project gave the community interest an initial advantage in defining the terrain that the partnership would occupy. What further strengthened its hand here was the general acceptance within Forum that the initiative's impact would depend on having a vibrant set of community partners. In spite of numerous tensions, the changes made over time to Forum's programme of work, to its organisational structure and to its operating style came to express the wishes of community actors as much as those of state partners.

What is also indisputable is that the resources that Forum provided were highly useful to Connemara West and other local community interests in adding to their facilities and to their overall capacity to bring about certain sorts of local change. Above all Forum, by focusing on the social needs of older people, became the means of establishing a new pattern of state-financed social care provision locally.

On the pessimistic side, it can be suggested that community interests within Forum have been turned into instruments of policy delivery largely on the state's terms. Moreover, while Forum may be operating for nearly 16 years now, there is still a sense (especially in its social care activity) in which it continues to function on a provisional basis. The fact that Forum's service delivery activity with older people depends on paid workers employed on temporary community employment schemes has left it vulnerable. Just how vulnerable it is became clear in 2005 when the broader threat to community enterprise schemes caused the entire basis of Forum's social care provision to be thrown into serious doubt.

Some further support for a pessimistic reading can be gained from the way innovations pioneered and maintained by Forum (and other Irish area partnerships (see Walsh, 2001, pp. 122-5) have yet to enter the mainstream of policy, at either the local or the national levels.

Comparing our Cases

In turning to compare our two instances of collective action as forms of potential countervailing power, we can begin by asking how close they come to our ideal-typical radical and pragmatic scenarios. On the surface level both Muintir and Connemara West have veered more towards pragmatism than radicalism in their conception of the people, in their analysis of large-scale forces, in the aims they set for themselves, in their approach to organisation (though reliance on local notables for leadership has by no means been total) and in their ideas about the benefits to be derived from partnership with the state.

This, however, conceals a great deal between them in their respective conceptions of "power over" forces and "power to" capabilities. Initially Muintir's conception of large-scale forces was very much influenced by conditions in the 1930s. How external forces have historically afflicted disadvantage on the remoter rural districts has been the contrasting focus of Connemara West. The notion that rural Ireland is under threat from large-scale urban forces may still be found in present-day Muintir, but this line of analysis is not nearly so prominent as it was in the early days.

At the outset both Muintir and Connemara West attributed their perceived relative powerlessness as much to the inability of their constituencies to act collectively as to their domination by "power over" forces. That said, it might be objected that the differences between our two sets of attempts to use collective action to build "power to" capabilities are so great as to raise the question of whether they can be usefully compared at all. After all, while Muintir has aspired to be a national movement, the concerns of Connemara West have been restricted to the well being of a single locality.

Such a basic difference as this would inevitably exert a profound influence on the sort of resources each has sought to mobilise and the sort of opportunities each has tried to exploit. At the same time, leadership has proved to be a hugely important resource in both cases, as has the creation of traditions of collective action built upon a distinctive analysis, learned and shared experience and a track record of being able to deliver a variety of public goods under changing conditions.

What is also clear is that Connemara West has been better able to build up its "power to" capabilities incrementally over time. While Muintir's ability to stay the course for 70 years is a remarkable achievement, its organisational progress has in important ways been more cyclical than cumulative in character.

Another discernible pattern is that both our cases do better in terms of capacity-building than in exerting control over large-scale "power over" forces. Both sets of activists have found that, in certain respects, they lacked the power to even restore or maintain the status quo (where the effect of different forms of structural rural decline were concerned, for instance). For this reason many of them would accept that the world changes in ways that they are powerless to alter, thus pointing to the limits to collective action as a form of countervailing power.

For all that, partnership with the state – or, more precisely, with different segments of it – has been seen in each of our cases as offering crucial opportunities. The pragmatic scenario assumes that there is always a good chance that community interests – especially those led by a competent local leadership – can create sufficient room to manoeuvre to be able to use the partnerships to their own advantage.

What the pragmatic scenario does not tell us of course is *why* one of our cases has been more effective than the other in its reliance on partnership. Partnership for Muintir has not proven to be a particularly effective means of organising a national movement around community councils, though it continues to be seen by Muintir activists as critical to the pursuit of such an aim. What Muintir has found is that reliance on state assistance to advance its work is mostly about "fitting in" with the state's priorities. We have seen how its negotiating power has proved to be greater in relation to Community Alert than in securing ongoing partnership-type funding for the sort of community development associated with its community councils. In contrast, social exclusion in the remote countryside has given Forum relatively more leverage in a context where social exclusion has been a rising policy priority that has found various institutional expression.

Although the differences in the experience of partnership and in using partnership effectively are very real between our two cases, it might be argued that in some respects they are each subject to the same dynamics. To the extent that the emerging pattern illustrates how the state has the power to bend community interests to its own purposes, what has transpired can be read as part of a general process of the state having succeeded in using partnership arrangements to turn community interests into service providers largely on its own terms (see Craig et al., 2004, pp. 221-2).

Such a pattern, echoing the pessimistic analysis of our radicals, suggests that what awaits community interests that involve themselves in partnership is incorporation (see Geddes, 2000, p. 797; Taylor, 2005, pp. 143-6). What is similarly evident, as the "working groups" in Forum and Community Alert in Muintir illustrate, is that the use of partnership to combat social exclusion has encouraged specialised community-based interests more than "whole community" interests (such as community councils) to come to the fore.

On the other hand, what the state wants from community interests and what these want for themselves can on occasion substantially converge. We find examples of this in the social care activity in Connemara and in Muintir's involvement in Community Alert. All this, in line with pragmatic reasoning, permits a more optimistic interpretation of events. Community interests (as has significantly been the case in Forum), on the basis of a favourable "balance of power", can get themselves into a position where they can use partnership to their own advantage. Arguably, this was also so in the 1970s for Muintir where its work with the community councils was concerned, but in the event this arrangement would not last.

Conclusion

Typically, instances of community action are embedded in quite different contexts. In the two cases we have been discussing, Muintir and Connemara West, both may have been concerned with threatening large-scale forces, but the nature of these forces was not always perceived to be the same. Nor, as we have seen, were the same "power to" capabilities relevant to the circumstances of our two cases. Rather than accept that these contextual differences are so great as to rule out meaningful comparison, our suggestion is that viewing collective action as a form of potential countervailing power can allow us explore the differences as well as the similarities between cases. The idea, in other words, is not to reduce the complexity of community action to a few basic categories. On the contrary, the interpretive framework outlined here is as much concerned with illuminating differences between cases as it is similarities.

The notion of collective action as a potential form of countervailing power lies at the base of our interpretive framework. In pursuing the possibility that the "power to" capabilities of collective action might be capable of negotiating "power over" relationships, we have explored some of the conditions under which this possibility might or might not be realised. Radical and pragmatic ideal-typical scenarios were introduced to help illuminate the direction community groups might take and how far they might go in attempting to turn collective action into forms of countervailing power. With these scenarios as our guides we were able to turn to our two cases with a number of questions in mind.

Did, we were able to ask, the early Muintir activists and the community interests behind Forum begin by seeing themselves as relatively powerless? Did they attribute their relative powerlessness to domination

by external "power over" forces as well as to their own lack of organisation? What was their conception of "power over" forces? How do they
see popular powerlessness being countered? How did they attempt to
mobilise resources and exploit opportunities so as to turn collective action into forms of countervailing power? What accounts for how well or
poorly our community actors have actually got on in their respective efforts to be effective?

We have also paid attention to the question of how well "partnership" might be used to add to the "power to" capabilities of community
actors, and to bringing "power over" forces more under popular control.
Our answer to this last question, based on the two cases briefly reviewed,
has been that it is not just a matter of choosing between pessimistic or
optimistic interpretations. The complexity of the situation we have described permits facets of both interpretations of partnership relations to
be regarded as equally valid.

References

Burger, T. (1987), *Max Weber's Theory of Concept Formation: History, Laws
and Ideal Types*, Durham: Duke University Press.

Commins, P. (1986), "Rural Social Change" in Clancy, P., Drudy, S., Lynch,
K., and O'Dowd, L., (eds.), *Ireland: A Sociological Profile*, Dublin: Institute of
Public Administration, pp. 47-69.

Craig, G., Taylor, M. and Parkes, T. (2004), "Protest or Partnership? The Voluntary and Community Sectors in the Policy Process", *Social Policy and Administration*, Vol. 38, No. 3, pp. 221-239.

Curtin, C. and Varley, T. (1995), "Community Action and the State" in Clancy,
P., Drudy, S., Lynch, K., and O'Dowd, L., (eds.), *Irish Society: Sociological
Perspectives*, Dublin: Institute of Public Administration, pp. 379-409.

Eipper, C. (1986), *The Holy Trinity: A Community Study of Church, State and
Business in Ireland*, Aldershot: Gower.

Fite, G.C. (1962), "The Historical Development of Agricultural Fundamentalism in the Nineteenth Century", *Journal of Farm Economics*, Vol. 44, pp. 1203-
1211.

Geddes, M. (2000), "Tackling Social Exclusion in the European Union? The
Limits to the New Orthodoxy of Local Partnership", *International Journal of
Urban and Regional Research*, Vol. 24, No. 4, pp. 782-800.

Kitching, G. (1989), *Development and Underdevelopment in Historical Perspective*, London: Routledge.

Lipton, M. (1977), *Why Poor People Stay Poor: A Study of Urban Bias in World Development*, London: Temple Smith.

McNabb, P. (1964), "Social Structure" in Newman, J. (ed.), *The Limerick Rural Survey*, Tipperary: Muintir na Tire Publications, pp. 193-242.

Morriss, P. (2002), *Power: A Philosophical Analysis* (2nd edn.), Manchester: Manchester University Press.

Muintir na Tíre. (1971), *Review Committee Report on Muintir na Tíre*, Tipperary: Muintir na Tíre Publications.

Ó Cinnéide, S. and Walsh, J. (1990), "Multiplication and Divisions: Trends in Community Development in Ireland since the 1960s", *Community Development Journal*, Vol. 24, pp. 326-336.

O'Hara, P. (1998), *Action on the Ground: Models of Practice in Rural Development*, Galway: Irish Rural Link.

Silverman, M. (2001), *An Irish Working Class: Explorations in Political Economy and Hegemony, 1800-1950*, Toronto: University of Toronto Press.

Taylor, G. (2005), *Negotiated Governance and Public Policy in Ireland*, Manchester: Manchester University Press.

Tierney, M. (2004), *The Story of Muintir na Tíre 1931–2001 – the First Seventy Years,* Tipperary: Muintir na Tíre Publications.

Tovey, H., Curtin, C. and Haase, T. (1996), "Poverty in Rural Ireland: Policy and Practice" in C. Curtin, Haase, T. and Tovey, H. (eds.), *Poverty in Rural Ireland: A Political Economy Approach*, Dublin: Oak Tree Press, pp. 307-321.

Varley, T. (2003), "Populism, the Europeanised State and Collective Action in Rural Ireland" in M. Blanc, (ed.), *Innovations, Institutions and Rural Change*, Luxembourg: Office for Official Publications of the European Communities, pp. 127-168.

Walsh, J. (2001), "Catalysts for Change: Public Policy Reform through Local Partnership in Ireland" in M. Geddes and Benington, J. (eds.), *Local Partnership and Social Exclusion in the European Union: New Forms of Local Social Governance?*, London: Routledge, pp. 111-133.

Notes

_____

[1]To some extent this radical analysis evokes the tenets of what has been called "agricultural fundamentalism" (Fite 1962, pp. 1203-4) or "rural fundamentalism" (Commins 1986, pp. 52-3).

[2]After Poverty 3 ended in 1994 Forum was accepted into the national Community Development Programme (CDP) and, in recognition of its circumstances, succeeded in securing double the normal CDP project funding.

Chapter 20

SOCIAL CAPITAL AND WELL-BEING IN IRELAND

Tom Healy[1]

The future of Irish society is uncertain. We have emerged from a period of extraordinarily rapid growth in measurable market income,
before which, we saw a period of extraordinary economic crisis characterised by high unemployment, emigration, stagnant or falling incomes
and continuing poverty for many.

Now we are at a crossroads.

What sort of society do we want for the future – our future in what
sort of world? And what sort of economy, education system, community
development, governance do we want and need to realise the society of
the future? Through education and other means, are we to "meet the
needs of the economy" or is "education", the "economy" and many other
things to meet the needs of real people in a society? These are tough
questions and involve a lot of thinking and a lot of hard work. They are
not necessarily the stuff of immediate response, marketable ideas and
measurable returns to investment.

We may start by trying to work out which are the right questions we
should be asking right now. In this chapter, I am speaking in a personal
capacity. No solutions are on offer – only questions – some of them on
the tough side perhaps. I begin by revisiting the notion of welfare or well-
being. Then I look at how societies – Irish society in particular – might

provide for well-being. Finally, I re-assess the role of "social capital" as one element in an overall social response to the well-being challenge.

How Are We Doing on Well-being?

Like many other things in life, the concept and term "well-being" is a slippery one. At its simplest, David Myers (1993) defines well-being as:

> . . . the pervasive sense that life has been and is good. It is an ongo-
> ing perception that this time in one's life, or even life as a whole, is
> fulfilling, meaningful, and pleasant.

However, well-being goes well beyond mental states of pleasure, happiness or satisfaction for individuals, important as that is. Social well-being concerns the match between our goals and the kind of life we experience. In other words, it concerns what we value and seek and how we evaluate our lives in this light. It concerns personal, collective and organisational values that, strictly speaking, are of no *controlling* concern of the state or the market.

But the notion of a "good society" is as old as the Greeks and still older. To simplify a long and tortuous debate about the nature of well-being, morality and the "good life" from Aristotle to latter-day philosophers like Amartya Sen we can say that well-being involves a coherence between the moral ends and chosen values of an individual or society, and the objective circumstances of life as perceived by them. It is as much about the *freedom to achieve* the life they perceive as best suited to them as the fact of particular achievements. This shifts the focus in studies of well-being from pre-determined outcomes such as health, education and income to the freedom to live a particular life in which people can flourish. Surely, health, education and income are vital components of, and means towards, a life well lived. However, income alone is an inadequate measure of well-being. In fact, there are thousands of studies to show that the returns to happiness from additional income for those above particular thresholds (I suspect most of the people reading this) is almost negative or negligible. All our striving after, competing, long hours and concerns over relativity and social status is ill-placed if you can believe what the "well-being" research is saying.

We are deemed to be a happy lot – at least up to recently. On every recent international survey of happiness/life satisfaction/subjective well-being,[2] the Irish emerge as being well above the European or international averages (refer to Table 20.1). The reasons for inter-country differences are complex. Certainly, health, income inequality and income are part of the explanation even if there is strong evidence for declining impact of income beyond particular thresholds of average income per capita. The quality of public governance and the nature of different value systems are also significant predictors as well as some aspects of "social capital". It is not proposed here to explore the extent to which cross-cultural or cross-country differences in social capital may be related to differences in levels of reported happiness or well-being.

Table 20.1: Well-Being, Social Capital and Income (OECD member countries, 1999-2002)

	GDP per Capita[1]	Average Satisfaction (scale 1-10)[2]	% Spending Time with Others[3]	% Respondents Who Do Unpaid Work for at Least One Group[4]
Luxembourg	49,154	7.87	n.a.	30.0
Norway	36,585	7.66	n.a.	n.a.
United States	34,953	7.65	96.3	64.7
Ireland	**29,810**	**8.15**	**96.1**	**28.4**
Canada	29,593	7.80	93.4	46.8
Switzerland	29,510	8.14	n.a.	n.a.
Denmark	29,218	8.24	96.3	33.2
Iceland	29,036	8.05	94.3	31.9
Netherlands	28,700	7.88	97.7	47.3
Austria	28,358	8.02	91.5	28.3
Australia	27,337	7.55	n.a.	n.a.
Belgium	27,098	7.56	93.2	31.4
UK	27,068	7.40	93.8	43.1*
Sweden	26,902	7.65	n.a.	53.9

France	26,562	6.93	90.3	21.9
Japan	26,538	6.48	83	15.6
Finland	26,355	7.87	92.1	36.5
Germany	25,465	7.61	96	19.5
Italy	25,378	7.17	90.7	25.0
Spain	21,348	7.04	91.8	15.6
New Zealand	21,228	n.a.	n.a.	n.a.
Portugal	17,913	6.98	89	11.6
Greece	17,016	6.67	96.1	38.0
Korea	15,916	6.21	91.3	47.1
Czech Repub.	14,861	7.06	88.8	29.8
Hungary	13,042	5.69	n.a.	14.3
Slovakia	11,323	6.03	n.a.	48.6
Poland	10,363	6.37	n.a.	12.1
Mexico	9,149	8.13	81.2	36.3
Turkey	6,046	5.62	n.a.	1.5
OECD average	24,061	7.30	92.1	31.2

Source: OECD (2005) Society at a Glance and World Values Survey 1999-2002, Inglehart et al. (2004). All of the data in the above table were obtained from: *http://www.oecd.org*

[1] Gross Domestic Product per capita in 2001 using Purchasing Power Parity values. Refer to Society at a Glance (OECD, 2005: 25) - Indicator GE1

[2] Refer to indicator C01 in OECD (2005:81)

[3] Refer to indicator C02 in OECD (2005:83). The data denote the proportion of survey respondents who "spend time with friends, or with colleagues from work, or with people from church, sport/cultural groups".

[4] Refer to indicator C03 in OECD (2005:85).

* Data for the United Kingdom refer to Great Britain only.

Turning to changes over time, the evidence indicates no definite trend in Ireland between 1981 and 1999 (Table 20.2). However, there does appear to have been an upward shift in reported levels of happiness by persons aged 50 or more (at the time of the survey) and a possible fall in respect of 18-29 and 40-49 year olds. Levels of reported happiness (or separate measures of life satisfaction) have not changed significantly, in the aggregate, over the last two decades. This is not to say that there are some very unhappy people in our midst and the data on rising numbers of people taking their own lives reveal another dimension to trends in well-being. Internationally, some of the countries with the highest re-ported *average* levels of well-being have, also, the highest levels of re-ported suicide. They also happen to have the highest *measured average* levels of social capital in terms of data on trust and civic engagement. There is more going on than appears on the surface.

Table 20.2: Levels of Reported Happiness in 1981, 1990 and 1999 in Ireland (% of adult population reporting that they are "very happy")

Age Group	1981 (N=1,500)	1990 (N=1,481)	1999 (N=982)
18-29	40	48	35
30-39	41	41	51
40-49	51	39	42
50-64	37	43	44
65 +	25	40	38
Total	39	43	42

Source: European Values Survey: Computer File (2003), Release 1, Tilburg University and Zentralarchiv für Empirische Sozialforschung, Cologne (ZA), Germany.

Is there a problem with the trends, level and distribution of well-being in Ireland? I suggest three reasons not to be complacent:

- It is possible, but not certain, that many of the factors that made for above-average happiness here are changing and even eroding. Hence, strength of family ties, marriage, religious belief, as well as institutional and cultural factors that have been helpful, cannot be taken for granted in the future.[3]

- The distribution of happiness is very uneven. People who are in poor health, unemployed and struggling to make ends meet as single par-ents or others on low income are well below the average (space does not permit to show in detail how various factors are related to reported subjective well-being in multivariate model — however, some summary bivariate indicators are shown in Table 20.3, below).

- A society composed of people who report happiness and satisfaction may contain within itself reserves of injustice, unhappiness for some as well as the seeds of future conflict and dysfunction.

Table 20.3: Levels of Self-reported Life Satisfaction in 2002*

	Average SWB Score	Standard Error
Gender	7.74	0.048
Male	7.57	0.072
Female	7.91	0.064
Age category		
18-29yrs	7.55	0.088
30-39yrs	7.82	0.108
40-49yrs	7.71	0.118
50-64yrs	7.75	0.112
65+yrs	8.05	0.112
Marital status		
Married/living with partner	8.02	0.061
Widowed	7.69	0.167
Never married	7.50	0.084
Separated/divorced	6.77	0.230
Residential location		
Dublin/large town (10,000 inhabitants+)	7.72	0.067
All other areas	7.75	0.071
Educational completion		
Below leaving Certificate	7.75	0.073
Leaving Certificate or higher	7.72	0.064
Religiosity		
Frequent Church attendance (monthly at least)	7.84	0.062
Less frequently	7.55	0.079

Owner-occupier		
Owns home	7.78	0.053
Does not own home	7.46	0.130
Employment status		
Paid employment	7.68	0.062
Retired	7.91	0.164
Unemployed	6.43	0.263
Domestic duties	8.11	0.103
Full-time student	7.81	0.141
Income (net weekly)		
First Quartile	7.73	0.174
Second Quartile	7.40	0.150
Third Quartile	7.61	0.120
Fourth Quartile	7.81	0.073

* ("All things considered, how satisfied are you with your life as a whole these days. Where would you place yourself in terms of overall satisfaction on a scale of 0 to 10 where '0' means you are 'very dissatisfied' to '10' which means you are 'very satisfied'?")

Source: Unpublished Thesis (Healy, 2005). Data are based on the National Economic and Social Forum Survey of adults undertaken by the ESRI in August 2002.

We need to pay closer attention to the "causes" of well-being as well as their implications for community practice and public policy. Research, including analysis of data from a survey of adults in Ireland (Healy, 2005), confirms the widely established finding that the extent and quality of inter-personal ties and social support are important explanatory variables of subjective well-being. In line with other international research, the analysis of Irish data confirms no statistical correlation between level of completed education and reported life satisfaction (taking other differences into account). In other words, on the face of it more education like more income does not make you happier if you have some already. Of course, it is worth increasing education and income – especially for those with relatively little. However it is defined, *some* measures of "social capital" (measured as inter-personal trust, social support and number of friends) are strong correlates of well-being. More about social capital later. First, there is a digression.

Staring Out from a Linear and Determined Universe . . .

Thinking in a world dominated by the print and, now especially, the image media we are used to following linear pathways. The following is a cartoon image. We start out with:

1. A well-defined problem – for example, poverty, young male suicide, low literacy levels, social dysfunction of one sort or another. Then . . .

2. We think about ways in which society – a society – could "fix" this problem in part or in whole. However . . .

3. An obvious way to "fix" this problem is to engage a more efficient public service delivery or to facilitate a solution based on market competition or a bit of both. Somewhere along the way, other entities get a mention – communities, families, voluntary groups and associations, etc. So . . .

4. The instruments to achieve a solution need to be carefully chosen. And, we need "evidence", "facts" (statistics!) and "research" of various kinds to tell us "how the problem is spread" and which things are associated with the problem so that we can think up effective strategies, responses, programmes, interventions, partnerships, etc to "fix" the problem or at least ameliorate some of its worst effects and attributes.

5. Living in a democratic society we need some measures of accountability – how well do our efforts and investments pay off? Especially, if we are guardians of some public service we need to be held to account. Hence, enter the world of "indicators", "target-setting", "performance measures", "evaluation of performance", etc. "Business planning" is everywhere and "evidence-based policy" is the new mantra.

6. Armed with "evidence" we can draw up "models of best practice". Like Michelangelo we can chip away at the stone until the "model", "The Model" begins to emerge. Note that we are not talking of

"models of good practice" but "best practice". Hence, every institution is on the way to "world class excellence", "leading edge innovation" and "premier customer service". But . . .

7. Every "model" needs to be tested. Hence, "indicators" – plenty of them – serve to test the performance of the model. Now, indicators do seven things:

    a. They *separate* things out into measurable components (the meaning of "analysis" is to break things down into components);

    b. They *standardise* people, events, relationships;

    c. They create a *unit* of measurement or *comparability*;

    d. They place everything on a *"linear"* scale (or a linear, non-linear scale for the mathematically inclined)[4];

    e. They allow people to identify *deterministic* and causal pathways/associations; and thereby

    f. They help us to *predict* the impacts of this or that intervention; and

    g. They enable other people to monitor, *control*, test.

8. Finally (!), the end goal of all of the above is the "satisfied customer" – whether satisfied through a market-based solution or a public service one or some combination of the two or some combination of the two with the "third sector".

Fixing Problems in a Linear Way and Top-down World . . .

Fixing problems – according to the above description is, ultimately, meant to be about controlling people, things and relationships for the customer. One set of people tend to prefer that public institutions do this on behalf of the people. Others tend to place greater reliance on impersonal markets to do job.

Most of us fall somewhere between these two poles. Lord Kelvin (William Thompson) – scientist and Ulsterman from the nineteenth century – summed it up in the following words ascribed to him:

> If we can't express what we know in the form of numbers, then we really don't know much about it, and if we don't know much about it we can't control it and if we can't control it, we are at the mercy of chance.

Lord Kelvin, if he were around today, might be MD of Kelvin Associates – consultant to governments, universities and enterprises.

Anyway, all of the above is perfectly reasonable, rational, self-evident and logical. It's linear, causal and control-based. I would argue that it is very necessary and unavoidable to some extent and in some ways. But, is it sufficient? As a way of thinking and acting it may not be sufficient to the extent that it does not cater for at least two awkward and essential realities in life:

- Concrete and complex human beings

- Concrete and complex human beings situated in concrete and complex networks of communities.

Mechanical systems from which the metaphor of social science draws are a poor representation of living, organic and messy eco-systems of which human and community development are an integral part. The empirical and "scientific" paradigm is seductive but stumbles over the sufficiency test. Hence, we need new ways of imagining, connecting and evaluating.

The emphasis in government action has, traditionally, been on uniformity of services, universality of access and centralised control over allocation of resources allied to enforced accountability of those in receipt of state support. However, given the complex nature of the environment in which Government policies and actions are developed, a "one-size-fits-all" model of service delivery is out of kilter with the way diverse communities function. The role of the state (whether at local, national or supra-national level) as sole arbitrator of decisions involving diverse communities and individuals is seriously open to question. This also has serious implications in some countries and for some parts of the education world for the development of curriculum, teaching methods and community education.

The prevailing models of public governance supported by empirical evidence all tend to focus on needs, wants and functionings in the market place or society as judged, measured and administered by someone other than the people being served. Efficient public administration or customer-focussed market service delights in the *needy* customer or recipient. It tends to miss out on the empowered citizen and community to *co-produce* solutions that linear pathway systems fail to imagine. My claim is that hierarchical, rigid and compartmental structures of public governance are ill-suited to the necessary task of reforming the public service system and helping it to relate more effectively to a renewed civil society. Centralised and over-controlling models of governance undermine the *motivational* base for actors other than Government. They fail to make effective use of the resources of other actors in decision-making and provision.

However, we are at a loss because it is easier to say what is lacking in the prevailing models of governance and research than to give examples of alternative or more inclusive approaches to understanding human development. The major challenge is to take a (a) whole-systems view in which we can see the connecting parts, and (b) recognise the actual and potential capacity of all human individuals and communities to be self-organisers. Which approaches or examples could be considered?

Helping Others to Define Their Own Capabilities and Solutions

How do we re-design policies to reflect better the realities of complexity, inter-relatedness and localism in which primacy is given to "self-organising networks of relatively autonomous players" (Stewart-Weeks, 2000)? A number of important design principles would be useful to consider:

1. Cultivating mutual help and self help;

2. A movement away from identifying "needs" only to identifying unique community "capabilities";

3. Promoting trust through equality and respect for rights;

4. Letting go of excessive and over-detailed control (empowering and trusting communities to be responsible);

5. Valuing, rewarding and recognising voluntary effort and achieve-
    ment.

In this way the state could move to being supportive and enabling more
than controlling. In any society, distance from power, lack of meaningful
consultation, absence of deliberative mechanisms and a general sense of
not being included in key decisions tend to generate a lack of trust and
engagement. Therefore, *letting go* and *empowering* emerge as critical
areas for urgent policy attention.

Creating a basis for equality and trust among various social groups
entails measures to raise basic income levels *and* to redistribute income
from the well-off to others. There is no free lunch. If we want Berlin-
type social services, free early childhood education, smaller classes in
schools, better quality school buildings, shorter hospital waiting times,
better and more integrated services to the old, the very young and the
sick, more opportunities for the long-term unemployed, persons with
disabilities . . . then someone has to pay. We either let the market do it
mainly or entirely in which case some people simply don't make it to the
finishing line because they don't even get a head start in an unequal
tournament, or we let the state do it mainly or entirely in which case we
can't afford to be around the bottom of the international tax league.
There is, also, a role for civil society – possibly in partnership with the
state and the market. However, there are no easy options or quick-fix
solutions here. Someone has to pay and responsibility needs to be taken
and appropriately shared.

But, achieving greater equality of well-being is about more than just
addressing low income or lack of employment and education opportunities. It also about practicing what I refer to as the four Rs. These are:

•   Recognition

•   Respect

•   Redistribution

•   Representation.

Recognising, naming and valuing difference is a liberating experience. Too often and especially in the past we didn't recognise particular groups or individuals in our communities. If we recognise human need and potential we must also respect it. This seems basic. But how often is real respect lacking in the way we deal with each other? Respect for people should be at the heart of every public policy and community initiative. I have mentioned redistribution. But redistributing things is about more than redistributing income or tangible wealth. It is also about redistributing power – real power – which is invisible, pervasive and intangible at many levels of Irish society and in many sectors of business, legal, church, public administration life. We prefer to avoid the obvious truths that stare us in the face and seek refuge in "customer-service" language when in truth many "customers" are not respected, recognised, empowered or represented. "Power is everywhere", as a sociologist once remarked. Access to power – decision-making – is more than just having the occasional focus group meeting or "consultation". One is weary from consultation. How about effective and effectual representation in the decisions that really matter?

What the National Economic and Social Forum described some years ago as "the unequal distribution in relationships of love, care and solidarity with others" has huge implications for participation by individuals and groups in society. The transparency, accountability and respect that authorities – political, civil, religious – demonstrate in their internal and external relationships has an important impact on trust as well as the capacity of individuals and groups to play a more active and effective role in society.

Some questions arise:

- Are we tapping into the various types of community energy and capability?

- Are we open to the needs of "others" as expressed through their voice and not just our own interpretative systems?

- Are we seeing "needs" only and not "capabilities"?

- Are their "needs" really "our needs" or is it that we are "needy" to control, help, fund, resource and feed others in their "neediness"?

- What does equality really mean to us?

The Place of Social Capital in All of This

After a digression I return to "social capital". So, where does "social capital" fit into all of this? Social capital is about social ties of trust, mutual obligation and engagement. Underlying these are the values – some we share and some we don't – that shape what we aim for and how we should get there. I find it useful to refer to this as "capital", not because "economics" should take over the world or because everything can be given a price (it cannot). "Capital", "power", "capability" and "agency" could be viewed as closely complementary.

Trust, voluntary endeavour, giving and solidarity have a real impact on people's well-being. People have rights – social, economic, cultural as well as fundamental rights to personal liberty, life and happiness. But for every right there is a responsibility. As a society in the twenty-first century we are still struggling like a new rich kid on the international block to figure out: Who is responsible? For what exactly? How? And Why? If we want to achieve a more just, a more equitable and a more caring society then we have to critically re-evaluate our own practice at many levels. The state cannot do it all. But it can do some things and it can do a lot differently to the way it is doing it now.

A series of sustained public conversations on values and the perspectives of various groups is needed. Places like the media, the Oireachtas, Third Level institutions and community fora are meant to be for this. But could we imagine more participatory forms of dialogue in which people genuinely seek to listen – possibly even places where people can be vulnerable to others. This might take a lot of social capital in the form of trust and reciprocity and could be dangerous without some level of prior trust and engagement. So, small steps are one way to begin – led by communities, young people . . .

A huge issue not touched on in this presentation is that of diversity – ethnic, identity, other. As Ireland becomes a more diverse society there is a major challenge to engage seriously with different ways of living, seeing and being community. We have hardly begun to address the issues from the standpoint of what it means for ethos, inclusion and cross-community links in various "public places" – schools, hospitals, public services, residential facilities, etc. Are we the welcoming, inclusive and friendly society that we like to believe that we have been? Were we not once strangers in a foreign place? A social capital perspective could help us to ask questions about the nature, depth and extent of contact, friendship, support, trust and expectation among various groups. In designing places in which to live, work and learn we will need to pay a lot greater attention to issues of "bridging social capital".[5]

It would be all too easy to go from one "deficit model" to another by reinventing "social capital" as a means of identifying that which communities lack and, therefore, need more of (whether from Government or some other source). An intelligent use of "social capital" could be about identifying what communities and individuals already have and which needs to be recognised, valued and "liberated". It is hard to do this if we want to keep things constantly under control and in a state of perpetual monitoring and form-filling.

There is a role and place for various "communities" – families in all their diversity, voluntary and community organisations, new social movements as well as cultural and sports movements that are an important life blood of villages and cities. Ultimately, well-being is everyone's business because your well-being is important to someone else – perhaps in a 100 years time. There is no magic programme for government to create new social capital over night or to replace old social capital that may be fraying. There are important design issues at the heart of most government programmes, policies and practices that impact in ways that we cannot yet fully understand.

Conclusions

Organisations, communities and governments are constantly faced with choices and decisions. Even individuals are: you and me. The nature and extent of impact of these choices and decisions in 10, 20 or 50 years is unsure. But that they have an impact *is* sure. Without a vision the people perish. We have only got ourselves to realise a vision.

References

Healy, T. (2005), "In Each Other's Shadow: What has been the impact of human and social capital on life satisfaction in Ireland?" Unpublished PhD Thesis, UCD.

Helliwell, J. (2004), "Well-being and social capital: Does suicide pose a puzzle?" National Bureau of Economic Research, Working Paper 10896.

Inglehart, R., Basanez, M., Diez-Medrano, J., Halman L., and Luijkx, R. (eds.) (2004), *Human Beliefs and Values: A cross-cultural sourcebook based on the 1999-2002 values surveys*, Siglo XXI Editores, México.

Myers, D. (1993), *The Pursuit of Happiness: Who is happy and why?* London: The Aquarian Press.

OECD (2005), *Society at a Glance.* Paris: Organisation for Economic Co-operation and Development.

Stewart-Weeks, M. (2000), "Trick or treat? Social capital, Leadership and the New Public Policy" in Ian Winters (ed.), *Social Capital and Public Policy in Australia.* Melbourne: Australian Institute of Family Studies.

Notes

---

[1] Senior Statistician at the Department of Education and Science and Research Associate at the Policy Institute, Trinity College Dublin. This paper is written in a personal capacity and any views expressed therein do not necessarily reflect those of others.

[2] All of these terms have slightly different meanings. See Healy (2005) for elaboration.

[3] There is a developing literature on the impact on well-being of inter-personal relationships, religion, trust, health and the overall state of governance in a region or country. See, for example, Helliwell (2004).

[4] This scale can be ordinal as in "bad", "good" "better" and "best".

[5] Ties among groups who are not "alike".

Chapter 21

THE ECONOMIC CHALLENGE
OF SUSTAINABILITY

Richard Douthwaite *and* **Emer O'Siochrú**

The Problem with Sustainable Development

Most people in Ireland think sustainability is highly desirable and sprinkle the adjective "sustainable" about with abandon, but are confused about what the concept really means. Their confusion can be traced back to the term "sustainable development" which was introduced to the public by the Brundtland Report, *Our Common Future*, in 1987. The basic Brundtland definition is clear enough: "Sustainable development is development that meets the needs of the present without compromising the ability of future generations to meet their own needs" but then the Report confuses the reader by attempting to make the principle less absolute:

> Meeting essential needs depends in part on achieving full growth potential, and sustainable development clearly requires economic growth in places where such needs are not being met. Elsewhere it can be consistent with economic growth provided the content of the growth reflects the broad principles of sustainability and non-exploitation of others.[1]

In other words, sustainable development is linked with growth, and since for many people, "development" and "growth" are synonyms, they think that "sustainable development" and "sustainable growth" are the same thing. And, of course, "sustainable growth" is not just a once-off increase in income levels that can reasonably be expected to be maintained indefinitely. It is a growth process that goes on increasing incomes reliably, year after year. In short, sustainability is linked in the public mind with something which is completely unsustainable.

Another flaw with the Brundtland Report is that it entirely ignores the possibility that limits to economic growth might exist and that humanity might have already exceeded them in some respects. Had Brundtland conceded this, the final sentence in the quotation above would have had to be changed radically because even if growth that "reflects the broad principals of sustainability" can be achieved, it ought not to be generated by rich countries while they remain unsustainable in almost every respect. This is because their economic growth necessarily involves the use of natural resources and, if technologies can be found which enable, say, twice as much output to be produced for the same level of resource input that does not mean that the extra output should come on stream. It would be far better for a country to keep its production at the current level and to halve its resource use, as that would move it towards sustainability rather than merely maintaining its unsustainable *status quo*.

The Growth Imperative

Unfortunately, under our current debt-based monetary system, no country has the option of foregoing growth because, without growth, it will fall into serious economic decline. The main reason for this is that if there is no growth in any year, the investments made the previous year have produced no return. Firms find themselves with lower profits and unused capacity, and this discourages them investing further, at least in those sectors in which the increased capacity has not been taken up. Less investment means less new bank loans being taken out and thus less money entering into circulation to replace that being removed as previous years' loans are repaid to the banks which made them. And less money in circulation means that there is less available for consumers to spend.

In normal years in industrialised economies, somewhere between 16 per cent (Sweden) and 31 per cent (Estonia) of GNP is invested in projects that, it is hoped, will enable the economy to grow the following year. A similar proportion of the labour force is employed on these projects. Consequently, if the expected growth fails to materialise and all further investments are cancelled, a fifth or more of a country's workers will find themselves without paid work. These newly unemployed people will be forced to cut their spending sharply, which in turn will cost other workers their jobs. The economy will enter a downward spiral, with each round of job losses leading to more.

The prospect of investment falling and creating widespread unemployment terrifies governments so much that they work very closely with their business sectors to ensure that their economies continue to grow almost regardless of any social or environmental damage the growth process may be causing. In other words, the need for growth to maintain short-term economic sustainability gets in the way of attending to more fundamental types of sustainability such as halting social decline or climate change.

In the present system, the only way to ensure that enough borrowing takes place to maintain the money supply and maintain employment is to ensure that enough growth occurs year after year to ensure that investors keep on investing. Studies have shown that in Britain a minimum of around 3 per cent growth is required to prevent unemployment increasing.

So although overall sustainability requires a long-term view, our particular money creation system is like a pair of spectacles which give short-term economic issues such prominence that they obscure our vision of the future. We concentrate on seeing that employees are paid at the end of the week, that interest is paid at the end of the half-year and that increased profits can be reported at year end. As a result, all too often, we fail to see that the natural environment is preserved, that capital equipment, buildings and infrastructure are kept up, that health is maintained, that knowledge and skills are preserved and passed on and that social structures such as families, friendships and neighbourhoods stay strong. These crucial concerns only get our attention when they begin to affect this year's economic performance.

A society that puts economic sustainability ahead of environmental and social sustainability because of a bug in its money-creation system is putting the cart before the horse. The economy should be merely the tool by which society supports itself, and the money system should be simply part of that tool. To be sustainable, a society has to put fundamental environmental sustainability above all else. The Earth does not accept the trade-offs so beloved of economists and politicians. Social sustainability comes a close second as even with environmental and resource security, no economy can survive for very long in conditions of chaos and strife created by gross inequality or unfair access to those resources. These laws are absolute.

The Economy as an Emergent System

Very few people understand that the workings of the economy are not "natural" in the sense of obeying relatively immutable and consistent laws but are "contingent" on the starting point and other factors. In other words, the rules which determine the results which an economy will deliver depend, amongst other things, on the economy's initial conditions, on the quantity and quality of the energy feeding it and on the medium used in interaction or exchange between the actors in the system. While the initial conditions were set in the past and cannot now be changed, the energy input and quality can. Moreover, the medium we use for interaction – money – is fully within our conscious design.

People thinking in systems-theory terms describe our current economy as an emergent structure arising from a complex reflexive system which oscilates between two basin attractors, one giving relatively slow steady growth and the other contraction and depression. Despite economists' best efforts, it is not possible to predict exactly when the switch from one basin attractor to the other will happen or how long the economy will stay in each basin, although patterns do repeat fairly regularly.

Recent advances in systems theory suggest that small adjustments in the amount or quality of the energy entering the system or changes in the algorithms of exchange or in the "stickiness" of interaction could cause the system cease its oscillations between the two basins and enter a different pattern – perhaps a more stable, sustainable one. Unfortunately, if the money system and the goal of preserving immediate, short-term economic sustainability are treated as sacrosanct, the world will be unable to escape the growth/depression cycle and find a type of economy which is much more sustainable in the very long term.

In Mesopotamia, in the Indus Valley and in the jungles of Mesoamerica, civilisations collapsed because they had undermined their environment. So did the Soviet and Roman empires. However, even though our system has so depleted the environmental resources it requires for long-term sustainability that it stands on the brink of collapse, we have greater scientific knowledge and political sophistication than the failures that went before us. Many governments see the warning signs and are aware of the need for policies to address them.

But governments will not take the radical steps required unless pushed to do so by their electorates. Like the frog in the hot water, it is hard to get sufficient political momentum to make sharp, uncomfortable changes to counter the slow growing, high impact threats we are facing such as climate change, loss of fertile soil, dropping water tables, shrinking biodiversity and human population growth. But, thankfully, another kind of environmental threat to economic, social and environmental sustainability is forcing its way up the list of government priorities, and it is one which there is potentially considerable public will to tackle. It is the imminent peak in oil and gas production.

Peak Oil and Energy Scarcity

Oilmen have been saying with increasing frequency recently that world oil production is about to reach a peak and then decline. Initially, it was retired petro-geologists – people like Ireland's Dr. Colin Campbell – who attempted to point this out, but top oil company executives are now saying so too and one company, Chevron, has spent a lot of money advertising the fact in magazines like *The Economist*, *Time* and *Newsweek*.

The problem Chevron has been highlighting is that enough new oil production has to come on-line each year to cover both the growth in world demand of at least two million barrels a day and the decline in production from existing fields of over four million barrels a day. "That's like a whole new Saudi Arabia [coming into production] every couple of years," Sadad al-Husseini, the retired head of exploration and production at the Saudi national oil company, Aramco, said in August 2005. "It's not sustainable." Figure 21.1 illustrates the problem.

*Figure 21.1: Supplying Oil and Gas Demand Will Require Major
Investment (millions of barrels per day of oil equivalent (MBDOE)*

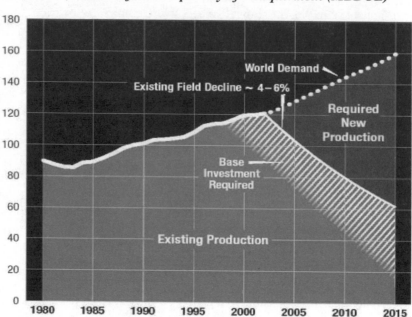

Source: Exxon-Mobil, 2004.

Unfortunately, the world's politicians have been let off the "we need-to-act-with-urgency" hook by economists, particularly those at the International Energy Agency, a branch of the OECD, whose duty is to advise governments on their energy policies. In common with most economists, those at the IEA regard oil as just another commodity and believe that its supply will increase if its price rises because the higher price means that more resources can be profitably devoted to its production. If sufficient investments (around $3 trillion) are made, the IEA says, world oil production will increase for at least another 25 years. Professor Kenneth Rogoff of Harvard and a former chief economist at the IMF concurs. "We might be running low on $20 oil, but for $60 we have adequate oil supplies for decades to come" he says. *The Economist,* which has consistently taken the IEA's line, wrote in April 2006:

> It is true that the big firms are struggling to replace reserves. But that
> does not mean the world is running out of oil, just that they do not

have access to the vast deposits of cheap and easy oil left in Russia
and members of OPEC.

In fact, no one is saying that the world is running out of oil. What the
oilmen worry about is whether supplies will be able to keep up with rising global demand. There is still plenty of oil in the ground but, despite
what the economists say, oil is not a commodity like any other. It is a
source of energy and, if it takes more energy to extract and refine it than
the oil itself delivers, that process will never be profitable, no matter how
high the price rises. As increasingly difficult oil sources have to be
tapped, the net energy gain, the energy return on energy invested
(EROEI) ratio, declines. At some point, throwing more resources – that
is to say, energy – into the effort to produce becomes pointless. When
that happens, world oil output will cease to increase, stay on a plateau for
a few years and then fall.

Note that both the oilmen and the economists are essentially saying
the same thing – that oil will be scarce in future. The IEA economists
believe that it will be possible to increase oil output at 1.6 per cent a year
for the next 25 years, which is much less than the rate at which global
demand is likely to grow if the world economy continues to expand at
the rate it did between 1993 and 2003, 3.6 per cent per annum. The oilmen, however, say that production is likely to start falling at between 4
per cent and 6 per cent a year some time within the next five or ten years.
If the economists are right, global growth will be severely checked. If the
oilmen are, then the global economy will contract.

As Figure 21.2 shows, there has been a very close correlation between the world's total output and its use of fossil energy, as measured
in terms of its carbon dioxide emissions. If less fossil energy is available,
it is going to be very difficult if not impossible for the world economy to
continue to grow each year.

Figure 21.2: World Annual % GDP:CO2, 1960–90

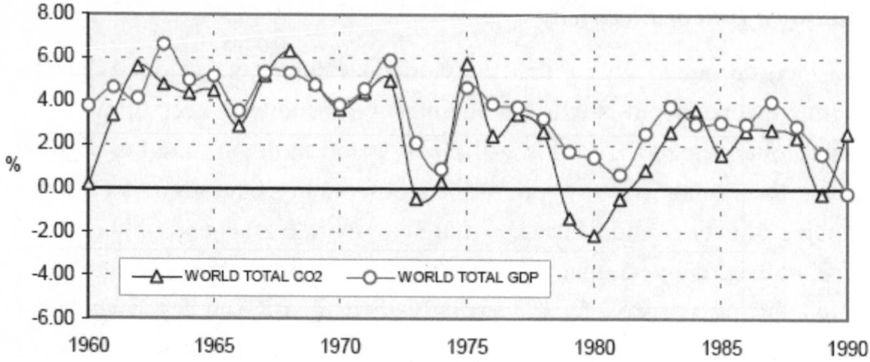

Source: Global Commons Institute, 1995.

Figure 21.2 shows the close link between global fossil fuel use, as represented by CO^2 emissions, and the rise in global incomes. The close link means that we can be sure that growth under business as usual will be slow or negative and the world economy is in severe danger of tripping into the depression attractor basin characteristic of our current structure.

Energy Price Inflation

One of the factors which makes the descent into depression highly likely is that the world's central banks don't understand that, as oil is getting scarcer, a fundamental shift is needed in the world economy to reflect this. When oil prices rise, the cost of all other forms of energy will rise too because, at least to some extent, one form of energy can be substituted for another. As a result, the prices of everything we buy will need to increase, but by differing amounts because of the differing amounts of energy required to make and deliver all the different goods and services we use. In other words, a new set of price relationships needs to be established to reflect the new cost structure. Inflation is the only relatively painless way that every price in the global economy can change by a different amount to reflect the new energy price level.

Figure 21.3 illustrates the number of seconds someone in an OECD country had to work to earn the price of a unit of electricity had fallen to less than a tenth of its 1920 level by the 1970s. We must now expect the time required to rise again.

Figure 21.3: Number of Seconds of Work Required to Earn the Money
to Buy a Unit of Electricity

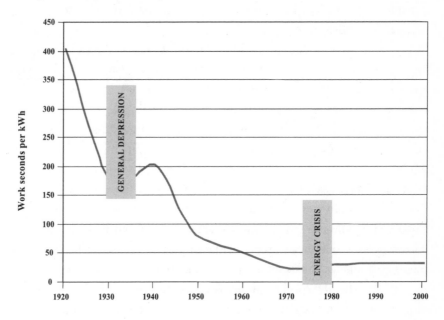

Source: Folke Gunther, 2002.

For the better off, the change will merely mean that they have less money to spend on luxuries. Holidays, dining out, prestige cars, savings and housing will be cut as they attempt to adjust to the new realities. But most people who are well-off now will still be able to live well.

It is the indirect effects of inflation that threaten them – and everyone else. The money system is not just a numeraire that keeps score in the economic system – it actively shapes the economy itself and gets shaped itself in turn. Inflation devalues money as a medium of exchange and as store of wealth and thus threatens the confidence with which it is held. Since money was decoupled from gold, a process that started at Bretton Woods after World War II and was finished by President Nixon in the early 1970s, it is has become virtual, backed only by public confidence. Almost certainly, the US Federal Bank and the European Central Bank Reserve will think it their duty to try to maintain this confidence by ensuring that the money people earn in wages and salaries will buy them almost as much as it did before oil prices began to rise.

To do this, they will continue increasing interest rates to damp down inflation. This is a dangerous strategy because raising the cost of borrowing money is itself inflationary since it raises the cost of running businesses. Only the exceptional firm manages without borrowed funds. Every business will react to the higher interest rates in the same way and attempt to put up its prices in an effort to preserve its profitability. This will cause more inflation, and the central banks will react with further interest rate rises. The cycle of price rises leading to interest rate increases leading to price rises could continue until most new projects became unviable and were scrapped because of the interest costs. This would cause demand to collapse and workers to be laid off. In the new climate, businesses reacting to the higher borrowing costs would find they could no longer pass them on to their customers. The resulting slowdown would cut property and share values far more effectively than allowing an inflation to proceed. It would also cause massive unemployment, thus cutting or eliminating the incomes of many people.

So while the decrease in oil production after the production peak will almost certainly cause the world economy to contract, that need not itself cause a recession. True, the purchasing power of people's incomes will decline, but the higher energy prices will create a lot of investment opportunities and there could be plenty of work about. Some sectors of the economy will do badly, others will rapidly expand. It will be the rise in interest rates to protect the money system that will cause any depression that comes along. An attempt to block inflation would be worse, far worse, than the disease. The US Federal Reserve and ECB should therefore adopt new inflation targets and allow relative prices to adjust so long as the inflation rate does not go too much above 8 per cent. This is the rate at which inflation begins to impose costs on the economy because firms find that they have to waste resources on continually adjusting their prices.

Despite the strong correlation between abundant energy use and economic growth, high energy prices can be a benign factor in the economy. We need to distinguish between a restriction in supply of energy which will certainly impede economic growth and higher energy prices which may not. Higher energy prices tend to shift spending away from consumption to the production of goods for export (in order to pay the higher cost of energy imports) and to capital investment in energy-saving and energy-producing technologies. Moreover, the inflation the higher energy prices generate helps the world economy by lowering the effective interest rate and thus makes investments in the new technologies even more attractive.

Land Value Tax

Of course, a lower effective interest rate will also make it more attractive to invest in property and shares. A buoyant stock market is a good thing as it would make it easier to finance the new energy companies. But a further increase in the price of property would be disastrous for first-time house buyers, most of whom already have to struggle to make their repayments. Anything disastrous for first-time buyers is eventually disastrous for the market as a whole, since it means that no one is getting on to the bottom of the ladder to allow the rest of us to move up, sideways or down as our circumstances change The resulting property crash would be from an even greater price level than at present and would bring the entire economy down with it.

Central banks seem truly to be caught in a quandary.

The solution to this problem is not within the remit of the central banks but the government – a carefully designed tax. This tax must not discourage investment in energy-saving improvements to buildings, services and settlements but simply make property less attractive as an investment. Such a tax is an annual land value tax (LVT) – the least worst tax according to economist Milton Friedman.[2] This tax would be set at a percentage of the value of the land element only of property and should be adjusted annually to remove any increase in the market value of the property not due to improvements by the owner.[3]

Its imposition would cause the value of property to fall to reflect the capitalised cost of the annual tax payment. But the construction industry would not collapse because the owners of land zoned for development would have to develop it or sell it on to a developer to avoid paying the tax year after year and seeing nor return. As a result, the price of development land will fall and builders will soon have no trouble acquiring land at prices that allow them a respectable profit on the sale of houses at the lower price. The number of new houses built might slow but the level of construction activity would be augmented by an increase in (untaxed) building improvements, i.e. the refurbishment and retrofitting of buildings to save energy that the high energy prices will spur.

Families who bought their houses at the height of the boom would not be burdened by the site tax at a time when they had lost purchasing power due to the higher energy prices and were facing high mortgage costs. This is because the LVT would be offset against their income tax until the property was sold or otherwise transferred.

Over time, the inflation would decrease the mortgage burden because, although people's incomes would lose purchasing power, they would nevertheless rise in money terms relative to the original loan. This way the construction sector could be kept working at near capacity until its efforts were switched to building the infrastructure required by a country that expects to have to manage without using any fossil energy at some time within the next 50 years.

Poverty and Famine

Just as the central bankers will be unable to preserve the purchasing power of money as energy prices rise, without causing an economic disaster, workers will be unable to preserve the purchasing power of their salaries and wages. Everything they buy will cost them more in terms of the number of minutes of work they have to do to earn the money to get it. As a result the world's poor will be very badly hit, especially the landless among them, as food will become increasingly scarce and expensive because of the large amount of energy required to produce it by industrialised methods. Moreover, huge areas of land are likely to be taken out of food production to produce energy crops.

Already the world's stocks of cereals are at the lowest level they have been since the early 1970s in terms of days of supply and they are being eroded further by the massive use of maize and wheat in the US for the production of bio-ethanol to add to petrol for cars. "Within four years, ethanol will be the nation's second-largest market for corn, running just behind feeding it to livestock", a spokesman for the National Corn Growers' Association told the *Wall Street Journal* in December 2005. The newspaper also reported that 30,000 stoves and boilers specifically made to burn maize had been sold in 2005, twice the number sold the previous year.

As Figure 21.4 shows, the world's grain stocks per person are lower than they have been at any time in the past thirty years. They are down to 69 days' supply. Despite this, increasing quantities are being used for fuel.

Figure 21.4: World Total Grain "Days of Supply"

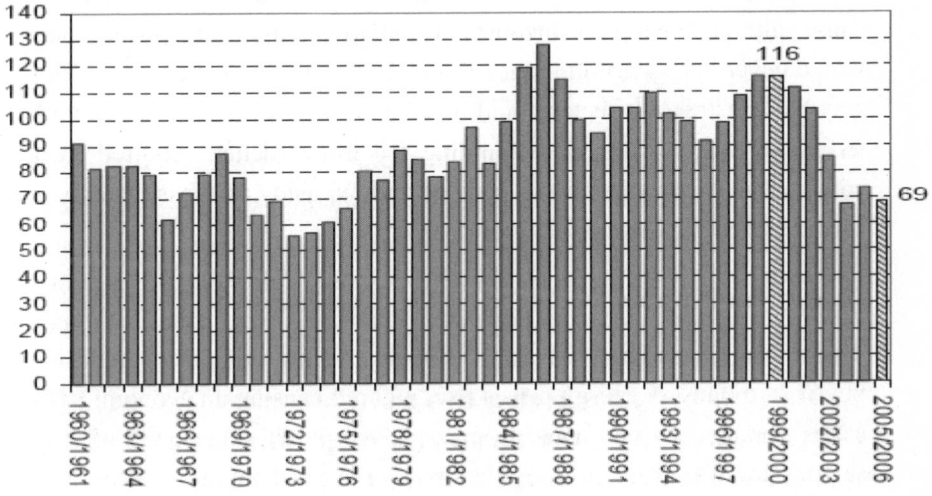

Source: National Farmers' Union of Canada, May, 2006

The situation has therefore already arisen in which the rich are running their cars and heating their homes using fuels that could otherwise have gone to feed the poor. The situation will get worse as market prices deny the poor the energy they need to make themselves more productive in their local economies. This poses serious problems for Irish and EU policies. The separation of energy and anti-poverty policies could be tolerated when energy costs were low but not when they are high and rising. A new paradigm for anti-poverty policies and structures requires new policy connections at the European level around energy, social cohesion and human rights.

The market economy we currently "enjoy" was once defined by the Australian writer Ted Trainer as "an ingenious device for ensuring that when things become scarce only the rich can get them". This will prove true about fossil energy as it becomes scarce unless we take action. The rich will have plenty of energy and use it, one way or another, to maintain their wealth and political power. But their enjoyment of it will be short-lived as when a society collapses in the way the civilisations did that we listed before, the rich do not avoid the fate of their poorer neighbours – they simply take longer to die. The poor in the South and amongst us in the North will not go quietly into the night; globalised communication has closed that option forever. Even the wealthiest, most carefully-guarded elite will have to accept that social justice is fundamental to their own survival in the short and in the long term.

Citizen Carbon Quota

In wartime, even governments with impeccable right-wing credentials do not leave the distribution of scarce, vital commodities to the free market. Instead, they introduce rationing.[4] If the poor are to be protected, a worldwide system of energy rationing is needed now, before attitudes harden as the scarcity grows more acute. Fortunately, a suitable rationing system is ready to hand, although it does need a little adapting.

The EU's Emissions Trading System is the cornerstone of the EU's effort to meet its Kyoto target. Its emission permits are as good a proxy for fossil fuel as you can invent. At present, these valuable rights to emit carbon dioxide into the atmosphere are being handed out free to some of the biggest users of fossil fuels in Europe.[5] If the recipient firms reduce their fossil fuel use and thus their emissions, they can sell their surplus permits on a new carbon market. Most companies in unregulated and captive markets such as that for electricity are charging the public for the permits they use in their production processes despite the fact that they get them free. This means that consumers are not only faced with higher energy costs because of the global scarcity, but that they are also paying for climate change measures which are failing to accomplish their goals. The EU's Lisbon strategy will expose more citizens to this form of legalised gouging as energy markets are steadily deregulated under it. The public, and most of their elected representatives, are totally ignorant about what is going on.

Given a little creativity and the courage to stand up to big business, the ETS could be redesigned to deliver on its climate targets and to protect the poor. It could thus ensure the social stability required to make the jump into a renewable energy future. Before anything can be traded, its ownership has to be established. Permits to emit greenhouse gases convey the right to use a natural resource, the earth's atmosphere, as a dump for a limited period and, if the permits were sold, they would produce an income for the rights-owner. The key question is therefore: who is the rights-owner? Is it the dump's current users, the state, or everyone on the planet? If each person's equal right to the use of the atmosphere was to be recognised, a new source of income would be created for every one, as energy companies would have to buy the permits from the rights-holders, the general population.

Predistribution versus Redistribution

Public policy on poverty in Ireland and Europe generally is still largely re-distributive, dispensing welfare benefits from tax revenues. New policy instruments like carbon trading open up new policy options. The current EU Emissions Trading System acts as a regressive tax with the revenue going to benefit businesses rather than the state or the people. However, carbon trading could be set up in such a way as to pre-distribute the limited rights to emit carbon/greenhouse gases to everyone, and then require businesses to buy those rights from the recipients. This would generate a citizens' income and compensate poor people for rising energy/carbon prices.

What if every adult EU resident got an equal share of whatever amount of emissions the EU as a whole was its target under the Kyoto Treaty? This "carbon quota" could be sold at a bank or post office at the current market rate, exactly as if the permits were a foreign currency. The banks and post offices would then sell the permits on to companies importing fossil fuels into the EU and those producing them here. Importers would be required to hand over to Customs enough permits to cover the eventual emissions from the fuel in a shipment whenever one came in. Oil, gas and coal producers in the EU would be monitored by inspectors who would collect permits for the emissions that their output would produce when burned. All very simple and cheap to administer compared to the current ETS system.

Obviously, the costs of our food, fuel and everything we buy would go up under this system but, if we lived in an energy frugal way and used less energy than the average in the EU, the amount we would receive when we sold our permits would be greater than the increased energy cost. Essentially, this could be the beginning of an EU citizen's income to protect the poor.

A Grown-Up Economy

It is imperative that we use our remaining fossil fuels as capital rather than income, investing it in projects which rapidly increase our renewable energy capacity until we reach a level that is self sustaining. This process cannot be achieved in a deep global depression as, quite apart from anything else, that would reduce the price of fossil energy to levels that made the switch to renewables uneconomic again.

At the same time as investing in energy generating capacity, we have to gradually redesign our settllements, retrofit our buildings, transform our agriculture and contain our population in order to substantially reduce total energy demand.[6] These objectives cannot be achieved in conditions of resource wars, famine and insecurity.

This chapter has outlined three economic tools to help society make the adjustment to a renewable energy future – energy price inflation, a site value tax and a citizen's carbon quota. Other tools are required, too, including the replacement of the debt-based money system with one in which provides a stable money stock. This would be achieved[7] by having a money which, rather than being lent into circulation by the banks, would be spent into circulation by the state and would remain in circulation until it was taxed out again. If such a money system was in place, the state would have no problem in picking up the slack if the economy was sliding into a recession by, for example, making grants to people wishing to get their houses up to a high energy standard – and thus, incidentally, keeping employment high in the building trade.

The adoption of just these four tools would set in train many of the necessary changes required for a more sustainable "grown up" economy. We offer them to policymakers in the hope that they will use them to avoid a major economic collapse because we want our collective journey to sustainability to start from where we stand now, rather from a situation in which most people would feel desperate and helpless.

Peak oil leaves us with no option but to move to a more sustainable, renewable, energy-fuelled economy. Getting there requires taking a running jump over a yawning chasm. There are no stepping stones. The world on the other side will be very different. It has to be. Radical changes, such as the four we have suggested, are therefore required. In the present circumstances, timid incrementalism, the making of small improvements to a failing system rather than revamping it entirely, just will not work.

Notes

[1] G.H. Brundtland (1987), *Our Common Future,* Oxford: Oxford University Press, 1987.

[2] "In my opinion, the least bad tax is the property tax on the unimproved value of land, the Henry George argument of many, many years ago." Friedmand, Milton, (November 18, 1978) *Human Events*, p. 14; see also the *Fortune Encyclopedia of Economics*, New York: Warner Books, 1993.

[3] For a more complete description of Land Value Tax in the Irish context see O'Siochrú, Emer (2004), "Land Value Tax: Unfinished Business", Healy, S. and Reynolds, B. (eds.) *A Fairer Tax system for a Fairer Ireland,* CORI Justice, pp.23-57.

[4] The case for using greenhouse emissions as the basis of a world system of energy rationing is made in *Energy Rationing and the Oil Price Crisis* (Feasta, Dublin, November 2005) Downloadable from http://www.feasta.org/energy.htm

[5] An analysis of the flaws in the EU Emissions Trading System and proposals for its reform along the lines suggested here can be found in *The Great Emissions Rights Give-Away* (Feasta, Dublin, March 2006). Downloadable from http://www.feasta.org/energy.htm.

[6] For a more complete description of challenge and remedies re fossil fuel scarcity see Douthwaite, R. (ed.) (2003) *Before the Wells Run Dry: Ireland's Transition to Renewable Energy*, Dublin, Feasta in association with Green Books and Lilliput Press.

[7] Proposals for a complete reform of the world's money systems can be found in Douthwaite, Richard, *The Ecology of Money*, Green Books, Totnes, Devon, 2006 (Revised edition). Downloadable from http://www.feasta.org

Chapter 22

THE ECONOMICS OF ALTRUISM
IN A TIME OF AFFLUENCE

John A. Healy *and* **Charles M.A. Clark**

Economics is often portrayed not only as a dismal science but also one which is based on selfish behaviour. It is interesting to look at what some of the leading thinkers in economics have said about whether people are intrinsically selfish or whether they are capable of promoting social objectives for the benefit of other people. This chapter sets out, against the background of Irish economic growth and a perceived move towards a more individualistic society, views by economists on altruism and the value of promoting a vision for a better society. In particular it seeks to address the following questions:

1. Does economics assume that we are all selfish?

2. Do governments have a role in delivering the altruistic preferences of individuals?

3. What are the choices that wealthy individuals face in promoting a better society?

After a period of rapid and unprecedented economic growth it is common to hear debate as to whether distributing resources and setting social goals to achieve outcomes from this growth will in turn kill the golden goose. Economics has tended to focus far more on production and consumption rather than distribution of resources, but it is interesting to review what thinkers like Adam Smith and Alfred Marshall the capacity of

both individuals and society to achieve objectives outside of the limited
scope of their own self interest. Finally, we highlight some areas where,
with leadership and the articulation of an attractive vision, progress
could be made towards achieving social goals which would also improve
the performance of the Irish economy.

Does Economic Theory Assume We Are Selfish?

The role of rational choice and the conception of people as self-interested
actors has been a central concern for economists for well over 200 years.
Most of the great economists have contributed to the debate on the role of
self-interested and altruistic preferences in determining behaviours. Recently economists have sought inspiration from biology, neuroscience and
psychology to help understand the choices that people make.

The conception of rationality used in economics and it association
with self-interest has long been a source of interest. Mandeville's (1714)
scandalous *Fable of the Bees: Private Vices, Public Virtues* shocked society by suggesting that self-interest would result in the optimum situation for society. This publication is sometimes viewed by historians,
most notably von Hayek, as an influence on Adam Smith's thinking on
libertarian thought and the role of self-interest. The intent and content of
the two analyses, however, are very different. Mandeville held that the
vice of luxury, no matter how deplorable, results in public benefits by
maintaining the prosperity of the economy. It is often argued that he was
engaged in mischief-making rather than serious social commentary
(Spiegel, 1991). Smith, on the other hand, saw the connection between
rational action and selfish behaviour as more complex. In the *Theory of
Moral Sentiments* he outlined the socialisation and the empathy needed
for social interactions to be fruitful and harmonious. Smith started the
Theory of Moral Sentiments by stating:

> How selfish soever man may be supposed, there are evidently some
> principles in his nature, which interest him in the fortune of others,
> and render their happiness necessary to him, though he derives noth-
> ing from it except the pleasure of seeing it. Of this kind is pity or
> compassion, the emotion which we feel for the misery of others,
> when we either see it, or are made to conceive it in a very lively
> manner. That we often derive sorrow from the sorrow of others, is a

matter of fact too obvious to require any instances to prove it; for this sentiment, like all the other original passions of human nature, is by no means confined to the virtuous and humane, though they perhaps may feel it with the most exquisite sensibility. The greatest ruffian, the most hardened violator of the laws of society, is not altogether without it (Smith, 1976, p. 7).

In *The Wealth of Nations,* however, he saw self-interest as the primary organising principle in the economy. For Adam Smith the role of self-interest was fundamental to the development of his method. He was extremely impressed by Newton's use of the principle of gravity to provide a unifying theory in astronomy. In particular, he agreed with the need to locate axioms, which are familiar to all mankind, deduce a theory of how phenomena operate and then test the theory by prediction. In his *Lectures on Rhetoric* (1762-3) he wrote of his pleasure at seeing

the phaenomena which we reckoned the most unaccountable all deduced from some principle (commonly a well-known one) all united in one chain, far superior to what we feel from the unconnected method where everything is accounted for by itself, without any reference to the others.

The apparent conflicting interpretations of self-interest in *The Wealth of Nations* and *The Theory of Moral Sentiments* are sometimes referred to as the "Adam Smith problem". The apparent conflict arises from the different levels of analysis of the two books. In *The Theory of Moral Sentiments* Smith is laying out the process by which individuals are socialised into a social system in which self-control is strong. It is this socialised individual that Smith introduces in *The Wealth of Nations*, a person who has considerable economic freedom because he also has considerable self-control. Smith is quite clear that there is a power which causes us to restrain ourselves and not always slavishly follow our self-interest:

It is a stronger power, a more forcible motive, which exerts itself upon such occasions. It is reason, principle, conscience, the inhabitant of the breast, the man within, the great judge and arbiter of our conduct. *It is he who, whenever we are about to act so as to affect the happiness of others, calls to us, with a voice capable of astonishing the most presumptuous of our passions, that we are but one of the multitude, in no respect better than any other in it; and that when*

we prefer ourselves so shamefully and so blindly to others, we be-
come the proper objects of resentment, abhorrence, and execration.
It is from him only that we learn the real littleness of ourselves, and
of whatever relates to ourselves, and the natural misrepresentations
of self-love can be corrected only by the eye of this impartial specta-
tor. It is he who shows us the propriety of generosity and the deformity of injustice; the propriety of resigning the greatest interests of our
own, for the yet greater interests of others, and the deformity of doing the smallest injury to another, in order to obtain the greatest
benefit to ourselves. (1976, p. 137, italics added).

Thus Smith's view of self-interest was not one of unfettered selfishness.
The rules which govern the marketplace and the social norms which pre-
vail in any given society will also strongly influence choices made in the
different spheres of life. Smith's contention that:

It is not for the benevolence of the butcher, the brewer or the baker,
that we expect our dinner, but for their regard to their own self-love
and never talk to them of our own necessities but of their own advantages (1937, p. 14).

is located firmly in the sphere of the impersonal market place. Similarly
he makes specific reference to industry when he states that:

He generally, indeed, neither intends to promote the public interest,
nor knows how much he is promoting it. By preferring the support of
domestic to that of foreign industry, he intend only his own security;
and by directing that industry in such a manner as its produce may be
of the greatest value, he intends only his own gain, and he is in this,
as in many other cases, led by an invisible hand to promote an end
which is no part of his intention (Ibid., p. 423).

Smith believed that self-interest, in the commercial realm and subject to
certain institutional limitations, played a key role in organising society in
an advantageous manner. There are institutional rules and norms which
govern competition and individual self-interest is not seen as boundless.
In the *Theory of Moral Sentiments* Smith makes more explicit the wider
social framework within which self-interested competition sits. His use
of an analogy of a race is particularly illuminating, where he sees the
individual runners as jostling aggressively for place but they do not cheat
and the rules and endpoint of the race determine the level of competition

that can take place. In this way we see that "the Adam Smith problem" is in fact a consistent account of the complex institutional framework and the certain spheres within which self-interest dominates.

The rise of utilitarian thought led to a simplification of the conception of self-interest. Jeremy Bentham (1982, p. 11) claimed that:

> Nature has placed mankind under the governance of two sovereign masters, pain and pleasure. It is for them alone to point out what we ought to do.

He thought that all pleasure was comparable and wrote that "Quantum of pleasure being equal, pushpin is as good as poetry". John Stuart Mill, the most famous of the utilitarians, disagreed and believed that some kinds of pleasure are more desirable than others. Similarly, Edgeworth (1881) believed that there were different capacities for enjoyment. Modern utility theory has, however, on the whole followed Bentham rather than Mill in not querying whether action has been inspired by higher order motives. Whilst Jevons did claim that there was a "higher moral calculus of right and wrong", he often quoted Bentham and developed his theory of marginal utility based on a conception of subjective self-interest.

Edgeworth (1881, p. 16) interestingly, writing approximately a century before Becker (1974) and Andreoni (1989) developed their models of altruism, wrote that

> Between the two extremes of Pure Egoistic and Pure Universalistic there may be an indefinite number of impure methods; wherein the happiness of others as compared by the agent (in a calm moment) with his own, neither counts for nothing, nor yet "counts as one", but counts for a fraction.

He had little doubt that there were motivations beyond narrow egotism which motivated individual and that analysis of these actions where within the proper subject area of economics and that analysis of altruistic behaviour could be formalised.

> We might suppose that the object which X (whose own utility is P) tends – in a calm, effective moment – to maximise, is not P, but $P + \lambda\pi$; where λ is a coefficient of effective sympathy (Edgeworth, 1881, p. 53).

Marshall believed that the study of altruism was not only within the remit of economics but that where possible it was the duty of the economist to try and understand this type of behaviour. He believed that it was very desirable for economists to apply rigorous scientific inquiry to philanthropic acts.

> No doubt men, even now are capable of much more unselfish service than they generally render: and the supreme aim of the economist is to discover how this latent social asset can be developed most quickly, and turned to account wisely (Marshall, 1920, p. 9).

He believed that it was deliberateness not selfishness which was the characteristic of the modern age and he makes reference to a growing "deliberate unselfishness" (Marshall, 1920, p. 6). He cautioned, however, that the economist's ability to study altruism empirically was limited due to the irregular nature of the actions and not because they are motivated by altruism.

> It is not the want of will but the want of power, that prevents economists from reckoning in the action of motives such as these; and they welcome the fact that some kinds of philanthropic action can be described in statistical returns, and can to a certain extent be reduced to law, if sufficiently broad averages are taken. For indeed there is scarcely any motive so fitful and irregular, but that some law cannot with regard to it can be detected with wide and patient observation. It would perhaps be possible even now to predict with tolerable closeness the subscriptions that a population of a hundred thousand Englishmen of average wealth will give to support hospitals and chapels and missions; and, in so far as this can be done, there is a basis for an economic discussion of supply and demand with reference to the services of hospital nurses, missionaries and other religious ministers (Marshall, 1920, p. 24).

Keynes (1936) held that a degree of self-interest in society was necessary and productive. He believed, however, that self-interest was to a certain degree a socialised behaviour. He believed that institutions were necessary to limit the extent to which individuals pursue and are rewarded for self-interested behaviour and that society ideally should be educated to reward less selfish forces.

> There are valuable human activities which require the motive of money-making and the environment of private wealth-ownership for their full fruition. . . . The task of transmuting human nature should not be confused with the task of managing it. Though in the ideal commonwealth men may have been taught or inspired or bred to take no interest in the stakes, it may still be wise and prudent statesmanship to allow the game to be played, subject to certain rules and limitations, so long as the average man, or even a significant section of the community is in fact strongly addicted to the money-making passion (Keynes, 1936, p. 374).

Becker (1976) compares the approaches of sociobiology and economics to explain the existence of altruism. He states that the existence of altruism has been the central theoretical problem of sociobiology and the central role of self-interest in economics has been reconciled with the persistence of altruism by ad hoc theorising. Sociobiologists usually explain the persistence of altruism using genetic fitness and group selection theories. Becker uses his economic theory of interaction to explain why altruism would persist.

Samuelson's revealed preference work is sometimes interpreted as divesting microeconomics of any need to discuss motivating factors. He himself however took a very different view and is scathing of economists who dismiss altruism as only self-interest in disguise:

> Mesmerized by Homo Economicus, who acts solely on egoism, economists shy away from altruism almost comically. Caught in a shameful act of heroism, they aver: "Shucks, it was only enlightened self-interest." Sometimes it is. At other times it may only be rationalization (spurious for card-carrying atheists): "If I rescue somebody's son, someone will rescue mine.
>
> I will not waste ink on face facing tautologies. When the governess of infants caught in a burning building reenters it unobserved in a hopeless mission of rescue casuists may argue: "She did it only to get the feeling of doing good. Because otherwise she wouldn't have done it." Such argumentation (in Wolfgang Pauli's scathing phrase) is not even wrong. It is just boring, irrelevant, and in the technical sense of old-fashioned logical positivism "meaningless". You do not understand the logic and the history of consumer demand theory – Pareto, W.E. Johnson, Slutsky, Allen-Hicks, Hotelling, Samuelson, Houthakker, . . . – if you think that is its content (Samuleson, 1993, p. 143).

We can see from the above limited review that many of the leading thinkers in the field of economics, from very differing schools of thought, have debated the role and scope of self-interest in determining behaviour. The content of the debate shows that not only is altruism an area which is considered an interesting area for economists to study, it is also recognised that this debate has profound impacts on the discussions on the appropriate role of government in delivering social or altruistic objectives.

Should Policy-makers Try to Deliver on Individuals' Altruistic Preferences?

Margaret Thatcher once famously quoted that there is no such thing as society:

> . . . there are individual men and women and there are families. No Government can do anything except through people, and people must look after themselves first.

If we accept methodological individualism as the appropriate model for analysing economic and political choices, it limits the role that governments and other institutions can play in terms of exercising leadership. Thatcher's view of society stems from the mechanistic view best exemplified by the Austrian school of economics. As Carl Menger noted:

> The phenomena of the national economy must, in theory, be reduced, in the last analysis, to individual efforts, that is to say, to its simplest constitutive elements, and explained in this way (quoted in Stark, 1963, p. 177).

Following the logic of methodological individuals and reducing all action to the level of individuals frequently meant ignoring the role of society and culture on individual behaviour, and promoting only self-interested actions as the only rational action (with altruism being irrational or non-rational). If society plays no active role in shaping human behaviour and outcomes, it is but a small step to the economic policies of Thatcher were the needs of the individual are placed above the common good (a phrase such a perspective could not comprehend). If the government only reacts to individual choice it limits capacity for government to make the case on behalf of certain social objectives. The obvious question is whether this is a desirable thing or not?

With altruistic preferences it is open to individuals to help those less fortunate if they so wish by transferring some of their income to those people they wish to help. If this is the case, what is the role for government? Economists have shown through using simple scenarios referred to as game theory that co-operation does not have a natural tendency to occur and that this can lead to individuals not working together to achieve social objectives. A simple example of two prisoners, both of whom will receive a much reduced sentence if they implicate the other whilst at the same time would be released due to lack of evidence if they remained silent, is often used to show that co-operation does not "naturally" occur even when it is in the self-interest of both parties. This lack of co-operation can be due to lack of information and lack of ways to enforce contracts. This is particularly the case when one is dealing with altruistic preferences as it can be very difficult to know what will truly make someone else better off and the way is open for potential donors to "free-ride" and leave it up to others.

Despite the potential for the government to intervene to remedy failures of the market to deliver social objectives, some conservative economists have emphasised the potential loss of liberty to individuals. When John Fitzgerald Kennedy called on Americans to ask not what the country can do for you, but instead ask what you can do for your country, Milton Friedman reacted quite negatively:

> Neither half of the statement expresses a relation between the citizen and his government that is worthy of the ideals of free men in a free society. . . . To the free man, the country is the collection of individuals who compose it, not something over and above them (Friedman, 1962, p. 1).

The basic proposition that someone could or would act in any way contrary to their self-interest is impossible to fit into Friedman's view of how the world works.

Less doctrinaire thinkers would accept that the government is in a better position through taxation to "enforce contracts" and through the democratic process is aware of public preferences and therefore less prone to confusion about what people actually want. In Irish society to-day there are a range of issues where government intervention could be justified not only to deliver on social objectives which polls show are popular but also to benefit the Irish economy. Below two illustrative areas are set out where it is proposed that government could develop comprehensive solutions that would not only deliver on altruistic/other related preferences which have been recorded through opinion polls, but also would help improve that performance of the Irish economy in a very real way.

Immigration

Ireland would seem to be at a crossroads in terms of the tenor of the debate around immigration. Ireland has become a country of net immigration over the last number of years with significant increases in the number of economic migrants, asylum seekers and foreign students entering the country. The initial lack of preparedness of the government for this rapid increase in immigration created an impression of a situation out of control. In the period 1995-2000 a quarter of a million people immigrated to Ireland. A period of rapid legislative reform ensued from 1996 when the *Refugee Act* was introduced. Prior to that there was a dependency on the *Aliens Act 1935*. There is evidence from both opinion polls and international studies of values that the Irish population has responded initially quite maturely to this transformation. That said, there are signs that misinformation and negative prejudice could skew the debate. Despite the fact that a 2005 survey by Lansdowne Marketing Research found that 40 per cent strongly disagreed and 25 per cent slightly disagreed with the statement that Ireland was better off before foreign nationals came to the country. There is a strong desire to enshrine a fair immigration system based on international norm and human rights with a system which helps sustain economic prosperity. Fifty-seven per cent strongly agreed that racism is going to be a significant problem in Ireland in the future. There is a strong evidence base to highlight the contribution which economic migrants have made to sustaining the economic prosperity that we currently enjoy and very little credible evidence to suggest displacement of Irish workers (Doyle, Hughes and Wadensjö, 2006). There is a need for the government to develop a comprehensive migration policy giving rights to migrant workers and their families whilst at the same time ensuring efficient and fair management of access and asylum policies. It is the role of government to develop and cost comprehensive and realistic solutions to emerging social phenomenon like immigration. If government abdicates itself from this debate or worse panders to suspicion and prejudice (e.g. in a tight election campaign) the tenor of the debate around migration in Ireland could change permanently. Not only would this lead to damage to society by not enshrining a fair immigration process based on due process (reflective of the current altruistic preferences of citizens), but also to the economy by reducing both the flexibility of the labour market and the attractiveness of Ireland as a home for skilled labour.

Improving Life Prospects for Disadvantaged Children

In Ireland today there is still significant social disadvantage being experienced by families. This results in almost one in five children living below the income poverty line for five years or more (Layte, Maitre, Nolan and Whelan, 2006). This not only results in these children experiencing social exclusion but also to a reduction in the potential for these children to acquire skills and opportunities to progress in education. Over the past number of budgets there has been a welcome shift towards emphasising increases in child benefit as the primary instrument to alleviate child income poverty. Given that child benefit is a universal payment to parents of all children, it does not suffer from the poverty traps or unemployment traps associated with other forms of welfare payments. It also is devoid of stigma associated with other forms of welfare payment. In a period of the growth of the tax base and budget surpluses, emphasising redistribution towards those who are less well off can be achieved within a defined period of time with far less political problems than redistribution where people are made worse off. There are indications from polls that the budgets which emphasised increases in child benefit were popular with the public. Income supports to parents should also be coupled with early intervention programmes. There is evidence from international evaluations that these programmes can have a lasting impact, if they are carefully designed. There is very credible and informative research which highlights the significant returns not only to the participants but also to wider society that these investments yield. The rate of return on the investment on early education is higher than for most public projects that are considered economic development (Rolnick and Grunewald, 2003). There is a strong economic rational for helping to develop the cognitive and non-cognitive abilities given that both are important for a productive workforce. Gaps that emerge early are difficult to change. "Skills beget skills and motivation begets motivation" (Heckman, 2006). Because skills are accumulated, starting early and over time investing in young children is an investment in future productivity and creates wider social benefits which far outweigh the cost of the programmes (Cunha, Heckman, Lochner and Masterov, 2005). A combination of prioritising child benefit and investing heavily in mainstreaming aspects of those pilot programmes which have been demonstrated to be effective (i.e. building on a solid evidence base) would dramatically alter the life chances of a large group of Irish citizens. By introducing a comprehensive plan to reduce childhood disadvantage by investing in both income supports and proven educational, health and parenting programmes, the government could radically alter the life chances of a group its citizens. Similar to immigration, there is a window of opportunity for the government to articulate an attractive vision for achieving a social goal but also that also has concrete benefits in terms of improving future national income.

The role of public policymakers in both of the examples highlighted above is to help inform and understand both the opportunities and costs involved in interventions to achieve social objectives. Government can also provide the institutions to help ensure that people contribute to fulfilling their altruistic desires and investing in future economic growth. It is important that government not only present the facts but also through the political democratic process present attractive visions which inspire people to action. In the cases of both migration and child poverty, the government needs to develop comprehensive proposals and present an attractive vision of these if we are to achieve the social objectives which most people say they aspire to achieve. These are just two illustrative examples which if promoted in political debate could help move us beyond reactionary discourse. This role of government in presenting comprehensive solutions and attractive visions to inspire people is similar to the role of other institutions such as non-profit organisations and for-profit companies where setting inspiring missions and realistic targeted objectives is becoming increasing commonplace.

What is the Role of Private Individuals in Achieving Social Goals?

As we have seen above, in economic theory the role of altruism in the preferences of individuals is an issue of some debate. Whilst in terms of achieving economic growth it is obvious that price signals (i.e. wages and incomes) are central to understanding the actions of individuals, it is less clear-cut whether altruism plays a significant role in how we distribute our income. The arguments imported from biology are that we are anxious to spread our genes and that therefore altruism to our families is carried over into wider society and that this is a legacy of evolution. Whilst these arguments might make sense in a setting where people are consuming to survive, they are less relevant in an age of affluence where some high net individuals are worried that their wealth might be a burden to their children. Again, where individuals wish to redistribute their own income to help achieve social objectives, whether they be charitable or otherwise, they can do this in a thoughtful way through targeting certain social problems or they can base their decisions on "warm glow" motivations. In Ireland the limited evidence available on charitable contributions suggest that the rich do not contribute as large proportion of their income to charity as in other countries. Again, it is interesting to look at how a number of economists who are often credited with instilling self-interest of individuals as the key organising principle of society view conspicuous consumption by the wealthy. Adam Smith in particular castigated the conspicuous consumption of large land owners as wasteful and vain:

> The high rate of profit seems everywhere to destroy that parsimony which in other circumstances is natural to the character of the merchant. When profits are high, that sober virtue seems to be superfluous (1776 [1937], p, 578).

Irish society has undergone a transformation both in terms of the size of our national income and the number of individuals who are now of a high net monetary worth. Outside of paying taxes (for those that reside within the state) these individuals face choices as to how they wish to consume or expend their wealth. Some will take the choice that attempting to spend a large proportion of their wealth is the way in which they will get the most personal satisfaction. Many of the twentieth century's richest people have found greater satisfaction through engaging in thoughtful acts of philanthropy with substantial proportions of their wealth. Andrew Carnegie articulated in detail in *The Gospel of Wealth* his view that the rich have both property rights as well as responsibilities. In terms of consuming/distributing their wealth, high net worth individuals in Ireland will face a choice as to whether they wish to

- Consume their wealth themselves

- Preserve it for their family's consumption with the inherent risks to their children

- Give to charities based on who they know or to improve their stature within society

- Target certain social objectives or social problems in a strategic way.

Private wealth can be in a unique position to fund the work of social entrepreneurs and non-profit leaders. These non-profit organisations can highlight unpopular issues, test and evaluate solutions to social problems and provide inspirational leadership to social change initiatives. In order to engage in thoughtful acts of philanthropy the rich need to find vibrant and energetic leaders of non-profit organisations who share their vision and passion for causes. Rationalising the actions of philanthropists within the lens of an economic choice one could make the case that the high net worth individuals in Ireland will face a trade-off between the latest model of the next Lear jet or helping improve Irish society in a meaningful way!

Conclusions

In many ways Irish society has come through a period of rapid transformation and it is only now that we are reflecting on what the rapid economic growth enables us to achieve both at a societal and individual level. It is interesting to look at how economic theory has understood the